DATE DUE

DEMCO 128-5046

SOMETHING ABOUT THE AUTHOR®

Something about
the Author *was named
an "Outstanding
Reference Source,"*
*the highest honor given
by the American
Library Association
Reference and Adult
Services Division.*

ISSN 0276-816X

R

SOMETHING ABOUT THE AUTHOR®

**Facts and Pictures about Authors
and Illustrators of Books for Young People**

EDITED BY
ALAN HEDBLAD

VOLUME 97

GALE

DETROIT · NEW YORK · LONDON

STAFF

Editor: Alan Hedblad
Associate Editor: Sheryl Ciccarelli
Assistant Editor: Melissa Hill

Sketchwriters/Copyeditors: Marie Ellavich, Ronie Garcia-Johnson, Mary Gillis, Motoko Fujishiro Huthwaite, Arlene M. Johnson, J. Sydney Jones, Thomas F. McMahon, Gerard J. Senick, Pamela L. Shelton, Crystal A. Towns, Arlene True, Stephen Thor Tschirhart, and Kathleen Witman

Managing Editor: Joyce Nakamura
Publisher: Hal May

Research Manager: Victoria B. Cariappa
Project Coordinator: Cheryl L. Warnock
Research Specialist: Maureen Richards
Research Associates: Tamara C. Nott, Tracie A. Richardson, Norma Sawaya
Research Assistants: Jeffrey D. Daniels, Talitha A. Jean, Corrine A. Stocker

Permissions Manager: Susan M. Trosky
Permissions Specialist: Maria L. Franklin
Permissions Associates: Edna M. Hedblad, Michele Lonoconus

Production Director: Mary Beth Trimper
Production Assistant: Shanna Heilveil

Desktop Publisher Assistant: Ninette Saad
Image Database Supervisor: Randy Bassett
Imaging Specialists: Robert Duncan, Michael Logusz
Photography Coordinator: Pamela A. Reed

This book is printed on acid-free paper that meets the minimum requirements of American National Standard for Information Sciences—Permanence Paper for Printed Library Materials, ANSI Z39.48-1984.

Library of Congress Catalog Card Number 72-27107

ISBN 0-7876-1150-6 ISSN 0276-816X

Printed in the United States of America

10 9 8 7 6 5 4 3 2 1

Contents

Authors in Forthcoming Volumes

Below are some of the authors and illustrators that will be featured in upcoming volumes of *SATA*. These include new entries on the swiftly rising stars of the field, as well as completely revised and updated entries (indicated with *) on some of the most notable and best-loved creators of books for children.

*Jan Andrews: The natural world serves as inspiration for this British-born Canadian author's picture books, which include *The Auction, Pumpkin Time,* and the highly praised *Very Last First Time,* as well as Andrews's young adult novel, *Keri.*

Edward Bloor: Bloor's first young adult novel, *Tangerine,* which combines elements of suspense, environmental concerns and a boy coping with a physical challenge, has garnered much critical acclaim.

*Rod Campbell: A prolific author and illustrator of books for preschoolers and early readers, Campbell is the creator of more than a hundred works that are noted for blending artistry and technology in an especially engaging manner.

Sharon M. Draper: Named 1997 National Teacher of the Year, Draper writes young adult novels aimed at contemporary urban teens. She received numerous honors for *Tears of a Tiger,* and her *Forged by Fire* earned her the prestigious 1998 Coretta Scott King Author Award.

Valeri Gorbachev: Well known in his native Ukraine, author/illustrator Gorbachev is making a name for himself in the United States. He hopes, through his gentle pen-and-ink watercolors and the appealing, human qualities of the characters he creates, to show the similarities among people all over the world.

Jessie Haas: The author of more than twenty novels and picture books for children, Haas often features horses, one of her reigning passions, as subjects in award-winning titles such as *Keeping Barney, Beware the Mare,* and *A Blue for Beware.*

Joanne Horniman: Horniman is a noted Australian author of novels and short stories for children and young adults centering on the realistic portrayal of unusual relationships. Her works, which include *Sand Monkeys, The Serpentine Belt,* and *Loving Athena,* are frequently set in the rainforest.

*Paul B. Janeczko: The experiences of young people are the focus of the poems included in more than a dozen anthologies that Janeczko has assembled. He has also penned his own collection of poetry, *Brickyard Summer,* about two teenage boys on summer vacation.

*Satoshi Kitamura: Kitamura is praised for his ability to interweave Japanese and Western visual traditions. His engaging illustrations add a whimsical, often unconventional touch to his own writing as well as the works of numerous children's authors.

Gail Carson Levine: Levine's *Ella Enchanted,* based on the Cinderella story, has been named a Newbery Honor Book and one of the best children's books of 1997 by the American Library Association.

Stephane Poulin: An award-winning Canadian writer-illustrator of children's books noted for colorful images, offbeat humor and sophisticated design, Poulin blends fantasy, reality, and humor with themes such as family, togetherness, and love. His popular *Josephine* series chronicles the adventures of a mischievous cat.

*Tor Seidler: In his highly imaginative novels for young readers, Seidler writes about fate and chance, and the personal risks that people sometimes take when their way of life is threatened. Each of these themes figures prominently in his books, which include *The Wainscott Weasel* and the acclaimed *Mean Margaret.*

Andrea Warren: Author/educator Warren tackles both fiction and nonfiction in her works for young people. In noted books such as *Pioneer Girl: Growing Up on the Prairie* and *Orphan Train Rider: One Boy's True Story,* young readers learn history while engrossed in the lives of Warren's characters.

Introduction

Something about the Author (*SATA*) is an ongoing reference series that examines the lives and works of authors and illustrators of books for children. *SATA* includes not only well-known writers and artists but also less prominent individuals whose works are just coming to be recognized. This series is often the only readily available information source on emerging authors and illustrators. You'll find *SATA* informative and entertaining, whether you are a student, a librarian, an English teacher, a parent, or simply an adult who enjoys children's literature.

What's Inside SATA

SATA provides detailed information about authors and illustrators who span the full time range of children's literature, from early figures like John Newbery and L. Frank Baum to contemporary figures like Judy Blume and Richard Peck. Authors in the series represent primarily English-speaking countries, particularly the United States, Canada, and the United Kingdom. Also included, however, are authors from around the world whose works are available in English translation. The writings represented in *SATA* include those created intentionally for children and young adults as well as those written for a general audience and known to interest younger readers. These writings cover the entire spectrum of children's literature, including picture books, humor, folk and fairy tales, animal stories, mystery and adventure, science fiction and fantasy, historical fiction, poetry and nonsense verse, drama, biography, and nonfiction.

Obituaries are also included in *SATA* and are intended not only as death notices but also as concise overviews of people's lives and work. Additionally, each edition features newly revised and updated entries for a selection of *SATA* listees who remain of interest to today's readers and who have been active enough to require extensive revisions of their earlier biographies.

Two Convenient Indexes

In response to suggestions from librarians, *SATA* indexes no longer appear in every volume but are included in alternate (odd-numbered) volumes of the series, beginning with Volume 57.

SATA continues to include two indexes that cumulate with each alternate volume: the Illustrations Index, arranged by the name of the illustrator, gives the number of the volume and page where the illustrator's work appears in the current volume as well as all preceding volumes in the series; the Author Index gives the number of the volume in which a person's Biographical Sketch or Obituary appears in the current volume as well as all preceding volumes in the series.

These indexes also include references to authors and illustrators who appear in Gale's *Yesterday's Authors of Books for Children, Children's Literature Review,* and *Something about the Author Autobiography Series.*

Easy-to-Use Entry Format

Whether you're already familiar with the *SATA* series or just getting acquainted, you will want to be aware of the kind of information that an entry provides. In every *SATA* entry the editors attempt to give as complete a picture of the person's life and work as possible. A typical entry in *SATA* includes the following clearly labeled information sections:

- *PERSONAL:* date and place of birth and death, parents' names and occupations, name of spouse, date of marriage, names of children, educational institutions attended, degrees received, religious and political affiliations, hobbies and other interests.

- *ADDRESSES:* complete home, office, electronic mail, and agent addresses, whenever available.

■ *CAREER:* name of employer, position, and dates for each career post; art exhibitions; military service; memberships and offices held in professional and civic organizations.

■ *AWARDS, HONORS:* literary and professional awards received.

■ *WRITINGS:* title-by-title chronological bibliography of books written and/or illustrated, listed by genre when known; lists of other notable publications, such as plays, screenplays, and periodical contributions.

■ *ADAPTATIONS:* a list of films, television programs, plays, CD-ROMs, recordings, and other media presentations that have been adapted from the author's work.

■ *WORK IN PROGRESS:* description of projects in progress.

■ *SIDELIGHTS:* a biographical portrait of the author or illustrator's development, either directly from the biographee—and often written specifically for the *SATA* entry—or gathered from diaries, letters, interviews, or other published sources.

■ *FOR MORE INFORMATION SEE:* references for further reading.

■ *EXTENSIVE ILLUSTRATIONS:* photographs, movie stills, book illustrations, and other interesting visual materials supplement the text.

How a SATA Entry Is Compiled

A *SATA* entry progresses through a series of steps. If the biographee is living, the *SATA* editors try to secure information directly from him or her through a questionnaire. From the information that the biographee supplies, the editors prepare an entry, filling in any essential missing details with research and/or telephone interviews. If possible, the author or illustrator is sent a copy of the entry to check for accuracy and completeness.

If the biographee is deceased or cannot be reached by questionnaire, the *SATA* editors examine a wide variety of published sources to gather information for an entry. Biographical and bibliographic sources are consulted, as are book reviews, feature articles, published interviews, and material sometimes obtained from the biographee's family, publishers, agent, or other associates.

Entries that have not been verified by the biographees or their representatives are marked with an asterisk (*).

Contact the Editor

We encourage our readers to examine the entire *SATA* series. Please write and tell us if we can make *SATA* even more helpful to you. Give your comments and suggestions to the editor:

BY MAIL: Editor, *Something about the Author,* Gale Research, 835 Penobscot Bldg., 645 Griswold St., Detroit, MI 48226-4094.

BY TELEPHONE: (800) 347-GALE

BY FAX: (313) 961-6599

Acknowledgments

Grateful acknowledgment is made to the following publishers, authors, and artists whose works appear in this volume.

ARRINGTON, STEPHEN. Arrington, Stephen, photograph. Reproduced by permission of Stephen Arrington.

BEERE, PETER. Wyatt, David, illustrator. From a cover of *Kiss of Death,* by Peter Beere. Scholastic Ltd., 1994. © David Wyatt, 1994. Reproduced by permission. / Beere, Peter, photograph. Reproduced by permission of Peter Beere.

BENNETT, CHERIE. Le Grou, Michel, photographer. From a cover of *Wild Hearts on Fire,* by Cherie Bennett. Pocket Books, 1994. Reproduced by permission of Pocket Books, a division of Simon & Schuster, Inc. / Cover of *Love Never Dies,* by Cherie Bennett. Avon Books, 1996. Reproduced by permission. / Cover of *Sunset Forever,* by Cherie Bennett. Berkley Books, 1997. Cover art © 1997 by General Licensing Company, Inc. Reproduced by permission of The Berkley Publishing Group, a member of Penguin Putnam Inc. / Watts, Stan, illustrator. From a jacket of *Life in the Fat Lane,* by Cherie Bennett. Delacorte Press, 1998. Jacket illustration © 1998 by Stan Watts. Reproduced by permission of Delacorte Press, a division of Bantam Doubleday Dell Publishing Group, Inc. / Bennett, Cherie, photograph by Nancy Andrews. Reproduced by permission of Cherie Bennett.

BISHOP, GAVIN. Bishop, Gavin, illustrator. From an illustration in *Maui and the Sun: A Maori Tale,* by Gavin Bishop. North-South Books, 1996. Text and illustrations © 1996 by Gavin Bishop. Reproduced by permission of North-South Books, Inc., New York. / Bishop, Gavin, illustrator. From an illustration in *Little Rabbit and the Sea,* by Gavin Bishop. North-South Books, 1997. Reproduced by permission of Gavin Bishop. / Bishop, Gavin, photograph by Bruce Foster. Reproduced by permission of Gavin Bishop.

BLEDSOE, LUCY JANE. Cover of *The Big Bike Race,* by Lucy Jane Bledsoe. Avon Books, 1997. Reproduced by permission. / Bledsoe, Lucy Jane, photograph by Phyllis Christopher. Reproduced by permission of Lucy Jane Bledsoe.

BOWEN, ANDY RUSSELL. Harvey, Lisa, illustrator. From an illustration in *A Head Full of Notions: A Story about Robert Fulton,* by Andy Russell Bowen. Carolrhoda Books, 1997. Illustrations © 1997 by Lisa Harvey. Reproduced by permission.

BRANCATO, ROBIN F. Mak, Kam, illustrator. From a cover of *Winning,* by Robin F. Brancato. Knopf, Inc., 1988. Cover art © 1988 by Kam Mak. Reproduced by permission of Random House, Inc. / Brancato, Robin F., photograph by Carol Kitman. Reproduced by permission of Robin F. Brancato.

BRANDENBERG, ALEXA. Brandenberg, Alexa, photograph by Marcy James. Reproduced by permission of Alexa Brandenberg.

BREWSTER, PATIENCE. Kroll, Steven, illustrator. From an illustration in *Queen of the May,* by Patience Brewster. Holiday House, 1993. Illustrations © 1993 by Patience Brewster. Reproduced by permission. / Brewster, Patience, illustrator. From an illustration in *Two Bushy Badgers,* by Patience Brewster. Little, Brown and Company, 1995. Copyright © 1995 by Patience Brewster. Reproduced by permission. / Brewster, Patience, photograph. Reproduced by permission of Patience Brewster.

BROWN, BEVERLY SWERDLOW. Brown, Beverly Swerdlow, photograph. Reproduced by permission of Beverly Swerdlow Brown.

BYALICK, MARCIA. Kahl, David, illustrator. From a cover of *It's a Matter of Trust,* by Marcia Byalick. Browndeer Press, 1995. Cover illustration © 1995 by David Kahl. Reproduced by permission of the illustrator. / Byalick, Marcia, photograph by Jane Schweiger. Reproduced by permission of Marcia Byalick.

CASWELL, BRIAN. Tanner, Jane, illustrator. From a cover of *Dreamslip,* by Brian Caswell. University of Queensland Press, 1994. Reproduced by permission. / Caswell, Brian, photograph. University of Queensland Press. Reproduced by permission.

CHAST, ROZ. Chast, Roz, illustrator. From an illustration in *Now Everybody Really Hates Me,* by Jane Read Martin and Patricia Marx. HarperCollins, 1993. Illustrations © 1993 by Roz Chast. Reproduced by permission of HarperCollins Publishers, Inc. In the British Commonwealth by The Wylie Agency, Inc. / Chast, Roz, illustrator. From an illustration in *Now I Will Never Leave the Dinner Table,* by Jane Read Martin and Patricia Marx. HarperCollins, 1996. Illustrations © 1996 by Roz Chast. Reproduced by permission of HarperCollins Publishers, Inc. In the British Commonwealth by The Wylie Agency, Inc. / Chast, Roz, photograph by Anne Hall. © Anne Hall. Reproduced by permission.

CLEMENT, ROD. Clement, Rod, illustrator. From an illustration in *Just Another Ordinary Day,* by Rod Clement. HarperCollins Publishers Australia, 1995, HarperCollins Publishers, Inc., 1996. Copyright © 1995 by Rod Clement. Reproduced by permission of HarperCollins Publishers Australia. In the U.S. by HarperCollins Publishers, Inc.

COOPER, ILENE. Wimmer, Mike, illustrator. From a jacket of *Mean Streak,* by Ilene Cooper. Morrow Junior Books, 1991. Jacket illustration © 1991 by Mike Wimmer. Reproduced by permission of Morrow Junior Books, a division of William Morrow & Company,

an illustration in *Old Home Day,* by Donald Hall. Browndeer Press, 1996. Illustrations © 1996 by Emily Arnold McCully. Reproduced by permission of Harcourt Brace & Company. / Moser, Barry, illustrator. From an illustration in *When Willard Met Babe Ruth,* by Donald Hall. Browndeer Press, 1996. Illustrations © 1996 by Barry Moser. Reproduced by permission of Harcourt Brace & Company. / Hall, Donald, photograph by Steven W. Lewis. Reproduced by permission of Donald Hall.

HARPER, JO. Harper, Jo, photograph by Loma Walker. Reproduced by permission of Jo Harper.

HAYNES, DAVID. Zinn, David, illustrator. From a cover of *The Gumma Wars,* by David Haynes. Milkweed Editions, 1997. © 1997, illustrations by David Zinn. Reproduced by permission.

HENEGHAN, JAMES. Lee, Paul, illustrator. From a jacket of *Wish Me Luck,* by James Heneghan. Frances Foster Books, 1997. Jacket art © 1997 by Paul Lee. Reproduced by permission of Farrar, Straus and Giroux, Inc. / Heneghan, James, photograph. Reproduced by permission of James Heneghan.

HEWITSON, JENNIFER. Hewitson, Jennifer, photograph. Reproduced by permission of Jennifer Hewitson.

HOFFMAN, MARY. Seeley, Laura L., illustrator. From an illustration in *The Four-Legged Ghosts,* by Mary Hoffman. Dial Books, 1993. Illustrations © Laura L. Seeley, 1993. Reproduced by permission of Dial Books for Young Readers, a division of Penguin Putnam Inc. / Jacket of *Henry's Baby,* by Mary Hoffman. Dorling Kindersley, Inc., 1993. Reproduced by permission. / Ray, Jane, illustrator. From an illustration in *Earth, Fire, Water, Air,* by Mary Hoffman. Orion Children's Books, 1995. Text © 1995 by Mary Hoffman. Illustrations © 1995 by Jane Ray. Reproduced by permission.

HONEYCUTT, NATALIE. Raymond, Larry, illustrator. From a jacket of *Ask Me Something Easy,* by Natalie Honeycutt. Orchard Books, 1991. Jacket illustration © 1991 by Larry Raymond. Reproduced by permission of Orchard Books, New York. / Ward, John, illustrator. From a jacket of *Twilight in Grace Falls,* by Natalie Honeycutt. Orchard Books, 1997. Jacket painting © 1997 by John Ward. Reproduced by permission of Orchard Books, New York. / Honeycutt, Natalie, photograph by Andrew Honeycutt. Reproduced by permission of Natalie Honeycutt.

HOPKINS, MARY RICE. Hopkins, Mary Rice, photograph. Reproduced by permission of Mary Rice Hopkins.

HOUK, RANDY. Houk, Randy, photograph by David Hiller. Reproduced by permission of Randy Houk.

JAMES, ELIZABETH. Weston, Martha, illustrator. From a cover of *The New Complete Babysitter's Handbook,* by Carol Barkin and Elizabeth James. Clarion Books, 1994. Cover illustration © 1995 by Martha Weston. Reproduced by permission of Houghton Mifflin Company. / Weston, Martha, illustrator. From a cover of *Social Smarts: Manners for Today's Kids,* by Elizabeth James and Carol Barkin. Clarion Books, 1996. Cover illustration © 1996 by Martha Weston. Reproduced by permission of Houghton Mifflin Company. / James, Elizabeth, photograph. Reproduced by permission of Elizabeth James.

KOMAIKO, LEAH. Carter, Abby, illustrator. From an illustration in *Annie Bananie Moves to Barry Avenue,* by Leah Komaiko. Delacorte Press, 1996. Illustrations © 1996 by Abby Carter. Reproduced by permission of Delacorte Press, a division of Bantam Doubleday Dell Publishing Group, Inc. In the British Commonwealth by the illustrator.

KOVALSKI, MARYANN. Kovalski, Maryann, illustrator. From an illustration in *Pizza for Breakfast,* by Maryann Kovalski. Kids Can Press, 1990, Morrow Junior Books, 1991. Copyright © 1990 by Maryann Kovalski. Reproduced by permission of Kids Can Press Ltd. In the U.S. by permission of Morrow Junior Books, a division of William Morrow and Company, Inc. / Kovalski, Maryann, illustrator. From an illustration in *Doctor Knickerbocker and Other Rhymes,* edited by David Booth. Ticknor & Fields, 1993, Kids Can Press, 1993. Selection © 1993 by David Booth. Illustrations © 1993 by Maryann Kovalski. Reproduced by permission of Houghton Mifflin Company. In the British Commonwealth by Kids Can Press Ltd. / Kovalski, Maryann, illustrator. From an illustration in *Princess Prunella and the Purple Peanut,* by Margaret Atwood. Workman Publishing, 1995. Illustration © 1995 by Maryann Kovalski. Reproduced by permission. / Kovalski, Maryann, photograph by Steven Jack. Reproduced by permission of Maryann Kovalski.

LADD, LOUISE. Cover of *Lost Valley,* by Louise Ladd. Berkley Books, 1996. Copyright © 1996 by Louise Ladd. Reproduced by permission of The Berkley Publishing Group, a member of Penguin Putnam Inc. / Ladd, Louise, photograph. Reproduced by permission of Louise Ladd.

LAUX, CONNIE. Laux, Connie, photograph. Reproduced by permission of Connie Laux.

LAVENDER, DAVID. "Pilgrims of the Plains," engraving. From an illustration in *The Santa Fe Trail,* by David Lavender. Holiday House, 1995. Reproduced by permission of The Huntington Library. / Trimble, Stephen, photographer. From a jacket of *Snowbound: The Tragic Story of the Donner Party,* by David Lavender. Holiday House, 1996. Photo © by Stephen Trimble. Reproduced by permission of the photographer. / Lavender, David, photograph. Reproduced by permission of David Lavender.

LESSEM, DON. Hamlin, Janet, illustrator. From a jacket of *Jack Horner: Living with Dinosaurs,* by Don Lessem. W. H. Freeman and Company, 1994. Illustrations copyright © 1994 by Janet Hamlin. Reproduced by permission of the illustrator. / Cover of *Supergiants,* by Don Lessem. Little, Brown and Company, 1997. Reproduced by permission of Little, Brown and Company. / Lessem, Don, photograph. Reproduced by permission of Don Lessem.

LEVIN, MIRIAM RAMSFELDER. Levin, Miriam Ramsfelder, photograph. Reproduced by permission of Miriam Ramsfelder Levin.

REEDER, CAROLYN. From a cover of *Shades of Gray,* by Carolyn Reeder. Avon Books, 1989. Reproduced by permission. / Reeder, Carolyn, photograph by deKun. Reproduced by permission of Carolyn Reeder.

RENDON, MARCIE R. Bellville, Cheryl Walsh, photographer. From a cover of *Powwow Summer: A Family Celebrates the Circle of Life,* by Marcie R. Rendon. Carolrhoda Books, 1996. Illustrations copyright © 1996 by Cheryl Walsh Bellville. Reproduced by permission.

RILEY, JAMES A. Cover of *The Negro Leagues,* by James A. Riley. Chelsea House Publishers, 1997. Reproduced by permission of NoirTech, Inc.

RODDA, EMILY. Young, Noela, illustrator. From a jacket of *The Timekeeper,* by Emily Rodda. Omnibus Books, 1992. Jacket art © 1992 by Noela Young. Reproduced by permission. / Kelly, Geoff, illustrator. From an illustration in *Power and Glory,* by Emily Rodda. Allen & Unwin Pty. Ltd., 1994. Illustrations © 1994 by Geoff Kelly. Reproduced by permission. / Smith, Craig, illustrator. From an illustration in *Yay!,* by Emily Rodda. Omnibus Books, 1996. Text © 1996 by Emily Rodda. Illustrations © 1996 by Craig Smith. Reproduced by permission.

RUURS, MARGRIET. Ruurs, Margriet, photograph. Reproduced by permission by Margriet Ruurs.

SAVAGE, JEFF. Daly, Paul, illustrator. From a cover of *Cowboys and Cow Towns of the Wild West,* by Jeff Savage. Enslow Publishers, Inc., 1995. Reproduced by permission. / Cover of *Barry Bonds: Mr. Excitement,* by Jeff Savage. First Avenue Editions, 1997. Reproduced by permission. / Savage, Jeff, photograph. Reproduced by permission of Jeff Savage.

SNYDER, BERNADETTE MCCARVER. Snyder, Bernadette McCarver, photograph. Reproduced by permission of Bernadette McCarver Snyder.

SOENTPIET, CHRIS K. Soentpiet, Chris, illustrator. From an illustration in *Around Town,* by Chris Soentpiet. Lothrop, Lee & Shepard, 1994. Copyright © 1994 by Chris K. Soentpiet. Reproduced by permission of Lothrop, Lee & Shepard Books, a division of William Morrow & Company, Inc. / Soentpiet, Chris K., photograph. Reproduced by permission of Chris K. Soentpiet.

THOMAS, ROB. Raschka, Chris, illustrator. From a jacket of *Rats Saw God,* by Rob Thomas. Simon & Schuster Books for Young Readers, 1996. Jacket illustration copyright © 1996 by Simon & Schuster. Reproduced by permission of Simon & Schuster Books for Young Readers, a division of Simon & Schuster, Inc. / Thomas, Rob, photograph by Stanley W. Hensley. Reproduced by permission of Rob Thomas.

WILLIAMS, MARCIA. Williams, Marcia, illustrator. From an illustration in *The Adventures of Robin Hood,* by Marcia Williams. Walker Books Ltd., 1995, Candlewick Press, 1997. Copyright © 1995 by Marcia Williams. Reproduced by permission of Walker Books Ltd. In the U.S. by Candlewick Press. / Williams, Marcia, photograph. Reproduced by permission of Marcia Williams.

WOOD, FRANCES M. Wood, Frances M., photograph by Brian J. Morton. Reproduced by permission.

WRIGHT, SUSAN KIMMEL. Wright, Susan Kimmel, photograph by Bill Metzger. Reproduced by permission of Susan Kimmel Wright.

ZAWADZKI, MAREK. Zawadzki, Marek, photograph. Reproduced by permission of Marek Zawadzki.

SOMETHING ABOUT THE AUTHOR®

ANDERSON, M. T(obin) 1968-

■ Personal

Born November 4, 1968, in Cambridge, MA; son of Will (an engineer) and Juliana (an Episcopal priest) Anderson. *Education:* Attended Harvard University, 1987; Cambridge University, B.A., 1991; Syracuse University, M.F.A., 1998.

■ Career

Writer. Candlewick Press, Cambridge, MA, editorial assistant, 1993-96; *Boston Review,* intern; WCUW-Radio, disc jockey. Has also worked as sales clerk at a department store.

■ Writings

Thirsty (horror novel), Candlewick Press (Cambridge, MA), 1997.

Reviews for *Improper Bostonian.*

■ Work in Progress

Burger Wuss, a "fast-food love story"; research on seventeenth- and eighteenth-century French and English history.

■ Sidelights

M. T. Anderson told *SATA:* "Writing is a kind of weakness, I think. We write because we can't decipher

things the first time around. As a reader, I like best those books in which the author, mulling things over for him or herself, enables readers to see a world anew.

"We are so used to the bizarre images, cabals, rituals, and rites that constitute our lives that they seem natural, even invisible, to us. I admire books that facilitate renewed awareness of the way we live, and this is what I'm attempting in my own work: renewed awareness both for myself and, I hope, for my readers. That's my goal, in any case."

Anderson's debut novel, *Thirsty,* set in a small town in Massachusetts, features a high school freshman named Chris who realizes that he is on the verge of growing into a vampire—despite his town's very elaborate and ritualistic attempts to fight the dreaded monsters, which seem to reap a steady New England harvest. "Chris's turbulent transformation ... is paralleled by and inextricable from the changes of adolescence: insatiable appetite, sleepless nights, and a deep sense of insecurity and isolation," noted *Horn Book* reviewer Lauren Adams, who added: "The unusual blend of camp horror and realistic adolescent turmoil and the suspenseful plot affirm a new talent worth watching." A *Kirkus Reviews* critic also praised *Thirsty* as a "startling, savagely funny debut."

■ Works Cited

Adams, Lauren, review of *Thirsty, Horn Book,* May-June, 1997, p. 313.
Review of *Thirsty, Kirkus Reviews,* January 1, 1997, p. 56.

■ For More Information See

PERIODICALS

Publishers Weekly, January 27, 1997, p. 108.

* * *

ARCHBOLD, Rick 1950-

■ Personal

Born in 1950.

■ Addresses

Agent—c/o Ann Rittenberg Literary Agency, Inc., 14 Montgomery Place, Brooklyn, NY 11215.

■ Career

Book editor; writer.

■ Writings

FOR YOUNG PEOPLE

(With Robert D. Ballard) *The Lost Wreck of the Isis*, Scholastic/Madison Press, 1990.
(With Ballard) *Exploring the Bismarck*, Scholastic, 1991.
Deep-Sea Explorer: The Story of Robert Ballard, Discoverer of the Titanic, Scholastic, 1994.

Also coauthor, with Robert Bateman, of *Safari*, 1998, and with Robert D. Ballard, *Ghost Lines*, 1998.

OTHER

(With Eugene Whelan) *Whelan: The Man in the Green Stetson*, Irwin Publishing (Toronto), 1986.
(With Robert D. Ballard) *The Discovery of the Titanic*, introduction by Walter Lord, illustrations by Ken Marschall, Warner Books, 1987.
(With Richard Earle and David Imrie) *Your Vitality Quotient: The Clinically Proven Program that Can Reduce Your Body Age—and Increase Your Zest for Life*, Warner Books, 1989.
Robert Bateman: An Artist in Nature, Random House, 1990.
(With Robert D. Ballard) *The Discovery of the Bismarck*, introduction by Ludovic Kennedy, illustrations by Ken Marschall, Warner Books, 1990.
(With Audrey McLaughlin) *A Woman's Place: My Life and Politics*, Macfarlane Walter & Ross (Toronto), 1992.
(With Robert D. Ballard) *Lost Ships of Guadalcanal*, Warner Books, 1993.
Hindenburg: An Illustrated History, Warner Books, 1994.
Robert Bateman: Natural Worlds, Simon & Schuster, 1996.
(With Dana McCauley) *Last Dinner on the Titanic*, Hyperion, 1997.
(With Robert D. Ballard) *Lost Liners: From the Titanic to the Andrea Doria the Ocean Floor Reveals Its*

Greatest Lost Ships, illustrations by Ken Marschall, Hyperion, 1998.

■ Sidelights

Canadian writer and editor Rick Archbold established his career in the 1980s and 1990s as author and coauthor of nonfiction books on subjects ranging from Canadian politics to the search for sunken ships. In 1987, Archbold began the first of many collaborative efforts with marine geologist Robert D. Ballard, producing the book *The Discovery of the Titanic*. Ballard was the man who found the legendary sunken ocean liner on September 1, 1985, after repeated attempts beginning in 1977. Exploring the wreck, he formed a theory about the cause of the sinking. The collision with the iceberg, in the words of *Washington Post Book World* reviewer Duncan Spencer, "popped a series of rivets between the iron plates that formed the skin of these prewelding ships. A long seam only three-quarters of an inch wide allowed the water to pour in so that the 'watertight' bulkheads were soon overtopped." Spencer adds that while the captain of the *Titanic*'s motives for steering into an icefield remain unknown, the book "has given us roundness and an end to one of the world's unforgettable soap operas."

Archbold's later works have further explored familiar subject areas. With Ballard, he has written more about sunken ships in *Lost Ships of Guadalcanal*, and for the juvenile audience *The Lost Wreck of the Isis*, *Exploring the Bismarck*, and *Deep-Sea Explorer: The Story of Robert Ballard, Discoverer of the Titanic*.

In *Deep-Sea Explorer*, Archbold chronicles the adventurous life of his frequent writing partner who also discovered the sunken German battleship Bismarck and shipwrecks from the Battle of Guadalcanal. Text and photographs reveal the dramatic excitement and danger encountered in unknown waters with a creative and bold explorer. A critic for *Kirkus Reviews* found the book "illuminating reading ... with well-chosen details." According to *Booklist*'s Merri Monks, Archbold's account is an "exciting portrait of the scientist/explorer." Although Deborah Stevenson of the *Bulletin of the Center for Children's Books* pointed to the author's tendency to "list facts rather than convey Ballard's personal life," she praised Archbold's coverage of Ballard's marine work as "clear and exciting."

■ Works Cited

Review of *Deep-Sea Explorer: The Story of Robert Ballard, Discoverer of the Titanic*, *Kirkus Reviews*, February 15, 1994, p. 222.
Monks, Merri, review of *Deep-Sea Explorer: The Story of Robert Ballard, Discoverer of the Titanic*, *Booklist*, March 1, 1994, p. 1247.
Spencer, Duncan, review of *The Discovery of the Titanic*, *Washington Post Book World*, November 6, 1987.
Stevenson, Deborah, review of *Deep-Sea Explorer: The Story of Robert Ballard, Discoverer of the Titanic*,

Bulletin of the Center for Children's Books, April, 1994, pp. 249-50.

■ For More Information See

PERIODICALS

Globe and Mail (Toronto), October 18, 1986.
New York Times Book Review, December 27, 1987, p. 19; April 9, 1989, pp. 30-31.

* * *

ARRINGTON, Stephen L(ee) 1948-

■ Personal

Born September 27, 1948, in Pasadena, CA; son of Richard (a banker) and Barbara (a mortgage broker) Arrington; married Cynthia Elizabeth Hamren, April 1, 1989; children: Stetcyn Lee, Cheyenne Summer, Chase Greystoke. *Education:* San Diego State University, A.S. *Politics:* Republican. *Religion:* Christian. *Hobbies and other interests:* Flying (private pilot's license), mountain biking, hiking, photography, gardening.

■ Addresses

Home—Paradise, CA. *Office*—P.O. Box 3234, Paradise, CA 95967. *Electronic mail*—drugsbit @ dcsi.net and (website) http://www.drugsbite.com.

■ Career

U.S. Navy, "frogman" in Navy bomb disposal unit, including service in Vietnam, 1966-71, leaving the service as chief petty officer; Boron Prison Camp, inmate fireman, 1982-85; College of Oceaneering, air diving supervisor, 1985-87; Cousteau Society, expedition leader and chief diver, 1987-93; motivational and drug education speaker and writer, 1993—. Special effects stuntperson for films, including *Top Gun* and *Oceans of Fire;* American Red Cross, instructor in cardiopulmonary resuscitation (CPR); also teaches karate and scuba diving. *Member:* Veterans of Foreign Wars.

■ Awards, Honors

Gold Medal from Worldfest and winner of "Silver Teli" award, best Christian video, 1995, for *Out of the Night Video.* Presidential Unit Citation, Naval Commendation Medal, and expert badges for pistol and rifle; Certificate of Merit for Lifesaving, American Red Cross.

■ Writings

Journey into Darkness: Nowhere to Land (memoir), Huntington House (Lafayette, LA), 1992.
Expedition and Diving Operations Handbook, Best Publishing (Flagstaff, AZ), 1993.

STEPHEN L. ARRINGTON

High on Adventure: Stories of Good, Clean, Spine-Tingling Fun, illustrated by Julie Pace, Huntington House, 1995.
High on Adventure II: Dreams Becoming Reality, illustrated by Margery Spielman, Huntington House, 1996.
High on Adventure III: Building the Adventure Machine, Huntington House, 1997.

Creator of *Out of the Night Video,* Wyland Group, 1995.

■ Work in Progress

High on Adventure IV, completion expected in 1998.

■ Sidelights

Stephen L. Arrington told *Something about the Author (SATA):* "Childhood dreams are the foundations for adult realities. This is a fact if people are willing to pursue their dreams. I look upon the human body as an adventure machine that can carry a person into a life quest full of challenge, wonder, and happiness. Our minds can be fine-tuned to think intelligently with deep insight and awareness. Who we are and what we will become in life is self-determined. All dreams are realizable through courage, moral commitment, discipline, and

Something about the Author, *Volume 97*

hard work. None of us is perfect, yet we should strive for perfection in all that we do. In life, if we make a mistake, it doesn't mean that we are a mistake. What is important is to learn from our errors and to try to grow toward being better and more caring people.

"A marijuana mistake led to my going to prison for three years. In my jail cell I made a commitment to pursue good works. Two years after my release I realized my childhood dream by becoming a chief diver for the Cousteau Society, and I don't even speak French!"

■ For More Information See

PERIODICALS

Bookwatch, May, 1993, p. 1.
Newsweek, November 1, 1982, p. 36.

B

THE BANJO
See PATERSON, A(ndrew) B(arton)

* * *

BARNE, Kitty
See BARNE, Marion Catherine

* * *

BARNE, Marion Catherine 1883-1957
(Kitty Barne)

■ Personal

Born 1883; died 1957; married Eric Streatfeild. *Education:* Royal College of Music, London, England. *Hobbies and other interests:* Musical activities for Girl Guides' Association.

■ Career

Writer of novels, nonfiction books, and plays, primarily for children. Also composed music. Worked in a hostel as a young adult. *Wartime Service:* Women's Voluntary Service during World War II: assisted in the reception of juvenile evacuees from London to Sussex.

■ Awards, Honors

Carnegie Medal, U.K. Library Association, 1940, for *Visitors from London.*

■ Writings

FICTION FOR CHILDREN

Tomorrow, illustrated by Ethel King-Martyn, Hodder and Stoughton (London), 1912.
The Easter Holidays, illustrated by Joan Kiddell-Monroe, Heinemann (London), 1935; published as *Secret of the Sandhills,* Dodd Mead (New York), 1949, Nelson (London), 1955.

Young Adventurers, illustrated by Ruth Gervis, Nelson, 1936.
She Shall Have Music, illustrated by Gervis, Dent (London), 1938, Dodd Mead, 1939.
Family Footlights, illustrated by Gervis, Dent, 1939, Dodd Mead, 1939.
Visitors from London, illustrated by Gervis, Dent, 1940, Dodd Mead, 1940.
May I Keep Dogs?, illustrated by Arnrid Johnston, Hamish Hamilton (London), 1941, Dodd Mead, 1942; published as *Bracken My Dog,* Dent, 1949.
We'll Meet in England, illustrated by Steven Spurrier, Hamish Hamilton, 1942, Dodd Mead, 1943.
Three and a Pigeon, illustrated by Spurrier, Hamish Hamilton and Dodd Mead, 1944.
In the Same Boat, illustrated by Ruth Gervis, Dent, 1945, Dodd Mead, 1945.
Musical Honours, illustrated by Gervis, Dent, 1947, Dodd Mead, 1947.
Dusty's Windmill, illustrated by Marcia Lane Foster, Dent, 1949; published as *The Windmill Mystery,* Dodd Mead, 1950.
Roly's Dogs, illustrated by Alice Molony, Dent, 1950; published as *Dog Stars,* Dodd Mead, 1951.
Barbie, illustrated by Marcia Lane Foster, Dent, 1952, Little Brown (Boston), 1969.
Admiral's Walk, illustrated by Mary Gurnat, Dent, 1953.
Rosina Copper, the Mystery Mare, illustrated by Alfons Purtscher, Evans (London), 1954, Dutton (New York), 1956.
Cousin Beatie Learns the Fiddle, Blackwell (Oxford, England), 1955.
Tann's Boarders, illustrated by Jill Crockford, Dent, 1955.
Rosina and Son, illustrated by Marcia Lane Foster, Evans Brothers (London), 1956.

PLAYS

(With D. W. Wheeler) *Tomorrow,* Curwen (London), 1910.
(With Wheeler) *Winds,* music by Kitty Barne, illustrated by Lucy Barne, Curwen, 1912.

(With Wheeler) *Timothy's Garden,* illustrated by Lucy Barne, Curwen, 1912.

(With Wheeler) *Celandine's Secret,* illustrated by J. M. Saunders, Curwen, 1914.

Peter and the Clock, Curwen, 1919.

Susie Pays a Visit, Curwen, 1921.

The Amber Gate: A Pageant Play, Curwen, 1925.

Philemon and Baucis, Gowans and Gray (London), Baker (Boston), 1926.

Madge: A Camp-Fire Play, Novello (London), 1928.

Adventurers: A Pageant Play, Deane (London), 1931, Baker, 1936.

(Adapter) *The Grand Party,* based on the novel *Holiday House,* by Catherine Sinclair, in *The Theatre Window: Plays for Schools,* edited by W. T. Cunningham, Arnold (London), 1933.

Two More Mimes from Folk Songs: The Wraggle, Taggle Gipsies, O!; Robin-a-Thrush, Curwen, 1936.

They Made the Royal Arms, Baker, 1937.

Shilling Teas, Deane, 1938, Baker, 1938.

Days of Glory: A Pageant Play, Deane, 1946.

The "Local Ass": A Documentary Pageant Play for Girl Guides, Girl Guides' Association (London), 1947.

Also author of *The Lost Birthday,* Curwen.

FICTION AND MISCELLANEOUS

The Amber Gate, illustrated by Ruth Gervis, Nelson (London and New York), 1933.

Elizabeth Fry: A Story Biography, illustrated by Gervis, Methuen (London), 1933, Penguin (London), 1950.

Songs and Stories for Acting, illustrated by Gervis, Brown and Ferguson (Glasgow, Scotland), 1939.

Listening to the Orchestra, Dent, 1941, revised edition, Bobbs Merrill (Indianapolis), 1946.

Here Come the Girl Guides, Girl Guides' Association, 1947.

Introducing Handel, illustrated by Jill Crockford, Dent, 1955, Roy (New York), 1957.

Introducing Mozart, illustrated by Crockford, Dent, 1955, Roy, 1957.

Introducing Schubert, illustrated by Crockford, Dent, 1957, Roy, 1957.

NOVELS

Mother at Large, Chapman and Hall (London), 1938.

While the Music Lasted, Chapman and Hall, 1943.

Enter Two Musicians, Chapman and Hall, 1944.

Duet for Sisters, Chapman and Hall, 1947.

Vespa, Chapman and Hall, 1950.

Music Perhaps, Chapman and Hall, 1957.

Many of Barne's writings for both children and adults have appeared under the name Kitty Barne.

■ Sidelights

A versatile writer for children and adults, Kitty Barne enjoyed a prolific career that was unified by the subject of music, as well as by topics such as animals and traditional English life. Her renown was at its height during World War II and the years surrounding it, when she was known as something of a pioneer in bringing realism to children's literature, a field which, up to that point, had been largely the province of escapist adventure, romance, and mystery. Though Barne retained many of the elements of standard children's fare in her work, she often presented them within realistic settings such as England during the blitz or Norway under Nazi occupation. Her protagonists also frequently confronted dilemmas that many young readers could identify with, such as the question of whether or not to pursue a certain activity; and her treatment of adult characters, such as the father in her 1947 novel, *Musical Honours,* was notable for its realistic blending of positive and negative qualities within a personality.

Having studied music as a child and having written and produced original dramas as early as elementary school, Barne undoubtedly had a sense of her calling from a very young age. Even so, she experienced a kind of struggle that many aspiring artists are familiar with: her early plays, though published, brought her little fame. It was when she turned to children's fiction in the late 1930s, perhaps at the urging of her husband's cousin, the popular children's writer Noel Streatfeild, that Barne's career took a marked upturn. The first of her novels for children was the 1935 volume *The Easter Holidays,* a mystery set in the Bristol countryside. On its republication in 1949 as *Secret of the Sandhills,* a critic in the *Saturday Review of Literature* commented that Barne's "skill in writing and her well-drawn characters lift what might have been just another mystery story out of the ordinary." *New York Times* reviewer Ellen Lewis Buell, on a similar note, said that "[a]s is not always the case in mystery stories, the characterization is incisively and amusingly drawn, and the background ... is charming."

On first publication, however, it was the 1938 *She Shall Have Music* that won Barne her reputation. The story

From *Rosina Copper, the Mystery Mare,* written by Marion Catherine "Kitty" Barne and illustrated by Alfons Purtscher.

concerns the struggle of a young Irish girl, Karen, to follow her musical calling despite her family's lack of resources. Several critics at the time found the family "amusing and likable," in the words of a *New York Times* reviewer. M. L. Becker, in *Books,* pointed out that the tale could be used as "a touchstone" by young readers who felt artistic callings themselves. Writing several decades later, Gary D. Schmidt, in the *Dictionary of Literary Biography,* commented unfavorably on the "fanciful" degree to which Karen's aspirations are gratified.

Barne's high point of official recognition came for her 1940 novel *Visitors from London,* the second in a series of books about a family named Farrar living on a Sussex farm called Steadings. The first volume in the series, *Family Footlights,* had won praise for its "lightness of touch" from a critic in the *Times Literary Supplement,* and from Buell in the *New York Times* for the author's "faculty of writing about large families so that every member has a distinct and interesting personality" and her penchant for "assuming intelligence and humor" on the part of young readers. *Visitors from London* surpassed *Family Footlights* both critically and commercially, in large part because of its gripping subject, the settlement of bombed-out London families in rural Britain during World War II. Becker, writing in *Books,* stated that adults as well as children would enjoy the work; *Library Journal's* Marian Herr even worried that the book might be too mature for children; however, a reviewer in the *New Yorker* called it "perfect for family reading aloud," and Buell, in the *New York Times,* presented the novel as a children's equivalent of such adult-oriented home-front novels as *Mrs. Miniver.* The novel won the Carnegie Award in 1940. Judging it retrospectively in 1989, Schmidt wrote in the *Dictionary of Literary Biography:* "This novel represents Kitty Barne at her best. Her characters are vividly drawn and realistic to the experiences of any child living in Britain during the war." Schmidt called *Visitors from London* "a celebration of British life, particularly country life."

Another Barne book set during World War II was *We'll Meet in England,* in which two Norwegian children escape their nation's occupation by sailing to England in an Englishman's boat, rescuing a downed R.A.F. pilot along the way. Reviewers at the time and since, noting that this book was more of an escapist adventure than *Visitors from England,* have nevertheless found it an enjoyable yarn for children that conveyed a patriotic excitement appropriate under the circumstances. Shortly after the war, when the war's effects on later civilian life could be measured, Barne produced what may be her most memorable work, *Musical Honours.* This 1947 novel deals with the return of a father to his family after having been a prisoner of war for several years. The father, Charley Redland, was formerly a musician, a vocation his children have wished to follow; but on his return, he decides that music is too unstable an occupation, and tries to steer the children into white-collar fields. Reviewer H. F. Griswold, writing in the *Christian Science Monitor,* called *Musical Honours* "an entrancing story about life in England ... during rationing and

reconstruction." Schmidt commended the achievement to a point: "All this is realistic: the uneasy return of the father into the family and the frustration of being told what one is to become when one is already embarked on a vocation." But he felt that Barne's resolution of such conflicts was not as realistic as her presentation of them: as in *She Shall Have Music,* success comes too easily for all the Redlands. Nevertheless, Schmidt asserts: "Barne's reputation as a pioneer in realistic fiction for children—insofar as such a reputation exists—rests on such a novel as *Musical Honours.*"

Barne described her own work as realistic in an autobiographical entry for *The Junior Book of Authors.* Explaining her intentions, she wrote, "I knew they [children] were sensible, critical, and not at all romantic about their own affairs .... Whether the heroes and heroines of my books are running a dogs' motel, escaping from the Gestapo in Norway, getting up a play, helping a Polish girl find her feet in an English school, or persuading a returned POW father to change his mind about their future careers, they are all independent, energetic people, making up their minds about what they want to do with their lives and going all out to do it." Though Schmidt believed that Barne had not completely fulfilled her intentions, he commented favorably, if somewhat ironically, on Barne's "ability to take the most dreadful, calamitous atmospheres and pit against them the secure, safe worlds of loving families and music and tea by the fire in cozy chairs."

Barne's nonfiction books include biographies of composers such as Handel, Mozart, and Schubert, and a 1941 opus, *Listening to the Orchestra.* Written during a time of wartime crisis, this popular book carried on Barne's personal tradition—which is also a very British tradition—of finding cause for bravery in the preservation of civilization and its comforts. Barne herself, in eloquent words quoted by Schmidt, saw herself as affirming life: "the music-lover looks for the expression of the eternal truths above the din and smoke of the martyred earth."

■ Works Cited

Becker, M. L., review of *She Shall Have Music, Books,* March 19, 1939, p. 8.

Becker, M. L., review of *Visitors from London, Books,* April 20, 1941, p. 8.

Buell, Ellen Lewis, review of *Family Footlights, New York Times,* January 21, 1940, p. 11.

Buell, Ellen Lewis, review of *Secret of the Sandhills, New York Times,* March 6, 1949, p. 32.

Buell, Ellen Lewis, review of *Visitors from London, New York Times,* March 2, 1941, p. 10.

Review of *Family Footlights, Times Literary Supplement,* October 7, 1939, p. 578.

Griswold, H. F., review of *Musical Honours, Christian Science Monitor,* December 18, 1947, p. 16.

Herr, Marian, review of *Visitors from London, Library Journal,* October 15, 1957, p. 152.

Schmidt, Gary D., *Dictionary of Literary Biography,
Volume 160: British Children's Writers, 1914-1960,*
Gale, 1996, pp. 30-35.
Review of *Secret of the Sandhills, Saturday Review of
Literature,* July 9, 1949.
Review of *She Shall Have Music, New York Times,* June
4, 1939, p. 10.
Review of *Visitors from London, New Yorker,* May 24,
1941.

■ For More Information See

BOOKS

Twentieth-Century Children's Writers, 4th edition, St.
James Press, 1995, pp. 64-65.
The Who's Who of Children's Literature, compiled and
edited by Brian Doyle, Schocken Books, 1968, pp.
19-20.

PERIODICALS

School Library Journal, April, 1989, p. 42.*

* * *

BEDDOWS, Eric
   See NUTT, Ken

* * *

BEERE, Peter 1951-

■ Personal

Born November 10, 1951, in Liverpool, England; son of
Stan (a government worker) and Elsie (a daycare super-
visor; maiden name, Grattan) Beere; married Jan,
March 31, 1979 (divorced March 6, 1987); married
Jacqueline Thornton (a lawyer), December 1, 1987.
Politics: "Left of center." *Religion:* Humanitarian. *Hob-
bies and other interests:* Angling, movies, ornithology,
classical music, jazz, reading Russian and Central
European literature in translation.

■ Addresses

Home—12 Sherman Dr., Rainhill, Merseyside L35
6PW, England.

■ Career

Writer, 1980—. Presents writing workshops; public
speaker. Manager of a night shelter for the homeless in
Lancaster, England, 1991-94; volunteer worker for an
adult literacy project. Also worked as laboratory assistant, gardener, truck driver, construction laborer, and
office worker.

■ Awards, Honors

Runner up, Children's Book of the Year, for *Crossfire*
and *Underworld.*

■ Writings

FOR YOUNG PEOPLE; SUSPENSE NOVELS

Crossfire, Scholastic, (England), 1991.
Underworld, Scholastic, 1992.
Underworld II, Scholastic, 1992.
Underworld III, Scholastic, 1992.

FOR YOUNG PEOPLE; CRIME NOVELS

School for Death, Scholastic, 1993, published in the
United States as *School for Terror,* Scholastic, 1994.
Kiss of Death ("Point Crime" series), Scholastic, 1994.
At Gehenna's Door, Scholastic, 1997.

FOR YOUNG PEOPLE; FANTASY NOVELS

Doom Sword, Scholastic, 1993.
Star Warriors, Scholastic, 1995.

SCIENCE FICTION NOVELS

Urban Prey, Arrow (England), 1984.
The Crucifixion Squad, Arrow, 1984.
Silent Slaughter, Arrow, 1985.

CRIME NOVELS

The Squad, MacDonald/Futura (England), 1987.
The Fifth Man, MacDonald/Futura, 1987.
The Sixth Day, MacDonald/Futura, 1988.

OTHER

Riot (juvenile drama), Scholastic (England), 1995.
Bod's Mum's Knickers (juvenile humor), Scholastic,
1995.

■ Work in Progress

Gangs, a contemporary "Romeo and Juliet story" for
teenagers; research on drug abuse and homelessness.

PETER BEERE

In Beere's mystery from the "Point Crime" series, a young heroine finds herself the recipient of anonymous threatening messages. (Cover illustration by David Wyatt.)

■ Sidelights

Peter Beere once commented: "I am not an 'arty' writer, although I admire many writers who are. I view myself primarily as a storyteller with something of a message. The message usually has something to do with being more humane, compassionate, less bigoted, more caring, and less stupid. There is a tendency in many of us, when in doubt, to act stupidly. I am not a 'run with the crowd' type, and I am anxious to promote the merits of self-determination and individuality. I usually try to conceal my message as much as possible: it isn't a good thing to get up on a soapbox.

"My writing style is terse, often to the point of being almost underwritten. I don't like waffle. I do like sardonic humor. I am not a great thinker: I go with my instincts and follow the flow. Forward planning of a book is something I find very difficult to do. If I already know it, what's the point in writing about it? All of this

adds a great deal of verve and pace to my writing. My books probably get read faster than most people's.

"My motivation for writing? It is better than a 'proper' job. It is more challenging, more difficult, and more rewarding. Familiarity is a curse. There is nothing familiar about writing: every page presents fresh problems and rewards. Few moments in life provide more exhilaration than when one breaks through a wall. I hate it at times. It depresses me often. Writing is a drug, though, seductive and demanding.

"I have always loved books. I have always thought that good writers are 'gods.' My own writing marks my (probably doomed) attempt to climb toward them. I am never satisfied. I never learn much. I keep looking.

"I only write during the hours of darkness. Writing is a process that should be kept secret. The rest of the day is one long tract of boredom."

■ For More Information See

PERIODICALS

Books for Keeps, January, 1995, p. 11.
Fantasy Review, February, 1986, p. 17.
School Librarian, November, 1993, p. 164; May, 1995, p. 76.
Voice of Youth Advocates, August, 1994, p. 142; October, 1995, p. 216.

*   *   *

BENNETT, Cherie 1960-

■ Personal

Born October 6, 1960, in Buffalo, NY; daughter of Bennett Berman (a writer) and Roslyn (Ozur) Cantor (an educator); married Jeff Gottesfeld (a writer and producer), February 4, 1991. *Education:* University of Michigan, B.A. *Religion:* Jewish.

■ Addresses

Home and office—P.O. Box 150326, Nashville, TN 37215. *Agents*—Curtis Brown Ltd., 10 Astor Place, New York, NY 10003; Writers and Artists Agency, 19 West 44th St., New York, NY 10036; Metropolitan Talent, Inc., 4526 Wilshire Blvd., Los Angeles, CA 90010; Don Buchwald & Associates, 10 East 44th St., New York, NY 10017.

■ Career

Author, playwright, and syndicated columnist. Performer in Broadway, Off-Broadway, and regional theater productions, including *Grease* and *When You Comin' Back, Red Ryder.* Theater director at regional and off-Broadway productions, including *Anne Frank & Me.* Has performed as a vocalist, singing backup for John Cougar Melloncamp and in her play, *Honk Tonk Angels.* Has appeared on television and radio talk shows and as

CHERIE BENNETT

a lecturer in schools. *Member:* Writers Guild East, Dramatists Guild, PEN American Center.

■ Awards, Honors

First Night award for best new play, RCI Festival of Emerging American Theater award, and Wing Walker Award, all 1993, and first place, Jackie White Memorial National Competition, 1995, all for *John Lennon and Me;* Children's Choice designation, Children's Book Council, and American Library Association distinction, both 1994, both for *Did You Hear about Amber?;* Dallas Shortfest! award, 1994, for *Sex and Rage in a Soho Loft;* Sholem Aleichem Commission award, 1994, and Bonderman Biennial award and First Night award, both 1995, all for *Anne Frank and Me;* New Visions/New Voices award, Kennedy Center for the Performing Arts, 1996, for *Cyra and Rocky;* New Visions/New Voices award, Kennedy Center for the Performing Arts, 1998, for *Searching for David's Heart;* first place, Jackie White Memorial Children's Playwriting Competition, 1998, for *Zink: The Myth, The Legend, The Zebra.*

■ Writings

FOR YOUNG ADULTS

Life in the Fat Lane (novel), Delacorte, 1998.

YOUNG ADULT NOVELS; MASS MARKET

Good-Bye, Best Friend (also see below), HarperCollins (New York), 1993.
Girls in Love, Scholastic (New York), 1996.
Bridesmaids, Scholastic, 1996.

Searching for David's Heart, Scholastic, 1998.

Also author of *With a Face Like Mine,* c. 1980.

YOUNG ADULT NOVELS; "SUNSET ISLAND" SERIES

Sunset Island, Berkley (New York), 1991.
Sunset Kiss, Berkley, 1991.
Sunset Dreams, Berkley, 1991.
Sunset Farewell, Berkley, 1991.
Sunset Reunion, Berkley, 1991.
Sunset Heat, Berkley, 1992.
Sunset Paradise, Berkley, 1992.
Sunset Promises, Berkley, 1992.
Sunset Scandal, Berkley, 1992.
Sunset Secrets, Berkley, 1992.
Sunset Whispers, Berkley, 1992.
Sunset after Dark, Berkley, 1993.
Sunset after Hours, Berkley, 1993.
Sunset after Midnight, Berkley, 1993.
Sunset Deceptions, Berkley, 1993.
Sunset Embrace, Berkley, 1993.
Sunset on the Road, Berkley, 1993.
Sunset Surf, Berkley, 1993.
Sunset Wishes, Berkley, 1993.
Sunset Touch, Berkley, 1993.
Sunset Wedding, Berkley, 1993.
Sunset Fantasy, Berkley, 1994.
Sunset Fire, Berkley, 1994.
Sunset Glitter, Berkley, 1994.
Sunset Heart, Berkley, 1994.
Sunset Illusions, Berkley, 1994.
Sunset Magic, Berkley, 1994.
Sunset Passion, Berkley, 1994.
Sunset Revenge, Berkley, 1994.
Sunset Sensation, Berkley, 1994.
Sunset Stranger, Berkley, 1994.
Sunset Fling, Berkley, 1995.
Sunset Love, Berkley, 1995.
Sunset Spirit, Berkley, 1995.
Sunset Tears, Berkley, 1995.
Sunset Forever, Berkley, 1997.

"Sunset Island" titles have been translated into several languages.

JUVENILE NOVELS; "CLUB SUNSET ISLAND" TRILOGY

Too Many Boys!, Berkley, 1994.
Dixie's First Kiss, Berkley, 1994.
Tori's Crush, Berkley, 1994.

YOUNG ADULT NOVELS; "SURVIVING SIXTEEN" TRILOGY

Did You Hear about Amber?, Puffin, 1993.
The Fall of the Perfect Girl, Puffin, 1993.
Only Love Can Break Your Heart, Puffin, 1994.

YOUNG ADULT NOVELS; "WILD HEARTS" SERIES

Hot Winter Nights, Pocket Books, 1994.
On the Edge, Pocket Books, 1994.
Passionate Kisses, Pocket Books, 1994.
Wild Hearts, Pocket Books, 1994.
Wild Hearts Forever, Pocket Books, 1994.
Wild Hearts on Fire, Pocket Books, 1994.

YOUNG ADULT NOVELS; "TEEN ANGELS" SERIES; CO-WRITTEN WITH HUSBAND, JEFF GOTTESFELD

Heaven Can't Wait, Avon, 1996.
Love Never Dies, Avon, 1996.
Angel Kisses, Avon, 1996.
Heaven Help Us!, Avon, 1996.
Nightmare in Heaven, Avon, 1996.
Love without End, Avon, 1996.

YOUNG ADULT NOVELS; "HOPE HOSPITAL" SERIES

Get Well Soon, Little Sister, Troll Communications, 1996.
The Initiation, Troll Communications, 1996.
The Accident, Troll Communications, 1997.

YOUNG ADULT NOVELS: "TRASH" SERIES; CO-WRITTEN WITH GOTTESFELD

Trash, Berkley, 1997.
Trash: Love, Lies, and Video, Berkley, 1997.
Trash: Good Girls, Bad Boys, Berkley, 1997.
Dirty Big Secrets, Berkley, 1997.
Trash: The Evil Twin, Berkley, 1997.
Trash: Truth or Scare, Berkley, 1998.

PLAYS

Honky Tonk Angels, produced in New York City, 1988, Boston, MA, 1990, and Charlotte, NC, 1991-92.
John Lennon and Me (also known as *Candy Store Window;* adapted from her novel *Good-Bye, Best Friend;* produced in Nashville, TN, 1993), Dramatic Publishing (Woodstock, IL), 1996.
Sex and Rage in a Soho Loft, produced in Nashville, 1994, Dallas, TX, 1994, and Columbia, SC, 1995.
Anne Frank and Me (produced in Nashville, 1995, produced off-Broadway, American Jewish Theater, 1996), Dramatic Publishing, 1997.
Cyra and Rocky (based on *Cyrano de Bergerac* by Edmund Rostand; produced in Washington, DC, at Kennedy Center for the Performing Arts, 1996), Dramatic Publishing, 1997.
Zink the So-Called Zebra (produced in Milwaukee, WI, 1997), Dramatic Publishing, 1998.
Searching for David's Heart (play; adapted from novel of the same name), produced in Washington, DC, at Kennedy Center for the Preforming Arts, 1998.

Author of screenplays *Angel from Montgomery* (New Line Cinema), 1993, and *Wild Hearts* (Lantana Publications), 1995.

OTHER

Also author of *Samantha Tyler's Younger Sister* (in German translation only), Cora-Verlag Press (Germany). Author of nationally syndicated advice column, "Hey Cherie!" Author of novels in series "The Party Line," under the pseudonym Carrie Austen. Creator and monitor of America Online's first online reader-written young adult novel, *Horror Ink,* 1997. Has written for National Broadcasting Company (NBC) television daytime drama *Another World.* Bennett's works have been translated into several languages, including French, German, Spanish, and Swedish.

■ **Adaptations**

Several novels and plays have been optioned for film and television, including *Honky Tonk Angels, John Lennon & Me, Wild Hearts, Teen Angels, Anne Frank & Me, Hope Hospital,* and *Cyra and Rocky.*

■ **Work in Progress**

A novelization of *Anne Frank & Me;* a new young adult fiction series entitled "Pageant" for Berkley.

■ **Sidelights**

A popular columnist and novelist read by young teens around the United States, Nashville-based author Cherie Bennett is as enthusiastic about entertaining her young audience as she is about the city she calls home. A former Broadway actress and singer, Bennett spends much of her non-writing time outside Tennessee, visiting with groups of teen girls in different parts of the

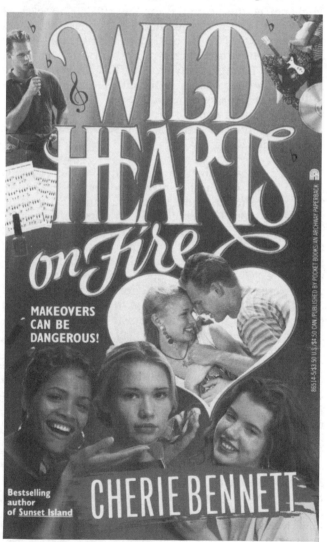

In Bennett's "Wild Hearts" series, New Yorker Jane McVay narrates tales about her new hometown of Nashville and her experiences in a country music band. (Cover photos by Michel Le Grou.)

United States. The upbeat author's discussions with adolescents are a constant reminder that growing up is a difficult time. "They [teen girls] worry most whether they are cute enough or thin enough," Bennett explained to *React for Teens* contributor Karen Pritzker. "Their lives become smaller. If I can write one book that saves a girl from that, I'm happy."

Born in 1960, Bennett spent her childhood years in Michigan, the only girl in a show-biz family. Her father worked as a writer for television shows, including *Twilight Zone, Route 66,* and Sid Caesar's *Show of Shows.* She explained to *Blast!* contributor Laura Matter that she started writing at a young age. "I wrote really, really bad poetry when I was a teenager," Bennett admitted. "This should give hope to kids out there who write poetry and think, 'This isn't any good.' I mean, my poetry stunk."

Bennett published her first novel, *With a Face Like Mine,* while she was a student at the University of Michigan at the beginning of the 1980s. However, it wasn't until she had graduated from college and spent several years in New York City as a singer and dancer that she returned to her writing seriously, first as a playwright. Bennett's play *Honky Tonk Angels* provided her with an introduction to the city she would one day call home. Featuring a group of women with dreams of becoming country music singing sensations, the play was produced in Nashville in 1988 and sold to Tri Star Pictures in 1992.

Bennett's long-running "Sunset Island" series of young adult novels, which she introduced in 1991, features teens Sam, Emma, and Carrie on a summer vacation that never ends. Taking place on an island off the coast of Maine, the novels follow the teens' efforts to find time for fun and friends while working as summer au pairs for vacationing families. In 1994 Bennett published the "Club Sunset Island" companion trilogy for younger readers. Featuring the novels *Too Many Boys, Dixie's First Kiss,* and *Tori's Crush,* the three-novel series features preteen protagonists coping with their first romantic experiences.

Other Bennett-penned series popular with teen readers include "Surviving Sixteen," a trilogy that debuted in 1993, and "Wild Hearts," which began in 1994. In *Wild Hearts,* the opening novel of the latter series, country music provides the backdrop to a New York City teen's growing appreciation for her new hometown of Nashville. Street-smart and cosmopolitan newcomer Jane McVay and her new friends—Savannah, Kimmy, and Sandra—eventually decide to form the band Wild Hearts, which serves as the series' focus. "Nashville provides a distinctive setting," noted a *Publishers Weekly* reviewer, who added that "Jane's wisecracking, first-person narrative . . . sets a rapid tempo." Silvia Makowski, in her review of the series premier in *Voice of Youth Advocates,* commented that "Bennett is in top form with this first installment . . . . Teens will feel sad and bad for [Jane] and identify with her predicament, caught between two exotic city cultures."

Angel Nicole Van Owen attempts to convince a sixteen-year-old girl that she is too young to have a baby in Bennett's second "Teen Angels" story.

Comprised of the novels *Did You Hear about Amber?, The Fall of the Perfect Girl,* and *Only Love Can Break Your Heart,* the "Surviving Sixteen" trilogy was praised by reviewers for its humor and lively style. Bennett's first-hand experience with rheumatoid arthritis serves as inspiration for her book *Did You Hear about Amber?* Published in 1993, the novel follows the beautiful but snobbish Amber, who makes up for living on the poor side of town by excelling at dance. Her talent and good looks gain her entry into the in-crowd until a diagnosis of rheumatoid arthritis cuts Amber's dreams of a career as a dancer short at age sixteen. In *The Fall of the Perfect Girl,* Bennett introduces readers to another teen with a less-than-ideal personality: Suzanne Elizabeth Wentworth Lafayette. As the length of her name might suggest, Bennett's protagonist is wealthy, worldly, and very spoiled. But the sixteen-year-old's perfect life comes crashing down around her after an indiscretion in her politically prominent father's past is publicly revealed. The family is scandalized with the discovery that Suzanne has a half-sister, Patsy, by her father's old girlfriend, and Suzanne's socialite mother indignantly leaves her husband. While noting that most readers will not find much to sympathize with in the novel's haughty heroine, Elaine S. Patterson stated in her *Kliatt* review that "girls should enjoy ... [watching] Suzanne becoming more thoughtful and mature." Noting that the novel was a "refreshing change of pace," *Voice of Youth Advocates* critic Beth Andersen maintained that *The Fall of the Perfect Girl* "is a good story about decent teens behaving in believable ways that do *not* involve substance abuse or promiscuity."

Bennett's "Teen Angels" novels, created and co-authored by her writer-producer husband, Jeff Gottesfeld, concern three older teens who meet untimely deaths and wind up in Teen Heaven, sent there by "Big Guy ... when they still had lessons of life to learn." The series begins with 1996's *Heaven Can't Wait,* as Cisco, Melody, and Nicole attempt to earn "Angel Points" by helping self-destructive musician Shayne Stone straighten out his life and end his dependance on drugs and alcohol. Averting a teen pregnancy becomes the focus of *Love Never Dies,* as angel Nicole is sent to "Ground Zero" (Earth) to convince a sixteen-year-old that motherhood should wait, no matter how much she loves her

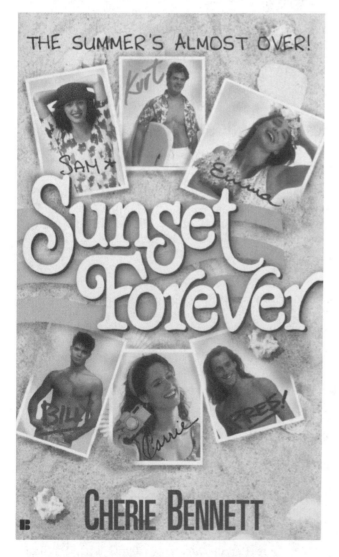

Part of Bennett's popular series set on an island off the coast of Maine, *Sunset Forever* follows three teens as they finish their summer jobs and contemplate future plans.

boyfriend. Observing that the series contains nondenominational references to religion despite its subject matter, Holly M. Ward, writing in *Voice of Youth Advocates,* praised the "Teen Angels" books as a "cute idea." Ward summarized the overall works as "light romance with the idea that one can make a positive difference in another's life." Similar in theme are Bennett's "Hope Hospital" books, which feature a trio of thirteen-year-olds who volunteer at a hospital in Hope, Michigan, and discover a great deal about life, death, and, of course, boys.

Bennett would make writing a family affair again with the "Trash" novel series begun in 1997. Working with her producer-husband Jeff Gottesfeld and drawing heavily on her daytime drama writing experience, Bennett created series protagonist Chelsea Jennings, the teen-age daughter of a convicted mass murderer. Hoping to conceal her past, Chelsea finds herself with a new boyfriend and a fashionable summer job in New York City, working behind the scenes on a scandalous TV talk show. The author "pulls out all the stops to snare female young adults looking for a read that's, well, just a trifle trashy," according to a *Publishers Weekly* critic in a review of the series' first installment, *Trash.*

Published in 1998, *Life in the Fat Lane* features a sixteen-year-old homecoming queen who lives the life many teens dream about: popularity in school, a perfect boyfriend, and excellent school marks. However, Lara Ardeche's ideal world slowly disintegrates as she begins to add pounds to her beauty pageant figure. Frustrated at her inexplicable weight gain, Lara tries fad diets, intense exercise sessions, and even fasting to shed the added pounds but nothing works. Only after coming to terms with her new size, and the incurable metabolic disorder behind it, is she able to regain her self-confidence confidence and appreciate the few true friends that remain with her. While talking about the damaging effects "unrealistic standards of beauty" have on teenagers, a *Kirkus Reviews* critic claimed that Bennett "lays out the issues with unusual clarity, sharp insight, and cutting irony." Calling the novel an "addicting experience," a contributor to *Publisher's Weekly* insists that Bennett's story about Lara's experience "is sure to hit a nerve" with readers.

In addition to her popular novel series, Bennett has written a number of stand-alone novels, and she continues to put her knowledge of the theater to good use in plays written for both adult and teen audiences. *John Lennon and Me,* a drama about a girl with cystic fibrosis based on her 1993 novel *Good-Bye, Best Friend,* received several awards after it was produced for the stage in 1992. Her play *Anne Frank and Me* about modern American teens, denial of the Holocaust, and the Nazi-occupation of Paris, was produced Off-Broadway by the American Jewish Theater in 1996. In a review for the *New York Times,* Lawrence Van Gelder hailed Bennett's reflection of Anne Frank's story through the eyes of modern—and skeptical—middle-schoolers assigned to perform a play based on Frank's diaries. The critic

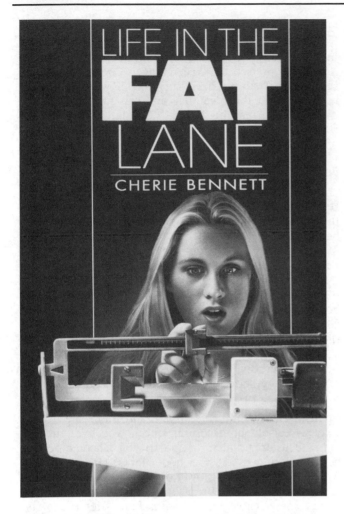

LIFE IN THE FAT LANE

CHERIE BENNETT

In Bennett's teen novel about self-image, beauty queen Lara Ardeche learns who her true friends are when a rare disease adds unwanted pounds to her svelte silhouette.

called the work "an eloquent and poignant play" that "deserves to be seen."

Receiving more than one hundred letters from fans of her columns and books each week, the prolific writer responds personally to each letter. "Garth Brooks taught me," Bennett explained, citing the country music superstar. "He told me early on that you must always respect the people who support you. And that's why anyone who sends me a fan letter gets my personal response. If a girl cares enough to read one of my books or my column, I owe it to her trust in me to write back."

■ Works Cited

Anderson, Beth, review of *The Fall of the Perfect Girl, Voice of Youth Advocates,* February, 1994, p. 364.
Bennett, Cherie, *Heaven Can't Wait,* Avon, 1996.
Review of *Life in the Fat Lane, Kirkus Reviews,* December 8, 1997, p. 73.
Review of *Life in the Fat Lane, Publishers Weekly,* December 15, 1997, p. 1832.
Makowski, Silvia, review of *Wild Hearts, Voice of Youth Advocates,* June, 1994, p. 80.
Matter, Laura, "Cherie Bennett Unplugged," *Blast! Magazine* (Nashville), April, 1993, pp. 18-19.
Patterson, Elaine S., review of *The Fall of the Perfect Girl, Kliatt,* November, 1993, p. 4.
Pritzker, Karen, "The Ultimate Pen Pal," *React for Teens,* January, 15-21, 1996, p. 13.
Review of *Trash, Publishers Weekly,* May 26, 1997, p. 86.
Van Gelder, Lawrence, review of *Anne Frank and Me, New York Times,* December 11, 1996.
Ward, Holly M., review of *Heaven Can't Wait* and *Love Never Dies, Voice of Youth Advocates,* June, 1996, p. 92.
Review of *Wild Hearts, Publishers Weekly,* January 17, 1994, p. 440.

■ For More Information See

PERIODICALS

Bulletin of the Center for Children's Books, February, 1998, pp. 194-95.
Horn Book, January-February, 1998, p. 69.
Kliatt, May, 1996, p. 12.
Publishers Weekly, June 14, 1993, p. 73.
Voice of Youth Advocates, December, 1993, pp. 286-87; April, 1996, p. 21.

*   *   *

BESTALL, A(lfred) E(dmeades) 1892-1986

■ Personal

Born December 14, 1892, in Mandalay, Burma; died January 15, 1986, in Wales. *Education:* Attended Birmingham Central School of Art, 1911-1913, and Central School of Art, London, 1914 and 1919-22.

■ Career

Illustrator, whose work appeared in periodicals including *Punch, Tatler, Bystander,* and *Passing Show;* wrote and illustrated the "Rupert" comic serial in the London *Daily Express,* 1935-65. *Military service:* Served in the British Army during World War I in Flanders.

■ Writings

SELF-ILLUSTRATED

Boys and Girls Book (annual; four volumes), Lane Publications (London, England), 1935-38.
Daily Express Rupert Annuals (forty-one volumes), Daily Express (London), 1936-76.
Rupert Adventure Series (fifty volumes), Daily Express, 1948-63.
Rupert Colour Library, Purnell (Maidenhead, Berkshire, England), 1976.
(With George Perry) *Rupert: A Bear's Life,* Pavilion, 1985.

Also author of two volumes of *Adventure Books;* contributor to *Daily Express Rupert Annuals* after 1976.

ILLUSTRATOR

Illustrator of *The Play's the Thing* by Enid Blyton, 1927, *A Book of Magic Rhymes* by Alfred Dunning, 1928, *Reading and Thinking* (seven volumes), 1928-1934, *Myths and Legends of Many Lands* by Evelyn Smith, 1930, *Tales from Many Lands* by D. V. Searle, 1930, *Kenilworth* by Sir Walter Scott, 1933, *The Pathfinder* by James Fenimore Cooper, 1933, *Thalaba the Destroyer* by Robert Southey, 1933, *The Black Tulip* by Alexandre Dumas, 1933, *The Three Musketeers* by Alexandre Dumas, 1933, *The Disappearing Trick* by Agnes Frome, 1933, *The Spanish Gold-Fish* by Dudley Glass, 1934, *New Times Reader 2*, 1934, *Mother Goose's Book of Nursery Rhymes,* 1936, *The Land of the Christmas Stocking* by Mabel Buchanan, 1936, *Salute to the Village* by Fay Inchfawn, 1943, *The Boy Next Door* by Enid Blyton, 1944, *Countryside [Animal, Strange] Tales from Blackwood* (three volumes), 1946-1950, *Folk Tales of Wales* by Eirwen Jones, 1947, *A Sprite at School* by Constance M. White, 1947, and *The Hive* by John Crompton, 1947.

■ Sidelights

British author and illustrator A. E. Bestall contributed work to periodicals during the 1930s and provided drawings for the works of many authors, including classics by James Fenimore Cooper and Alexandre Dumas as well as volumes by the popular British children's writer Enid Blyton. He is best remembered, however, for his years as the creative force behind the children's comic strip "Rupert" in the London *Daily Express.* Though Rupert the Bear and several of his friends were the creation of Mary Tourtel, Bestall took over the strip when failing eyesight forced Tourtel to relinquish the task in 1935. Bestall himself retired from the day-to-day job of writing and drawing "Rupert" for the newspaper in 1965, but continued to contribute adventures to the annual Rupert books published by the *Daily Express* until his death in 1986.

In Tourtel's hands, Rupert had fantasy-oriented adventures, encountering what Mary Cadogan described in *Twentieth-Century Children's Writers* as "weird castles and caves that seemed to spring up like mushrooms or mirages in the meadows near his home." Tourtel also endowed her hero with her own love of airplanes and other instruments of flight. When Bestall began writing and drawing Rupert's adventures, he retained Tourtel's emphasis on flight, but gave the stories more of a science fiction flavor. He also added new characters to Rupert's circle of friends and led the bear into more mystery-solving situations than had Tourtel. Bestall kept the series current; in a 1980 episode, Rupert rode in a flying saucer.

Shortly before his death, Bestall collaborated with George Perry on a history of the Rupert character, *Rupert: A Bear's Life.* In these pages, the pair recount Tourtel's creation of Rupert and recall that Bestall did not sign the strip for several years after taking it over. As Humphrey Carpenter explained, reviewing *A Bear's Life* in the *Times Literary Supplement,* this was "out of

respect for Mrs. Tourtel, who was still alive." Carpenter further noted that the volume contains several Rupert stories and concluded that "Rupert ... is really a timeless folk-hero."

Rupert is still popular, and Bestall's *Rupert Annuals* continue to be reprinted. Reviewing a 1991 facsimile of 1939's *The Adventures of Rupert* in the *Spectator,* Juliet Townsend remarked that the volume was "wonderfully cosy and reassuring." Carpenter and others have mentioned that they preferred Bestall's work on Rupert over Tourtel's, but Byron Rogers, writing in the *Times,* preferred what he labeled as the "pure romance" of the strips and stories done by the bear's creator. He did, however, profess his admiration for Bestall's illustrations, calling him "a wonderful artist." Not all critics share an affection for Rupert, however; Peter Campbell, discussing the bear and his comic strip friends in a *London Review of Books* article, called "mystifying ... the appeal which characters of stultifying banality exercise for generation after generation of children." Perry and Bestall themselves, however, predicted in *A Bear's Life* that "the odds are on a recognisable Rupert Bear being present in the first issue of the *Daily Express* to appear in the 21st century."

■ Works Cited

Bestall, A. E., and George Perry, *A Bear's Life,* Pavilion, 1985.

Cadogan, Mary, *Twentieth-Century Children's Writers,* 4th edition, St. James Press, 1995.

Campbell, Peter, *London Review of Books,* December 5, 1985, p. 18.

Carpenter, Humphrey, review of *A Bear's Life, Times Literary Supplement,* December 20, 1985, p. 1460.

Rogers, Byron, *Times* (London), December 5, 1985.

Townsend, Juliet, review of *The Adventures of Rupert, Spectator,* November 30, 1991, p. 54.

*   *   *

BISHOP, Gavin 1946-

■ Personal

Born February 13, 1946, in Invercargill, New Zealand; son of Stanley Alan (a railway employee) and Doris Hinepau (McKay) Bishop; married Vivien Carol Edwards (a teacher and artist), August 27, 1966; children: Cressida, Charlotte, Alexandra. *Education:* University of Canterbury, Diploma of Fine Arts (with honors), 1967; Christchurch Teachers' College, diploma, 1968. *Politics:* Liberal. *Hobbies and other interests:* Reading, movies, gardening (in fits and starts), travel, food.

■ Addresses

Home and office—11 Cracroft Ter., Christchurch 2, New Zealand. *Agent*—Studio Godwin Sturges, 154 West Newton St., Boston, MA 02118. *Electronic mail*—gavinbishop @ netaccess.co.nz

■ Career

Illustrator, author, educator. Linwood High School, Christchurch, New Zealand, art teacher and department chair, 1969-89; Christ's College, Christchurch, head of art department, 1989—. Rhode Island School of Design, Providence, RI, professor, 1996; UNESCO children's literature workshop leader in China, 1992, and Indonesia, 1996. *Member:* New Zealand Society of Authors (PEN New Zealand Inc.), New Zealand Illustrators' Guild.

■ Awards, Honors

Russell Clark Medal for Illustration, New Zealand Library Association, 1982, for *Mrs. McGinty and the Bizarre Plant;* New Zealand Children's Picture Book of the Year, New Zealand Government Publishers and New Zealand Literary Fund, 1983, for *Mr. Fox;* Grand Prix, Noma Concours, UNESCO and Kodansha International, 1984, for illustrations in *Mr. Fox;* Russell Clark Medal finalist, 1991, for *Katarina;* AIM Award for Children's Picture Book of the Year, 1994, for *Hinepau.*

■ Writings

FOR CHILDREN; SELF-ILLUSTRATED

Mrs. McGinty and the Bizarre Plant, Oxford University Press, 1981.
Bidibidi, Oxford University Press, 1982.
Mr. Fox, Oxford University Press, 1982.
Chicken Licken, Oxford University Press, 1984.
The Horror of Hickory Bay, Oxford University Press, 1984.
Mother Hubbard, Oxford University Press, 1984.
A Apple Pie, Oxford University Press, 1987.

GAVIN BISHOP

The Three Little Pigs, Ashton Scholastic (New York), 1989.
Katarina, Random House (New York City), 1990.
Hinepau, Ashton Scholastic, 1993.
Maui and the Sun: A Maori Tale, North-South Books (New York), 1996.
Little Rabbit and the Sea, North-South Books, 1997.
Maui and the Goddess of Fire, Scholastic (New Zealand), forthcoming.

ILLUSTRATOR

Katherine O'Brien, *The Year of the Yelvertons,* Oxford University Press, 1981.
Kathleen Leverich, *The Hungry Fox,* Houghton (Boston), 1986.
Beverley Dietz, *The Lion and the Jackal,* Simon & Schuster (New York), 1991.
Jeffrey Leask, *Little Red Rocking Hood,* Ashton Scholastic, 1992.
Philip Bailey, *The Wedding of Mistress Fox,* North South, 1994.
Kana Riley, *A Moose Is Loose,* Brown Publishing Network, 1994.
Philip Bailey (reteller), *The Wedding of Mistress Fox,* North-South Books, 1994.
Joy Cowley, *The Bears' Picnic,* Shortlands, 1995.

OTHER

Author of libretto for *Terrible Tom,* a ballet commissioned by Royal New Zealand Ballet Company, 1985, and *Te Maia and the Sea-Devil,* a ballet, Royal New Zealand Ballet Company, 1986; author of scripts for TVNZ television series *Bidibidi,* broadcast November and December, 1990, and *Bidibidi to the Rescue,* broadcast November and December, 1991, both based on his book, *Bidibidi;* author of numerous readers published by Wendy Pye Limited, including *Spider, There Is a Planet, I Like to Find Things, The Cracker Jack, Good Luck Elephant, Cabbage Caterpillar,* and *The Secret Lives of Mr. and Mrs. Smith.*

■ Sidelights

Gavin Bishop is an illustrator noted for his attention to background details in pictures that augment, often humorously, the stories they accompany. In addition to providing illustrations that are considered colorful and lively, Bishop has made a name for himself as an effective reteller of such traditional tales as *The Three Pigs* and *Mother Hubbard,* though these works are often appreciated more for their artwork than for the stories they illustrate. Bishop's storytelling ambitions have further extended to encompass narratives that highlight the native Maori culture of his homeland of New Zealand.

Born in Invercargill, the southernmost city in New Zealand, Bishop lived with his parents in his grandmother's little house "with a big rhododendron in front." He started school when the family moved to Kingston, "a tiny collection of houses at the end of the railway line from Invercargill," Bishop told *Something about the Author (SATA),* where they lived until he was eight. "At the single-teacher school in Kingston, there were only eleven pupils, and I was the only one in my class. Some days I got a ride to school on the back of a huge horse with two other kids. We had to climb the school gate to get onto its back," Bishop recollected. "I had a dog called Smudge and a cat called Calla Callutsa, which was given to us by some Greek neighbors when they shifted to Wellington.

"In Kingston, we had no electricity or telephone, and we didn't have a car," Bishop continued. "Our radio ran on a car battery, but reception was poor because of the surrounding mountains. The *Southland Times* arrived spasmodically on the freight train from Lumsden. It was the *Auckland Weekly* news, though, that excited us all, with the pictures of the young Queen Elizabeth's coronation in 1953—the pageantry and the crown jewels."

At the age of eight, Bishop returned with his family to Invercargill, where he discovered the joys of a free library system and joined the public library. He was introduced to Tolkien's *The Hobbit* through an extract in a magazine when he was nine. "I have read it several times since and still find it a source of inspiration," Bishop noted. At the age of eighteen, he enrolled at the Canterbury University School of Fine Arts in Christchurch to study painting. "I was fortunate to be a student there when Russell Clark, a well-known New Zealand illustrator, taught there," Bishop added. After graduating with honours in painting in 1967, he spent a year at the Christchurch Secondary Teachers' College. "From early in my life, I wanted to be an art teacher," Bishop reflected, "and that is what I am now." The two interests which have remained constant throughout his life, Bishop notes, are his love of teaching and children's literature. "Books, stories, and pictures have provided a lifelong fascination for me. Children's picture books in particular, with their intertwined rhythms of pictures and words combining to tell a story in an often deceptively simple way, have always interested me."

Bishop's first self-illustrated children's book, *Mrs. McGinty and the Bizarre Plant,* won an award for illustration from the New Zealand Library Association. In this story, the butt of the neighborhood children's jokes becomes a local hero of sorts when the plant she buys at the store grows to enormous proportions, eventually attracting the attention of a team of botanists, who airlift the giant plant for their collection. Zena Sutherland of the *Bulletin of the Center for Children's Books* found this an "amusing" plot, but offered greater praise for Bishop's illustrations, calling them "boldly designed, usually dramatically composed, nicely detailed." A critic for *Junior Bookshelf* similarly singled out Bishop's artwork, stating that he "most effectively and subtly depicts the transformation of Mrs. McGinty's character and outlook." "I love gardening and growing things," the author admitted. "My wife and I have times when we talk and read about nothing else. On other occasions, however, we avoid the garden for months on end."

Bishop followed this first effort with several adaptations of traditional stories for children. His illustrations for *Mr. Fox* drew comparisons to Maurice Sendak from Marcus Crouch in *Junior Bookshelf,* and Margery Fisher of *Growing Point* likewise noted that Bishop's "idiosyncratic illustrations" add an element of "implied social satire" to the story that "lifts the folk-tale far away from its simple origins." Similarly, the "vigor and humor" of Bishop's illustrations steal the show, according to a reviewer for *Bulletin of the Center for Children's Books,* in the author's retelling *Chicken Licken,* the tale of a chick who thinks the sky is falling when an acorn lands on her head. "The traditional tale may be slight," wrote Ralph Lavender in *School Librarian,* "but the superbly autumnal pictures make it into something which is quite

From *Little Rabbit and the Sea*, written and illustrated by Gavin Bishop.

Maui and his brothers returned home and went fishing. Now they would have plenty of daylight to catch all the fish they wanted.

Maui attempts to capture the sun and stretch the daylight hours in Bishop's self-illustrated retelling of a Polynesian folktale. (From *Maui and the Sun: A Maori Tale.*)

special." A review of Bishop's *Mother Hubbard* garnered the following comment from Marcus Crouch of *Junior Bookshelf:* "Gavin Bishop's distinguishing mark, apart from his brilliant technique, is his attention to detail . . . . These pictures are for reading." And a *Kirkus Reviews* commentator, who began by noting that there is little need for another version of the story of *The Three Pigs,* ended by concluding his review of Bishop's rendering, "Why not another version, if it's this good?"

Bishop has traveled extensively, not only throughout New Zealand, but also to many countries overseas— England, France, Italy, Germany, Australia, Greece, Holland, Canada, and Malaysia. He has been to Japan four times, and in 1990 he and his youngest daughter took part in a cultural exchange on the island of Sakhalin in the Soviet Far East. In 1992, he went to Beijing and Shanghai at the invitation of UNESCO to give lectures and run workshops on children's literature. In 1997 he went to Indonesia to work again for UNESCO. He has visited the United States several times and in the spring of 1996 taught at the Rhode Island School of Design in Providence.

"In recent years," Bishop continued to *SATA,* "I have become more and more interested in sifting through the memories of my own childhood in search of useful material for stories and ideas for pictures.

"The ballet libretto for 'Terrible Tom,' commissioned by the Royal New Zealand Ballet in 1985, is loosely based on incidents from my early years in Invercargill.

"In 'Katarina' I explored the family stories and verbal histories that I was told by my mother about her Aunt Kate who had shifted down south from the Waikato in the 1860s. 'Hinepau' is a legend-like story that I named after my mother whose family were Maori/Scots.

"I would in the future like to produce more work of a bicultural nature. New Zealand children should know and feel comfortable with their Maori heritage. Besides creating a better understanding of Maori-Pakeha values, a knowledge of Taha-Maori would provide a richer and more stimulating country in which to live."

■ Works Cited

Review of *Chicken Licken, Bulletin of the Center for Children's Books,* April, 1985, p. 141.

Crouch, Marcus, review of *Mother Hubbard, Junior Bookshelf,* February, 1988, p. 18.

Crouch, Marcus, review of *Mr. Fox, Junior Bookshelf,* June, 1983, p. 107.

Fisher, Margery, review of *Mr. Fox, Growing Point,* May, 1983, p. 4080.

Lavender, Ralph, review of *Chicken Licken, School Librarian,* June, 1985, p. 133.

Review of *Mrs. McGinty and the Bizarre Plant, Junior Bookshelf,* August, 1982, pp. 128-29.

Sutherland, Zena, review of *Mrs. McGinty and the Bizarre Plant, Bulletin of the Center for Children's Books,* May, 1983, p. 163.

Review of *The Three Little Pigs, Kirkus Reviews,* January 15, 1990, pp. 101-02.

■ For More Information See

PERIODICALS

Booklist, May 1, 1996, p. 1508.
Growing Point, July, 1987, p. 4837.
Publishers Weekly, November 28, 1994, p. 61.
School Library Journal, March, 1990, p. 188; December, 1994, pp. 122-23; July, 1996, p. 77.

BLEDSOE, Lucy Jane 1957-

■ Personal

Born February 1, 1957, in Portland, OR; daughter of John P. and Helen (Wieman) Bledsoe; companion of Patricia E. Mullan. *Education:* Attended Williams College, 1975-77; University of California at Berkeley, B.A., 1979. *Hobbies and other interests:* Cycling, mountaineering, literacy programs.

■ Career

Writer. Martin Luther King Junior High, Berkeley, CA, California Poets in the Schools residency, 1990; Tenderloin Women Writers Workshop, San Francisco, CA, facilitator, 1990-92; George Lucas Education Foundation, Skywalker Ranch, Marin County, CA, script and story writer, 1992; Globe Book Company, Paramus, NJ, textbook and story writer, 1992-95. Conducts creative writing workshops for adult literacy programs in Richmond, San Francisco, Oakland, and Berkeley, CA. *Member:* PEN, National Writers Union, Media Alliance.

■ Awards, Honors

Youthgrant from National Endowment for the Humanities, 1982; PEN Syndicated Fiction Award, 1985; semifinalist, San Francisco Foundation's Joseph Henry Jackson Award for Fiction, 1987 and 1988; grant from Poets and Writers Readings/Workshop, 1989; creative writing fellowship from Money for Women/Barbara Deming Memorial Fund, 1989; honorable mention, *Literacy Lights* fiction contest, 1990; honorable mention, *New Letters* Literacy Awards, 1995, for essay "Above Treeline."

■ Writings

FOR CHILDREN

The Big Bike Race, illustrated by Sterling Brown, Holiday House, 1995.
Tracks in the Snow, Holiday House, 1997.

"AN AMERICAN FAMILY" SERIES

Colony of Fear, Fearon Education (Belmont, CA), 1989.
A Matter of Pride, Fearon Education, 1989.
Two Kinds of Patriots, Fearon Education, 1989.
The Journey Home, Fearon Education, 1989.
Rhino Wars, Fearon/Janus/Quercus, 1993.
Sweat: Stories and a Novella, Seal Press (Seattle), 1995.
Working Parts, Seal Press, 1997.

OTHER

Break Away, David S. Lake Publishers (Belmont, CA), 1986.
A Question of Freedom, David S. Lake Publishers, 1987.
Amelia Earhart (biography), Fearon/Janus/Quercus (Belmont, CA), 1987.

Contributor to books, including *Combat Zone,* Fearon Education, 1990; *Fearon's Amazing Adventures,* Fearon/

LUCY JANE BLEDSOE

Janus/Quercus, 1993; *Growing Up Gay: A Literary Anthology,* edited by Bennett L. Singer, New Press of New York, 1993; *Another Wilderness,* edited by Susan Fox Rogers, Seal Press, 1994; *Sportsdykes,* edited by Susan Fox Rogers, St. Martins, 1994; *Tomboys!,* edited by Lynne Yamaguchi and Karen Barber, Alyson, 1995; and *Women on Women 3,* edited by Joan Nestle and Naomi Holoch, Plume Books, 1995. Also contributor of numerous articles to magazines, including *Newsday, Conditions, Northwest Literary Forum, Lesbian Short Fiction, Lambda Book Report, California Bicyclist,* and *Frontiers.*

EDITOR

Goddesses We Ain't: Tenderloin Women Writers, Freedom Voices Publications (San Francisco, CA), 1992.
Let the Spirit Flow: Writings on Communications and Freedom, Berkeley Reads (Berkeley, CA), June, 1994.
Heatwave: Women in Love and Lust (anthology), Alyson (Los Angeles), 1995.
Leaping 50 Stories High, (Richmond, CA), 1995.

■ Sidelights

An accomplished nonfiction, textbook, and essay writer, Lucy Jane Bledsoe has also written works for children. In her well-received story *The Big Bike Race,* Ernest and his sister, Melissa, are being raised by their grandmother in Washington, DC, and Ernest desperately wants a sleek, new racing bicycle for his tenth birthday. His grandmother scrapes together enough money to buy Ernest a bike—a big, clunky, yellow bike. Although embarrassed by the bike, Ernest is touched by his grandmother's generosity and is determined to win the Citywide Cup race with his new bicycle. *The Big Bike Race* is based on experiences Bledsoe had as a child when she also received a big, used, yellow bike.

Critics have praised *The Big Bike Race* for its depiction of a loving African-American family that succeeds despite poverty. *Booklist* reviewer Lauren Peterson comments that this type of "dignified portrayal ... is something not seen enough in mainstream children's literature." The book has also been praised as more than a simple story of wishes granted. Margaret A. Bush of *Horn Book* writes that a "nice twist veers events away from a predictable outcome to a more complex and satisfying conclusion."

Bledsoe once commented that "my primary motivation for writing is to make sense of the world. Creating—stories, paintings, dance, music, art of any kind—is the only way I know how to combat forces of destruction and feelings of alienation. I read widely and am

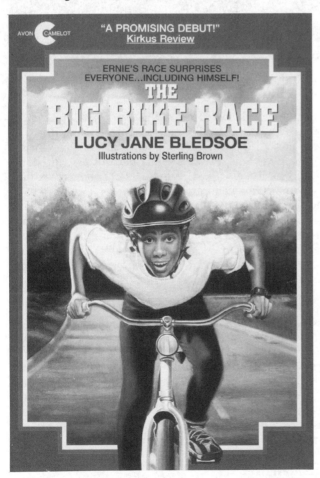

AVON CAMELOT

"A PROMISING DEBUT!"
Kirkus Review

ERNIE'S RACE SURPRISES EVERYONE...INCLUDING HIMSELF!

THE
BIG BIKE RACE
LUCY JANE BLEDSOE

Illustrations by Sterling Brown

Ernie decides that his secondhand bike won't stop him from proving himself a skillful bike racer in Bledsoe's warmhearted book for young readers.

influenced by everything I read. Each month I have different favorite authors, both contemporary and classic. I teach creative writing classes in literacy—that's *literacy,* not literary—programs, and I sincerely believe adults who are learning to read and write for the first time are the best writing teachers I have had. They teach me about the bones of language and about the absolute necessity of a story.

"I write fiction every day and all morning. I am not an outline writer, though I usually try to write a string of scenes before beginning a first draft. (These synopses always change drastically in the course of writing a story or book.) Then I write the first draft pretty much all the way through. The real work begins after the first draft is complete. I rewrite a tremendous amount: every story or chapter goes through dozens of drafts.

"I write textbooks for a living. About fifty percent of the textbook writing I do is in the sciences. I love reading about physics and earth science, both of which teach me what a blip we are in the history of the universe. We don't have time for anything but the truth. So I try to tell the truth. I do that better with fiction than with nonfiction.

"I am also inspired by courageous people and nutty people, and most of all, by people who are both."

■ Works Cited

Bush, Margaret A., review of *The Big Bike Race, Horn Book,* January, 1996, p. 72.
Peterson, Lauren, review of *The Big Bike Race, Booklist,* October 1, 1995, p. 313.

■ For More Information See

PERIODICALS

Bulletin of the Center for Children's Books, December, 1995, p. 119.
Kirkus Reviews, October 15, 1995, p. 1487.
Library Journal, October 1, 1995, p. 122.
Publishers Weekly, August 7, 1995, p. 456.
School Library Journal, November, 1995, p. 96.

*   *   *

BOND, B. J.
See HENEGHAN, James

*   *   *

BOWEN, Alexandria Russell
(Andy Russell Bowen)

■ Personal

Born in St. Paul, MN; married; children: a daughter and stepdaughter. *Education:* Wellesley College, B.A.; University of Michigan, M.A. *Hobbies and other interests:* Painting (watercolor, acrylic), world travel (annual trips to Africa), the outdoors, canoeing, camping, walking in Great Britain.

■ Addresses

Home and office—Minneapolis, MN.

■ Career

Writer for children. Minnesota Conservatory of Performing Arts (private secondary school), St. Paul, founder and member of board of directors, also worked as interim director and development director. *Member:* Midwest Authors Association, Children's Reading Round Table.

■ Writings

FOR CHILDREN; AS ANDY RUSSELL BOWEN

A World of Knowing: A Story about Thomas Hopkins Gallaudet, illustrated by Elaine Wadsworth, Carolrhoda (Minneapolis, MN), 1995.

A Head Full of Notions: A Story about Robert Fulton, illustrated by Lisa Harvey, Carolrhoda, 1996.

The Back of the Beyond: A Story about Lewis and Clark, illustrated by Ralph L. Ramstad, Carolrhoda, 1996.

Flying against the Wind: A Story about Beryl Markham, Carolrhoda, 1998.

Author, under name Alexandria Bowen, of children's plays, including *Rascals and Riverboats,* adaptations of *Grimms' Fairy Tales, 'Twas the Night before Christmas,* and *Arcadia's Dream* (operetta with rhymed text), all produced in Minneapolis in the 1980s.

■ Work in Progress

More biographies for children.

■ Sidelights

Alexandria Russell Bowen told *SATA:* "I was born and raised in St. Paul, Minnesota, went to Wellesley College and the University of Michigan. I have lived in Cambridge, Massachusetts, and Cambridge, England (where I acted in a Gilbert and Sullivan company and played violin in a string orchestra), Ann Arbor, Michigan, and now Minneapolis.

"I have traveled widely (still do), including seven safaris to East, Central, and Southern Africa to see animals, birds, scenery. I drive around in open vehicles with knowledgeable guides, take photographs, and stay in camps or simple lodges. I love the excitement, the beauty, the smells and sounds of the bush, and the privilege of seeing and living among wildlife in its own natural habitat.

"I also travel often to England, Ireland, Scotland, and Wales for canal boat trips, week-long walks, the London theater, visits with friends. We (my husband, daughter, and I) also travel frequently to Central and South America for educational trips and/or winter breaks. I

also went to China last fall on a science museum trip, visiting Beijing, Sian, and other cities and spending a week on a boat on the Yangtze River.

"I take a lot of pictures and paint watercolors from my photographs. I have made two family recipe books for my daughter and stepdaughter, with watercolor paintings to accompany each recipe, and I have just completed a picture book for a step-granddaughter. I am also learning about acrylics and have recently painted a small pine chest and several clay pots. I am definitely an amateur at this painting business, but I love it. It's wonderful fun and all-absorbing.

"Much of what I do—writing, painting, traveling to out-of-the-way places—starts out as a challenge and a matter of curiosity. 'I've never done this before,' then 'I wonder if I could do it ... I'm going to try,' then 'Oh, my God, what have I gotten myself into!' That is the usual pattern, and it has brought many adventures and personal satisfactions into my life.

"Many of my activities during childhood and adulthood have centered around music (violin, piano, large and small choral groups), the outdoors, and children. I

From *A Head Full of Notions,* Andy Russell Bowen's biography of Robert Fulton, inventor of the steamboat. (Illustrated by Lisa Harvey.)

started writing stories for my own children when they were very young and went on from there. One of the qualities I like best in myself and others is a spirit of playfulness, which is especially meaningful to me if there is behind it an individual, like me, who has experienced difficult times. I am healthy and incredibly blessed with loving family and friends. I have worked hard for this."

■ For More Information See

PERIODICALS

Booklist, January 1, 1996, p. 820.
School Library Journal, January, 1996, p. 114.

* * *

BOWEN, Andy Russell
See BOWEN, Alexandria Russell

* * *

BRANCATO, Robin F. 1936-

■ Personal

Born March 19, 1936, in Reading, PA; daughter of W. Robert (a telephone company worker) and Margretta (Neuroth) Fidler; married John J. Brancato (a teacher), December 17, 1960; children: Christopher Jay, Gregory Robert. *Education:* University of Pennsylvania, B.A., 1958; City College of the City University of New York, M.A., 1976.

■ Addresses

Home—Teaneck, NJ.

■ Career

John Wiley & Sons, New York City, copyeditor, 1959-61; Hackensack High School, Hackensack, NJ, teacher of English, journalism, and creative writing, 1967-79, 1985, part-time teacher, 1979-84; currently teaching in Teaneck, NJ. Kean College of New Jersey, writer in residence, c. 1985.

■ Awards, Honors

Best Books, American Library Association, 1977, for *Winning,* 1980, for *Come Alive at 505,* and 1982, for *Sweet Bells Jangled out of Tune;* New Jersey Authors Award, New Jersey Institute of Technology, 1988, for *Uneasy Money,* and 1990, for *Winning.* Brancato was also honored as an Outstanding Pennsylvania Author by the Pennsylvania School Librarians Association in 1983.

■ Writings

Don't Sit under the Apple Tree, Knopf, 1975.
Something Left to Lose, Knopf, 1976.

Winning, Knopf, 1977.
Blinded by the Light, Knopf, 1978.
Come Alive at 505, Knopf, 1980.
Sweet Bells Jangled out of Tune, Knopf, 1982.
Facing Up, Knopf, 1984.
Uneasy Money, Knopf, 1986.

Also contributor of short stories "Fourth of July," in *Sixteen,* edited by Donald Gallo, Dell, 1984, and "White Chocolate," in *Connections,* edited by Gallo, Dell, 1989; contributor of one-act play, "War of the Words," in *Centerstage,* edited by Gallo, HarperCollins, 1990.

■ Adaptations

Blinded by the Light was made into a television "Movie of the Week" for the Columbia Broadcasting System (CBS), December, 1980.

■ Work in Progress

An untitled young adult novel.

■ Sidelights

Preferring realistic fiction over fantasy, Robin F. Brancato has established a solid reputation as an author of straightforward novels featuring teenage characters struggling with personal crises. Her stories reflect both her memories of her own childhood and her experiences as an educator and mother of two. Thus, although her books are often categorized as being for young adults, she once commented, "I like to think that I write *about*

ROBIN F. BRANCATO

young people but not exclusively *for* them. Down with distinctions.... Well-written stories that happen to be about the young can and should be read without apology by adults." "The novels of Robin Brancato," asserted Louise A. DeSalvo in *Media and Methods,* "mark signposts in the stages that children must live through in learning about adversity, and the way-stations they must pass through in coping with hardship. Her novels ... teach young people about their own capacities for coping with problems without relinquishing the joys that come with living."

Compared to most of her fictional characters, who endure various trials in their lives, Brancato was fortunate enough to have a very stable family life as a child. Most of Brancato's early memories are of her days spent in the Reading, Pennsylvania, suburb of Wyomissing. "Wyomissing was then and is now a wonderful place for children," the author reflected in *Speaking for Ourselves: Autobiographical Sketches by Notable Authors of Books for Young Adults.* "Within walking distance from my house were a school I loved, a good library, a playground and swimming pool, woods and a creek to explore, and a main street with lots of shops." In an essay Brancato also noted, "My world as a child seemed large and safe. My mother stayed home and took care of us, as all the other mothers did, and my father worked from nine to five for the telephone company."

Even World War II seemed remote to Brancato, although years later she realized the great effect of this difficult period. As a child, her exposure to the outside world came instead through the books that she borrowed from the nearby library or received from her relatives as gifts. Brancato did not like to read fantasy stories as much as she liked to learn about the next adventures of the Bobbsey Twins or Nancy Drew; and when she was in high school she came to love such novels as Margaret Mitchell's *Gone with the Wind* and John Steinbeck's *Grapes of Wrath.* These books left an indelible impression on the future writer.

"My entrance into adolescence was gradual and relatively untraumatic," Brancato admitted in her autobiographical essay. Like many other junior high school students, she played sports such as basketball, dated, and had a small circle of close friends. This happy, sheltered life was shaken when Brancato's father was transferred to another city and the family had to move to the coal-mining town of Shamokin, Pennsylvania. The house on the tranquil, tree-lined street near the woods was replaced by one on a busy street next to an unsightly coal bank "where a perpetual fire smoldered near a sign that said 'Glen-Burn Colliery.'" Leaving her school and all her friends seemed like a major tragedy to the fifteen-year-old Brancato, but she later came to realize that the experience was important to her personal growth because it opened her eyes to other lifestyles. In Wyomissing the people all generally came from English or German, Protestant, affluent backgrounds, but in Shamokin she came across a more diverse assortment of ethnic, working-class people. Brancato also came to enjoy her new school, where she had

several excellent teachers, broadened her reading horizons, and saw her first Shakespearean play during a school trip. Even her bouts with loneliness had their advantage: when she was by herself, Brancato would read and practice her writing more.

Before her senior year in high school, Brancato moved with her family again, this time to Camp Hill near Harrisburg, Pennsylvania's capital city. Moving the second time was not nearly as traumatic for Brancato. She gained quick acceptance among her new classmates by playing basketball and field hockey and by developing a "modest reputation as a satirist," which she earned by writing and publishing a small newspaper called the *Moosettes Home Journal* and by writing skits for a school stage production. In college Brancato continued to enjoy writing humor, and she developed a taste for musical comedies.

Attending the University of Pennsylvania on a scholarship that paid for half her tuition, Brancato worked various odd jobs to help pay for the rest of her college costs. For her course of study she chose creative writing "because it allowed for more electives and fewer requirements than a major in English." But the demands on her writing—nine thousand words were required each semester—were more stringent. "I wrote mostly short, realistic prose pieces and a one-act musical comedy, complete with lyrics by me and music by a male friend. The musical was given a staged reading at a seminar session, and some of my short pieces ended up in the *Pennsylvania Literary Review,* but I wasn't particularly proud of any one thing that I wrote at that time."

Brancato also contributed to the *Pennsylvania News*—the female-run counterpart to the university's male-run *Daily Pennsylvanian* at a time when such distinctions were still common—and the school's humor magazine, *Pennpix,* which was later renamed *Highball.* Her involvement with these projects led her to become the only woman contributor to Mask and Wig, the university's drama group. "Of all my experiences at Penn," Brancato reflected, "this was the most heady." She enjoyed the theater and became involved with the stage by acting in some of the school's productions; her dream was to write lyrics for musical comedies as good as those of the renowned Oscar Hammerstein.

After graduating from the University of Pennsylvania, Brancato and one of her close friends decided to explore Europe together. They traveled on a shoestring budget, cutting expenses by staying with relatives or friends whenever possible, or in the cheapest youth hostels and pensions. Brancato kept a journal of her trip, "but it seems a pale document when I look at it now, full of 'We saw this, we ate that. Tomorrow we're going to....' I would like to have written more reflectively, but I didn't. Knowing that my days as a student were over and it was now time to start being a writer, I felt frightened. There I was, seeing with my own eyes some of the greatest works of mankind. Was I *feeling* deeply enough? I kept wondering. What could I say about Europe that hadn't already been said?"

Her ambitions of becoming a professional writer put on temporary hold, Brancato settled in New York City and got a job as a textbook copyeditor. However, it quickly became apparent to her that this job was going to be extremely dull. Textbooks did not stimulate her imagination as much as fiction, and she found herself wishing more and more that she could return to her days in school. Recalling how much fun she had as an instructor when she worked as a counselor at summer camp, Brancato hit upon the idea of going back to college so she could get a master's degree and teach English, thereby combining her passion for literature with teaching. She continued her copyediting job while attending classes and, whenever possible, squeezed in time for writing. Some of the work she accomplished at the time included poetry and a collection of children's stories that was rejected by two publishers before she put it permanently in her files.

Despite Brancato's busy schedule filled with work, school, writing, and friends, she still harbored a sense of loneliness. Then one day in 1960 she met John Brancato, a fellow student at Hunter College. They were married within the year and set out together to begin dual careers in teaching. "Our being in the same profession always seemed an advantage," the author observed. "We've hardly ever gotten bored listening to each other's shoptalk." Settling in New Jersey, Brancato found a job at Hackensack High School teaching English and writing. For two years she worked full time until the birth of her sons Chris in 1962 and Greg in 1964. She decided to stay home during the daytime to take care of the children while her husband worked. To help make ends meet, she taught classes at night and did some freelance copyediting during the day.

When Brancato's husband won a Fulbright grant to teach in Italy for two years, the family rented out their New Jersey home and moved to Modena. In this city, not far from Bologna, the Brancatos fell in love with all things Italian, including opera, food, and the language, which they learned to speak fluently. As she looked after her children and the apartment and held a part-time teaching job at a nearby elementary school—where she taught the children to speak English—writing was once again set on the back burner for some other time. But that time was starting to draw near for Brancato.

Upon her return to New Jersey, Brancato was able to get her old job back at Hackensack High School, where, in addition to teaching English, she began instructing students in journalism and world literature and was an adviser for the student newspaper. During this time she tried composing some poetry and a few short stories, but their publication in small newspapers and magazines did not satisfy Brancato's desire to be a successful author. Then, one day, she was introduced by a good friend to Agatha Young, the author of such books as *The Hospital* and other stories about the medical world, who recommended that Brancato try her hand at writing a

novel. Brancato resolved to do just that. The only problem was she did not know what to write about. She searched through all the material she had written before in the hope of finding something to inspire her, until she stumbled upon a short piece about one of her elementary school teachers. "This fragment set off a chain reaction of childhood memories, so that in the next few hours I made a plan for a whole novel. I hadn't decided in advance to write for children, and at first I wasn't sure for whom I was writing. All I knew was that this was the story I wanted to tell. It was about a child like myself, growing up in a small town in Pennsylvania at the end of World War II, and facing the loss of a loved one for the first time."

Not only was the background for the tale similar to the author's own, but the thematic concern was also very personal, for Brancato's greatest fear as a child was the fear of losing someone close to her. Feverishly writing the book over the summer of 1973, the aspiring novelist

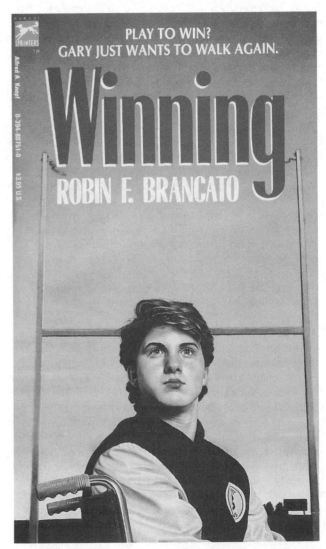

High school football player Gary Madden, paralyzed from a spinal injury, touches the life of recently-widowed teacher Ann Treer in Brancato's novel about overcoming adversity and loss. (Cover illustration by Kam Mak.)

completed all but the last three chapters of her project before her family went on a three-week vacation to England. Brancato knew full well that once she returned to teaching in the fall she would not be able to work on her book, so she spent her last few days in Cornwall finishing the manuscript. The result was *Don't Sit under the Apple Tree,* published two years later by Alfred A. Knopf, Inc.

Don't Sit under the Apple Tree is about a girl named Ellis Carpenter who lives in Wissining, Pennsylvania. During the summer of 1945, as the war draws to a close in distant Europe, Ellis comes to terms with her first experiences with death and the beginnings of sexual awareness. But, more importantly, she learns from her grandmother—who passes away by the story's end—that people should not feel guilty about enjoying life after a loved one has died. Reviews of this first novel were generally favorable. For example, *School Library Journal* critic Cyrisse Jaffee called *Don't Sit under the Apple Tree* a "modest yet satisfying story," and she praised the author for her "sensitive and humorous" characterizations.

Brancato's second novel, *Something Left to Lose,* was also based on her childhood experiences. This time the author recalls in fictionalized form the year when she moved away from her home in Wyomissing. At first, Brancato planned to write more about the move and how it affected her main character, Jane Ann, but when it became apparent that Rebbie and Lydia, two of Jane Ann's friends, were important to the story, Brancato decided to make the novel about all the events leading up to—but not including—the move. "So I wrote about the bonds that tie three friends together and left the move and its aftermath for a novel I haven't written yet," Brancato commented.

The author packs her story full of events and character conflicts, including Jane Ann's role in the school play, her first involvement with a young boy, and her unusual friendship with Rebbie. In Jane Ann and Rebbie, Brancato offers the reader a look at how completely opposite personalities might interact. Rebbie, as the name implies, is a rebel who experiments with smoking and drinking and believes in astrology; Jane Ann, on the other hand, has a strong sense of responsibility. Both characters have their own problems, however, which they deal with in their own way. Rebbie pretends that her mother's alcoholism does not bother her and that she is happy to lead a footloose lifestyle. But her belief in the abilities of astrology to predict events reveals her inner desire to find a controlling force in her life. Jane Ann seems to come from a comfortable, stable, middle-class home, yet she suffers from problems with self-identity that cause her to have fits of anxiety. DeSalvo lauded Brancato's comparison of Jane Ann and Rebbie for demonstrating that everyone, whether or not they come from troubled families, has problems of one kind or another: "we are delusional if we think that we can banish [adversity] by creating isolated paradises of peace and tranquility for our children to grow in."

The idea that hardships are a universal problem is central to the themes in all of Brancato's books. "Instead of protecting kids from adversity," commented DeSalvo, "the implicit message in each of Brancato's novels is that we need to help them develop their resources for coping with it." Another common aspect of the author's novels is that she likes to end her stories without coming to any firm conclusions about the issues she presents. "I like the idea of writing stories that raise questions for readers to think about in terms of themselves," Brancato once said. "I write my books *to ask the questions,*" she later added, "not necessarily to provide all the answers. Above all, I hope that my readers will be carried along by the heart, spirit, and humor of the characters and will realize only after the fact that I've sneaked in a few important things to ponder."

Brancato's books became more issue oriented with her third novel, *Winning,* which was also the first book she wrote that involved a subject that was not directly related to her own life, though it was inspired by an actual event. By the mid-1970s both of Brancato's sons were playing football, and this caused her to recall how in 1972 one of the athletes at Hackensack High School was in an accident that injured his spinal cord. Although she herself had been involved in many sports as a student, Brancato could not help worrying about the possibilities that one of her children would be hurt. She became interested in writing a novel about a high school football player who becomes paralyzed, but she did not know a lot about the medical facts such an injury entailed or how it might personally affect those involved. This meant she had a lot of research to do.

"The period that I spent researching and writing *Winning* was one of the most fascinating in my life as a writer," Brancato revealed. Deciding not to interview the student who was in the accident at Hackensack because she "wanted to avoid any appearance of exploiting someone else's trouble," the author interviewed numerous other accident victims instead. She also interviewed doctors and therapists and read volumes on psychology and sports medicine. "Although I had started out as a person who could barely tolerate visiting a hospital," Brancato concluded about the experience, "I ended up enjoying my research, loving the people I met, and developing a deep interest in the field of rehabilitation medicine."

Winning involves the struggles of not only Gary Madden, the paralyzed high school football player, but also his English teacher, Ann Treer, who is going through a painful time after the death of her husband. Working together as tutor and student, the two find that they need each other's help. Ann helps Gary to cope with the fact that his disability is permanent, and by helping Gary, Ann is able to once again get in touch with feelings she has suppressed since the loss of her husband. *Winning* received a warm welcome from a number of critics who complimented Brancato on her ability to write about such an emotional topic without being overly sentimental. One *Booklist* reviewer lauded Brancato's ability to show how Gary's situation affects those around him, commenting that *Winning* is a "generally moving and involving junior novel that avoids being maudlin." A *Publishers Weekly* contributor commended the "realistically portrayed" characters and called the novel "a superior work."

The research that went into Brancato's next novel, *Blinded by the Light,* was not only fascinating for the author, but also a little bit risky. This novel concerns religious cults in America, a topic that Brancato has been interested in since she was a college student. While at the University of Pennsylvania, she even attended a couple of dinners hosted by a group led by a man called Father Divine, whom his followers believed to be the incarnation of God on Earth. Brancato continued to be curious about cults after she graduated, but it was not until such groups began to gain regular media attention during the 1970s that the author felt it was time to write a story about them. As with *Winning,* Brancato researched her topic thoroughly through visits to the library and interviews, mainly focusing her attention on the Unification Church—also known as the "Moonies," after the cult's leader, Reverend Sun Myung Moon—because it was the most prominent cult at the time. Many people believed that such religious groups brainwashed and otherwise manipulated people into becoming loyal followers. Brancato concluded that the only way to find this out for certain was to pretend to be interested in joining a cult herself.

After some coaching from a newspaper reporter in Philadelphia who had once infiltrated a cult for one of his stories, Brancato attended a meeting of the Unification Church and signed up for a three-day workshop. Being careful to note the spot in Westchester County, New York, where the workshop was to be held, the author told her husband where to meet her in case she had trouble leaving. Staying with the cult for two days, Brancato found the members to be exploitative, but not in the way she expected. "I hated my two days there because of the ways in which we recruits were manipulated. There was no physical threat at all, and even the psychological threats seemed mild, but the attempts at making us dependent, accepting, and like-minded were strong enough so that I yearned to go home." She managed to leave a day early, having learned as much as she cared to about cult life.

In writing *Blinded by the Light,* Brancato took advantage of much of her experience with the cult and turned it into a story about a college senior, Jim Brower, who joins a group called the Light of the World Church—the L.O.W.—just a few weeks before he is to graduate. When he disappears his family fears that he may have been kidnapped, so his younger sister Gail sets out to find him. Gail discovers that he is with the L.O.W. and infiltrates the group in order to try to convince Jim to return home. But Gail herself is in danger of becoming brainwashed by the cult's techniques of depriving their recruits of food and rest, until her boyfriend rescues her just before she pledges her loyalty to the L.O.W. The novel ends with Gail finally meeting and talking with Jim, but—in one of Brancato's typically ambiguous

conclusions—she is unable to convince him to come home.

This fictitious tale parallels in some ways the story of a cult member whom Brancato met while she was with the Moonies. The woman had come to take her daughter away from the Unification Church, but the mother ironically ended up staying herself. In her novel, Brancato tried to capture this power that cults have to lure new members. Some critics have felt that Brancato's presentation of arguments of the cult versus non-cult members may be too one-sided and oversimplified, but a *Booklist* contributor added that the author "manages to convey the frightening ease with which someone ... can be converted." And Peter S. Prescott remarked in a *Newsweek* review that *Blinded by the Light* "is dramatic and convincing."

Coincidentally, one month after the publication of *Blinded by the Light* in 1978, followers of cult leader Jim Jones were forced into drinking cyanide-laced Kool-aid in a small settlement in Guyana, South America. Nine hundred people died. Not only did the story make front page news, but it also sparked interest in Brancato's book. It was consequently made into a television movie that, in turn, created even more publicity for the author's novel. Although many authors are often unhappy with the results when their books are turned into movies, Brancato was not disappointed. "Even though details were changed," she wrote, "the spirit of the book was captured. It was fun to see the results of my work translated to another medium."

Brancato wrote *Blinded by the Light* while teaching full-time; her earlier books had all been written during leaves of absence from her high school job. With her next couple of novels she compromised and taught part-time. Her ongoing involvement with school showed its influence in the plot of her next book, *Come Alive at 505,* which also reflects Brancato's longtime interest in radio that goes back to the time when she was eight years old and had the chance to perform in a radio drama for children that was broadcast on a small station. Though she was never destined to make it big in radio—it was the author's first and only experience in the medium—she never forgot the fun she had. Her enthusiasm is carried over into *Come Alive at 505.*

The plot of *Come Alive at 505* involves high school senior Dan Fetzer and his relationship with an over-weight but attractive girl named Mimi Alman. Dan is a radio enthusiast who wants to pursue a career as a disc jockey, instead of applying for college as his parents wish. His knowledge of broadcasting also helps him to contrive a plan to campaign for an imaginary student as his high school's class president. To help him with the hoax, Dan enlists the help of his friend, George, and Mimi. The novel comes to a head when Mimi's confession that George had given her illegal drugs to help her lose weight is accidentally taped on Dan's equipment. Full of action and lively dialogue, the book was promoted by the publisher as being especially geared toward modern media-oriented teenagers. But *New York*

Times Book Review critic Kathleen Leverich claimed that "the book's true genre ... is neither media-oriented, trendy nor Today.... [It] is an old-fashioned, optimistic adventure-romance."

Brancato continued to write steadily during the 1980s, completing novels such as *Sweet Bells Jangled out of Tune* and *Facing Up.* The author addresses the issue of the plight of street people in *Sweet Bells Jangled out of Tune,* which involves a young girl named Ellen whose eccentric Grandmother Eva has become a bag lady. Once a prosperous and respected member of the community, Eva has somehow lost everything and becomes a thief and object of scorn in the town. When Ellen decides to help her grandmother any way she can, she places herself at odds with her mother, who has forbidden Ellen to visit Eva. Ellen does so anyway, and soon comes to realize that her grandmother's dilemma is the result of psychological problems that must be treated at a hospital. *Sweet Bells Jangled out of Tune* was praised by a number of reviewers, including one *Publishers Weekly* critic who commented: "Brancato has produced a topnotch drama about 'different' people." *Best Sellers* contributor Russell H. Goodyear commended the author's portrayal of Eva: "Seldom does a writer of adolescent literature provide as much insight into psychological cause and effect as Robin Brancato has."

Some reviews for Brancato's next novel, *Facing Up,* were less enthusiastic than those for *Sweet Bells Jangled out of Tune.* The story of a teenage love triangle that ends in one boy's accidental death that leaves his friend to struggle with nearly unbearable guilt was called "pulpish" by *Best Sellers* critic Aaron I. Michelson; and Constance Allen complained in *School Library Journal* about the book's "stereotyped characters." Nevertheless, Ann A. Flowers commented in *Horn Book* that "Dave's struggle to regain his equilibrium is told in a tight, clean narrative," adding that the story contains much "vitality and interest."

Uneasy Money—the story of an eighteen-year-old who wins over two million dollars in a state lottery and gets carried away with his new-found wealth—is considerably more light-hearted than many of Brancato's other novels. However, it is a typical example of Brancato's method of placing young characters in situations that pose important questions while still offering opportunities for humor and wit. With all her experience in teaching and in raising children, writing for young adults has been—and will likely remain—Brancato's primary goal. The author says that whenever she is asked why she does not write for adults, she replies: "'I'd be delighted—*if* I am ever swept away by an idea that is clearly of interest to adults.' So far, every time I have been consumed by something, to the extent that I *know* I have to write about it, that something has been connected with adolescence."

■ Works Cited

Allen, Constance, review of *Facing Up, School Library Journal,* April, 1984, p. 122.

Review of *Blinded by the Light, Booklist,* September 15, 1978, p. 175.

Brancato, Robin F., essay in *Something about the Author Autobiography Series,* Volume 9, Gale, 1990, pp. 53-68.

DeSalvo, Louise A., "The Uses of Adversity," *Media and Methods,* April, 1979, pp. 16, 18, 50-51.

Flowers, Ann A., review of *Facing Up, Horn Book,* April, 1984, pp. 199-200.

Gallo, Donald R., *Speaking for Ourselves: Autobiographical Sketches by Notable Authors of Books for Young Adults,* National Council of Teachers of English, 1990, pp. 28-29.

Goodyear, Russell H., review of *Sweet Bells Jangled out of Tune, Best Sellers,* June, 1982, p. 118.

Jaffee, Cyrisse, review of *Don't Sit under the Apple Tree, School Library Journal,* May, 1975, p. 52.

Leverich, Kathleen, review of *Come Alive at 505, New York Times Book Review,* April 27, 1980, p. 65.

Michelson, Aaron I., review of *Facing Up, Best Sellers,* June, 1984, p. 115.

Prescott, Peter S., review of *Blinded by the Light, Newsweek,* December 18, 1978, p. 102.

Review of *Sweet Bells Jangled out of Tune, Publishers Weekly,* January 15, 1982, p. 99.

Review of *Winning, Booklist,* September 1, 1977, p. 30.

Review of *Winning, Publishers Weekly,* January 2, 1978, p. 65.

■ For More Information See

BOOKS

Contemporary Literary Criticism, Volume 35, Gale, 1985, pp. 65-70.

Twentieth-Century Young Adult Writers, St. James Press, 1994, pp. 74-75.*

*   *   *

BRANDENBERG, Alexa (Demetria) 1966-

■ Personal

Born June 7, 1966, in New York, NY; daughter of Franz (an author) and Aliki (an author and illustrator; maiden name, Liacouras) Brandenberg; married Jeffrey Odefey, May 11, 1996. *Education:* William Smith College, B.A., 1988.

■ Addresses

Home—New York. *Electronic mail*—bigsky @ best-web.net

■ Career

Author and illustrator of children's books.

■ Writings

SELF-ILLUSTRATED

I Am Me!, Harcourt (San Diego, CA), 1996.

ALEXA BRANDENBERG

Chop, Simmer, Season: A Day at the Top Notch Restaurant, Harcourt, 1997.

ILLUSTRATOR

Franz Brandenberg, *A Fun Weekend,* Greenwillow (New York City), 1991.

Suzanne Fletcher, *The Pot Game: The Art of Communication,* Holistic Press (Pasadena, CA), 1992.

Jeffrey Odefey, *The Mentor Handbook,* Women's Opportunity and Resource Development (Missoula, MT), 1996.

Tony Johnston, *We Love the Dirt,* Cartwheel Books (New York City), 1997.

■ **Sidelights**

Alexa Brandenberg told *Something about the Author* (*SATA*): "My whole life has been permeated with children's books, due partly to the fact that both my parents are in the field. From a young age I would wander into bookstores to look for my parents' works and stayed until all the other children's books had been read. I do the same now and I recognize it as a fortuitous honor to be actually part of this world myself.

"My objective as a children's book author and illustrator is to make children respond to my books. I would like to inspire children to explore their uniqueness and to make them notice that each of them can think in his or her own individual way. I want to make children smile and laugh, and to encourage them to savor their early years."

Brandenberg's initial contributions to children's literature have been well-received. Her first book, *I Am Me!,* shows nine different preschool children of various races, each dreaming of what they want to be when they grow up and already demonstrating their aptitude and skills. *School Library Journal* reviewer Judith Constantinides remarked, "An excellent offering for toddlers," while a *Kirkus Reviews* critic lauded the breakdown of gender stereotypes, calling Brandenberg's book "rudimentary, but effective." A *Publishers Weekly* writer observed that the simple figures and composition resembled the work of the author/illustrator's noted mother, Aliki, "implying yet another factor in choosing a career."

With her second self-illustrated book, *Chop, Simmer, Season,* Brandenberg introduces the world of two restaurant chefs who demonstrate, through choice verbs, how to prepare an entire meal, complete with soup, main course, salad, bread, and dessert. "One of the wonderful things about the book," reviewer Carolyn Jenks of *School Library Journal* points out, "is that it does not try to do too much, thus giving children an opportunity to create their own understanding."

■ **Works Cited**

Constantinides, Judith, review of *I Am Me!, School Library Journal,* December, 1996, pp. 84-85.

Review of *I Am Me!, Kirkus Reviews,* August 1, 1996, p. 1147.

Review of *I Am Me!, Publishers Weekly,* August 19, 1996, p. 65.

Jenks, Carolyn, review of *Chop, Simmer, Season, School Library Journal,* May, 1997, p. 93.

■ **For More Information See**

PERIODICALS

Booklist, April 15, 1997, p. 1434.
School Library Journal, June, 1991, p. 72.

*   *   *

BREWSTER, Patience 1952-

■ **Personal**

Born October 26, 1952, in Plymouth, MA; daughter of Spencer Hatch (deceased) and Marietta (a teacher of horse riding, carriage driving, and dressage; maiden name, Withington) Brewster; married Holland Chauncey Gregg III (a television producer), June 18, 1977; children: Holland Chauncey IV, Marietta Brewster. *Education:* Philadelphia College of Art, B.F.A., 1974.

■ **Addresses**

Home—Jordan Road, Skaneateles, NY 13152.

■ Career

Author and illustrator. Harlow House, Plymouth, MA, guide to Pilgrim living and crafts, 1964-73; salesperson and graphic artist, 1973-78; freelance artist in calligraphy and advertising, 1974—; part-time waitress and cook, 1974-77; author and illustrator of children's books, 1979—. Lecturer in writing and illustrating and on creativity. Creator of posters for Opera Theater of Syracuse, NY; Skaneateles Festival, NY; "The Original Art" Show, New York City, 1983; "Every Page," Master Eagle Gallery, New York City, 1985; and Houghton Mifflin publishing company. Creator of puzzles for Creative Playthings. Designer of cards, journals, and gift books for Marcel Schurman and Thomas Nelson. *Exhibitions:* Harriet Griffin Gallery, New York City, 1975-77; Renaissance Gallery, Ithaca, NY 1977; Main Street Gallery, Nantucket, MA, 1978-82; "The Original Art," Master Eagle Gallery, New York City, 1982-85; Chilmark Gallery, Martha's Vineyard, MA, 1985; Schweinfurth Museum, Auburn, NY; Memorial Art Gallery, Rochester, NY; Original Art Exhibition, Society of Illustrators; Pastabilities, Syracuse, NY; McKenzie Art Gallery, Corning, NY; Storyopolis, Los Angeles, CA; Elizabeth Stone Gallery, Birmingham, MI.

■ Awards, Honors

California Reader's Choice Award and *Booklist*'s Editors' Choice selection, both 1982, both for illustrations in *Good as New;* exhibition at Bologna International Book Fair, 1985, and Golden Sower Award (K-3), 1988, both for illustrations in *Don't Touch My Room;* Golden Sower nomination and Children's Choice Award, Children's Book Council, both for *Bear and Mrs. Duck;* Junior Literary Guild selections for *Ellsworth and the Cats from Mars, Nobody,* and *Good as New.*

■ Writings

FOR CHILDREN; SELF-ILLUSTRATED

(Reteller) *Dame Wiggins of Lee and Her Seven Wonderful Cats,* Crowell, 1980.
Ellsworth and the Cats from Mars, Houghton Mifflin/Clarion, 1981.
Nobody, Clarion, 1982.
Rabbit Inn, Little, Brown, 1991.
Two Bushy Badgers, Little, Brown, 1995.
Too Many Puppies, Scholastic, 1997.

ILLUSTRATOR

Barbara Douglass, *Good as New,* Lothrop, 1982.
Story Time (anthology), Reader's Digest, 1982.
Morse Hamilton, *Who's Afraid of the Dark?,* Avon, 1983.
Hamilton, *How Do You Do, Mr. Birdsteps?,* Avon, 1983.
Selma Boyd and Pauline Boyd, *I Met a Polar Bear,* Lothrop, 1983.
Cathy Warren, *Victoria's ABC Adventure,* Lothrop, 1984.
Nikki Yektai, *Sun Rain,* Four Winds, 1984.
Patricia Lakin, *Don't Touch My Room,* Little, Brown, 1985.

PATIENCE BREWSTER

Lakin, *Oh, Brother!,* Little, Brown, 1987.
Myra C. Livingston (editor), *Valentine Poems,* Holiday House, 1987.
Sue Alexander, *"There's More, Much More,"* Said Squirrel, Harcourt, 1987.
Elizabeth Winthrop, *Bear and Mrs. Duck,* Holiday House, 1988.
Patricia Lakin, *Just like Me,* Little, Brown, 1989.
Steven Kroll, *Princess Abigail and the Wonderful Hat,* Holiday House, 1991.
Elizabeth Winthrop, *Bear's Christmas Surprise,* Holiday House, 1991.
Mary Blocksma, *Yoo Hoo, Moon,* Bantam, 1992.
Steven Kroll, *Queen of the May,* Holiday House, 1993.
Joan Scoby, *The Fannie Farmer Junior Cookbook,* Little, Brown, 1993.
Elizabeth Winthrop, *Bear and Roly-Poly,* Holiday House, 1996.

Also author and illustrator of "A Pampers Blue Ribbon Baby Goes through the Bunny Hole" (advertising). Illustrator of *A.M.A. Family Health Cookbook,* Pocket Books, 1997. Illustrator of textbooks for Houghton Mifflin and Harcourt Brace Jovanovich. Contributor of illustrations to *Cricket* and *Lady Bug* magazines. Brewster's books have been published in England, Australia, France, China, and South Africa, and printed in French and Chinese.

■ Sidelights

Patience Brewster is an award-winning author and illustrator of several children's books and the illustrator of books written by authors such as Elizabeth Winthrop, Steven Kroll, Patricia Lakin, and Myra Cohn Livingston. Working with pencil, paint, ink, and watercolors, she is the creator of colorful characters—most often animals, especially cats—that have charmed critics. While, for the most part, Brewster's illustrations accompany works of fiction, her art can also be found in the *Fannie Farmer Junior Cookbook,* textbooks, and children's magazines. As an illustrator, Brewster provides pictures that range from pastel watercolors to bright, full-page illustrations in near-psychedelic colors. She is well known for her borders as well as for the decorative details that enhance her works; critics occasionally regard Brewster's art more highly than the texts of the books that she illustrates.

Brewster grew up in Plymouth, Massachusetts, near a dairy farm. She lived with five siblings and, as she explained to *Something about the Author (SATA),* "an ever-growing menagerie consisting of several horses and dogs and any combination of cows, sheep, goats, donkeys, chickens, peacocks, pigs, rabbits, and cats." Brewster was encouraged to pursue her love of art at home. She noted, "I got great inspiration from the talents of my parents and grandparents. We were all encouraged in our various interests. I never enrolled in art classes at school but preferred working at home, drawing and dabbling with an older sister's college art supplies. My high school teachers, therefore, were not too supportive of my idea of going to an art college. But my family and friends were . . . ." Brewster decided to attend the Philadelphia College of Art. "Once there," she wrote, "I had my first real exposure to city life and full-time concentration on art. I graduated as a printmaking major, but my four years included a lot of drawing, painting, and a thesis on bookmaking."

After graduating from college, Brewster supported herself with various jobs and worked in advertising and with calligraphy. She presented her art work in shows in New York and Massachusetts before she was convinced by her husband Holland to share it with children's book publishers in New York. "I'd always been told I ought to get involved in children's books, but I never knew where to begin. Holly made appointments for me to show my work to several publishers in New York and forced me out the door. I prepared for painful rejection but we found a warm reception everywhere. That sent me into a state of elated shock."

Brewster made her first contribution to children's literature with her adaptation of *Dame Wiggins of Lee and Her Seven Wonderful Cats,* a poem written by John Ruskin in 1885; Ruskin based his verses on a poem he first wrote in 1823, "A Humorous Tale Written Principally by a Lady of Ninety." The story consists of several verses about an old woman and her charismatic cats, which learn to sing and ice skate, among other activities. "Brewster gives the rhyming nonsense boisterous charm with neatly limned drawings of a dotty old woman and her talented cats," wrote a *Publishers Weekly* critic, who found the cats "simply wonderful." A *Kirkus Reviews*

critic described the book as "fetchingly designed" and "cunningly illustrated."

Brewster provided both the text and the pictures for her next book, *Ellsworth and the Cats from Mars.* When Ellsworth, a yellow kitten, looks into his yard one day, he sees green Martian cats with antennae. He finds a space hat and puts it on, and begins communicating with one of the cats. For his explanation of Earth-cat life, the space cat provides Ellsworth with a spaceship of his own, and Ellsworth zooms to Mars. However, he gets lost and has to be rescued by his alien friends. "Brewster makes a delightful debut," commented a *Publishers Weekly* reviewer, who described the story as "a soundly structured fantasy" that is "suspensefully funny." "An amusing and delightful book," concluded Ann A. Flowers of *Horn Book.*

Brewster explained to *SATA* that her first two books were created with the help of her young son Holland, who was born during the production of her first book. "*Dame Wiggins of Lee and Her Seven Wonderful Cats* offered many opportunities to incorporate some of my growing son's expressions and positions into those of the cats in the old-fashioned nonsense verse. In *Ellsworth and the Cats from Mars,* I used his humor even more. He was beginning to talk and commented and laughed at the 'funny pictures' that occupied much of my time." Brewster also noted, "My daughter, Marietta, as well as

Brewster provides the pictures for Steven Kroll's Cinderella tale of an overworked young girl who becomes queen of the May Day celebration. (From *Queen of the May,* written by Steven Kroll and illustrated by Brewster.)

The eensy speck of pie
Flew right across the room
And landed with a *plop*
Beside a dirty broom.

Two badger friends fight and reconcile in Brewster's book of rhyming text and 1950s-inspired illustrations. (From *Two Bushy Badgers,* written and illustrated by Brewster.)

my son are great sources of information as well as painfully honest critics of manuscripts and art work going in and out of my studio."

Rabbit Inn is another of Brewster's self-illustrated books featuring animal characters. Pandora and Bob, rabbits who run an inn, spend a month preparing for some special guests. They enlist the other guests at the inn (other small to medium-sized animals) to clean and polish along with them. All the while, the toiling guests are left to wonder who is coming to visit. Soon enough, they learn that the guests are Pandora and Bob's new baby bunnies. According to a reviewer in *Publishers Weekly,* Brewster's "airy watercolors are packed with delicate, amusing details; the inn's furnishings are worthy of Laura Ashley." A *Kirkus Reviews* critic remarked, "The text's amiable spirit of cooperation and anticipation is beautifully extended in the illustrations; these rabbits, with their expressive, elongated ears, are captivating."

Brewster's picture book *Two Bushy Badgers* is a rhyming story with pink, lavender, orange and turquoise illustrations about two animals, Arthur and Ollie, who vow to be friends to the end. When the pair move in together, the badgers find themselves becoming increasingly unpleasant to one another, and as Ruth K. MacDonald of *School Library Journal* noted, the friends "enter a silent, cold war." However, at the end of the story the badgers decide that their feud is a waste of time and go back to being devoted pals. The illustrations

in this book are often considered quite unusual: aside from the brown-hued badgers, the other characters and details in the story are delineated in an array of rainbow colors. MacDonald called the pictures "a wild, bebop, rock-and-roll motif out of the 50s, done in a Pepto-Bismol pink and a ubiquitous aqua...." While a reviewer in *Publishers Weekly* wrote that "Borders and decorative touches are Brewster's forte," the critic described the work as "[u]naccountably bizarre."

In 1982, Brewster began to illustrate the works of other authors. *Don't Touch My Room* and *Oh, Brother!,* both written by Patricia Lakin, feature Aaron and his younger brother Benjii. In the latter book, Aaron tires of his situation as the older brother, and resents the fact that Benjii gets what he wants so frequently, so Aaron tries to scare Benjii with stories until their parents intervene. A *Publishers Weekly* critic described Brewster's illustrated characters as "likable." "Brewster's colorful and detailed illustrations will endear this book to children," commented Lee Bock of *School Library Journal.*

Brewster provided the illustrations for the "Bear" series of picture books written by Elizabeth Winthrop: *Bear and Mrs. Duck, Bear's Christmas Surprise,* and *Bear and Roly-Poly. Bear and Mrs. Duck* begins when Mrs. Duck arrives to care for Bear (a small, stuffed brown bear). Bear does not like his baby-sitter. He tries to ignore her, but he finally takes her suggestion and begins to draw. Mrs. Duck impresses him by flying and swimming. By the time his owner, Nora, returns, Bear has changed his mind about Mrs. Duck. "Brewster's pastels push this sweetly winning story along," commented a *Publishers Weekly* critic. In *Bear and Roly-Poly,* Bear learns that he will have a baby sister. However, Nora brings him a large panda, not the small bear he is expecting. Bear is surprised at first, but gradually, he and his new sister become good friends. Stephanie Zvirin of *Booklist* explained that because Brewster presents the new sister as "a giant," she "gives countenance to the feelings of awe and insignificance children often experience" upon the arrival of a sibling. "Charming illustrations and believable characters make this ... story right on target" for children who have unrealistic expectations about new siblings, concluded Virginia Opocensky in *School Library Journal.*

Brewster has also illustrated the original fairy tales of Steven Kroll. *Princess Abigail and the Wonderful Hat* describes how a king who wants a new hat promises to reward the maker of the best hat with his daughter's hand in marriage. When the horrible Prince Grindstone fashions the best hat, Princess Abigail flees. She meets a huge lizard who makes a hat for the king from natural objects; when the king tries on the hat, he declares that the lizard is the true winner of the contest. As Abigail cries with joy, her tear drops fall on the lizard, who turns into a handsome prince. According to Marilyn Iarusso of *School Library Journal,* Brewster's colorful illustrations contain "many romantically swirling tendrils of plants, hair, and ribbons." With *Queen of the May,* Kroll and Brewster present young readers with a variation of Cinderella in which a young girl is helped to become Queen of the May by a crow, a beaver, and a chipmunk after she has been kind to them. Writing in *School Library Journal,* Christine A. Moesch stated, "The pastel watercolor illustrations help convey the beauty of spring."

Mary Blocksma's *Yoo Hoo, Moon!,* which Brewster illustrated, begins when Bear realizes he can't sleep because the moon is not out. He sings to the moon, and wakes up some other animals. They all sing together until the wind blows away the clouds. When the moon finally shines, Bear has fallen asleep. Sharron McElmeel of *School Library Journal* wrote that Brewster's work is the "best part" of the book, while Karen Hutt of *Booklist* commented that young children "will like the ... brightly colored illustrations."

Brewster told *SATA,* "After years of juggling part-time illustrating with motherhood, I'm finally seeing the time approaching when, with both children in school, I will attend to writing more of my own books to illustrate. I am dreaming of the day when my calendar will be empty, my house quiet, animals fed, and my studio clean so I can walk in and begin a work based totally on inspiration. I also want to do this in secret so that I will have no deadline to meet."

Brewster advises aspiring illustrators to "Use good materials. The best brushes, paints and paper. Work hard on a small portfolio that you feel proud of and then go after the best publishers first. Take advice and *don't give up."*

■ Works Cited

Review of *Bear and Mrs. Duck, Publishers Weekly,* October 28, 1988, p. 77.

Bock, Lee, review of *Oh, Brother!, School Library Journal,* June-July, 1987, pp. 84-85.

Review of *Dame Wiggins of Lee and Her Seven Wonderful Cats, Kirkus Reviews,* October 1, 1980, p. 1291.

Review of *Dame Wiggins of Lee and Her Seven Wonderful Cats, Publishers Weekly,* October 31, 1980, p. 86.

Review of *Ellsworth and the Cats from Mars, Publishers Weekly,* January 30, 1981, p. 76.

Flowers, Ann A., review of *Ellsworth and the Cats from Mars, Horn Book,* June, 1981, p. 291.

Hutt, Karen, review of *Yoo Hoo, Moon!, Booklist,* April 1, 1992, p. 1459.

Iarusso, Marilyn, review of *Princess Abigail and the Wonderful Hat, School Library Journal,* July, 1991, p. 59.

MacDonald, Ruth K., review of *Two Bushy Badgers, School Library Journal,* June, 1995, p. 78.

McElmeel, Sharron, review of *Yoo Hoo, Moon!, School Library Journal,* March, 1992, p. 208.

Moesch, Christine A., review of *Queen of the May, School Library Journal,* July, 1993, p. 62.

Review of *Oh, Brother!, Publishers Weekly,* April 24, 1987, p. 68.

Opocensky, Virginia, review of *Bear and Roly-Poly, School Library Journal,* May, 1996, p. 101.

Review of *Rabbit Inn, Kirkus Reviews,* March 15, 1991, p. 392.

Review of *Rabbit Inn, Publishers Weekly,* March 15, 1991, p. 57.

Review of *Two Bushy Badgers, Publishers Weekly,* April 24, 1995, p. 71.

Zvirin, Stephanie, review of *Bear and Roly-Poly, Booklist,* March 1, 1996, p. 1189.

■ For More Information See

BOOKS

Cummins, Julie, editor, *Children's Book Illustration and Design,* PBC International, 1992.

PERIODICALS

Children's Digest, July-August, 1996, p. 34.
Horn Book, April, 1982, p. 154.
Kirkus Reviews, August 15, 1982, p. 933.
New York Times Book Review, September 19, 1991, p. 27.
School Library Journal, October, 1991, p. 35.

BROWN, Beverly Swerdlow

■ Personal

Born in Los Angeles, CA; daughter of Albert (in sales) and Ida (Yudell) Swerdlow; married Alvin T. Brown (a bacteriologist and microbiologist), May 17, 1953; children: Elizabeth A., Michael S. *Education:* Los Angeles City College, A.A.; also attended University of California, Los Angeles. *Hobbies and other interests:* Greek and Balkan dancing, white-water river rafting, play-going, working out, club historian.

■ Addresses

Home—P.O. Box 64812, Los Angeles, CA 90064.

■ Career

Writer. *Member:* Society of Children's Book Writers and Illustrators.

■ Writings

The Myth-Adventures of Kraken, illustrated by Carol Louise Koplan, Brasch & Brasch (Ontario, CA), 1978.
Erica, the Ecologist, May Davenport (Los Altos, CA), 1984.
The Secret at Morgan Manor, January Productions, 1989.
The Springtime Ghost, January Productions, 1989.
The House on Winchester Lane, January Productions, 1989.
Tricky Train Ride Mystery, January Productions, 1989.
Smile Soup, Kendall/Hunt (Dubuque, IA), 1993.
Brothers and the Broom, Kendall/Hunt, 1993.
The Foolproof Tool Kit, Kendall/Hunt, 1993.
The Traveling Pillow, illustrated by Margot Jane Ott, Greene Bark Press, 1994.
Mouse's Baby Blanket, illustrated by Suzanne Aull, Seedling (Columbus, OH), 1996.
Oliver's High Five, Health Press, 1997.
Panda's Birthday Surprise, Seedling, 1998.

Contributor to magazines, including *Tiger Beat, Highlights for Children, True West, Teacher, Popular Archaeology, Country Journal,* and *Wee Wisdom.*

■ Work in Progress

A modern-day fairy tale; a collection of stories and poems; a mini-mystery series.

■ Sidelights

Beverly S. Brown told *Something about the Author* (*SATA*): "I wrote my very first book, which was bound with string, in my third-grade class. I 'illustrated' it to the theme of transportation. Years later, I did research on things that interested me: the soda fountain and how it all began, the La Brea Tar Pits (where I was a volunteer, digging out fossils), folk dancing (after I saw

BEVERLY SWERDLOW BROWN

the movie *Zorba the Greek,* I knew I had to learn the art of Greek dancing).

"The dancing began as a class at the Extension of the University of California, Los Angeles, and segued into a fifteen-year weekly grouping of men and women enjoying the music and intricate steps of Greek dancing. The weekly gatherings came to an end, but I still get together with friends and dance at various Greek restaurants. It is an emotional and physical experience we all savor.

"Any kind of writing is difficult to do, and rejections do sting; but this special dance has taught me to persevere—to stand my ground and move forward, and not to be intimidated by others. I love writing for children, and I send my work all over the world. I'm very pleased that most of my material has been accepted for books and magazines. I look forward to book signings, because they keep me in touch with parents and children—my audience, my inspiration."

■ For More Information See

PERIODICALS

Children's Book Watch, July, 1996, p. 4.
School Library Journal, April, 1979, p. 40.
West Coast Review of Books, May, 1979, p. 38.

BUSH, Anne Kelleher 1959-

■ Personal

Born March 31, 1959, in Ocean City, NJ; daughter of Michael J. (an engineering consultant) and Frances Kelly (an administrator; maiden name, Castaldi) Kelleher; married Raymond G. Bush, March 16, 1980 (marriage ended, February 1, 1996); children: Katherine, James, Margaret, Abigail. *Education:* Johns Hopkins University, B.A., 1982.

■ Addresses

Home—Bethlehem, PA. *Agent*—Donald Maas, Donald Maas Literary Agency, 157 West 57th St., Suite 1003, New York, NY 10019. *Electronic mail*— AHAY72a @prodigy.com.

■ Career

Writer.

■ Writings

SCIENCE FICTION/FANTASY NOVELS

Daughter of Prophecy, Warner Books, 1995.
Children of Enchantment, Warner Books, 1996.
The Misbegotten King, Warner Books, 1996.

■ Sidelights

Anne Kelleher Bush's fantasy tale, *Daughter of Prophecy,* revolves around Nydia Farhallen, a witch living in the rubble of twenty-eighth-century America. Nydia holds the magic formula for the powers that caused destruction in America and around the world. King Abelard saves her from burning at the stake, but tragedy ensues when Nydia shares her secret with the ambitious king. *Kliatt* contributor Susan Cromby maintained: "Strong Arthurian themes thread their way through this novel; the power-hungry King, his faithful companion, and a prophecy concerning the future."

■ Works Cited

Cromby, Susan, review of *Daughter of Prophecy, Kliatt,* July, 1995, p. 14.

■ For More Information See

PERIODICALS

Locus, February, 1995, p. 29.
Publishers Weekly, February 6, 1995, p. 81.
Voice of Youth Advocates, June, 1995, p. 102.*

BYALICK, Marcia 1947-

■ Personal

Born April 9, 1947, in Brooklyn, NY; daughter of Al (a dry cleaner) and Mona (Goldsmith) Finkelstein; married Robert Byalick (a psychologist), November 22, 1967; children: Jennifer, Carrie. *Education:* Brooklyn College of the City University of New York, M.A., 1969. *Politics:* Liberal Democrat. *Religion:* Jewish. *Hobbies and other interests:* Theater, exercise, "any excuse to get together with friends and family."

■ Addresses

Home and office—22 Lydia Ct., Searingtown, NY 11507.

■ Career

Writer. Editor in chief, *Women's Record,* 1985-93. Columnist, feature writer, *Spotlight, Distinction,* 1996—. Hofstra University, C. W. Post writing teacher, 1993—. Journalist, Long Island section of the *New York Times.*

■ Awards, Honors

Seven awards from Long Island Press Club, 1986-93, for work as a columnist; Books for the Teen Age, New York Public Library, 1996, for *It's a Matter of Trust.*

MARCIA BYALICK

■ Writings

FOR YOUNG ADULTS

It's a Matter of Trust, Harcourt (Orlando, FL), 1995.

OTHER

(With Linda Saslow) *The Three Career Couple: Mastering the Art of Juggling Work, Home, and Family* (humorous self-help), Peterson's Press (Princeton, NJ), 1993.

(With Saslow) *How Come I Feel So Disconnected If This Is Such a User Friendly World? Reconnecting With Your Family, Your Friends—and Your Life,* Peterson's Press, 1995.

(With Ronald A. Ruden) *The Craving Brain: The Biobalance Approach to Controlling Addictions,* HarperCollins, 1997.

Author of the young adult novels *Reel Life,* 1993, and *Whose Eyes Are These?,* 1997.

■ Sidelights

Marcia Byalick's young adult novel *It's a Matter of Trust* concerns the life of sixteen-year-old Erika Gershon and what happens to her when her father is indicted for racketeering. Erika copes with the intrusion of the media upon her family, the gossip of her friends, and the death of a beloved uncle. "Young readers will find a wealth of issues to discuss in this unsettling, thought-provoking novel," maintained *School Library Journal* contributor Jana R. Fine. Readers will empathize with Erika's turmoil over cheating during a tennis match and then lying about it, as well as her realization that she has developed romantic feelings for her camp mate Greg. "YA girls will find much to like about Erika and her story of maturation," asserted *Voice of Youth Advocates* contributor Lucy Marx.

"Even though my book is fiction," Byalick said in an interview with Ramin P. Jaleshgari in the *New York Times,* "I wanted to write something indicative of what modern kids are coping with. True, not everyone has an accused criminal for a father, but many kids deal with issues that are just as serious. Acne, clothes and friends are not all today's teens are concerned with."

"My ultimate goal is to help teens become comfortable dealing with hard issues," Byalick continued. "Young people need to know that time always brings change. Through my writing I'd like to teach them that coping with those changes positively is always within their control."

When police indict her father on racketeering charges, sixteen-year-old Erika endures emotional turmoil, outrageous gossip, and unwanted media attention. (Cover illustration by David Kahl.)

■ Works Cited

Fine, Jana R., review of *It's a Matter of Trust, School Library Journal,* December, 1995, p. 128.

Byalick, Marcia, in an interview with Ramin P. Jaleshgari, *New York Times,* January 21, 1996, p. 14.

Marx, Lucy, review of *It's a Matter of Trust, Voice of Youth Advocates,* February, 1996, p. 368.

■ For More Information See

PERIODICALS

Bulletin of the Center for Children's Books, January, 1996, p. 156.

C

CARROLL, Elizabeth
See JAMES, Elizabeth

*   *   *

CASWELL, Brian 1954-

■ Personal

Born January 13, 1954, in Wales; son of George Harry
(a courier) and Jean (maiden name, Hignett; present
surname, McGrath) Caswell; married Marlene Gerada
(a homemaker), February 23, 1974; children: Michael,
Claire, Nicholas and Benjamin (twins). *Education:* University of New South Wales, B.A., 1975, Dip. Ed., 1976.
Politics: "Slightly left of centre." *Religion:* Roman
Catholic.

■ Addresses

Home and office—17 Wagstaff St., Edensor Park, New
South Wales 2176, Australia. *Agent*—Rick Raftos Management, P.O. Box 445, Paddington, New South Wales
2021, Australia.

■ Career

New South Wales Department of Education, high
school teacher of English and history, 1976-91. Univer-
sity of Western Sydney, writer in residence. Lector and
Eucharistic minister for local church. Royals Basketball
Club (youth club), coach. *Member:* New South Wales
Teachers Federation, University of New South Wales
Alumni Association, Australian Society of Authors,
Australasian Performing Right Association.

■ Awards, Honors

Honour Book, Book of the Year Awards, Children's
Book Council of Australia, 1990, for *Merryll of the
Stones;* shortlist, Book of the Year Awards, Children's
Book Council of Australia, 1993, for *A Cage of Butter-
flies,* and 1996, for *Deucalion;* Notable Books, Chil-
dren's Book Council of Australia, 1992, for *A Dream of*

BRIAN CASWELL

Stars, 1994, for *Mike,* 1995, for both *Lisdalia* and
Dreamslip, 1996, for *Maddie,* and 1997, for *Asturias;*
fellow of Australia Council, 1994, 1996; selected for
Australia Council screenwriting attachment, Australian
Film, Television, and Radio School, 1995; Australian
Multi-Cultural Children's Literature Award, 1995, and
Highly Commended citation, Australian Human Rights
Award—Children's Literature, both for *Lisdalia;* Aus-
tralian Children's Peace Literature Award, 1995, for
Deucalion, and shortlist, 1997, for *Asturias;* Aurealis
Speculative Fiction Award, 1996, for *Deucalion;* Nota-
ble new books, International Youth Library, 1997, for
Asturias.

■ Writings

FOR YOUNG ADULTS

Merryll of the Stones, University of Queensland Press (St. Lucia, Australia), 1989.
A Dream of Stars, University of Queensland Press, 1991.
A Cage of Butterflies, University of Queensland Press, 1992.
Dreamslip, University of Queensland Press, 1994.
Deucalion, University of Queensland Press, 1995.
Asturias, University of Queensland Press, 1996.
(With David Phu An Chiem) *Only the Heart,* University of Queensland Press, 1997.

"BOUNDARY PARK" TRILOGY; FOR CHILDREN

Mike (first volume), University of Queensland Press, 1993.
Lisdalia (second volume), University of Queensland Press, 1994.
Maddie (third volume), University of Queensland Press, 1995.

OTHER

(Contributor) Agnes Nieuwenhuizen, editor, *The Written World: Youth and Literature,* Thorpe (Melbourne, Australia), 1994.
Relax Max! (for children), illustrated by Kurt Hedridge, University of Queensland Press, 1997.

Contributor to periodicals.

■ Work in Progress

Alien Zones, a humorous science fiction series for children; *Rookies* and *Bloodlines,* young adult novels, completion expected in 1998; *The View from Ararat,* young adult novel; adapting *Only the Heart* for a screenplay, with An Chiem.

■ Sidelights

Brian Caswell told *Something about the Author* (*SATA*): "After an early childhood spent in Wales and England, I arrived in Australia in 1966. My youth was split fairly evenly between the music industry, school, and sports. Then I trained as a teacher at the University of New South Wales, graduating in 1976, and began a sixteen-year career as a teacher of English and history and a high school basketball coach (not the exalted position in Australia that it is in the United States!). I regard all of this as the best possible apprenticeship for a writer of children's and young adult literature.

"I began writing seriously in 1987, in an effort to create a story that would speak to the teenagers I was involved with. These were teenagers from the western suburbs of Sydney, Australia, for whom much of the traditionally 'popular' canon of youth literature was becoming increasingly inaccessible and irrelevant. I quickly realized, however, that this was a more universal problem. I had chosen to write for the first generation born into the

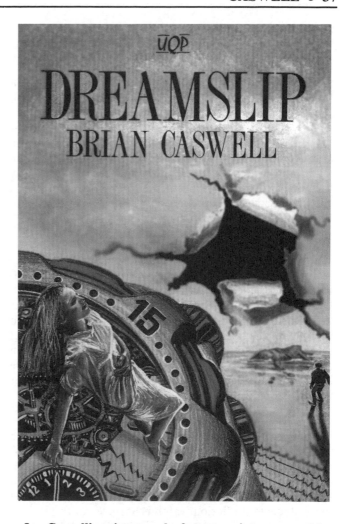

In Caswell's time-travel fantasy, sixteen-year-old Martin searches for his twin sister, who is lost somewhere in history. (Cover illustration by Jane Tanner.)

world of the communications revolution, what I came to call the post-Spielberg generation.

"Living in this world, with its 'quick bite' philosophy in news and story, as well as in eating habits, this generation has a markedly different perception of narrative from those (like myself) born into less frenetic times. If books are to remain an important part of their culture, a new narrative must be developed to retain all that is best in traditional forms, but also to speak to the new generation in a form it recognizes and to which it can respond.

"In the past few years, through thirteen published books, I have developed (and continue to develop) a narrative style, which (I hope!) mirrors and complements the complex multi-media culture that surrounds us. This has gained me a pleasing degree of popularity among my chosen readership in Australia, and I hope soon to expand it to include the United States and England. I tell stories of groups, rather than individuals, and I allow different members of the group to tell their parts of the story, in the way a film might. I am still very aware, however, that I am writing a novel or short story, which must do far more than a film in some areas.

"Since 1991 I have been writing full-time, working at home and occasionally touring Australia to speak at schools, universities, and conferences. I have been a writer in residence at the University of Western Sydney and a writer attached to the Australian Film, Television, and Radio School. I coach my twin sons' basketball team and watch far too many movies. In my early forties, I am having the best time of my life, and I live in constant fear that someone will notice how much fun I'm having and force me to take my old life back.

"In Australia I am sought after as a speaker on narrative technique and new directions in young people's literature, and I have had articles published on the subject. On the other side of the ledger, of the awards my books have garnered, a large number are based, not only on literary merit, but on social factors. This indicates that the content, as well as the form of my work, has been considered worthy of note by a number of people involved in selecting and monitoring literature for young people.

"I believe in the capacities of young people, and I refuse to 'write down' to them simply because common 'wisdom' is willing to assign to them a sophistication in emotional terms which it is unwilling to acknowledge in the area of reading technique. Such an attitude can tend to produce youth fiction which is at once confrontational and disturbing, yet technically and artistically simplistic and intellectually limiting. Our youth deserve more respect than this.

"What we must aim for is, I believe, the creation of a form of 'literary' youth fiction that is technically and artistically demanding, yet culturally relevant in both form and content. It must also recognize the fact that, though youth fiction is different from adult fiction in purpose and audience, it is in no way 'inferior.' My greatest pleasure is that I have found a willing readership—in Australia, at least—not only among teenagers, but among their parents, teachers, and librarians. These readers allow me to raise some of the questions about their world and themselves that it is the job of literature to raise."

■ For More Information See

PERIODICALS

Horn Book, July-August, 1992, p. 497.
Magpies, September, 1992, p. 33; November, 1993, p. 32; July, 1994, p. 24; November, 1994, pp. 31, 33; September, 1995, p. 34; September, 1996, p. 36.
Reading Time, November, 1997, p. 32.

CHAST, Roz 1954-

■ Personal

Born November 26, 1954, in Brooklyn, NY; daughter of George (a teacher of French and Spanish) and Elizabeth (an assistant principal; maiden name, Buchman) Chast; married William Franzen (a writer), September 22, 1984; children: Ian, Nina. *Education:* Attended Manhattan Art Students League; Rhode Island School of Design, B.F.A., 1977.

■ Addresses

Home—Ridgefield, CT. *Office*—c/o *New Yorker* Cartoonists, 25 W. 23rd St., New York, NY 10036.

■ Career

Cartoonist and book illustrator. *New Yorker,* New York City, cartoonist, 1979—. Has also provided art for advertising agencies. *Exhibitions:* Exhibitor at the Illustration Gallery, New York City.

■ Writings

ILLUSTRATOR; FOR CHILDREN

Jane Read Martin and Patricia Marx, *Now Everybody Really Hates Me,* Harper, 1993.

ROZ CHAST

Alfa-Betty Olsen and Marshall Efron, *Gabby the Shrew*, Random House, 1994.

Jane Read Martin and Patricia Marx, *Now I Will Never Leave the Dinner Table*, HarperCollins, 1995.

CARTOON COLLECTIONS

Unscientific Americans, Dial, 1982.

Parallel Universes: An Assortment of Cartoons, Harper, 1984.

Mondo Boxo: Cartoon Stories, Harper, 1987.

The Four Elements, Harper, 1988.

Proof of Life on Earth, HarperCollins, 1991.

Childproof: Cartoons about Parents and Children, Hyperion, 1997.

OTHER

(Illustrator) Allia Zobel, *The Joy of Being Single*, Workman, 1992.

Contributor of cartoons to periodicals, including *New Yorker, Christopher Street, Village Voice, Money,* and *National Lampoon*.

■ Work in Progress

Illustrations for *Meet My Staff* by Patricia Marx for HarperCollins.

■ Sidelights

Hailed by William Goldstein of *Publishers Weekly* as "probably the funniest woman in the world," Roz Chast is a cartoonist whose humorous, offbeat drawings about the absurdities of everyday life have made her one of the most popular staff artists for the *New Yorker* as well as a well-received newcomer to the field of children's books. Chast has published several collections of her cartoons for adults and has provided the illustrations for picture books for young readers that feature distinctive human and animal characters. Blending sophisticated ideas with a drawing style that is often described as childlike, Chast, according to Pope Brock in *People Weekly*, "looks at the world with a child's fixity and a child's fears." Additionally, Chast includes in her work what is considered an unusually high number of words. Written in her own distinctive handwriting, as she related to Goldstein, Chast calls the drawings in her collection *Mondo Boxo* "cartoon short stories." Reviewers often laud Chast as an especially gifted observer of humanity. When she first began submitting cartoons to the *New Yorker*, claimed Brock, "No one had ever seen characters quite like Chast's before—hunch-shouldered geeks with bad haircuts, sporting thrift-shop clothing and poleaxed expressions. Even more peculiar was Chast's drawing style, which is scrawny and childlike."

In his *Booklist* review of her first collection of cartoons, *Unscientific Americans*, Alan Moores noted that Chast is "wise in her sense of the absurdities of modern life," while Ben Reuven of the *Los Angeles Times Book Review* called the book "outrageous, inspired, ever-so-slightly demented." Chast's next collection, *Parallel Universes*, was deemed "wickedly funny" by Jonathan

I will never sleep in my bed again. I will sleep on the floor at all times. Except when I sleep in the fort in my closet. And I will put thumbtacks around my fort to make it Theodore-proof.

With a wealth of humorous detail, Chast's illustrations enhance the story of Patty Jane, a young girl who vows to stay in her room forever after being sent there as punishment. (From *Now Everybody Really Hates Me*, written by Jane Read Martin and Patricia Marx.)

Yardley in *Book World*. In his review of *Proof of Life on Earth*, Ralph Sassone said that Chast "can be counted on to decode and recontextualize the small talk, inflated claims, and petty impulses that make up life on this planet—and to make it a hoot"; Sassone summed up Chast's work as "a sharp yet democratic vision in which everything under the sun gets a chance to fulfill its absurd potential." Brock quoted *New Yorker* cartoon editor Lee Lorenz as saying that Chast's "best cartoons are a perfect blend of drawing and idea. I can't imagine her cartoons being drawn any other way."

Chast was born in Brooklyn, New York, and grew up as an only child in the Flatbush area of the city. She started drawing as a child and recalled in *People Weekly*, "My first and biggest cartoon love was Charles Addams. I like the creepiness in his cartoons." Addams, the creator of "The Addams Family," was one of the *New Yorker*'s most famous cartoonists. Chast recounted an important grade-school experience for Goldstein in *Publishers Weekly*: "The teacher had some kind of contest for drawing, I don't know what it was. But you know those things that when ladies would put their sweater over their shoulders, to keep them from falling off, there'd be this little kind of chain attached? Well I won one of those! So that kind of really inspired me—'Wow, if this is what drawing can do, I'll just stay with it.'" She continued, "I guess I sort of started drawing cartoon-like things when I was about fourteen or something like that." Chast always read comics, but remembers that her parents, educators in the Brooklyn public schools, forbade her to read the "*Archie and Veronica* variety; they weren't educational enough." Instead, her parents would buy her the "Classics Illustrated" type of comics—"you know, *The Ox-Bow Incident* in living color," she said—which Chast disliked intensely; however, she had a friend with a stack of comics three feet high who exposed her to *Mad* and other less highbrow publications.

While she was in high school, Chast attended classes at the Art Students League in Manhattan, where, she remembered, "I really learned a lot ... [They] had the strangest models.... Young people, really old people, people that were incredibly skinny but they had this really weird pot belly. I mean the strangest collection of people from the most beautifully proportioned men and women to people whose stomachs were very square in a certain way." Considering a career as a painter, she earned a bachelor's degree in fine arts from the Rhode Island School of Design (RISD); however, Chast decided not to become a fine artist because, she said, "I missed the words." After she left RISD, Chast "knew what I really loved to do was cartoons and stuff like that, but I thought that was completely impractical and I'd never be able to do it." Chast compiled a portfolio of her work and sought a position as a magazine illustrator, a career that she abandoned after a few months when she started to draw cartoons. Riding home on the subway one day, she saw a copy of *Christopher Street* and was pleased to discover that it included cartoons as a regular feature; a short time later, Chast sold her first cartoon to *Christopher Street* for ten dollars. In 1978, she sold her first drawing to the *New Yorker,* eventually procuring a contract from them for first rights to all of her works and, in the early 1990s, becoming one of only two female staff cartoonists at the magazine. At the *New Yorker,* Chast met her husband, William Franzen, who was working on the staff first as a messenger and later as a humor writer; the couple were married in 1984 and have two children, Ian and Nina. Franzen has also written a book of short stories, *Hearing from Wayne.*

After publishing five collections of her cartoons and illustrating Allia Zobel's humorous book *The Joy of Being Single,* Chast entered the field of children's literature when she provided the pictures for Jane Read Martin and Patricia Marx's collaboration *Now Everybody Really Hates Me,* published in 1993. In the story, Patty Jane Pepper is sent to her room for assaulting her younger brother during his birthday party—or as Patty Jane says, "I did not hit Theodore. I touched him hard." *Now Everybody Really Hates Me* explores the heroine's fantasies of staying in her room forever—except maybe for visits to her friends. Patty, who muses on the many ways she can avenge herself on her family, is finally coaxed out of her room by the offer of birthday cake and ice cream. Critics generally appreciated *Now Everybody Really Hates Me* for capturing a familiar childhood

Joy never has what I call fun. Joy does not like to do spider art. Joy does not like to get dizzy with our little brother, Theodore, and me. Joy does not even like mud.

Chast lends witty illustrations to another tale of Patty Jane, who denounces her babysitting sister after she confines Patty Jane to the table for refusing to eat her spinach. (From *Now I Will Never Leave the Dinner Table,* written by Jane Read Martin and Patricia Marx.)

experience as well as for the portrayal of stubborn Patty Jane; in addition, reviewers praised Chast for her line-and-wash drawings, which are credited for successfully mirroring the events of the story while adding humorous details and funny asides. *Booklist* reviewer Stephanie Zvirin maintained that Chast "uses expressive, snappy, slightly sophisticated drawings, washed in watercolor, to interpret Patty's tale of childhood woe." Caroline Parr of *School Library Journal* claimed that it is "Chast's cartoons that make this book stand out." *New York Times* reviewer Andrea Barnet noted that the "deadpan humor of the authors ... is perfectly suited to Roz Chast's wonderfully waggish illustrations. In fact, the marriage of text and pictures is so seamless it seems surprising that Ms. Chast ... has never done a children's book before."

Following *Now Everybody Really Hates Me,* Chast illustrated *Gabby the Shrew,* a story by Alfa-Betty Olsen and Marshall Efron about a young shrew whose constant hunger leads him into a situation where he disrupts a human family before being discovered by his mother. *School Library Journal* reviewer Marilyn Taniguchi asserted, "Chast's clever cartoon illustrations are in tune with the text's hyperbole," while *Booklist* critic Lauren

Peterson observed, "Chast's delightfully silly cartoons with occasional sound effects ... nicely reflect the story's slapstick flavor."

With *Now I Will Never Leave the Dinner Table,* Chast again joins forces with authors Jane Read Martin and Patricia Marx. In this book, a sequel to *Now Everybody Really Hates Me,* Patty Jane is stranded at the dinner table facing a huge pile of spinach at the insistence of her baby-sitter, perfect older sister Joy, who has accused Patty Jane of hiding her portion of spinach in her pocket. Patty Jane digs in her heels, saying "I will never finish my spinach. Even if that means sitting here until I am grown up with children of my own." While she sulks, Patty Jane freely assassinates her sister's character while imagining how she can get Joy out of her life forever; in the end, Patty Jane "allows" Joy to stay. Mary M. Burns of *Horn Book* called *Now I Will Never Leave the Dinner Table* "a guffaw-a-minute sitcom with no laugh track needed" and added, "Watercolor-and-line illustrations effectively augment the deadpan text with flamboyant, detailed images to match Patty Jane's unbridled style." *Booklist* reviewer Stephanie Zvirin said that "Chast's sophisticated cartoonlike artwork ... evokes Patty Jane in all her disagreeable glory and provides fine reinforcement for the sardonic humor of the tale," while *Publishers Weekly* concluded, "Chast makes hay with the hyperbolic text."

■ Works Cited

Barnet, Andrea, review of *Now Everybody Really Hates Me, New York Times Book Review,* April 24, 1994, p. 24.

Brock, Pope, "Drawing on Anxiety," *People Weekly,* December 2, 1991, pp. 169-70, 172.

Burns, Mary M., review of *Now I Will Never Leave the Dinner Table, Horn Book,* September-October, 1996, pp. 582-83.

Goldstein, William, "Chast-Izing the World: An Interview with *The New Yorker*'s Funniest Cartoonist," *Publishers Weekly,* August 14, 1987, pp. 82-83.

Martin, Jane Read, and Patricia Marx, *Now Everybody Really Hates Me,* Harper, 1993.

Martin, Jane Read, and Patricia Marx, *Now I Will Never Leave the Dinner Table,* HarperCollins, 1995.

Moores, Alan, review of *Unscientific Americans, Booklist,* November 15, 1982, p. 420.

Review of *Now I Will Never Leave the Dinner Table, Publishers Weekly,* March 11, 1996, p. 63.

Parr, Caroline, review of *Now Everybody Really Hates Me, School Library Journal,* March, 1994, p. 205.

Peterson, Lauren, review of *Gabby the Shrew, Booklist,* January 1, 1995, p. 826.

Reuven, Ben, review of *Unscientific Americans, Los Angeles Times Book Review,* October 3, 1982, p. 6.

Sassone, Ralph, review of *Proof of Life on Earth, Village Voice Literary Supplement,* December, 1991, p. 10.

Taniguchi, Marilyn, review of *Gabby the Shrew, School Library Journal,* February, 1995, p. 78.

Yardley, Jonathan, review of *Parallel Universes, Book World—The Washington Post,* September 23, 1984, p. 12.

Zvirin, Stephanie, review of *Now Everybody Really Hates Me, Booklist,* October 15, 1993, p. 453.

Zvirin, Stephanie, review of *Now I Will Never Leave the Dinner Table, Booklist,* April 1, 1996, pp. 1371-72.

■ For More Information See

BOOKS

Legends in Their Own Time, Prentice Hall, 1994.
Newsmakers 92, Gale, 1992.

PERIODICALS

Ms., December, 1982, p. 16.
New York Times, November 27, 1988, pp. 44-45, 62-65.
New York Times Book Review, October 31, 1982, p. 35; February 28, 1988, p. 20; April 21, 1992, p. 24.
Village Voice Literary Supplement, November 27, 1984, p. 53.
Wilson Library Bulletin, April, 1994, p. 118.*

—*Sketch by Gerard J. Senick*

*   *   *

CLEMENT, Rod

■ Addresses

Home—Sydney, Australia.

■ Career

Author, illustrator, and cartoonist. Caricaturist for several Australian newspapers and periodicals, including the *Australian Financial Review.*

■ Awards, Honors

Shortlist, Picture Book of the Year, Children's Book Council of Australia, 1996, for *Just Another Ordinary Day.*

■ Writings

FOR CHILDREN

Counting on Frank, Collins (Sydney, Australia), 1990, Gareth Stevens (Milwaukee), 1991.
Eyes in Disguise, Collins, 1992.
Just Another Ordinary Day, Angus & Robertson (Pymble, New South Wales), 1995, HarperCollins, 1997.
Grandad's Teeth, Angus & Robertson, 1997, as *Grandpa's Teeth,* HarperCollins, 1998.

ILLUSTRATOR

Hazel Edwards, *The Imaginary Menagerie,* Lothian (Melbourne, Australia), 1984.
Hazel Edwards, *Snail Mail,* Collins, 1986.
Nick Greaves, *When Hippo Was Hairy, and Other Tales from Africa,* Collins, 1988, Barron's (New York City), 1988.
Sheena Knowles, *Edwina the Emu,* Collins, 1988.
Nick Greaves, *When Lion Could Fly, and Other Tales from Africa,* Barron's (Hauppauge, NY), 1993.

■ Sidelights

Beginning his career in children's literature as an illustrator in the early 1980s, Rod Clement has expanded his talents into the realm of storytelling. From his home in Australia, Clement has both written and created artwork for such highly praised works as *Counting on Frank, Eyes in Disguise,* and *Grandad's Teeth,* all featuring the author/illustrator's offbeat sense of fun.

Hazel Edwards's 1984 story *The Imaginary Menagerie* was the first published work featuring Clement's unique illustrations. The success of his efforts prompted other assignments, including work on Edwards's *Snail Mail,* Sheena Knowles's humorous *Edwina the Emu,* and two popular anthologies of African folktales, *When Hippo Was Hairy, and Other Tales from Africa* and the companion volume *When Lion Could Fly, and Other Tales from Africa.* "The stories are amusing, the artwork wonderful," lauded Sheilamae O'Hara in a review of *When Lion Could Fly* for *Booklist.* O'Hara added that the work was "a bonanza for folktale enthusiasts and wild animal lovers alike."

In 1990 Clement published his first solo volume, *Counting on Frank.* As its title suggests, the book features mathematical games, which are played by a clever dog named Frank with the help of his young owner. Praised by Margot Tyrrell in *Magpies* for its ability to humorously capture "children's ways of approaching ideas of space and time and encourag[ing] them to think about ... [such] concepts," *Counting on Frank* was followed by the fish story *Eyes in Disguise.* In this work, Clement's scaly picture-book protagonists Bernice and Ian are considered outsiders because of their unusual markings. Deciding to make for a different shore, the big-eyed pair swim off in search of other fish more like themselves, encountering adventures along the way. Commenting favorably on the book's effectiveness in appealing to young readers on many levels, Albert Brgoc noted in his *Magpies* review: "Visually the book is stunning.... Children are always interested in the charismatic fish and what will happen to them." Among Clement's other picture book projects have been *Just Another Ordinary Day,* featuring illustrations that a *Teaching and Learning Literature* critic described as "deliciously zany," and *Grandad's Teeth,* a tongue-in-cheek mystery about a set of chompers and the intensive police investigation that ensues after they are swiped during their nighttime soak in the glass next to Grandpa's bed. "Clement's toothy cast should get everyone grinning as his caricatured townsfolk, parrots, dolls, teddy bears, and even the fish on ice flash their pearly whites," maintained Elizabeth Bush of the *Bulletin of the Center for Children's Books.* "In Rod Clement's

Every morning she got a lift to school with Mrs. Ellsworth.
Mrs. Ellsworth was the oldest person on the block and told amazing stories about life in the old days. She also drove the oldest car in the world, so they were never on time.

Rod Clement's illustrations relate outlandish details in ironic counterpart to his understated text about Amanda's not-so-ordinary life. (From *Just Another Ordinary Day,* written and illustrated by Clement.)

■ Awards, Honors

IRA Children's Choice award, for *Choosing Sides;* Best Books designation, *Chicago Tribune,* 1995, for *Buddy Love—Now on Video,* and 1997, for *The Dead Sea Scrolls.*

■ Writings

NOVELS

The Winning of Miss Lynn Ryan, illustrated by Susan Magurn, Morrow (New York), 1987.
Buddy Love—Now on Video, HarperCollins (New York), 1995.
I'll See You in My Dreams, Viking Penguin (New York), 1997.

NOVELS; "KIDS FROM KENNEDY MIDDLE SCHOOL" SERIES

Queen of the Sixth Grade, Morrow, 1988.
Choosing Sides, Morrow, 1990.
Mean Streak, Morrow, 1991.
The New, Improved Gretchen Hubbard, Morrow, 1992.

NOVELS; "FRANCES IN THE FOURTH GRADE" SERIES

Frances Takes a Chance, Bullseye Books (New York), 1991.
Frances Dances, Bullseye Books, 1991.
Frances Four-Eyes, Bullseye Books, 1991.
Frances and Friends, illustrated by Vilma Ortiz, Bullseye Books, 1991.

NOVELS; "HOLLYWOOD WARS" SERIES

Lights, Camera, Attitude, Puffin (New York), 1993.
My Co-Star, My Enemy, Puffin, 1993.
Seeing Red, Puffin, 1993.
Trouble in Paradise, Puffin, 1993.

NOVELS; "HOLIDAY FIVE" SERIES

Trick or Trouble, Viking (New York), 1994.
The Worst Noel, Viking, 1994.
Stupid Cupid, Viking, 1995.
Star Spangled Summer, Viking, 1996.
No-Thanks Thanksgiving, Viking, 1996.

OTHER

Susan B. Anthony (biography), F. Watts, 1984.
(Editor, with Denise Wilms) *Guide to Non-Sexist Children's Books,* Volume II: *1976-1985,* Academy Chicago (Chicago), 1987.
The Dead Sea Scrolls, illustrated by John Thompson, Morrow, 1997.

Has also written for television series, including *American Playhouse* and *The Jeffersons;* author of teleplay *Under the Biltmore Clock,* 1983.

■ Work in Progress

A book about young people in the Bible.

■ Sidelights

A distinguished critic of children's books for the magazine *Booklist,* Ilene Cooper's name is also known to teen and pre-teen readers as a popular novelist. The author of the humorous novel *Buddy Love—Now on Video* as well as the "Kids from Kennedy Middle School" and "Hollywood Wars" series, Cooper has also researched and written several works of nonfiction that follow her interest in both women's history and her own religious roots.

Cooper's most popular novel series—"Kids from Kennedy Middle School," first introduced to teen readers in 1988—delves into the inner politics of the "in-crowd." In *Queen of the Sixth Grade,* Veronica Volner, the self-proclaimed reigning queen of the "Awesome Kennedy Girls" (or AKG), commands that another girl, Robin, be cast out of the group when it becomes apparent that a boy Veronica likes favors her former best friend. "Sixth-grade meanness has rarely been better portrayed," commented Roger Sutton in *Bulletin of the Center for Children's Books.* Critic Nancy Vasilakis, writing in *Horn Book,* declared that Cooper "probes with excellent

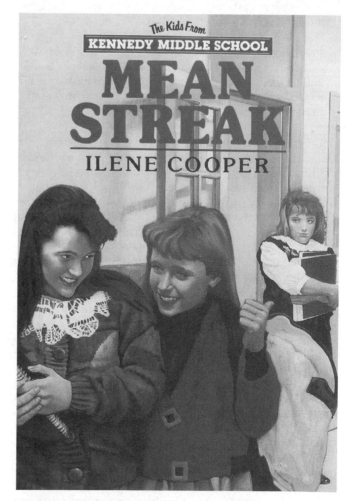

Concerned about her popularity at school, sixth-grader Veronica Volner hides her true feelings about her parents' divorce. (Cover illustration by Mike Wimmer.)

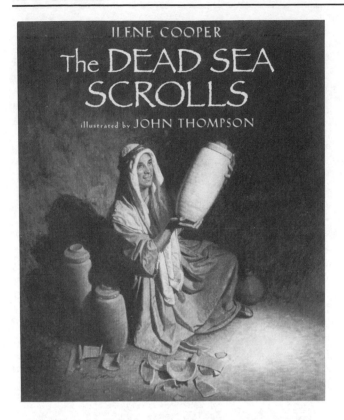

Published to commemorate the fiftieth anniversary of the discovery of the Dead Sea Scrolls, Cooper's book investigates scholars' attempts to authenticate and understand one of the most significant archeological finds of the twentieth century.

understanding a specific problem of interpersonal relationships facing many schoolchildren." The devilry continues in *Choosing Sides* and *Mean Streak,* as testy Veronica attempts to hide her discombobulated home-life by causing problems for her romantic rivals, especially for Gretchen Hubbard, the fattest girl in the sixth grade. Sutton remarked that while Veronica is an unsavory character, she is an engaging one that "captures our interest and sympathy, and ... leaves us with some hope that she is capable of change."

Cooper's "Hollywood Wars" series also deals with the social pressures of teen life. In *My Co-Star, My Enemy,* fifteen-year-old Alison Blake suddenly finds herself with a role in a television show. Unfortunately, Alison's good luck results in the animosity of fellow cast-member Jamie, also fifteen, whose six-year acting career seems to be near an end. In addition to providing a look at how a television show is filmed, the series follows the changes that rising popularity makes in Alison's formerly quiet life.

Published in 1995, *Buddy Love—Now on Video* features a thirteen-year-old protagonist who is desperate to find that one thing that will inspire him; so far, only girls and television have really caught his attention. Ultimately, Buddy finds a way to combine his two main interests after his father buys a video recorder and lets his son use it. Seeing his world through the viewfinder while

mastering his filmmaking skills, Buddy eventually begins to view his life differently and find new appreciation for his family. "Cooper's sure touch paints the emotions of early adolescence accurately," noted *Voice of Youth Advocates* reviewer Faye H. Gottschall, who also praised the author's ability to imbue the story with humor. Critic Roger Sutton appreciated Cooper's use of comedy as well and called the author's sense of "middle-school reality ... upbeat but sheared of didacticism" in his review in *Bulletin of the Center for Children's Books.*

Older teens take center stage in Cooper's 1997 suspense novel, *I'll See You in My Dreams.* Years after suffering a spell of nightmares that occurred just before her father's tragic death in a car accident, sixteen-year-old Karen Genovese's dreams of a cute new boy at school begin to turn dark. Sensing that something bad is about to befall her new classmate, Mark Kennedy, and Mark's younger brother Brian, Karen sets about trying to avert another tragedy. While a *Publishers Weekly* reviewer claimed that "readers anticipating eerie renditions of psychic experiences may be disappointed" in the direction of the novel, a *Kirkus Reviews* contributor considered *I'll See You in My Dreams* a fun book for teen readers that has "a spooky atmosphere and a few surprising plot twists."

In addition to her novels for adolescents, Cooper has published several works for younger readers, including her four-volume "Frances in the Fourth Grade" series and the novel *The Winning of Miss Lynn Ryan.* Revolving around a class of fifth grade students' efforts to curry favor with a pretty and poised new teacher who demands perfection, Cooper's 1987 work illustrates how a teacher can "help her students see what is best in themselves or ... stifle their better instincts," according to *Horn Book* contributor Nancy Vasilakis. Readers gain a sense of the schoolchildren's struggle through the perspectives of characters such as Carrie, whose messy work will never pass Miss Ryan's muster, and ultra-brainy but equally unpopular "Luke the Puke."

Cooper's *The Dead Sea Scrolls,* published in 1997, was only her second work of nonfiction in fifteen years. The book explores the history behind the collection of religious documents discovered by a shepherd in 1947 in a cave on the shore of the Dead Sea. Cooper recounts the efforts of scientists, translators, and scholars to authenticate and understand what many consider to be the most significant archaeological find of the twentieth century. The volume, which commemorates the fiftieth anniversary of the scrolls' discovery, contains a great deal of research that ranges from studying the techniques of archaeologists and computer scientists to learning the history of Judeo-Christianity and the Middle East. This wealth of factual information is presented in order to allow young readers to understand the many facets of a tale that encompasses two thousand years of human history.

The Dead Sea Scrolls was well received by critics. "This fascinating story takes on new life," stated *Book Links* reviewer Judy O'Malley. "Despite the unavoidable jumping back and forth in time ... [the text is] clear and accessible," noted Jennifer M. Brabander in her critique of the volume for *Horn Book*. The critic added that Cooper's work "dynamically proves that biblical history is anything but dead." Cooper commented on the writing of *The Dead Sea Scrolls* in a *Book Links* essay: "A special moment for me was my trip to Israel, when I finally got to the Dead Sea caves and Qumran, where excavations are still in progress. No matter how many books and articles I read, nothing could match actually climbing those limestone cliffs myself. There is a Hebrew word, *beshert*, that roughly translates as fate or something that is meant to be. The discovery of the scrolls in those desolate caves makes the word *beshert* come alive for me."

"Kids always ask me where I get my ideas," Cooper once told *SATA*. "Most of them come from my own childhood and teenage years. Although many things have changed since I was young, the hopes and fears and feelings seem to remain the same."

■ Works Cited

Brabander, Jennifer M., review of *The Dead Sea Scrolls, Horn Book,* September/October, 1997, pp. 590-91.

Cooper, Ilene, "The Dead Sea Scrolls," *Book Links,* May, 1997, pp. 16-20.

Gottschall, Faye H., review of *Buddy Love—Now on Video, Voice of Youth Advocates,* April, 1996, p. 24.

Review of *I'll See You in My Dreams, Kirkus Reviews,* June 1, 1997, p. 870.

Review of *I'll See You in My Dreams, Publishers Weekly,* June 2, 1997, p. 72.

O'Malley, Judy, review of *The Dead Sea Scrolls, Book Links,* May, 1997, p. 16.

Sutton, Roger, review of *Queen of the Sixth Grade, Bulletin of the Center for Children's Books,* November, 1988, p. 68.

Sutton, Roger, review of *Mean Streak, Bulletin of the Center for Children's Books,* April, 1991, p. 188.

Sutton, Roger, review of *Buddy Love—Now on Video, Bulletin of the Center for Children's Books,* December, 1995, pp. 123-24.

Vasilakis, Nancy, review of *The Winning of Miss Ryan, Horn Book,* January, 1988, p. 62.

Vasilakis, Nancy, review of *Queen of the Sixth Grade, Horn Book,* January, 1989, p. 68.

■ For More Information See

PERIODICALS

Booklist, May 15, 1991, p. 1798; August, 1992, p. 2010; May 1, 1993, p. 1580; March 1, 1997, p. 1157.

Bulletin of the Center for Children's Books, October, 1987, pp. 25-26; September, 1990, pp. 4-5; November, 1992, p. 70; September, 1997, pp. 8-9.

Kirkus Reviews, May 15, 1991, p. 669; June 15, 1991, p. 787; August 15, 1994, p. 1142.

Publishers Weekly, June 14, 1991, p. 47; May 10, 1993, p. 72; July 4, 1994, p. 64.

School Library Journal, August, 1984, p. 82; May, 1990, p. 103.

COTTRINGER, Anne 1952-

■ Personal

Born May 28, 1952, in Niagara Falls, Ontario, Canada; children: Joseph, Freddy. *Education:* University of Western Ontario, B.A.; Slade School of Fine Art, London, England, Dip.Ad.; Royal College of Art, London, M.A.

■ Addresses

Home and office—13 Almington St., London N4 3BP, England.

■ Career

Freelance cinematographer and director for films and television, 1980—.

■ Writings

Ella and the Naughty Lion, illustrated by Russell Ayto, Houghton (Boston, MA), 1996.

Contributor to magazines. Member of editorial board, *Vertigo,* a film and television magazine.

■ Work in Progress

Friends and Avatars; Danny and the Great White Bear for Macmillan; *Flip Flap! Who's That?* for Penguin.

ANNE COTTRINGER

■ Sidelights

In Anne Cottringer's first book, *Ella and the Naughty Lion,* little Ella, sister of newborn baby Jasper, watches closely as a rambunctious lion pushes the baby out of his crib, tears up his teddy bear, and acts out all her mean feelings, "an alter ego on the loose," as a *Kirkus Reviews* critic remarked. When Jasper is really in danger, however, Ella comes to the rescue and discovers the pride and joy of being Big Sister and heroine of the day. The *Kirkus Reviews* commentator maintained: "[Cottringer's] language is vigorous and the telling is sharp." Janice Del Negro of the *Bulletin of the Center for Children's Books* observed that the author's apt depictions of Ella's apparent jealousy amounted to "more than just 'new baby' bibliotherapy," and warmly praised her "great readaloud rhythm."

■ Works Cited

Del Negro, Janice, review of *Ella and the Naughty Lion, Bulletin of the Center for Children's Books,* October, 1996, pp. 52-53.
Review of *Ella and the Naughty Lion, Kirkus Reviews,* July 15, 1996, p. 1046.

■ For More Information See

PERIODICALS

Booklist, September 1, 1996, p. 141.
Publishers Weekly, September 2, 1996, p. 130.
School Librarian, November, 1996, p. 145.
School Library Journal, December, 1996, p. 91.

*   *   *

CREWS, Nina 1963-

■ Personal

Born May 19, 1963, in Frankfurt, Germany; daughter of Donald (an author/illustrator) and Ann (an author/illustrator; maiden name, Jonas) Crews. *Education:* Yale University, B.A., 1985.

■ Addresses

Home and office—Brooklyn, NY.

■ Career

Author and illustrator of children's books; animator. Freelance animation artist/coordinator, 1986-94, and illustrator, 1991—. Ink Tank (animation studio), New York City, producer, 1995-97.

■ Writings

One Hot Summer Day, with photographs by the author, Greenwillow, 1995.
I'll Catch the Moon, illustrated with photographs and drawings by the author, Greenwillow, 1996.
Snowball, Greenwillow, 1997.

OTHER

Contributor of illustrations to newspapers, including the *Village Voice,* and magazines, including *Parenting.*

■ Work in Progress

You Are Here, for Greenwillow.

■ Sidelights

The daughter of respected author/illustrators Donald Crews and Ann Jonas, Nina Crews has established a reputation of her own as a talented contributor to the field of children's literature. Combining simple stories with arresting photographic collages, Crews creates picture books that are considered notable for reflecting the thoughts, feelings, and experiences of young children while celebrating the urban environment that is the background of her works. Born in Frankfurt, Germany, Crews was raised in an artistic atmosphere in Manhattan's West Village. Regarding New York City, Crews said in a promotional piece for Greenwillow Books, "I think I've always loved it . . . . I enjoyed the city and all its variety. The people, the neighborhoods, all of the city's quirkiness were endlessly exciting. I started taking pictures at an early age, and the city was my first subject." As a child, Crews and her sister were encouraged by their parents in their art projects. As a teenager, Crews attended the Music and Art High School in New York City and went to Yale University to major in art and study photography. She commented, "I had well-rounded art training in high school but became more focused on photography in college. Since then, I have

NINA CREWS

My mother tells me to play inside games. She has the fan on high.

Using collages of photographs, Crews illustrates the simple tale of a young girl's enjoyment of a sudden rainstorm on a sweltering day in the city. (From *One Hot Summer Day,* written and illustrated by Crews.)

been working in commercial animation production and doing freelance photo-collage illustration."

In an interview with Shannon Maughan in *Publishers Weekly,* Crews recalled, "My father always said, 'You should do a children's book.'" When friends made disparaging remarks about New York City not being a good place to raise children, Crews was prompted to create the concept book *One Hot Summer Day.* She explained in *Publishers Weekly,* "I wanted to do a book about an urban child's existence. I wanted to reflect the energy of the city environment, the textures of it. It's something that I love. This book came out of remembering those days of big thunderstorms when the whole world changes from one thing into another." Using a family friend as a model for her collage photographs, Crews depicted a lively, happy African American girl dressed in purple overalls who describes her city neighborhood as she plays on a sweltering day. Engaging in activities like eating popsicles, playing on the swings, and trying to fry an egg on the sidewalk, the narrator finally dances among the raindrops of a sudden thunderstorm. In her review of *One Hot Summer Day* in *Horn Book,* Mary M. Burns commented that Crews's illustrations are an "intriguing combination of realistic images imaginatively redefined in unexpected juxtaposition.... In this context, the camera is as much a painter's tool as palette and brush...." Burns concluded that *One Hot Summer Day* is a "wonderful concept book" and an "auspicious debut." A reviewer in *Publishers Weekly* concurred, calling the book a "promising debut" and noting that Crews "skillfully captures the childlike wonder at and appreciation of small delights." A *Kirkus Reviews* commentator heralded "the debut of a welcome new voice and vision," and praised "the fresh and intriguing way these snapshots are collaged with other media into an urban narrative for very young children." When asked by *Publishers Weekly* about the

reaction of her parents to her book, Crews said, "They gave me my space and were really encouraging."

In her next concept book, *I'll Catch the Moon,* Crews renders her collages in a style that is both reminiscent of and different from the one in *One Hot Summer Day.* In this work, the artist uses toned black-and-white background photos to create a dreamlike fantasy about climbing a ladder to the moon. Narrated by a seven-year-old girl with a missing front tooth, the story describes the child's fantasy as she looks out her window at New York City by night. She imagines herself climbing a ladder to the moon and dancing among the stars before heading home to bed. Crews uses a photo-collage technique that mixes actual photos from NASA with those taken by the artist. Writing in *Horn Book,* Elizabeth S. Watson called *I'll Catch the Moon* a "knockout in both concept and execution" and added that both "the photographs themselves and their placement in the overall design are outstanding." *Bulletin of the Center for Children's Books* reviewer Deborah Stevenson claimed, "As nighttime journeys go ... this is an unusual one, and kids may enjoy the tantalizingly realistic bedtime fantasy." A *Kirkus Reviews* critic added that the narrator's wish "is vividly brought to life," and concluded, "In style and setting, this book is virtually a repeat of Crews's *One Hot Summer Day,* but its star-drenched, dreamlike mood gives it a totally different emotional content."

In her promotional piece for Greenwillow, Crews stated, "I love making collages. Some of my favorite artists— Romare Bearden, Hannah Hoch, and Man Ray—combined photography and collage. Collage allows me to use photography playfully and to tell a story on many levels. I enjoy photographing children. The interaction always adds something to the project; their performances always give me new ideas. I try to keep the photography session as loose as possible. Collaging the images allows mc a great deal of freedom. Basically, almost anything can happen. Writing the book is another kind of challenge. I try to find a good balance between the written story and the visual story. Each one should help the other. Picture books are the combination of two forms of poetry, written and visual, and their flow should be musical. I find myself reading a lot of poetry while I work on ideas."

"As a child," Crews concluded, "I loved books and I loved to look. The more there was to see in any one image, the better. I also loved books that were set in city places. I hope that a new generation will get these same pleasures from my books."

■ Works Cited

Burns, Mary M., review of *One Hot Summer Day, Horn Book,* July-August, 1995, p. 448.

Crews, Nina, promotional piece for Greenwillow Books.

Review of *I'll Catch the Moon, Kirkus Reviews,* April 15, 1996, p. 600.

Maughan, Shannon, interview with Nina Crews in "Flying Starts," *Publishers Weekly,* July 3, 1995, p. 33.

Review of *One Hot Summer Day, Kirkus Reviews,* May 1, 1995, p. 633.

Review of *One Hot Summer Day, Publishers Weekly,* June 12, 1995, p. 60.

Stevenson, Deborah, review of *I'll Catch the Moon, Bulletin of the Center for Children's Books,* May, 1996, p. 297.

Watson, Elizabeth S., review of *I'll Catch the Moon, Horn Book,* May-June, 1996, pp. 321-22.

■ For More Information See

PERIODICALS

Booklist, June 1, 1995, p. 1776.

Publishers Weekly, May 13, 1996, p. 75; November 10, 1997, p. 73.

School Library Journal, June, 1995, p. 79; May, 1996, p. 85.

—Sketch by Gerard J. Senick

D

DANIELS, Zoe
See LAUX, Constance

*   *   *

DARIAN, Shea 1959-

■ Personal

Given name is pronounced "Shay"; born December 30, 1959, in Jefferson City, MO; daughter of Charles Strother (in insurance sales) and Demetra Anne (an administrative assistant; maiden name, Woodyard) Bagbey; married Andrew Hughes (now Darian; a teacher), August 16, 1986; children: Morgan, Willa. *Education:* Iowa State University, B.A., 1983; Garrett-Evangelical Seminary, M.Div., 1986; attended Waldorf Institute of Sunbridge College, 1996. *Hobbies and other interests:* Drama, dance, community building, multi-faith celebrations, family spirituality and celebrations.

■ Addresses

Home—3880 Lilly Rd., Brookfield, WI 53005.

■ Career

Ordained United Methodist minister, 1985; youth minister of United Methodist church in Urbandale, IA, 1982-83; minister through the arts at a community church, Evanston, IL, 1984-86; Waldorf School of Louisville, Louisville, KY, founder, 1992, administrator, 1992-94; Passageways for Parents, parent educator, 1994—; Minister through the Arts, Wauwatosa Avenue United Methodist Church, 1998—. Singer and songwriter, 1972—; co-founder and singer, Avalon Acappella Ensemble, 1993—.

■ Writings

Seven Times the Sun: Guiding Your Child through the Rhythms of the Day, Innisfree Press (Philadelphia, PA), 1994.

Grandpa's Garden, illustrated by Karlyn Holman, Dawn Publications, 1996.

Contributor to *Mothering.*

■ Work in Progress

Sanctuaries for the Soul: Guiding Your Child Toward Spiritual Wisdom; Grandma's Kitchen, a companion to *Grandpa's Garden;* research on "celebrating death with children" and on rites of passage for children of all ages.

■ Sidelights

Shea Darian told *Something about the Author* (*SATA*): "A few months before my partner, Andrew, and I celebrated our wedding ceremony, I remember telling one of my graduate school instructors that I was unsure about my future career plans. When my instructor asked me if I had ever considered becoming a writer, I was delighted. Writing had been a secret passion of mine since I was a child. When the instructor went on to suggest that perhaps I would write about my experiences as a wife and (eventually) a mother, I was offended. I remember thinking, though I didn't have the courage to say it at the time, 'If I choose to be a writer, I'll write about something *really* important!'

"Yet, here I am, over a decade later, writing and speaking about my experiences of family life. I recognize now that this work I am doing, to help create a healthy family and inspire others to do so, is the most important work I may ever do. It is also work that has strongly influenced my development as a writer. It is my children who have taught me (what I believe to be) the single most important lesson for a writer (and a parent) to learn—to live in the present and open one's eyes, one's heart and soul to the subtlest movements of creation. My children have taught me to participate in and to observe life in such a way that every ordinary moment, every day holds for me an opportunity for learning, for deepening my understanding of myself and life.

"As a child, my grandfather was the person who modeled for me this ability to live in the present, to reap spiritual meaning from ordinary endeavors. My memories of sharing ordinary moments with my grandfather are filled with his wisdom, his insight, his humor and love. A desire to preserve my grandfather's gifts for reaping the harvest of ordinary moments was the catalyst for writing my first children's book, *Grandpa's Garden*. It is my wish that every child has the privilege of knowing someone like my grandfather, an adult who gives a child hope and vision that the ability to live in the present, to open oneself fully to creation's more subtle gestures within and around us, need not fade with maturity. This, too, is my vision as a writer—to inspire myself and others to recognize that the great mystery of life ever so gently, in ordinary moments, is dropping us hints all the time."

■ For More Information See

PERIODICALS

Catholic Library World, December, 1996, p. 56.

*   *   *

DARLING, Sandra
See DAY, Alexandra

*   *   *

DAY, Alexandra 1941-
(Sandra Darling)

■ Personal

Real name Sandra Louise Woodward Darling; born in 1941, in Cincinnati, Ohio; daughter of Charles Lawson (an artist) and Esther Arabella (a homemaker; maiden name, Claflin) Woodward; married Harold Darling (a cinema/bookstore owner and publisher) 1967; children: Sacheverell, Rabindranath Tagore, Lafcadio Hearn, Christina. *Education:* Graduated from Swarthmore College; trained as an artist at the Art Students' League in New York City.

■ Addresses

Home—Seattle, WA. *Office*—Blue Lantern Studio, Seattle, WA.

■ Career

Green Tiger Press, San Diego, CA, founder and owner with husband, Harold Darling, note cards and stationery designer, 1970-86; children's author and illustrator, 1985—; Blue Lantern Studio, San Diego, owner with H. Darling, 1986-93, Seattle, WA, 1993—; Blue Lantern Books and the Laughing Elephant, San Diego, owner with H. Darling, 1992-93, Seattle, 1993—. Young Men's Hebrew Association, New York City crafts teacher.

■ Awards, Honors

Special mention, Children's Jury, Bologna Book Fair, Children's Choice Award, International Reading Association and Children's Book Council, 1984, both for *The Teddy Bears' Picnic;* Parents' Choice Award for Illustration, 1984, for *The Blue Faience Hippopotamus.*

■ Writings

SELF-ILLUSTRATED "CARL" BOOKS

Good Dog, Carl, Green Tiger, 1985.
Carl Goes Shopping, Farrar, Straus, and Giroux, 1989.
Carl's Christmas, Farrar, Straus, and Giroux, 1990.
Carl's Afternoon in the Park, Farrar, Straus, and Giroux, 1991, published in Spanish as *Carlito en el parque una tarde,* Farrar, Straus, and Giroux, 1992.
Carl's Masquerade, Farrar, Straus, and Giroux, 1992.
Carl Goes to Daycare, Farrar, Straus, and Giroux, 1993.
Carl Makes a Scrapbook, Farrar, Straus, and Giroux, 1994.
Carl Pops Up (also with illustrations by Vicki Teague Cooper), Simon & Schuster, 1994.
Carl's Birthday, Farrar, Straus, and Giroux, 1995.
Carl's Baby Journal, Farrar, Straus, and Giroux, 1996.

OTHER SELF-ILLUSTRATED BOOKS

Frank and Ernest, Scholastic, 1988.
Paddy's Pay-Day, Viking, 1989.
Frank and Ernest Play Ball, Scholastic, 1990.
River Parade, Viking, 1990.
Frank and Ernest on the Road, Scholastic, 1994.
A Bouquet, Blue Lantern Studio, 1996.

ILLUSTRATOR

Jimmy Kennedy, *The Teddy Bears' Picnic* (book and record set), Green Tiger, 1983.
Joan Marshall Grant, *The Blue Faience Hippopotamus,* Green Tiger, 1984.
Cooper Edens, *Children of Wonder* (Volume 1: *Helping the Sun,* Volume 2: *Helping the Animals,* Volume 3: *Helping the Flowers & Trees,* Volume 4: *Helping the Night),* Green Tiger, 1987.
Ned Washington, *When You Wish Upon A Star,* Green Tiger, 1987.
Abigail Darling, *Teddy Bears' Picnic Cookbook,* Puffin Books, 1993.
Christina Darling, *Mirror,* Farrar, Straus & Giroux, 1997.
Cooper Edens, *The Christmas We Moved to the Barn,* HarperCollins, 1997.

OTHER

(With Cooper Edens and Welleran Poltarnees), *Children from the Golden Age, 1880-1930,* Green Tiger, 1987.
(Editor with Welleran Poltarnees) *A. B. C. of Fashionable Animals,* Green Tiger, 1989.

Also author and illustrator of *My Puppy's Record Book,* Farrar, Straus & Giroux, and illustrator of Cooper Eden's *Taffy's Family,* Michael di Capua Books.

ALEXANDRA DAY

■ Sidelights

Author and artist Alexandra Day is a favorite—with critics, parents, and children—for her quiet "Carl" books, which feature a large Rotweiller dog and a baby named Madeleine. "Alexandra Day" is really Sandra Darling and, sometimes, her husband, Harold Darling. As "Day" explained in *Something about the Author Autobiography Series* (*SAAS*), "When I sign my pen name it is with the understanding that it includes both of our contributions." In any case, Sandra Darling is more than the creator of *Good Dog, Carl* and its successors. She has authored and illustrated a number of other books, including the Frank and Ernest books (about a bear and an elephant) and has illustrated picture books with texts by other authors, such as *The Teddy Bears' Picnic*. With her husband, Day has owned and operated a publishing company, the Green Tiger Press, and the Blue Lantern Studio.

As the granddaughter of an architect and the daughter of a painter, Day grew up immersed in a family in which art was important. She recalled in *SAAS*, "my home was always well supplied with those things necessary for creation, repair, and transformation—pencils, chalk, paint, brushes, paper, tools, wire, nails, glue, and so on. My sisters and I were always made to feel that these

materials were there to be freely used. Even more significant was the assumption in our family that if you wanted something, whether it was a kite, a strawberry pie, a prom dress, or a tree house, with a little ingenuity and application (and help, if necessary) you could make it."

Day also read a great deal during her childhood. She told *SAAS* that she read "Nancy Drew, the Black Stallion books, Laura Ingalls Wilder, E. Nesbit, and wept with *Black Beauty* and *Little Women*." Her favorite authors included George Macdonald, C. S. Lewis, G. K. Chesterton, J. R. R. Tolkien, and Charles Williams. These authors, who posed fantastic stories, affected Day's later work: "I think that one of the reasons my illustrations have appealed to people is that they can sense my sincerity. I have no trouble at all in believing that dogs can read, stuffed animals come alive, or a bear and elephant run a business."

After attending Swarthmore College, where she majored in English literature, Day moved to New York City and worked at the Young Men's Hebrew Association as a crafts teacher. She also took classes in figure drawing and painting at the Art Students' League and from Will Barnet. On a trip to California, she met Harold Darling, who owned a cinema and book store (housed in the same building), and they were married in 1967. Day cxplained in *SAAS* that Harold had three children (Harold Jr., Abigail, and Benjamin) and that, from 1969 to 1973, the Darlings had four more children, each named after lesser known but excellent authors the Darlings admired.

In 1970, the Darlings founded the Green Tiger Press in San Diego, California, to support their growing family and to engage their combined interests and talents. They went from publishing postcards and notecards and bookmarks to books written and illustrated by others. According to Day in *SAAS,* the Darlings "had been publishers for twelve years," but it "had never occurred to [her] to illustrate a book." When Day needed an illustrator for an old song, "The Teddy Bears' Picnic," with music by John Bratton and words by Jimmy Kennedy, she decided to do the work herself. It took her about one year to complete the paintings for the book, using her son's teddy bears for models. The book was a success, and Day went on to illustrate other books published by the Darlings' press.

Day revealed the origins of *Good Dog, Carl,* in her *SAAS* essay. On a trip in Zurich, Switzerland, the Darlings saw an old book which featured a story about a poodle and a baby playing while the baby should have been napping. Charmed by the idea, the Darlings decided to create a similar work, "but using our Rottweiler in place of the poodle," and that was "serious and lovely in approach." *Good Dog, Carl,* which Day began in 1984, was pub-

Day's immensely popular series of "Carl" books feature the Rottweiler and baby Madeleine in whimsical adventures. (From *Carl's Masquerade,* written and illustrated by Day.)

lished in 1985 and was, in the words of Day, "an even larger success than *The Teddy Bears' Picnic.* It, and its sequels, continue to sell enormously, and I have to fight off the pressure to make a career of babies and dogs." Still, since 1989, when the first sequel to *Good Dog, Carl, Carl Goes Shopping,* was published, Day has published a Carl book each year. Like the first one, they contain few words (the mother telling Carl to watch the baby, the mother's words of praise upon her return, "Good dog, Carl!"), and the illustrations tell the story. Over time, the beloved models for Carl (the Darlings' Rottweiler dogs) have passed on, and Day has changed her paints and techniques.

In *Carl Goes Shopping,* Carl (rendered in paint on gray paper) watches over a toddler and carries her into various departments in the store. Calling the book a "thoroughly enjoyable adventure," a reviewer in *Horn Book* suggested that Day offers "the most pinchable baby and pettable dog of the season." After wreaking havoc everywhere they go, they return before the mother does. *Carl's Christmas,* in the words of a *Publishers Weekly* critic, was "imbued with enough 'good will towards man' to warm a whole town." Carl takes care of a puppy and a baby in *Carl's Afternoon in the Park.* "The dogs are as charmingly true to life as ever," wrote a *Kirkus Reviews* critic about Day's oil paintings.

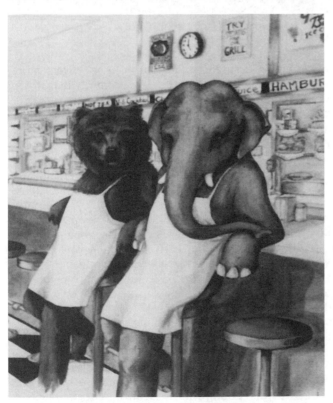

First in Day's series about the unique friendship between a bear and elephant, *Frank and Ernest* finds the pair running a 1950s-style diner.

Carl and the baby follow the baby's parents to a costume party in *Carl's Masquerade.* According to Roger Sutton of *Bulletin of the Center for Children's Books,* the setting of this book "allows Day free rein for her deliberately *outre,* painterly style and whimsical turn of imagination." In *Carl Goes to Daycare,* Carl runs baby Madeleine's class when the teacher is locked outside; Ellen Mandel of *Booklist* asserted that this book "is sure to be a favorite in a deservedly popular series." A *Publishers Weekly* critic wrote that "everyone's favorite Rottweiler is back in top form" in *Carl's Birthday,* in which Carl and Madeleine secretly aid her mother's party preparations.

Another of Day's series features a bear, Frank, and an elephant, Ernest. In the first book, *Frank and Ernest,* the watercolor-illustrated pair runs a '50s style diner, using amusing diner dialogue (which is explained in a glossary). Trev Jones of *School Library Journal* concluded that the book is "bound to become standard fare for story hour specials." *Frank and Ernest Play Ball* finds the pair managing a baseball team and using a dictionary to understand their job. In *Frank and Ernest on the Road,* they find work as truckers using CB radio and its vocabulary. "Fans of the dynamic duo's previous adventures will appreciate this exploration of a new linguistic frontier," wrote Zena Sutherland in *Bulletin of the Center for Children's Books.*

Surrounded by family and friends, the Darlings live in Seattle, Washington. There, they run the Blue Lantern Studio. While Day continues to work on her books, their production is still a family affair. She illustrated a cook book written by her stepdaughter Abigail, and *Mirror,* illustrated by Day, was written by her youngest daughter, Christina. In a *Publishers Weekly* starred review, a critic wrote that this fantasy storybook is a "good reflection on this mother/daughter team."

■ Works Cited

Review of *Carl's Afternoon in the Park, Kirkus Reviews,* September 15, 1991, p. 1230.
Review of *Carl's Birthday, Publishers Weekly,* October 23, 1995, p. 67.
Review of *Carl's Christmas, Publishers Weekly,* September 14, 1990, p. 123.
Review of *Carl Goes Shopping, Horn Book,* January-February, 1990, p. 50.
Day, Alexandra, *Something about the Author Autobiography Series,* Gale, Volume 19, 1995, pp. 133-49.
Jones, Trev, review of *Frank and Ernest, School Library Journal,* August, 1988, p. 80.
Mandel, Ellen, review of *Carl Goes to Daycare, Booklist,* December 15, 1993, p. 763.
Review of *Mirror, Publishers Weekly,* January 13, 1997, p. 75.
Sutherland, Zena, review of *Frank and Ernest on the Road, Bulletin of the Center for Children's Books,* March, 1994, p. 219.
Sutton, Roger, review of *Carl's Masquerade, Bulletin of the Center for Children's Books,* December, 1992, p. 109.

■ For More Information See

BOOKS

Silvey, Anita, editor, *Children's Books and Their Creators,* Houghton, 1995, p. 190.

PERIODICALS

Booklist, November 15, 1994, p. 610; January 1, 1996, p. 843; March 1, 1997, p. 1170.
Bulletin of the Center for Children's Books, January, 1990, p. 108.
Kirkus Reviews, October 15, 1994, p. 1406.
Publishers Weekly, November 22, 1993, p. 63; August 22, 1994, p. 54.
School Library Journal, February, 1994, p. 83; November, 1994, p. 74; December, 1995, p. 79.

—Sketch by Ronie Garcia-Johnson

*   *   *

DEGEN, Bruce 1945-

■ Personal

Born June 14, 1945, in Brooklyn, NY; married Christine Bostard (a teacher and illustrator); children: Benjamin, Alexander. *Education:* Cooper Union, B.F.A., 1966; Pratt Institute, M.F.A., 1975.

■ Addresses

Home—Newtown, CT.

■ Career

Author and illustrator. Director of an artists' lithography studio in Ein Hod, Israel, beginning 1971. Writing instructor and illustrator of books for children at School of Visual Arts, New York City; has also worked as an opera scenery painter, advertising designer, printmaker, and teacher of life-drawing, printmaking, and calligraphy to advanced high school students and adults. *Exhibitions:* Degen's illustrations have been exhibited in New York City at the Master Eagle Gallery and the Hempstead Municipal Gallery. *Member:* Society of Children's Book Writers and Illustrators.

■ Awards, Honors

Children's Choice selection, International Reading Association and Children's Book Council, 1982, for *Little Chick's Big Day,* and 1985, for *My Mother Didn't Kiss Me Good-Night;* Garden State Children's Book Award (Easy-to-Read category), New Jersey Library Association, 1983, for *Commander Toad in Space,* 1992, for *The Magic School Bus inside the Human Body,* and 1993, for *The Magic School Bus Lost in the Solar System;* Editors' Choice, *Booklist,* 1983, for *Jamberry;* Children's Books of the Year, Child Study Association of America, 1985, for *Jamberry,* and 1987, for *The Josefina Story Quilt;* Boston Globe-Horn Book nonfiction honor, 1987, for *The Magic School Bus at the*

Mouse's house is too small to accommodate all the friends who visit for his birthday. (From *Mouse's Birthday*, written by Jane Yolen and illustrated by Bruce Degen.)

Waterworks. Winner of many further child-selected awards.

■ Writings

FOR CHILDREN; SELF-ILLUSTRATED

Aunt Possum and the Pumpkin Man, Harper, 1977.
The Little Witch and the Riddle, Harper, 1980.
Jamberry, Harper, 1983.
Teddy Bear Towers, Harper Collins, 1991.
Sailaway Home, Scholastic, 1996.

ILLUSTRATOR

Malcolm Hall, *Forecast,* Coward, 1977.
Stephen Krensky, *A Big Day for Sceptres,* Atheneum, 1977.
Malcolm Hall, *Caricatures,* Coward, 1978.
Carol Chapman, *Ig Lives in a Cave,* Dutton, 1979.
Judy Delton, *Brimhall Turns to Magic,* Lothrop, 1979.
Marjorie Weinman Sharmat, *Mr. Jameson and Mr. Phillips,* Harper, 1979.
Claudia Louise Lewis, *Up and Down the River: Boat Poems,* Harper, 1979.
Jane Yolen, *Commander Toad in Space,* Coward, 1980.
Charlotte Herman, *My Mother Didn't Kiss Me Good-Night,* Dutton, 1980.
Donald J. Sobol, *Encyclopedia Brown's Second Record Book of Weird and Wonderful Facts,* Delacorte, 1981.
Mary Kwitz, *Little Chick's Big Day,* Harper, 1981.
Clyde Robert Bulla, *Dandelion Hill,* Dutton, 1982.

Jane Yolen, *Commander Toad and the Planet of the Grapes,* Coward, 1982.
Joel L. Schwartz, *Upchuck Summer,* Delacorte, 1982.
Malcolm Hall, *Deadlines,* Coward, 1982.
Mary Kwitz, *Little Chick's Breakfast,* Harper, 1983.
Jane Yolen, *Commander Toad and the Big Black Hole,* Coward, 1983.
Lyn Littlefield Hoopes, *Daddy's Coming Home!,* Harper, 1984.
Jane Yolen, *Commander Toad and the Dis-Asteroid,* Coward, 1985.
Joseph Slate, *Lonely Lula Cat,* Harper, 1985.
Bonnie Pryor, *Grandpa Bear,* Morrow, 1985.
Joel L. Schwartz, *Best Friends Don't Come in Threes,* Dell, 1985.
Eleanor Coerr, *The Josefina Story Quilt,* Harper, 1986.
Jane Yolen, *Commander Toad and the Intergalactic Spy,* Coward, 1986.
Diane Stanley, *The Good-Luck Pencil,* Four Winds, 1986.
Bonnie Pryor, *Grandpa Bear's Christmas,* Morrow, 1986.
Nancy White Carlstrom, *Jesse Bear, What Will You Wear?,* Macmillan, 1986.
Joanna Cole, *The Magic School Bus at the Waterworks,* Scholastic, 1986.
(With wife, Chris Degen) Aileen Lucia Fisher, *When It Comes to Bugs: Poems,* Harper, 1986.
Larry Weinberg, *The Forgetful Bears Meet Mr. Memory,* Scholastic, 1987.

Joanna Cole, *The Magic School Bus inside the Earth,* Scholastic, 1987.

Jane Yolen, *Commander Toad and the Space Pirates,* Putnam, 1987.

Nancy White Carlstrom, *Better Not Get Wet, Jesse Bear,* Macmillan, 1988.

Larry Weinberg, *The Forgetful Bears Help Santa,* Scholastic, 1988.

Joan Lowery Nixon, *If You Were a Writer,* Four Winds, 1988.

Mike Thaler, *In the Middle of the Puddle,* Harper, 1988.

Jan Wahl, *Tim Kitten and the Red Cupboard,* Simon & Schuster, 1988.

Barbara Brenner and William H. Hooks, *Lion and Lamb,* Bantam, 1989.

Joanna Cole, *The Magic School Bus inside the Human Body,* Scholastic, 1989.

Barbara Brenner and William H. Hooks, *Lion and Lamb Step Out,* Bantam, 1990.

Nancy White Carlstrom, *It's about Time, Jesse Bear,* Macmillan, 1990.

Joanna Cole, *Dinosaur Dances,* Putnam, 1990.

Joanna Cole, *The Magic School Bus Lost in the Solar System,* Scholastic, 1990.

Barbara Brenner and William H. Hooks, *Ups and Downs with Lion and Lamb,* Bantam, 1991.

Tony Johnston, *Goblin Walk,* Putnam, 1991.

Nancy White Carlstrom, *How Do You Say It Today, Jesse Bear?,* Macmillan, 1992.

Mary DeBall Kwitz, *Little Chick's Friend, Duckling,* HarperCollins, 1992.

Joanna Cole, *The Magic School Bus on the Ocean Floor,* Scholastic, 1992.

Jane Yolen, *Mouse's Birthday,* Putnam, 1993.

John Archambault, *A Beautiful Feast for a Big King Cat,* HarperCollins, 1994.

Joan Lowery Nixon, *Will You Give Me a Dream?,* Four Winds, 1994.

Joanna Cole, *The Magic School Bus in the Time of the Dinosaurs,* Scholastic, 1994.

Nancy White Carlstrom, *Jesse Bear's Tra-La Tub,* Aladdin Books, 1994.

Nancy White Carlstrom, *Jesse Bear's Tum-Tum Tickle,* Aladdin Books, 1994.

Nancy White Carlstrom, *Jesse Bear's Yum-Yum Crumble,* Aladdin Books, 1994.

Nancy White Carlstrom, *Happy Birthday, Jesse Bear,* Macmillan, 1994.

Joanna Cole, *The Magic School Bus inside a Hurricane,* Scholastic, 1995.

Joanna Cole, *The Magic School Bus Meets the Rot Squad: A Book about Decomposition,* Scholastic, 1995.

Nancy White Carlstrom, *Let's Count It Out, Jesse Bear,* Simon & Schuster, 1996.

Joanna Cole, *The Magic School Bus inside a Beehive,* Scholastic, 1996.

Joanna Cole, *The Magic School Bus Going Batty: A Book about Bats,* Scholastic, 1996.

Joanna Cole, *The Magic School Bus Out of This World,* Scholastic, 1996.

Nancy White Carlstrom, *Guess Who's Coming, Jesse Bear?,* Simon & Schuster, 1997.

Jane Yolen, *Commander Toad and the Voyage Home,* Putnam, 1997.

Nancy White Carlstrom, *I Love You, Mama, Any Time of the Year,* Simon & Schuster, 1997.

Nancy White Carlstrom, *I Love You, Papa, In All Kinds of Weather,* Simon & Schuster, 1997.

Joanna Cole, *The Magic School Bus Gets Planted,* Scholastic, 1997.

Joanna Cole, *The Magic School Bus Goes Upstream,* Scholastic, 1997.

Joanna Cole, *The Magic School Bus Shows & Tells,* Scholastic, 1997.

Joanna Cole, *The Magic School Bus Ups & Downs,* Scholastic, 1997.

Joanna Cole, *The Magic School Bus and the Electric Field Trip,* Scholastic, 1997.

■ Adaptations

Jamberry was adapted as a cassette by Live Oak Media, 1986. Degen's illustrations for Joanna Cole's "Magic School Bus" series served as the basis for the PBS-TV animated series of the same title.

■ Sidelights

Bruce Degen, an illustrator best known for his work for the "Commander Toad" series by Jane Yolen and Joanna Cole's "Magic School Bus" books, first discovered his talent as a young child. He was encouraged by his elementary school teacher to pursue his interest in drawing, which eventually led him to two degrees in the fine arts. After graduating from Cooper Union with a bachelor's degree, he worked as a director of an artists' lithography studio in Ein Hod, Israel. A number of other jobs followed, including work as a teacher. Two years after receiving his master's degree from the Pratt Institute, Degen published his first book for children.

Although not formally trained as an illustrator, Degen has had a fondness for books since he was a child growing up in New York City. "I have always loved books," he once told *Something about the Author* (*SATA*). "As a child I would love to go to the library. If it was a nice day I wouldn't wait until I got home to read my books. I had to stop in the little park and begin my books under a tree." So, as he also once related, Degen was irresistibly drawn to children's book illustration. "After doing many different things in the field of art I decided to go back to the root of what made drawing fun for me as a child—children's books."

Degen prefers to illustrate with line drawings and watercolors. His trademark cartoon-style spreads, filled with details and sight gags that supplement the text, showcase the artist's whimsical sense of humor and love of children's books. His style is considered especially well suited for Joanna Cole's 'Magic School Bus" series, which aims to teach children about scientific facts with the help of humor and fantasy. "Collaborating with Joanna Cole on the 'Magic School Bus' series, Degen epitomized visual silliness," according to Suzy Schmidt in *Children's Books and Their Creators.* Schmidt added:

"The crowded pages are absorbing as they display action, text, bubble-dialogue, and school reports. The result is an endlessly entertaining set of books with a wide and loyal readership—a remarkable achievement for a science series." Degen's illustrations for the series have been roundly praised by reviewers. "Degen's [drawings] ... fill the pages with plenty of action and intriguing details," said Carolyn Phelan in a *Booklist* review of *The Magic School Bus inside a Beehive.* And Stephanie Zvirin, writing in another *Booklist* review, noted that Degen's illustrations help in "clarifying the concepts and adding comic relief" to Cole's text.

Degen has also collaborated with other authors on series books with continuing characters, including the "Little Chick" stories by Mary DeBall Kwitz, the "Grandpa Bear" books by Bonnie Pryor, the "Lion and Lamb" books by Barbara Brenner and William H. Hooks, the "Forgetful Bears" by Larry Weinberg, and the "Jesse Bear" series by Nancy White Carlstrom. Of these, the "Jesse Bear" books have received the most attention.

Carlstrom's books, full of exuberant, creative rhymes, proved a perfect vehicle for some of Degen's best work. Schmidt has noted that Degen's strength is in his ability to collaborate well with authors: "[Degen's] work has contributed most to children's literature not by drawing attention to itself but by providing strong accompaniment to the texts." In a review of *Jesse Bear, What Will You Wear? School Library Journal* contributor Liza Bliss asserted that text and illustrations "interplay beautifully, each enhancing the other's brightness." Degen displays his usual sense of humor in the "Jesse Bear" books, too. In *Better Not Get Wet, Jesse Bear,* for example, a portrait on the wall reacts in astonishment to Jesse Bear's watery mess.

Degen tends to illustrate animal characters more frequently than humans, and some of his finest work, including his own *Jamberry* as well as the "Jesse Bear" books, has bears as featured characters. "People often ask me why I use animals," Degen once told *SATA.* "I think it is because they allow an easy fantasy identifica-

In Degen's self-illustrated *Sailaway Home*, a little pig takes an imaginary adventure, then gratefully returns to the security of his family.

Degen's illustrative style is featured in Joanna Cole's "Magic School Bus" series, which aims to teach children about scientific facts with the help of humor and fantasy. (From *The Magic School Bus in the Time of Dinosaurs.*)

tion, and the change of scale is cozy and attractive to children." Degen also does well creating pictures to accompany rhymes, including Yolen's *Mouse's Birthday.* As one *Publishers Weekly* reviewer wrote, "Degen's art is the ideal match for Yolen's jaunty rhyme."

Along with *Jamberry,* Degen has written and illustrated several of his own children's books. One of the more recent of these, *Sailaway Home,* is a simple rhyming story in which a young pig imagines a number of adventures while remaining safely near home. Calling the illustrations and rhymes "sweetly cheerful," *School Library Journal* commentator Lisa Dennis observed that in any other writer/illustrator's hands, the result would be "an unappealingly saccharine picture book, but in Degen's accomplished hands, these ingredients are melded into a delightful story." Having now illustrated scores of books for children, Degen hopes to continue his career indefinitely. "I believe that good children's book art will delight the child, and this is the work of lasting interest," he once remarked. "Being able to read to children, I can see by the children's candid reactions which elements truly communicate. Since I began, this work has involved me totally, and I hope I will be doing it as long as I can hold a pencil."

■ Works Cited

Bliss, Liza, review of *Jesse Bear, What Will You Wear?,* *School Library Journal,* April, 1986, pp. 68-69.

Dennis, Lisa, review of *Sailaway Home, School Library Journal,* March, 1996, p. 167.

Review of *Mouse's Birthday, Publishers Weekly,* March 8, 1993, p. 76.

Phelan, Carolyn, review of *The Magic School Bus inside a Beehive, Booklist,* September 1, 1996, p. 121.

Schmidt, Suzy, "Bruce Degen," *Children's Books and Their Creators,* edited by Anita Silvey, Houghton Mifflin, 1995, pp. 191-92.

Zvirin, Stephanie, review of *The Magic School Bus inside a Hurricane, Booklist,* June 1-15, 1995, p. 1776.

■ For More Information See

BOOKS

Sixth Book of Junior Authors and Illustrators, Wilson, 1989, pp. 74-76.

PERIODICALS

Booklist, January 15, 1993, p. 925; April 1, 1994, p. 1461; July, 1994, p. 1952; August, 1994, p. 2045.

Bulletin of the Center for Children's Books, May, 1986, p. 162; October, 1996, p. 51.

Horn Book Magazine, May-June, 1988, pp. 338-39; January-February, 1991, p. 94; November-December, 1995, p. 760; November-December, 1996, p. 757.

Publishers Weekly, March 11, 1988, p. 102; May 20, 1994, p. 55.

School Library Journal, May, 1988, p. 81; April, 1992, p. 89; August, 1992, p. 151; November, 1992, p. 72.

* * *

DEKA, Connie
See LAUX, Constance

* * *

De LEON, Nephtali 1945-

■ Personal

Born May 9, 1945, in Laredo, TX; son of Francisco De Leon Cordero (a migrant worker) and Maria Guadalupe De Leon-Gonzalez (a migrant worker); children: Aide. *Education:* Attended Texas Technological University, Our Lady of the Lake University of San Antonio, Instituto de Alianza Francesa, and University of Mexico City.

■ Career

La Voz de los Llanos (bilingual weekly journal; title means "The Voice of the Plains"), Lubbock, TX, editor, 1968-73; freelance poet, writer, painter, and sculptor, c. 1973—. President of Le Cercle Francais; director of Teatro Chicano del Barrio; vice chair of American Civil Liberties Union, and Ciudadanos Pro Justicia Social. Has given poetry readings on television. *Military service:* U.S. Army. *Member:* Hispanic Writers Guild, Revolucion Artistica y Accion Social, Royal Chicano Air Force (affiliate), Congreso de Artistas Cosmicos de Aztlan (affiliate).

■ Awards, Honors

Ford fellowship, 1975; award from Canto Al Pueblo Commission, 1976; award from National Hispanic Writers Guild, 1977; first place award from Le Cercle Francais.

■ Writings

FOR CHILDREN

(And illustrator) *I Will Catch the Sun* (play; first produced in San Antonio, TX, at Our Lady of the Lake University's Thiry Auditorium, 1979), Trucha Publications, 1973.

I Color My Garden, Tri-County Housing (Shallowater, TX), 1973.

(With Carlos Gonzalez and Alfredo Aleman) *El Segundo de Febrero* (historical play for children), Centro Cultural Aztlan, 1983.

Sparky y su Gang, Nosotros, 1985.

OTHER

(And illustrator) *Chicanos: Our Background and Our Pride* (essays), Trucha Publications, 1972.

Five Plays (contains "The Death of Ernesto Nerios," "Chicanos! The Living and the Dead," "Play Number Nine," "The Judging of Man," and "The Flies"), Totinem Publications, 1972 (also see below).

(And illustrator) *Chicano Poet: With Images and Visions of the Poet* (poetry; includes "Coca Cola Dream" [also see below]), Trucha Publications, 1973.

The Flies (play), first produced in El Paso, TX, at University of Texas-El Paso, 1973.

(And illustrator) *Coca Cola Dream* (poetry), Trucha Publications, 1973, 2nd edition, 1976.

Chicanos! The Living and the Dead (play), first produced in Hagerman, NM, 1974.

Play Number Nine, first produced in Boulder, CO, at University of Colorado, 1976.

El tesoro de Pancho Villa (play), first produced in Lubbock, TX, 1977.

La muerte de Ernesto Nerios (play; also titled *The Death of Ernesto Nerios*), first produced in San Antonio, TX, at San Pedro Playhouse, 1978.

Tequila Mockingbird; or, The Ghost of Unemployment (play), Trucha Publications, 1979.

Guadalupe Blues (poetry), privately printed, 1985.

Artemia: La Loca del River Walk: An Allegory of the Arts in San Antonio, Educators' Roundtable, 1986.

El pollito amarillo: Baby Chick Yellow, Educators' Roundtable, 1987.

Also author of *Hey, Mr. President Man: On the Eve of the Bicentennial,* Trucha Publications, 1975, *Poems by Nephtali,* 1977, and *Getting It Together,* 1980. Contributor to anthologies, including *We Are Chicanos: An Anthology of Mexican-American Literature,* edited by Philip D. Ortego, Washington Square Press, 1973; *Floricanto,* edited by Mary Ann Pacheco, University of California, Los Angeles, 1974; *Floricanto II,* University of Texas, Austin, 1975; and *El Quetzal Emplumece,* edited by Carmela Montalvo and others, Mexican-American Cultural Center (San Antonio, TX), 1976. Contributor of articles and poems to periodicals, including *Texas Observer, Reverberations, American Dawn, La Luz, Noticias, New Blood, Grito del Sol, New Morning, El Regional, El Sol of Houston, La Voz de Texas, Floricante, Caracol, El Tecolote, La Guardia, Tiempo,* and *Canto Al Pueblo.*

■ Sidelights

Nephtali De Leon is a Chicano writer of poems, plays, essays, and children's stories. A sculptor and painter, he has also illustrated many of his books. Although these diverse artistic activities keep him busy, De Leon nonetheless considers himself a Chicano activist first. His passion for justice and equality for his people was first aroused during childhood when as a migrant worker in Texas he witnessed the cruel treatment of illegal aliens by American border patrolmen. As an adult activist, De Leon has primarily focused his efforts on improving the quality of education for young Chicanos by writing books for them and by working with school systems in the Southwest. In addition, De Leon has supported Chicanos by helping establish Trucha Publications, a small press founded in 1970 by barrio residents of Lubbock, Texas, for the purpose of supporting emerging Chicano writers. Trucha published many of De Leon's early books, most of which center on the author's interest in promoting equal opportunity for Chicanos. "De Leon writes mainly to express the dreams, desires, and aspirations of the Chicano people," wrote Jean S. Chittenden in *Dictionary of Literary Biography*. "His motivation in writing is to give an honest and truthful representation of the plight of the Chicano, which he sees as the result of a historical process."

Whether based on historical events or his own musings, De Leon's writings advocate Chicano liberation from all forms of repression. His play "Chicanos! The Living and the Dead," for instance, involves Chicano protestors rallying against the abuses of Americans and their system of government; "Play Number Nine" compares the mythological Prometheus, who is seeking physical freedom, with the Chicanos seeking cultural freedom through improved education; and "The Flies" equates downtrodden Chicanos with squashed flies. De Leon's call for liberation continues in his poetry, where his imaginative works typically promote a world of peace and happiness beyond the life of injustice and discrimination Chicanos often experience in America. One of his more notable poems, "Coca Cola Dream," attacks American materialism for preventing humans from achieving Christian kindness and a full understanding of each other.

In his concern for Chicano school children, whom he considers "kickouts" rather than "dropouts," De Leon tried to write school materials that would instill pride in their heritage. One poem, "In the Plaza We Walk," has been used in junior high schools from the 1985 edition of *Patterns in Literature: America Reads*. Other titles, which have been used from Minnesota and Wisconsin to New Mexico and California, Nebraska, Colorado, and Utah, include *Chicanos: Our Background and Our Pride, I Will Catch the Sun,* and *I Color My Garden*. In *I Will Catch the Sun,* a Chicano boy is humiliated when others make fun of him for responding "I will catch the sun," when asked by the teacher for his chief ambition. He gains everyone's respect, however, when he catches the reflection of the sun in a pan of water. De Leon's second book for children, *I Color My Garden,* is a bilingual, bicultural edition composed of seventeen informative poems about different vegetables. Children are encouraged to color in the pictures and through various activities are taught not only reading but writing, spelling, science, and arithmetic. As an activist, writer, and artist, De Leon has not only improved the

quality of education for Chicano children, but has personally served as a role model to follow.

■ Works Cited

Chittenden, Jean S., *Dictionary of Literary Biography, Volume 82: Chicano Writers, First Series,* Gale, 1989, p. 99.*

*   *   *

DOKEY, Cameron 1956-

■ Personal

Born August 14, 1956, in Stockton, CA; daughter of Richard (a writer and teacher) and Charron (a teacher; maiden name, Johnson) Dokey; married James F. Verdery (a theater manager), September 23, 1984. *Education:* University of Washington, B.A. (magna cum laude).

■ Addresses

Home—Seattle, WA; fax 206-283-0417. *Agent*—Fran Lebowitz, Writers House, Inc., 21 West 26th St., New York, NY 10010.

■ Career

Oregon Shakespeare Festival, Ashland, actor, 1977-81; Pacific Science Center, Seattle, WA, exhibit copywriter, 1989-93; novelist, 1993—. *Member:* Romance Writers of America.

CAMERON DOKEY

■ Writings

Eternally Yours (young adult horror novel), Kensington Publishing (Kalamazoo, MI), 1994.
The Talisman (young adult horror novel), Kensington Publishing, 1994.
New Year, New Love, Avon, 1996.
Be Mine: A Romantic Quartet of Special Valentines to Capture Your Heart, Avon Books, 1997.
Graveside Tales, Andrews & McMeel, 1997.
Midnight Mysteries, Andrews & McMeel, 1997.
Together Forever, Bantam, 1997.

"MYSTERY DATE" SERIES; SUPERNATURAL ROMANCE NOVELS; FOR YOUNG ADULTS

Love Me, Love Me Not, Zebra Books (New York), 1995.
Blue Moon, Kensington Publishing, 1995.
Heart's Desire, Kensington Publishing, 1995.

"HEARTS AND DREAMS" SERIES; HISTORICAL NOVELS; FOR YOUNG ADULTS

Katherine, Heart of Freedom, Avon (New York), 1997.
Charlotte, Heart of Hope, Avon, 1997.
Stephanie, Heart of Gold, Avon, 1998.
Carrie, Heart of Courage, Avon, 1998.

OTHER

Co-author of educational materials based on the cable television series *Beakman's World.*

■ Sidelights

Cameron Dokey comments: "The truth is, I've always wanted to be a writer, even though I haven't always known what I wanted to write. When I was growing up, my father taught high school and my mother taught kindergarten. (The totally cool thing about having parents who were teachers was that all of us got the summers off. We'd go camping, which my father loved and my mother hated.) Every weekday evening during the school year, from eight o'clock to ten o'clock, my father would go to his study and write. I'm not sure I thought about it much at the time. It was just the way things worked at our house. Gradually, however, I began to realize that my father was doing something special. Once I'd realized that, the certainty began to grow upon me that, someday, I would be a writer, too.

"I did many things before I became a full-time writer. I worked as an actor in professional repertory theater, and I worked at a lot of secretarial and retail jobs. The turning point came when I was hired to be the exhibit writer at the Pacific Science Center in Seattle, Washington. At last, I was fulfilling my dream of being a writer. Naturally, I began to look around to see what other kind of writer I could be.

"Friends from my acting days were writing young adult fiction. When I expressed an interest, they agreed to mentor me. In 1993 I was offered my first contract, and I've been writing young adult fiction ever since. In many ways, it makes a lot of sense that I've landed in the young people's corner. I was a voracious reader as a young person. Every two weeks, my mom and I would

In this installment of Cameron Dokey's historical fiction series about a hope chest passed down through many generations, Charlotte finds danger, excitement, and romance in Baltimore during the War of 1812.

make the trip to the library. She would check out books for her class, and I'd check out as many books as I could for myself. I think the number was ten. Two weeks later, I'd return those ten books, all read, and go home with ten more. The librarians loved me (except when my books were overdue!).

"My own books reflect my personal interests, as well as a couple of publisher requests. My first two titles are horror novels, which caused some people who know me to raise their eyebrows and throw up their hands in dismay. Why was I writing horror novels, they wondered. Weren't those always horribly violent, particularly toward young women? Didn't I want to write anything where good things happened? Didn't I want to write things that were uplifting and worthwhile?

"'Read my books,' I'd answer. I think you'll find that they are not gratuitously violent. You'll find that my girls are strong characters who overcome great odds. They grow and change throughout the course of their stories. They become more self-aware. They refuse to become victims, and their words and actions say so. I *am* writing something where good things happen. I am writing something worthwhile, and I am particularly pleased to find my own views about my work reflected in special mentions by librarians.

"I've moved on to historical fiction at the moment, but the same rules apply. I want to be interested in the people I create. I want to watch them grow. If I really wanted to get cosmic about all this, I could say that I try to expect the same things of my characters as I do of myself. I need to grow and change as a writer. I need to take on new things.

"Writing is a process. I'm interested in all of it."

■ For More Information See

PERIODICALS

Publishers Weekly, July 3, 1995, p. 62; February 3, 1997, p. 107.

ADELE DUECK

DUECK, Adele 1955-

■ Personal

Born April 7, 1955, in Outlook, Saskatchewan, Canada; daughter of Frank and Lona (Jensen) Loken; married Raymond Dueck (a farmer), December 28, 1974; children: Lisa, Cheryl, Philip, Jeanette, Alison. *Education:* Attended Saskatchewan Technical Institute, 1974-75. *Religion:* Christian.

■ Addresses

Home—Box 152, Lucky Lake, Saskatchewan, Canada S0L 1Z0.

■ Career

Freelance writer; also serves the family farm as an accountant and secretary. Wheatland Regional Library, member of board of directors, Lucky Lake branch, 1993—; Lucky Lake Community Band, treasurer, 1995-97. *Member:* Canadian Society of Authors, Illustrators, and Performers (associate member), Saskatchewan Writers Guild, Saskatchewan Children's Writers Round Robin.

■ Awards, Honors

Three children's literature awards, Saskatchewan Writers Guild, 1987, 1990, and 1993, for unpublished works.

■ Writings

Anywhere But Here (young adult novel), Orca Book Publishers (Victoria, British Columbia), 1996.

Author of "Homefront," a column in *Western People,* 1986-90.

■ Work in Progress

A nonfiction picture book about farming; a sequel to *Anywhere But Here;* a novel for adults; short stories for children.

■ Sidelights

Adele Dueck told *Something about the Author (SATA):* "I fell in love with books when I was about twelve. My decision to become a writer came very shortly afterward. What I'm sure would have been a spectacular career took a severe setback when I was eighteen. I assume now that I believed writing was something to do in one's spare time. I wish someone had given me a catalog to a journalism school.

"No one did, so I began several never finished novels and entertained relatives with long, humorous letters. Then my husband and I had children, and I had to keep them entertained so they would stay in the garden long enough to pick the beans. I wrote some of those stories down, and one thing led to another. There I was taking what I used to write home to mother and putting it in a newspaper column instead.

"Being a naturally shy person, my decision to go public was not easy; I seriously considered using a pseudonym. Only my certainty that the pieces would be rejected finally let me submit them under my own name. To my amazement, they were accepted and grew into a regular column. Inspired by this success, I tried a couple more novels for adults, one of which I actually finished, and started working seriously on the stories I told the kids.

"We are very busy on our farm, too busy sometimes. My novel *Anywhere But Here* was begun to show my eldest daughter, when she was about ten, that other families were busy, too. Unfortunately, life was so busy that she was eighteen when it was published. The book changed in those years. I wanted to show city kids why the weather was important and some of the freedoms that came with living on a farm, and I wanted rural kids to see their own lives between covers. The challenge was that I didn't want the kids to know I was doing any of this. I needed to write a book they would read just because it was fun. What was more fun than a mystery?

"Now I find that I want to write more farm stories. Although I did not grow up on a farm, it seems like the perfect place to spend a childhood. There's room for adventure. I can bring in the importance of families working together toward a common goal, an appreciation of the world God made, and a recognition that farming is important to everyone, because everyone eats.

"Because of the farm, my writing time is slotted into the only season of the year when we're not busy. I do almost all my writing between January first and April thirtieth. It's not an ideal situation, but much as I like writing, I can't give up living to do it.

"Though I started my professional writing career on my own, I keep at it because of the support and encouragement of the Saskatchewan Children's Writers Round Robin. I strongly encourage beginning writers to join some kind of writing group, preferably one that contains published, as well as aspiring, writers. Living in an isolated area as I do, the Round Robin suits me perfectly. We correspond throughout the year, meeting in person once in the spring and once in the fall.

"When I was beginning, I found reading books about writing beneficial. They taught me the things that seem so obvious now, but about which I didn't have a clue then—simple things like type on one side of the paper, double-space, send self-addressed stamped envelopes—and creative hints like let the protagonist solve the problem and don't be afraid to use big words just because you're writing for small children.

"It's not any easier finding time to write now than it ever was, but I feel a greater compulsion. When I receive a letter from a ten-year-old on the other side of the country asking for a list of my books so she can read them all, I really regret having to disappoint her."

■ **For More Information See**

PERIODICALS

Quill & Quire (Toronto), May, 1996, p. 33.

*   *   *

**DUVAL, Katherine
  See JAMES, Elizabeth**

*   *   *

DYGARD, Thomas J. 1931-1996

■ Personal

Born August 10, 1931, in Little Rock, AR; son of Thomas J. (a tailor) and Nannie (a musician; maiden name, Smith) Dygard; died October 1, 1996, in Hazelton, PA; married Patricia Redditt, November 23, 1951; children: Thomas J., Nancy Adams Stevens. *Education:* Attended Little Rock Junior College, 1949-50, 1950-51; University of Arkansas, Fayetteville, B.A., 1953. *Politics:* Independent. *Religion:* Episcopal.

■ Career

Arkansas Gazette, Little Rock, sportswriter and reporter, 1949-53; Associated Press, reporter in Little Rock, 1954-56, Detroit, MI, 1956-58, Birmingham, AL, 1958-62, and New Orleans, LA, 1962-64, bureau chief in Little Rock, 1964-66, Indianapolis, IN, 1966-71, Chicago, IL, 1971-85, and Tokyo, Japan, 1985-1993. *Member:* Chicago Headline Club (president, 1974), Chicago Press Club (president, 1978), Foreign Correspondents' Club of Japan.

■ Awards, Honors

Books for the Teen Age, New York Public Library, 1980, for *Outside Shooter,* 1981, for *Point Spread,* and 1982, for *Soccer Duel; Halfback Tough* was selected one of the Child Study Association of America's Children's Books of the Year, 1987.

■ Writings

NOVELS

Running Scared, Morrow, 1977.
Winning Kicker, Morrow, 1978.
Outside Shooter, Morrow, 1979.
Point Spread, Morrow, 1980.
Soccer Duel, Morrow, 1981.
Quarterback Walk-On, Morrow, 1982.
Rebound Caper, Morrow, 1983.
Tournament Upstart, Morrow, 1984.
Wilderness Peril, Morrow, 1985.
Halfback Tough, Morrow, 1986.
The Rookie Arrives, Morrow, 1988.

THOMAS J. DYGARD

Forward Pass, Morrow, 1989.
Backfield Package, Morrow, 1992.
Game Plan, Morrow, 1993.
The Rebounder, Morrow, 1994.
Infield Hit, Morrow, 1994.
Running Wild, Morrow, 1996.

■ Sidelights

"I was born in Little Rock, Arkansas, a town of about 100,000 people," Thomas J. Dygard commented in an interview for *Authors and Artists for Young Adults.* "Looking back on it, I must have had a horribly 'normal' childhood. I did what most kids did—went to school and played ball. My father, a tailor, died when I was ten. He had been ill for five of those years, so I don't remember very much about him. I was an only child, and, of course, when your father dies, you become worried and frightened, but people have a way of surviving that sort of thing. It probably sounds worse now than it actually appeared to me then." Dygard's mother was a musician who taught the piano and played it, at times, professionally. She died when he was nineteen.

"I was an average student in school, always had trouble with mathematics, and always liked English and history. I've been a voracious reader ever since I first learned how, and I think that's what led me into writing. The idea that I could write something that would interest somebody as much as books had interested me sounded like a very satisfying prospect."

Growing up in Little Rock, Dygard went through the usual set of dream careers. "Army officer, journalist, professional baseball player, novelist, commercial artist, architect, etc., etc. The journalist dream stuck." By age twelve, he was editor of the *Neighbor News,* a neighborhood paper concerned with "local gossip unless something major was happening (like World War II). Then we'd listen to the radio and write our stories."

Dygard's work on his high school's paper led to an apprenticeship with the *Arkansas Gazette.* "I have always been intensely interested in all sorts of writing," he has said. "The principal of the high school called me in one day to tell me that the sports editor of the *Gazette* was looking for what they called a junior sports writer. It was night work—from five in the afternoon to eleven at night. The *Gazette* was a morning newspaper. The principal asked if I would be interested. I sure was. I went down to talk with the sports editor and he hired me.

"During the first couple of years with the paper in Little Rock, I covered baseball, football, basketball, tennis, golf—just about every sport except jai-alai. I had played football, basketball, and baseball in high school, but was never varsity. Still, I was quite interested in sports, and since it was the area of the news I was covering, I made myself more interested. Of course, a lot of sports writing is talking to coaches and players, trying to find out what's going on in their heads. So I learned as I went along.

"It seemed there were fewer people in the world of sports who took themselves as seriously as people in politics or government. They enjoyed themselves, and, I might add, it was a lot of fun to work with them. I became aware of it after I left sports writing and went into general reporting.

"I was interested in everything I could learn about newspapers, not just reporting and writing, but how the paper was put out, how make-up was handled, how headlines were written, why it was important to do certain things at certain times a certain way. My goal was to be a good newspaper man."

Dygard enrolled at Little Rock Junior College, all the while continuing with his newspaper work. "I covered the football team at school the first year I was there and had a lucky break when they went undefeated to the Little Rose Bowl in Pasadena. I was, after all, going to school with these players and the coach lived on campus, so I got to know them all well. That was a great experience, and a very exciting season to cover."

While Dygard was in school, his mother died. "I was nineteen when she died of cancer. She had been quite ill for about four years and unable to work for two of those years. So it was a pretty frightening time. She was a very courageous woman who was in and out of the hospital all the time but never complained," Dygard related.

He eventually earned his degree from the University of Arkansas, Fayetteville, "two hundred miles away from Little Rock, but I still worked for the *Gazette,* covering sports and also writing some feature stories. I married a fellow Little Rock Junior College student. Marriage, I found out, will change your life. I'd been living in the fraternity house, and after the marriage, settled in an apartment.

"Suddenly, things like getting through school and getting something out of it seemed a great deal more serious to me. Because I had been very much on my own with no one supporting me for a couple of years, I guess the responsibility of marriage wasn't as jarring a thing for me as it might be for some people.

"After I graduated I went back to Little Rock and worked for the *Gazette.* After about six months, I quit and went to work for the University of Arkansas, Fayetteville, in the editorial division of the Institute of Science and Technology. My main goal was to get a Master's degree. I felt that I wasn't making a lot of headway at the newspaper so when I was offered this job, I took the opportunity to work on a Master's in history. I had been there about six months when the Associated Press bureau chief in Little Rock called and offered me a job with the A.P. They were familiar with my work. I was quite excited about working for the A.P. because it was a worldwide news organization.

"The Associated Press is a non-profit, cooperative venture of American newspapers. Nobody owns it. Almost 1800 daily newspapers in the United States are organized into this corporation which maintains news bureaus all over the world. Each paper pays an assessment based on its circulation. The assessments support the operation. So the bigger papers pay more than the smaller papers. There are around 140 bureaus in the United States, and about eighty overseas. I started out in Little Rock writing some sports and covering the state capital."

Dygard's career with the Associated Press spanned decades. "I've been a reporter, editor, rewrite man, and now I'm an executive," he explained. "I've always had that kind of romantic vision of journalism, but it's not all trench coats and beautiful brunettes. There's an awful lot of nitty gritty that goes into it. Fortunately, I've enjoyed the nitty gritty, too.

"I worked in the Birmingham, Alabama, bureau during the time of the Freedom Riders and the Ku Klux Klan. The Blacks, called Negroes then, were trying to integrate places like lunch counters, bus stations, waiting rooms, rest rooms, and water fountains, but the Klan was determined to stop them. There were a lot of bloody riots. I witnessed some of them. They were unforgettable experiences. It was big news at the time—every day you knew you were writing a front-page story.

"You see people at their best, and you see people at their worst, and there was a little bit of both in that situation. Freedom Riders were willing to get their heads caved in

trying to win a point. They were certainly very dedicated."

Dygard and his colleagues demonstrated their own courage during this time. "That would have been the only time in my career that I felt physically threatened. The Klan was after the press, and, as a matter of fact, when we knew there was going to be trouble, we would try to disguise ourselves by wearing the Ku Klux Klan uniform—khaki pants and a white T-shirt."

Dygard's career took him around the United States as well as around the world. He related these experiences: "I've enjoyed being able to live in different areas— Little Rock, Detroit, Birmingham, New Orleans, Indianapolis, and Chicago. The best place to live and raise a family is Indianapolis. They have nice neighborhoods, good schools, reasonable prices. It has just about everything going for it if you are a young person with children.

"My wife and I started foreign travel as a hobby about twenty years ago and have been to more than thirty

When Joe Mitchell begins to get offers from first-rate colleges, he rethinks his decision to attend a small school just so he can continue to play footfall with his high school friends. (Cover illustration by Stephen Marchesi.)

countries. Living in Asia, of course, has offered a great opportunity to go to places like China, Bangkok, Hong Kong, and Singapore. We've traveled to Russia and have been to Europe five times. Whether you're going to Europe or Asia, people live in cultures very different from those of us who grew up in the United States. Each country produces different kinds of people, and most of them, I've found, are extraordinarily nice. Even in China, which I had always viewed as big and monolithic and full of terror and horror, people were very nice and friendly. The same was true in Moscow. Every day you read in the news what their governments are doing, but the people are generally nice folks."

In 1985, Dygard became Chief of the Tokyo Bureau of the Associated Press. "One day, the phone rang and the president of the company asked if I would go to Japan. My wife and I decided to go. I enjoy living in Tokyo. Almost everything about it is completely different from the United States: the culture, the language. It's crowded, expensive, noisy, and dirty but there's a fascination about it. The people think differently. 'The company' represents family, and they spend a lot more time at their jobs than they need to (and a lot more time than most people in the world do). Their co-workers are almost like brothers and sisters. It's an attitude I had never seen before. And everything is very, very crowded. They live in very small, cramped quarters and tend to go out instead of having people in."

Though Dygard's career provided him with endless experience and satisfaction, it wasn't until 1977 that he was able to accomplish another of his childhood dreams, when he published his first sports novel, *Running Scared.* "I had tried writing a novel a number of times, but always reached a point where I got bored with it. I realized that if the writer is bored, the reader is going to be bored," he explained. "Then one night in a motel in Champaign, Illinois, where I was left to my own devices, I thought, 'Well, I've always said I'll do it—I will start a book and go all the way through to the finish, no matter what.' I wrote the first chapter that night and eventually went all the way through to the finish, telling myself that it may never get published. I finally finished it, which was a scary thing because now I had to do something with it. I let my wife read it; she was less than enthusiastic. 'I've read worse,' said she. (She's not a great sports fan.)

"I went to the library and gathered up about ten books that looked like what I had written, and wrote to their publishers. I heard back from only about half of them, with one or two saying 'Thanks, but no thanks.' The others recommended sending it along and 'we'll take a look at it.' So I started mailing it off. Morrow Junior Books sent my manuscript back with a three-page letter, saying 'We almost took this book, but it's got some flaws.'

"The flaws were things that never would have dawned on me because I'd had no experience in this. Writing fiction was a bigger leap from journalism than I had expected. One problem was point of view. I would have

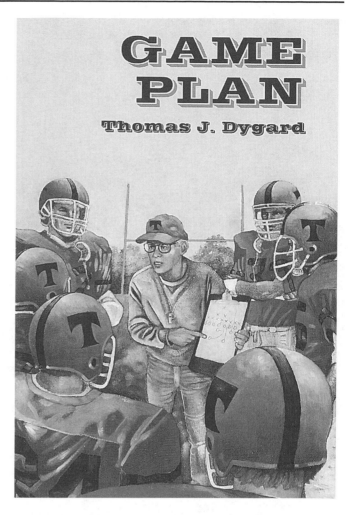

When the football coach of Barton High School is injured, student manager Hubert Hatton is forced to take charge and discovers that coaching presents him with tests of his courage and confidence. (Cover illustration by Stephen Marchesi.)

two characters talking and reading each other's mind. 'That's a "no no,"' according to Morrow. 'You can only see through one set of eyes. If two people are talking, one of them knows what he's thinking, but he should have no idea what the other one is thinking.' I also revealed something at the end of the book that wasn't fair to keep from the reader. You've got to give some hint of it. 'Foreshadowing,' they called it.

"So I took their letter as an invitation and wrote back saying, 'I don't have any arguments with the flaws you cited; I can fix them. Will you look at it again?' They agreed. It did not mean throwing the whole manuscript away and rewriting it. All it involved really was inserting one chapter and rewriting certain portions, which literally took me only one weekend. I sent it back and they bought it. Then they asked if I could do it again."

Dygard did do it again, writing several popular novels: *Winning Kicker, Outside Shooter, Point Spread, Soccer Duel,* and *Halfback Tough,* dealing with virtually every aspect of sports. He explained: "The editors were very

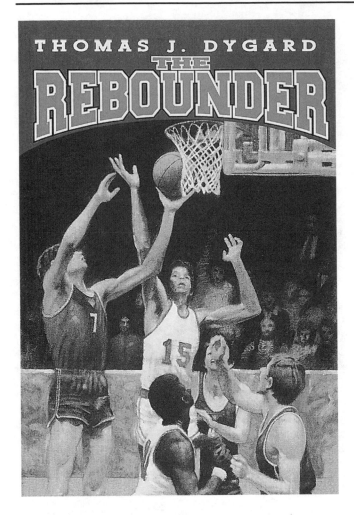

THOMAS J. DYGARD
THE REBOUNDER

Another title in Dygard's list of exciting sports novels, this book relates the story of Chris Patton, a young student who struggles against problems in his past to be a winning basketball player. (Cover illustration by Mike Wimmer.)

good. I was impressed, and always have been, with their suggestions. It's been an education.

"I wrote my first book as an adult novel, but when I finished and reread it, I thought of it more as a book for teenagers. My approach to my readership was from the viewpoint of a fourteen-year-old boy entitled to a story that helps him look ahead to adulthood. I've always tried to keep that in mind as I've written. The books may be called young adult novels, but the reader is entitled to an adult story.

"The number one thing about writing is clarity, which applies to fiction and journalism alike. If the reader doesn't understand something, you've completely missed the boat. The reader can always turn on the television and you will probably lose him. So the writing has got to be abundantly clear, interesting, and thoughtful, and the basic idea has got to have drama. You present your character in a situation where he 'wants' something, and then you present him with obstacles to be overcome. If it's done correctly, the character will

overcome these obstacles only to find more obstacles, which may lead him to change his goal."

Dygard's books contain elements of a deeper nature than the mere pursuit of athleticism, such as the insecurity Joe Atkins, the protagonist of *Halfback Tough,* feels over his bad record in a new school, or the courage of the football star's choice of soccer over football in *Soccer Duel.* Dygard shows great sensitivity for the young adults in his novels. "Well, I used to be one, so I draw rather heavily upon that. I think that a lot of people at fourteen, fifteen, and even twenty, can have a lot of lonely, uncertain moments when they feel like an outsider or feel not as good as they ought to about something. I don't find it difficult to relate to that kind of feeling. It may sound like childishness when a kid says 'I want to do this or that,' but he's actually making important decisions. Joe Atkins felt like an outsider, but he also felt hope about a new beginning and decided that the old way had not been much fun and that maybe he ought to try another approach."

Dygard saw athletics as a healthy aspect of a young adult's life, if it is viewed realistically. Today's youth, he recommended, should not have sport careers as singular goals. "Every kid in the world probably went through some period where he thought he'd like to play short-stop for the Yankees, but I'm sure most of them outgrew it. There are an awful lot of young people these days deciding to make sports a career. Sports can be enjoyable and have real value, as well, but it's all got to be held in perspective. The fact is only a very small percentage of college athletes ever make it in professional sports," he related.

Notwithstanding, Dygard remained a sports fan. "I still like watching football at the college level. It's better than high school and it's not as automatic as professional football. College ball has a lot more human drama. But I don't really have a least favorite sport. I enjoy them all and always have."

Some of his books required a certain amount of research. "I wrote *Soccer Duel* at the request of Morrow Junior Books. They asked if I could write a book on soccer, but I had never even seen a soccer match. To me, soccer was a game played by Argentines, Italians, and the girls in gym class. I called the soccer coach in my daughter's high school and told him I needed help. He took to it with great enthusiasm. I attended a number of their practice sessions, and a whole season of matches. After the matches, he and I would go out together and he'd tell me why they'd lost. And in the end, I gave him the manuscript of *Soccer Duel* to make sure I hadn't made some horrible technical error. I was quite flattered that he actually picked up a play that I had written and put it in his playbook.

"A lot of my story ideas and happenings, as it is with anybody trying to recreate life-like situations, are certainly reflections of what I have seen, heard, or read. I've been fortunate to be in journalism where my job has been to see and hear those things.

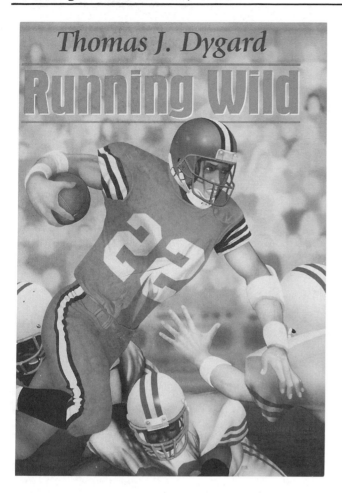

Pete Holman joins the football team as a way of avoiding trouble with the law, but his friendship with a tough gang proves a strong temptation to adopt his old ways. (Cover illustration by Jon Weiman.)

"I do most of my writing from eight until about noon on most Saturday and Sunday mornings. A rather famous writer once said there's nothing to writing, you just sit down and bleed through the pores. Actually, it's not torture for me. I enjoy writing. Of course, an awful lot of it is wadding up pieces of paper and throwing them in the wastebasket. I'm not so much a writer as a rewriter. I tend to write one draft as fast as I can from beginning to end. I'll go back and pick out bits and pieces to revise. Then I'll go back and rewrite the whole thing from page one, then revise again. I outline only in my mind. I tried a written outline once and it fouled me up. My characters would go one way and my outline would go another, so I decided to go 'with the characters.' When I start, I know what the story is about and roughly what's going to happen and where it's going to end, and from there I try to create something. I enjoy the process of seeing a character develop, and come out at the end of a day of writing feeling not exhausted, but like I've had fun. I also get an enormous feeling of satisfaction when a book comes out and I can lay my hands on it for the first time. It's a real upper.

"I try to write one book a year. I've written one outdoor adventure, *Wilderness Peril,* but I guess it's also a sports

story. I have toyed with the idea of doing a mystery, but since my writing time is very limited, I continue with sports stories. I'm working on a football story at the moment, called *Backfield Package,* about four boys in a high school backfield who decide to go to college and stick together, but then everything starts falling apart."

In two of Dygard's more recent books, the main characters are athletes who transfer to new schools and must overcome feelings of self-doubt. *The Rebounder* features six-foot six-inch Chris, who for obvious reasons is approached by the basketball coach. Chris refuses to join the team because he accidentally injured an opposing player the previous season. Coach Fulton is very caring and supportive, helping Chris overcome his aversion and return to playing basketball. The fictional Hal, whose father was a well-known big league baseball player, is the main character of *Infield Hit.* After his parents' divorce, Hal moves with his mother, transfering to a new school midway through his junior year. To meet new friends, he joins the baseball team. Tiring of always being compared to his father and placed in the same playing position (third base), Hal attempts to conceal the identity of his father. Although his new coach knew Hal's father, he helps Hal find a more suitable playing position—second base—and bats him lead-off. Some of Hal's teammates assume he's been given this position because of his famous father. Hal proves that he is, in his own right, a good baseball player, and in using some top-notch diplomacy, helps the team come together as a group. Todd Morning of *School Library Journal* called *Infield Hit* a "solid sports novel with some effective extras thrown in."

Dygard's books have been very popular with his readers. He explained: "I get one or two letters a week from kids. There are a few questions that keep recurring. 'Was this story based on real people?' is one. I say, 'No, not at all.' Another question is, 'Did you ever know anyone who had this problem?' Some of the letters are remarkably thoughtful from kids who are obviously interested in writing themselves. They ask a lot of questions about the mechanics of writing books, such as, 'How long did it take you?'

"The one thing I hope my books do is help make lifetime readers of kids. I think there's something a person can get out of a book that he can't get from movies or television. I'm afraid a lot of people go through life never discovering what that is. A reader is much more apt to think than someone staring at television. Someone who reads a book sometimes slips into real thinking."

■ Works Cited

Dygard, Thomas J., in an interview with Dieter Miller for *Authors and Artists for Young Adults,* Volume 7, Gale, 1991.

Morning, Todd, review of *Infield Hit, School Library Journal,* March, 1995, p. 222.

■ For More Information See

PERIODICALS

Booklist, September 1, 1994, p. 35; April 15, 1995, p. 1493.

Voice of Youth Advocates, August, 1995, p. 156.

E

ELLIOTT, Joey
  See HOUK, Randy

* * *

ENGLE, Marion
  See LADD, Louise

* * *

EPHRAIM, Shelly S(chonebaum) 1952-

■ Personal

Born October 16, 1952, in Baltimore, MD; daughter of Jacob (a grocer) and Ruth (Leikach) Schonebaum; married Lon Ephraim (a musician), March 9, 1980; children: Jascha, Theo. *Education:* Maryland Institute College of Art, B.F.A., 1975. *Hobbies and other interests:* Folkdancing, computer graphics, collecting ruby glass and Roseville pottery.

■ Addresses

Home—3822 Palmira Lane, Silver Spring, MD 20906.

■ Career

Ayres Art Studio, Baltimore, MD, paste-up and layout artist, 1975-77; Bolton Hill Frame Shop, Baltimore, picture framer, 1977-80; Koenig Art Emporium, Gaithersburg, MD, picture framer, 1989-90; Benner & Mulshine Medical Office, Silver Spring, MD, medical secretary, 1996—, Cherry Blossom Music, computer graphic illustrator, 1987—.

■ Illustrator

Daniel J. Swartz, *Bim and Bom: A Shabbat Tale,* Kar-Ben (Rockville, MD), 1996.

Also provided illustrations for the videotape *A Very Special Present,* Uffington Productions, 1994.

SHELLY S. EPHRAIM

■ Sidelights

Shelly S. Ephraim told *Something about the Author* (*SATA*): "I have been drawing since earliest memory. When I was very small, before I could read and write, my mother had me draw her shopping list. She would then take it and 'read' it over the phone to my dad, who was a grocer. Having my talent recognized and nurtured at an early age was so important to me. This kind of encouragement by my parents continued and grew over the years."

ERICKSON, Betty J(ean) 1923-

■ Personal

Born October 11, 1923, in Taft, CA; daughter of John Cooper Henderson Douglas Young (a cabinetmaker, truck driver, mushroom farmer, oil rig driller and realtor) and Erva Edna (Lincoln) Young (deceased, 1938); stepdaughter of Kathleen Ricky Young (a teacher and musician); married Richard Baldwin Erickson (in United States Air Force), November 29, 1952; children: Terry A. Erickson Dodson, Gregory S., John Jeffrey, Mark K., Pamela S. Erickson Escarsega, Timothy F., Donn Bradley, Sara J. Erickson Parry, Caris A. Erickson Goryachev. *Education:* College (now University) of the Pacific, B.A., 1945; Mills College, M.A., 1952. *Politics:* "Moderate Republican." *Religion:* United Methodist.

■ Addresses

Home—14611 North Anderson St., Woodbridge, VA 22193. *Office*—Springwoods Elementary School, 3815 Marquis Pl., Woodbridge, VA 22192. *Electronic mail*—read@erols.com.

■ Career

Educator, writer. Master teacher at public schools in Stockton, CA, and Alhambra, CA, 1945-51; Mills College, demonstration teacher, summers, 1947-51; Teaching Fellow, Mills College, 1951-52; elementary teacher, Bellevue, NE, 1966-68; Title I teacher, reading specialist, Reading Recovery Teacher, Prince William County Schools, VA, 1968-94. Volunteer reading recovery teacher, Springwoods Elementary School, Woodbridge, VA, 1994—. *Member:* Reading Recovery Council of North America, Phi Delta Kappa.

■ Awards, Honors

Named teacher of the year, Battlefield chapter, Phi Delta Kappa, 1996; Performance Award, Prince William County Schools, 1997.

■ Writings

Oh, No, Sherman!, illustrated by Kristine Dillard, Seedling Publications (Columbus, OH), 1996.
Play Ball, Sherman!, illustrated by Dillard, Seedling Publications, 1996.
Use Your Beak, Seedling Publications, in press.
Big Bad Rex, Seedling Publications, in press.

Contributor to periodicals, including *Reading in Virginia, Reading Teacher,* and *First Teacher.* Has also coauthored, coillustrated, and coedited sets of eight-page books published for beginning readers by Prince William County Schools, VA.

■ Work in Progress

Collection of animal stories for young readers, holiday nonfiction for beginning readers, magazine stories for

BETTY J. ERICKSON

middle-grade readers, and a middle-grade mystery novel.

■ Sidelights

Betty J. Erickson told *Something about the Author* (*SATA*): "In the years B.C. (Before Computer), my ideas vanished before I could capture them on paper, and cutting and pasting with actual scissors and tape was tedious. In 1983, I met my first computer, bonded with it, and became a prolific writer. I could think and write simultaneously, and I had work space and tools for reshaping, clarifying, and correcting. My trusty monitor displayed gems, aberrations, and fuzzy images.

"Since I was, and probably always will be, a reading teacher, my audience was the children I served. When text in a particular genre, subject, or level of difficulty was not available, I wrote it using language I deemed appropriate. In the 1980s my captive audience read my books without complaint. Today's children select from a wide variety of titles and authors, and they are more discriminating.

"In the 1980s, I discovered a selection of books for beginning readers written by New Zealand author Joy Cowley. Joy writes from the child's point of view. Her youngest or smallest character sparks children's interests by overcoming obstacles, meeting challenges, winning races or prizes, and becoming the hero. Obviously, her books had charm and appeal that mine lacked. I deposited my children's books in the incinerator and started over. In 1992, Trudy Larson, a representative from the Wright Group, brought Joy Cowley to my classroom. Since that time, Joy and her husband, Terry Coles, have become my friends and have encouraged me to hone my craft as a children's writer despite the 'tick-tock' of my clock!

"I write nearly six hours a day during the summer. My study, a converted bedroom, is crammed with two computers, two printers, a work table, art supplies, paper cutter, copier, and shelves of children's books and magazines. When school is in session, I write on Saturdays. Most writing during the week is done for immediate use at Springwoods Elementary School, where I tutor Reading Recovery students and work with small groups of first and second graders who need extra support in reading. Children are candid and reliable critics, and they keep me supplied with fresh ideas. Our eleven grandchildren serve up an abundant supply of story material. My experiences as mother of nine, one inherited and eight begats, can be triggered in a heartbeat. Also, my own childhood experiences are on automatic redial.

"*Oh, No, Sherman!* is based on an incident involving our son Donn when he was a paper boy. *Play Ball, Sherman!* is a true account of the antics of the family pet at our grandson's soccer game. Amazingly, Kristine Dillard illustrated the scene as accurately as if she had been a witness. Even her car resembled Niecy, the family Nissan. She captured the flavor of both stories, and children give her glowing accolades.

"An account of a male cardinal caring for his fledgling, entitled *Use Your Beak,* and a story describing tyrannosaurus rex through analogy and comparisons familiar to young children, entitled *Big Bad Rex,* are due soon."

*   *   *

ESBENSEN, Barbara J(uster) 1925-1996

■ Personal

Born April 28, 1925, in Madison, WI; died, 1996; daughter of Eugene M. (a physician) and Isabel S. (a singer; maiden name, Sinaiko) Juster; married Thorwald S. Esbensen (a developer of educational programs for microcomputers), June 24, 1953; children: Julie, Peter (deceased), Daniel, Jane, George, Kai. *Education:* University of Wisconsin, B.S., 1947.

■ Career

Madison Public Schools, Madison, WI, art teacher, 1947-49; Shorewood Hills Schools, Shorewood Hills, WI, art teacher, 1949-50; South Shore Community School, Port Wing, WI, art and creative writing teacher, 1953-56; Trust Territory of the Pacific Islands, Truk, Eastern Caroline Islands, art and creative writing teacher, 1956-58; Eureka Public Schools, Eureka, CA, ele-

BARBARA J. ESBENSEN

mentary school teacher, 1960-63; College of St. Scholastica, Duluth, MN, art and creative writing methods teacher, 1964-66, creative arts consultant, 1970-71. Writer, 1965—. Eureka newspapers, Eureka, CA, advertising designer, 1959-60. Edina Chorale, member of board of directors, 1988-90.

■ Awards, Honors

Teacher's Choice, National Council of Teachers of English, 1987, for *Words with Wrinkled Knees,* and 1988, for *The Star Maiden;* Finalist, Minnesota Book Award, 1988, for *The Star Maiden;* Notable Children's Trade Book in the Field of Social Studies, National Council for Social Studies and Children's Book Council, 1989, for *Ladder to the Sky.*

■ Writings

POETRY

Swing around the Sun, Lerner, 1965.
Cold Stars and Fireflies: Poems of the Four Seasons, illustrated by Susan Bonners, Crowell, 1984.
Words With Wrinkled Knees: Animal Poems, illustrated by John Stadler, Crowell, 1986.
Who Shrank My Grandmother's House? Poems of Discovery, illustrated by Eric Beddows, HarperCollins, 1992.
Dance with Me, illustrated by Megan Lloyd, HarperCollins, 1995.
Echoes for the Eye: Poems to Celebrate Patterns in Nature, illustrated by Helen K. Davie, HarperCollins, 1996.

RETELLINGS

The Star Maiden: An Ojibway Tale, illustrated by Helen
   K. Davie, Little, Brown, 1988.
*Ladder to the Sky: How the Gift of Healing Came to the
   Ojibway Nation: A Legend Retold,* illustrated by
   Helen K. Davie, Little, Brown, 1989.
*The Great Buffalo Race: How the Buffalo Got Its Hump:
   A Seneca Tale,* Illustrated by Helen K. Davie, Little,
   Brown, 1994.
The Dream Mouse: A Lullaby Tale from Old Latvia,
   illustrated by Judith Mitchell, Little, Brown, 1995.

NONFICTION

Great Northern Diver: The Loon, illustrated by Mary
   Barrett Brown, Little, Brown, 1990.
Tiger with Wings: The Great Horned Owl, illustrated by
   Mary Barrett Brown, Orchard Books, 1991.
Playful Slider: The North American River Otter, illus-
   trated by Mary Barrett Brown, Little, Brown, 1993.
Sponges are Skeletons ("Let's-Read-And-Find-Out Sci-
   ence" series), illustrated by Holly Keller, Harper-
   Collins, 1993.
Baby Whales Drink Milk ("Let's-Read-And-Find-Out
   Science" series), illustrated by Lambert Davis,
   HarperCollins, 1994.
Swift as the Wind: The Cheetah, illustrated by Jean
   Cassels, Orchard Books, 1996.

OTHER

A Celebration of Bees: Helping Children Write Poetry,
   Winston Press, 1975, published with a foreword by
   Lee Bennett Hopkins, Holt, 1995.

CONTRIBUTOR TO ANTHOLOGIES

Myra Cohn Livingston, *Thanksgiving Poems,* Holiday
   House, 1985.
Livingston, *Poems for Jewish Holidays,* Holiday House,
   1986.
Livingston, *Valentine Poems,* Holiday House, 1987.
Caroline Bauer, *Windy Day Stories and Poems,* Lippin-
   cott, 1988.
Livingston, *Halloween Poems,* Holiday House, 1989.
Bobbye S. Goldstein, *Bear in Mind,* Viking/Kestrel,
   1989.

Also author of *The Night Rainbow: Images of the
Northern Lights from Around the World* (poems), illustrated by Simon Ng, 1996. Esbensen's manuscripts are
housed in the Kerlan Collection, University of Minnesota, and the Central Missouri State University Collection
of Literature for Children, Warrensburg, MO.

■ Sidelights

Barbara Esbensen, as she once revealed to *Something
about the Author (SATA),* began to consider herself a
writer when she was ten years old. Esbensen, who was
also a teacher and a singer, spent much of her time
writing. Over the course of thirty years at work as a
professional writer, Esbensen contributed collections of
poetry, retold tales, and eloquent books about animals
to children's literature. In all of her works, Esbensen
called upon the power of the image. She told *SATA,*

From *Tiger with Wings: The Great Horned Owl,* written
by Esbensen and illustrated by Mary Barrett Brown.

"Words can be combined in fresh, unexpected ways and
when this happens, the result is a quiet explosion of
delight for the reader. Whether I am writing prose or
poetry, I like to find those word combinations and then
watch the sentences catch fire and shower down
sparks!"

Esbensen became a writer when she was just fourteen
years old, in 1939. When "Russia invaded Finland," she
explained to *SATA,* "I was so upset at that international
event that I wrote an anti-war poem and showed it to
my English teacher the next day. She was a journalist
and a published poet. 'Barbara,' she said, 'you are a
writer.' From that moment, even though I took many art
courses, majored in art at the University of Wisconsin,
and taught art for years, I thought of myself as 'A
WRITER.' ... Writing is my great joy."

Esbensen's poetry has won praise from critics. *Words
With Wrinkled Knees* is a collection of twenty-one
poems which relates the names of animals (from owls to
elephants, snakes and giraffes) to their characteristics
and habits. According to a reviewer for the *Junior
Bookshelf,* these poems "are witty and sometimes beautiful and perceptive" and are replete with images.
Richard Brown of *School Librarian* found the work
"quirky, finely-honed, and altogether ... successful."
"Word-lovers will applaud Esbensen's unique poems,"
asserted a *Publishers Weekly* critic. *Cold Stars and
Fireflies,* as *School Library Journal* contributor Lee
Bock explained, is a "merry journey through the seasons." Forty-three short poems move from autumn,
with the first day of school and Halloween, to winter,
spring, and summer. "A splendid collection for sharing," wrote Barbara Elleman of *Booklist. Dance with Me*
presents fifteen poems in which the poet interprets the
movement of people, natural forces, and objects as

dance. In the words of *School Library Journal* contributor Barbara Kiefer, the poems "reveal unexpected images in the most delightful ways." *Who Shrank My Grandmother's House?* shows children how to discover the wonder in everyday moments and objects with twenty-three poems. Lauralyn Persson, writing in *School Library Journal,* described the collection as "an invitation to enter the sphere of daydreaming" and "creativity." A *Publishers Weekly* critic noted Esbensen's imagery and wrote that her "sophisticated verses glisten." "The images here are clean, simple, and surprising," related Betsy Hearne of the *Bulletin of the Center for Children's Books.*

Most of Esbensen's retold tales are drawn from Native American folklore and mythology. *The Star Maiden* and *Ladder to the Sky,* both from the Ojibway Nation, have won Esbensen recognition. *The Star Maiden* tells how a star-girl living in the sky hopes to live on the earth. First, she takes the form of a rose, and then that of a prairie plant, but neither form is suitable. Finally, seeing her reflection in the water of a lake, she and her friends decide to move there, and they become water lilies. "The author retells the simple *pourquoi* story with dignity and imbues the text with a dreamlike and poetic mystery," observed *Horn Book* commentator Ethel R. Twichell. *The Star Maiden* won a Teacher's Choice award from the National Council of Teachers of English.

Ladder to the Sky explains how the Ojibway gained the power to heal. It describes a time in which the people are never sick, and they never die. Instead, spiritual messengers escort elderly people up a magic vine to the sky. Things change when a young man is favored by the spirits. The people grow envious, and, to save him, the spirits take him up to the sky. The young man's grandmother, heartbroken, climbs up the vine to bring him back, even though it is forbidden for a mortal, alone, to do so. The vine breaks, and pain, disease, and death come to the people. Still, the Great Spirit gives the knowledge of natural substances and power to heal to the Medicine People. "Esbensen's rhythmic and powerful blank verse ... gets its message across," wrote a *Publishers Weekly* critic.

Esbensen's books about animals contain facts and scientific information sometimes presented in a style that *Horn Book* critic Ellen Fader, in a review of *Great Northern Diver,* called "lyrical." *Great Northern Diver* tells about the loon, where it lives, its habits, and its life cycle. "Esbensen never tips the factual balance by becoming self-indulgently poetic," noted Betsy Hearne of the *Bulletin of the Center for Children's Books. Tiger with Wings: The Great Horned Owl* describes one of nature's great predators. This book, according to a *Kirkus Reviews* critic, provides an "even more detailed and better-balanced portrait" than *Great Northern Diver. Playful Slider* focuses on the North American river otter and explains how they hunt, fight, and play on land and in water. *Sponges are Skeletons* brings a seemingly less active sea animal to the attention of readers. "The text is simple and thought provoking," remarked Annie

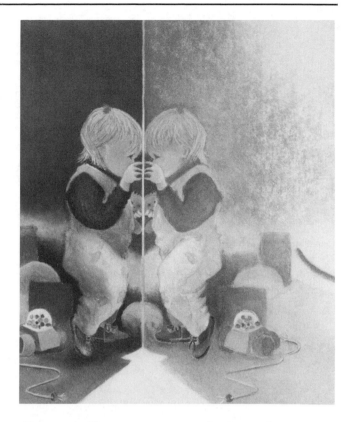

Esbensen's fifteen poems capture the dance of nature in the everyday world. (From *Dance with Me,* illustrated by Megan Lloyd.)

Ayres of *Booklist. Baby Whales Drink Milk* helps children understand that whales are not fish but mammals like humans.

Describing her writing process in an interview with Jeffrey S. Copeland for *Speaking of Poets,* Esbensen commented: "Sometimes I just sit and scribble things on a piece of paper to get my brain going, and many times in that process something occurs to me that I put someplace else in the poem. Then after I do a couple of rough drafts, I realize that such and such can start the poem, so it isn't always that my brain started them that way. I save my rough drafts and they really are a mess.... When kids ask about my writing process, I can show them that sometimes a poem starts with none of this good stuff. I can show them thirty pages of scratches and then the three pages that worked out the way I wanted. It shows them we all need to write, write, and then write some more before we end up with the best we can do."

■ Works Cited

Ayres, Annie, review of *Sponges Are Skeletons, Booklist,* December 1, 1993, p. 694.

Bock, Lee, review of *Cold Stars and Fireflies, School Library Journal,* October, 1984, p. 156.

Brown, Richard, review of *Words With Wrinkled Knees, School Librarian,* February, 1992, p. 27.

Elleman, Barbara, review of *Cold Stars and Fireflies, Booklist,* October 15, 1984, p. 305.

Esbensen, Barbara Juster, in an interview with Jeffrey S. Copeland, *Speaking of Poets: Interviews with Poets Who Write for Children and Young Adults,* National Council of Teachers of English, 1993, pp. 104-12.

Fader, Ellen, review of *Great Northern Diver, Horn Book,* May-June, 1990, p. 347.

Hearne, Betsy, review of *Great Northern Diver, Bulletin of the Center for Children's Books,* March, 1990, p. 158.

Hearne, Betsy, review of *Who Shrank My Grandmother's House, Bulletin of the Center for Children's Books,* April, 1992, p. 204.

Kiefer, Barbara, review of *Dance With Me, School Library Journal,* October, 1995, p. 146.

Review of *Ladder to the Sky, Publishers Weekly,* October 27, 1989.

Persson, Lauralyn, review of *Who Shrank My Grandmother's House, School Library Journal,* April, 1992, pp. 104-05.

Review of *Tiger With Wings, Kirkus Reviews,* July 1, 1991, p. 863.

Twichell, Ethel R., review of *The Star Maiden, Horn Book,* July-August, 1988, p. 506.

Review of *Who Shrank My Grandmother's House, Publishers Weekly,* March 23, 1992, pp. 73-74.

Review of *Words With Wrinkled Knees, Junior Bookshelf,* December, 1991, p. 261.

Review of *Words With Wrinkled Knees, Publishers Weekly,* December 12, 1986, p. 54.

■ For More Information See

PERIODICALS

Booklist, December 1, 1993, pp. 692, 694.

Horn Book, September-October, 1991, p. 610.

School Library Journal, November, 1994, p. 97; May, 1995, p. 99.

—*Sketch by Ronie Garcia-Johnson*

F

FIELD, Dorothy 1944-

■ Personal

Born October 2, 1944, in New York, NY; daughter of Harold C. (an editor) and Jane M. (an art therapist) Field; married R. L. van der Vegt (a teacher), February 13, 1975; children: Cicely. *Education:* University of Rochester, B.A., 1966; University of California, Berkeley, M.A., 1971. *Religion:* Jewish.

■ Addresses

Home—R.R.1, Cobble Hill, British Columbia, Canada V0R 1L0.

■ Career

Freelance artist, using artist-made paper as a medium for sculptural work and books.

■ Writings

FOR CHILDREN

In the Street of the Temple Cloth Printers, Orca Book Publishers (Victoria, British Columbia), 1996.

OTHER

Meditations at the Edge: Paper and Spirit, limited letterpress edition, Peter and Donna Thomas (Santa Cruz, CA), 1996.

Author of articles and reviews on papermaking and traditional Asian culture.

■ Work in Progress

Through a Paper Lens: Glimpses of Tradition and Change in Nepal, 1984-96, publication of a limited edition by the magazine *Portfolio* expected in 1998.

■ For More Information See

PERIODICALS

Quill and Quire, June, 1996, p. 56.*

*   *   *

FITZSIMONS, Cecilia (A. L.) 1952-

■ Personal

Born May 28, 1952, in Welling, Kent, England; daughter of Martin and Eileen King; married Steve Fitzsimons (a lecturer), 1973; children: a son and a daughter. *Education:* Westfield College, University of London, B.Sc. (Honors), 1973; University of Leicester, postgraduate research, 1973-74; Portsmouth University, Ph.D., 1981.

■ Addresses

Office—25 Hazelgrove, Portsmouth, Hampshire, P08 0LE, England.

■ Career

Author and illustrator.

■ Writings

Step-by-Step 50 Nature Projects for Kids, photographs by Anthony Pickhaver, Smithmark, 1995.
Animal Habitats, illustrated by Adam Hook, Raintree Steck-Vaughn (Austin, TX), 1996.
Animal Lives, illustrated by Adam Hook, Raintree Steck-Vaughn, 1996.
Creatures of the Past, illustrated by Chris Forsey, Raintree Steck-Vaughn, 1996.
Water Life, illustrated by Helen Ward, Raintree Steck-Vaughn, 1996.
(With Marion Elliot and Petra Boase) *100 Things for Kids to Make and Do,* Ultimate Editions (London, England), 1996.

CECILIA FITZSIMONS

SELF-ILLUSTRATED

Pop-Up Field Guides: My First Birds, Harper and Row, 1985.

Pop-Up Field Guides: My First Butterflies, Harper and Row, 1985.

Pop-Up Field Guides: My First Fishes and Other Waterlife, Harper and Row, 1987.

Pop-Up Field Guides: My First Insects, Spiders and Crawlers, Harper and Row, 1987.

Seashore Life of North America, Bonanza (New York), 1989.

What Can I See? In the Field, Hamish Hamilton, 1990.

What Can I See? In the Playground, Hamish Hamilton, 1990.

What Can I See? In the Woods, Hamish Hamilton, 1990.

What Can I See? At the Seaside, Hamish Hamilton, 1990.

Sainsbury's Book of the Sea, Walker, 1991.

Pocket Pull-Outs: Rivers and Ponds, Studio Editions (London, England), 1992.

Pocket Pull-Outs: The Seashore, Studio Editions, 1992.

Pocket Pull-Outs: Trees and Woodlands, Studio Editions, 1992.

Pocket Pull-Outs: Animals in Danger: A Nature Guide, Studio Editions, 1993.

Sainsbury's Book of Birds, Walker, 1994.

Clever Clogs, Wild Animals, Henderson, 1994.

Sainsbury's Animals of the World, Shaw's, 1995.

All about Food: Fruit, Silver Burdett (Parsippany, NJ), 1996.

All about Food: Vegetables and Herbs, Silver Burdett, 1997.

All about Food: Cereals, Nuts and Spices, Zoe (Winchester, England), 1997.

All about Food: Dairy Foods and Drinks, Zoe, 1997.

Sainsbury's Dangerous Animals, Shaw's, 1997.

ILLUSTRATOR

Pamela Forey, *Wild Flowers: Learning to Identify,* Macdonald (London, England), 1984.

Eleanor Lawrence, *An Instant Guide to Trees,* Bonanza, 1985.

Ron Wilson, *The New Dictionary of Dinosaurs,* Grafton (London, England), 1986.

Ron Wilson, *100 Dinosaurs from A to Z,* Grosset & Dunlap, 1986.

Pamela Forey, *An Instant Guide to Mammals: The Most Familiar Species: North American Mammals,* Bonanza, 1986.

Pamela Forey, *An Instant Guide to Wildflowers: The Most Familiar Species: North American Wildflowers,* Bonanza, 1986.

Jennifer Cockrane, *Air Ecology,* Watts, 1987.

Jennifer Cockrane, *Land Ecology,* Watts, 1987.

Jennifer Cockrane, *Plant Ecology,* Watts, 1987.

Jennifer Cockrane, *Water Ecology,* Watts, 1987.

Claire Littlejohn, *The Modern Ark: The Endangered Wildlife of Our Planet,* Dial, 1989, World International (Manchester, England), 1989.

Andreas Bubel, *Microstructure and Function of Cells: Electron Micrographs Cell Ultrastructure,* Simon & Schuster, 1989, E. Horwood (Chicester, England), 1989.

Pamela Forey, *Letts Pocket Guide to Wild Flowers,* Letts (London, England), 1990.

Rosie Harlow and Kuo Kang Chen, *Energy and Growth,* Warwick Press (New York), 1991, Kingfisher Books—Colophon, 1991.

Pamela Forey, *Letts Pocket Guide to Stars and Planets,* Letts, 1991.

Eva Fejer and Steve Frampton, *Letts Pocket Guide to Rocks and Minerals,* Letts, 1991.

Simon Perry, *A First Guide to Insects,* Hodder and Stoughton, 1991.

Simon Perry, *A First Guide to Trees,* Hodder and Stoughton, 1991.

Philip Steele, *Extinct Insects,* Watts, 1992.

Philip Steele, *Extinct Land Mammals,* Watts, 1992.

Jane Charman, *Life Goes On, and On . . . ,* Thornes, 1992.

Henry Gee and Steve McCormick, *Letts Pocket Guide to Fossils,* Letts, 1992.

Pamela Forey, *Letts Pocket Guide to Insects,* Letts, 1992.

Simon Perry, *A First Guide to Garden Birds,* Hodder and Stoughton, 1993.

Simon Perry, *A First Guide to Pond Life,* Hodder and Stoughton, 1993.

Pamela Forey, *Letts Pocket Guide to Sea and Seashore Life: The Most Common Species of European Fish and Other Marine Life,* Letts, 1994.

Lewis Peake, *Your Body,* Henderson (Woodbridge, England), 1994.

Sue Finnie, *Countries of the World,* Henderson, 1995.

Philip Steele and David Hogg, *Deserts,* Carolrhoda Books (Minneapolis, MN), 1996.

■ Sidelights

Cecilia Fitzsimons writes and illustrates science books for children and young adults, garnering praise both for the photographic clarity of her line drawings and watercolor paintings of plant, sea, and animal life, and for her straightforward, informative texts. Working with both standard formats and paper engineering like pop-ups and pull-outs, the prolific Fitzsimons creates field guides on a variety of subjects in the natural world, such as animals, birds, insects, fish, trees, and bodies of water; she also addresses such topics as food and nature projects for children. As an illustrator, Fitzsimons has provided the pictures for informational books for children and adults by such writers as Ron Wilson, Pamela Forey, Jennifer Cockrane, Simon Perry, and Philip Steele; these writers explain about such subjects as dinosaurs, ecology, cells, the human body, and countries of the world. Regarding the books for which she has provided both text and pictures, Fitzsimons is acknowledged for creating attractive, well-designed works that are both educational and entertaining. Several of her self-illustrated books have captured high marks as works fit for both indoor reading and for taking into the field as an aid to observation. Fitzsimons is consistently praised for creating works with the potential to inspire children to explore the natural world; in several of her works, in fact, Fitzsimons includes space for children to keep a record of their sightings. In general, Fitzsimons's numerous science and nature titles for children are warmly received for their brightly colored pictures and interesting texts; several volumes, in particular those which utilize the pop-up format, are especially well regarded for their ability to draw in reluctant readers.

Born in Kent, England, Fitzsimons was trained as a scientist. She received a degree in the biological sciences (zoology, botany, and paleontology) from the University of London and her Ph.D. in marine cell biology research from Portsmouth University; in addition, she did post-graduate work at the University of Leicester studying insects from Malayan rainforests. She began her publishing career as an illustrator, and her pictures are often said to be a positive addition to science texts aimed at middle-grade readers. In a *School Library Journal* review of Philip Steele's *Extinct Insects* and *Extinct Land Mammals,* Barbara B. Murphy praised Fitzsimons's contribution to the books, saying the illustrator's "eye-catching, colorful illustrations ... highlight every page." Fitzsimons's "What Can I See?" series amply fits the bill on both accounts, according to some critics. In a *Junior Bookshelf* review of *What Can I See? In the Playground,* a book in which a number of views of the same playground scene highlight a variety of plants and animal life that the watchful observer may find, the critic wrote: "This is a beautifully presented information book," and particularly praised the illustrations,

which are characterized as having "the clarity and detail of photographs." Similar qualities were found by *Growing Point* reviewer Margery Fisher regarding *What Can I See? At the Seaside* and *What Can I See? In the Field;* Fisher characterized these books as capable of fostering the interest of nature-minded children through text and pictures that are "essentially simple but in no way pedestrian or condescending."

Fitzsimons' first creations as an author/illustrator are pop-up field guides, a series that, while aimed at an audience in the early primary grades, are also deemed useful in drawing in older reluctant young scientists due to the popularity of the pop-up format. A contributor to *Publishers Weekly* reviewing *My First Butterflies* and its companion volume, *My First Birds,* which was dubbed "equally marvelous" by the critic, claimed, "Fitzsimons is a gifted artist [who creates] beautiful full-color paintings." The critic was enthusiastic about these first installments in the pop-up series, noting that they present "accurate and readily accessible information as well as esthetic rewards," courtesy of the author-artist's colorful, detailed paintings of numerous butterflies in their natural habitats. Likewise, a reviewer of *My First Fishes and Other Waterlife* in *Publishers Weekly* called this book "a field guide in the best sense, one that appeals to the armchair reader or someone observing the creatures firsthand." Reviewing *My First Insects, Spiders and Crawlers* in the *Christian Science Monitor,* Diane Manuel predicted that the book "could provide hours of entertainment in a meadow or beside a pond.... [A] good start for the fearless explorer." Fitzsimons offers practical advice to dedicated young scientists in *Step-by-Step 50 Nature Projects for Kids* (1995), a book that includes science experiments and artistic activities for both indoor and outdoor settings. According to *School library Journal* reviewer Kristin Lott, Fitzsimons "emphasizes safety, nature conservation, and the importance of respecting property rights when exploring" in this work.

■ Works Cited

Fisher, Margery, review of *What Can I See? At the Seaside* and *What Can I See? In the Field, Growing Point,* July, 1990, p. 5372.

Review of *What Can I See? In the Playground, Junior Bookshelf,* February, 1991, p. 21.

Lott, Kristin, review of *Step-by-Step: 50 Nature Projects for Kids, School Library Journal,* January, 1996, p. 117.

Manuel, Diane, review of *My First Insects, Christian Science Monitor,* August 7, 1987, p. B6.

Murphy, Barbara B., review of *Extinct Insects* and *Extinct Land Mammals, School Library Journal,* August, 1992, p. 174.

Review of *My First Butterflies, Publishers Weekly,* January 25, 1985, p. 94.

Review of *My First Fishes and Other Waterlife, Publishers Weekly,* June 12, 1987, p. 84.

■ **For More Information See**

PERIODICALS

Junior Bookshelf, October, 1985, p. 217.
School Librarian, November, 1996, p. 162.
School Library Journal, February, 1987, p. 86; February, 1988, p. 78.
Science Books, November, 1985, p. 74; May, 1996, p. 114.

G

NORMA GAFFRON

GAFFRON, Norma (Bondeson) 1931-

■ Personal

Born November 5, 1931, in Minneapolis, MN; daughter of Peter Albert (a baker and bakery shop owner) and Minnie (a homemaker; maiden name, Gaustad) Bondeson; married Bernard W. Gaffron (an engineer and laboratory director), June 6, 1953; children: Michael, Timothy, Patricia. *Education:* Winona State Teachers College (now State University), A.Ed., 1951; University of Minnesota, B.S. in Education, 1976. *Hobbies and other interests:* Reading, knitting, calligraphy, sewing, drawing.

■ Addresses

Home—2060 16th Terr. N.W., New Brighton, MN 55112.

■ Career

Elementary schoolteacher in Dodge Center, MN, 1951-53, Duluth, MN, 1954-56, Mounds View, MN, 1956-59. Kerlan Collection of Children's Literature volunteer at Minneapolis Children's Theatre; also appointed to the Board of the Friends of the Kerlan Collection. Presents workshops on writing fiction for children. *Member:* Society of Children's Book Writers and Illustrators, Thimble Collectors International.

■ Awards, Honors

Anna Cross Giblin Nonfiction Research Grant from Society of Children's Book Writers and Illustrators, 1992.

■ Writings

The Bermuda Triangle: Opposing Viewpoints, Greenhaven Press (St. Paul, MN), 1988, revised edition, 1995.
Bigfoot: Opposing Viewpoints, Greenhaven Press, 1989.
Unicorns: Opposing Viewpoints, Greenhaven Press, 1989.
Dealing with Death, Lucent Books (San Diego, CA), 1989.
El Dorado, Land of Gold: Opposing Viewpoints, Greenhaven Press, 1990.

Contributor to magazines and newspapers, including *Field and Stream, SAIL, Children's Magic Window, Jack and Jill, Children's Digest,* and *Life and Health.*

■ Work in Progress

A novel about a boy and an old lady who have a dream; three picture books, tentatively titled *The Sky Blue*

Barn, Kevin's Long Winter, and *Greenwood;* research for a history of carousels.

■ Sidelights

Norma Gaffron told *Something about the Author* (*SATA*): "Many years ago, when I was teaching third grade in Dodge Center, Minnesota, a little boy named Danny smiled up at me as I finished reading a story to the class. 'You could read to us all day, couldn't you, Miss Bondeson?' he asked. 'Yes,' I answered, because it was true. I loved to read, to share the joys of what can be found in books. I still love to read and to share what I learn. I rejoice whenever a child takes the time to write to me about one of my books.

"Most of the letters (and some are from adults) are in response to *The Bermuda Triangle.* This topic fascinated me, not only because of the myriad theories of why and how boats and planes and people have disappeared in this area, but because of the continued interest it holds for countless people. With my family, I had bareboat chartered and sailed in the region more than once. I admit I decided to do the book because I wanted a solid reason to read all about the area.

"The first version came out in 1988. Then, when some airplane wreckage was discovered off the coast of Florida in 1991, my publisher, Greenhaven Press, asked me to update my first book. I did so, adding the new information and getting the opportunity to do something most authors never have a chance to do: to rewrite and 'polish' parts of the book that I now felt were a bit rough.

"One of the wonderful things about writing nonfiction is the joy of the search. One source leads to another. Often one finds facts, theories, and anecdotes in unlikely places. For example, when I was on jury duty, a fellow juror saw what I was reading (an article on the Bermuda Triangle) and felt he could talk to me about the UFO he had seen. I listened, and in the course of our conversation he told me about a magazine called *Fate* that turned out to be another good source of information for my book.

"After writing four books in the 'Great Mysteries' series, and *Dealing with Death* for the 'Overview' series, I felt I really needed a change of pace. For the last few years I have been writing fiction. I am now writing the stories I want to write. Picture books are fun. Learning to think visually is a challenge, and so far I have encouraging letters from editors. As every writer knows, however, it is getting the contract that counts. My children's novels, too, are in the formative stage. As a child, I always dreamed that someday I would write a wonderful book of fiction. I still might.

"Writing to people, interviewing on the phone, as well as in person, takes me away from the word processor for a welcome break from the solitude of a writer's day. I also occasionally speak to groups of school children, usually sixth- to eighth-graders, the age group for which my published books are written, and each winter for the past few years I have been teaching an adult class in writing for children in Punta Gorda, Florida. My advice to all of them is: practice. Writing takes discipline. The more you write, the more you feel like writing. The less you write, the easier it is to become involved in other things. Pursue your dream. Persist. When my daughter Patty, our youngest child, left home, I turned her room into my office. Yet I continue to write—at the dining room table, on my lap while the clothes wash, and from notes scrawled on scraps of paper throughout the day."

■ For More Information See

PERIODICALS

School Library Journal, March, 1988, p. 207; March, 1990, p. 242; April, 1990, p. 129.

*   *   *

GILBERT, Barbara Snow 1954-

■ Personal

Born April 9, 1954, in Oklahoma City, OK; married; children: two daughters. *Education:* Colorado College, B.A. (magna cum laude), 1976; University of Texas at Austin, J.D. (with honors), 1979. *Hobbies and other interests:* Piano.

BARBARA SNOW GILBERT

■ Addresses

Home and Office—1121 Fenwick Pl., Oklahoma City, OK 73116. *Electronic mail*—hbsa.gilbert @ world net.att.net.

■ Career

Attorney, mediator, and writer. Lawyer in Oklahoma City, OK, 1980—; mediator, Oklahoma City, 1994—. Has worked on various political staffs, including those of the Speaker of the U.S. House of Representatives and the Governor of Oklahoma, and is a member of the mediation panel for the U.S. District Court for the Western District of Oklahoma. *Member:* Society of Children's Book Writers and Illustrators, Oklahoma Bar Association, Phi Beta Kappa, Kappa Alpha Theta.

■ Awards, Honors

Oklahoma Book Award, Oklahoma Center for the Book, 1997, Best Books of 1996, *School Library Journal,* and Books for the Teen Age, New York Public Library, 1997, all for *Stone Water.*

■ Writings

Stone Water, Front Street (Arden, NC), 1996.
Broken Chords, Front Street, 1997.

■ Work in Progress

Paper Trail (tentative title).

■ Sidelights

Attorney Barbara Snow Gilbert's first book for young adults, *Stone Water,* presents the agonizing dilemma teenaged Grant faces in desiring to help his grandfather die with dignity. The son of a busy lawyer father and a mother who is a judge, the protagonist wrestles with the moral and legal complications of whether or not to follow his beloved grandfather's wishes to assist with his suicide. Deborah Stevenson of the *Bulletin of the Center for Children's Books* praised Gilbert's "smooth and capable" writing and described *Stone Water* as an "intellectually challenging" look at a "compelling issue." Michael Cart, writing in *Booklist,* applauded Gilbert's "tackling the thorny subject ... with courage and candor" and predicted the book will "stimulate thought and invite discussion" on a topic of significant current importance. *Voice of Youth Advocates* contributor Janet R. Mura asserted: "This excellent, poignant book should be on all school and public library shelves."

■ Works Cited

Cart, Michael, review of *Stone Water, Booklist,* December 15, 1996, p. 721.
Mura, Janet R., review of *Stone Water, Voice of Youth Advocates,* April, 1997, pp. 28-29.

Stevenson, Deborah, review of *Stone Water, Bulletin of the Center for Children's Books,* January, 1997, p. 170.

■ For More Information See

PERIODICALS

Children's Book Review Service, November, 1996, p. 34.
Kirkus Reviews, October 15, 1996, p. 1532.
Publishers Weekly, November 18, 1996, p. 76.
School Library Journal, December, 1996, pp. 29, 136.

* * *

GILBERT, Suzie 1956-
(Elizabeth T. Vulture)

■ Personal

Born October 26, 1956, in Glen Cove, NY; daughter of Francis B., Jr. (an investment counselor) and Sandra (Still) Gilbert; married John Horgan (a writer), June 3, 1989; children: Mac, Skye. *Education:* Columbia University, B.A., 1983. *Politics:* Independent. *Religion:* None.

■ Addresses

Home and office—20 Cat Rock Rd., Garrison, NY 10524. *Electronic mail*—Gilbert @ highlands.com.

■ Career

Writer. Hudson Valley Raptor Center (sanctuary for birds of prey), member of board of directors and volunteer. Has previously worked in a variety of occupations, including photographer, travel agent, dog trainer, chicken and turkey raiser, and for the National Hockey League.

■ Awards, Honors

New York Press Association Award, best creative nonfiction column, second place, 1996; *Hawk Hill* was cited by *Smithsonian* as a notable book for children, 1996.

■ Writings

Hawk Hill, illustrated by Sylvia Long, Chronicle Books (San Francisco, CA), 1996.

Author of an environmental column, under pseudonym Elizabeth T. Vulture, for Taconic Media, Inc. Author of three optioned screenplays, not yet produced.

■ Sidelights

Suzie Gilbert told *Something about the Author (SATA):* "Now I'm a writer, but before that ... drifter? I've never had a career until a few years ago. Before that I just traveled around and moved from job to job. I worked for a travel agency in Florida, with a photographer in California and Hong Kong, waitressed and

Suzie Gilbert with Blondie.

painted boats in St. Croix, galloped racehorses on Long Island, raised free-range chickens and turkeys in Maine, and trained dogs, sold Ferraris, and worked for the National Hockey League in New York City. Now I have two children, so I'm not going anywhere.

"I wish I could say my writing started with an inspirational bolt from the blue, but truthfully, I had returned to college after a long absence and couldn't think of any other major. After I received my degree, I didn't write anything until years later, when I had a story I wanted to tell and thought it would be funniest as a screenplay. I bought a book called *How to Write a Screenplay,* managed to find an agent, and was then tortured by Hollywood for five years.

"I've always enjoyed birds and animals. In 1990 my husband and I moved out of New York City to the Hudson Valley, and I discovered a sanctuary for birds of prey. I think I had the equivalent of a religious conversion. My appreciation of birds has become an obsession. I think they are the most beautiful and magical creatures in the world, and I have become an activist for their protection, as well as the protection of all wildlife.

"I write our raptor center's newsletter, and *Hawk Hill* grew out of a paragraph I wrote about one of our injured hawks. I had never written anything for children before,

but I know that, during certain stages of their lives, some kids can have a special bond with an animal that they can't have with another person. They know that animals have a lot to tell them, and they instinctively know how to listen.

"I hope my book, and any future children's books I write, will encourage an appreciation of nature and the wild world. I have been taking birds from the raptor center to my book signings for *Hawk Hill,* and it is incredible to see the look of awe on children's faces the first time they see a bird of prey at close range. It gives me hope for the future of wildlife.

"Here's my advice to aspiring writers: if you really believe in your work, don't give up. *Hawk Hill* was rejected by fifty-two publishers. Several said, 'It's too long. If you cut it down to standard picture book length, we'll take it.' Of course, cutting it down would have destroyed the story. One publisher said, 'Obviously this woman knows nothing about writing a children's book.' This was true, but it didn't stop me. My other advice is: find someone else who believes in your work, and lean on them for support. I would never have survived the process (from writing to publication took five years) if my husband hadn't kept repeating, 'Something that good has to be published.'"

■ For More Information See

PERIODICALS

Booklist, November 1, 1996, p. 497.
Publishers Weekly, October 7, 1996, p. 74.
School Library Journal, November, 1996, p. 80.
Skipping Stones, March-April, 1997, p. 8.

* * *

GILDEN, Mel 1947-

■ Personal

Born in 1947.

■ Addresses

Office—c/o Pocket Books, Simon & Schuster Bldg., 1230 Avenue of the Americas, New York, NY 10020.

■ Career

Writer.

■ Writings

The Return of Captain Conquer, Houghton, 1986.
Pokey to the Rescue, illustrated by Dick Codor and Carol Bouman, Wanderer Books (New York City), 1987.
RV and the Haunted Garage, illustrated by Dick Codor and Carol Bouman, Wanderer Books, 1987.
Harry Newberry and the Raiders of the Red Drink, Holt, 1989.

Outer Space, and All That Junk, illustrated by Daniel LaVigne, Lippincott, 1989.

The Planetoid of Amazement, HarperCollins, 1991.

Boogeymen ("Star Trek: The Next Generation" series), Pocket Books, 1991.

The Starship Trap ("Star Trek" series), Pocket Books, 1993.

The Jungle Book: A Novelization (based on script by Stephen Sommers and the novel by Rudyard Kipling), HarperPaperbacks, 1994.

The Pet ("Star Trek: Deep Space Nine" series), Pocket Books, 1994.

The Pumpkins of Time (sequel to *Outer Space, and All That Junk*), Browndeer, 1994.

My Brother Blubb, Pocket Books, 1994.

Blubb and the Chocolate Treasure, Pocket Books, 1995.

Blubb and the Amazing Morphing Machine, Pocket Books, 1996.

"FIFTH GRADE MONSTERS" SERIES

M Is for Monster, illustrated by John Pierard, Avon, 1987.

Born to Howl, Avon, 1987.

The Pet of Frankenstein, Avon, 1988.

Z Is for Zombie, Avon, 1988.

Monster Mashers, Avon, 1989.

Things That Go Bark in the Park, Avon, 1989.

Yuckers!, Avon, 1989.

The Monster in Creeps Head Bay, Avon, 1990.

How to Be a Vampire in One Easy Lesson, illustrated by John Pierard, Avon, 1990.

Island of the Weird, Avon, 1990.

Werewolf, Come Home, Avon, 1990.

Monster Boy, Avon, 1991.

Troll Patrol, Avon, 1991.

The Secret of Dinosaur Bog, Avon, 1991.

"ZOOT MARLOWE" SERIES

Surfing Samurai Robots, Lynx Press (New York City), 1988.

Hawaiian U.F.O. Aliens, Roc (New York City), 1991.

Tubular Android Superheroes, Roc, 1991.

"BEVERLY HILLS 90210" SERIES; NOVELIZATIONS OF TELEPLAYS; ALL PUBLISHED BY HARPERPAPERBACKS

Beverly Hills, 90210, 1991.

No Secrets, 1991.

'Tis the Season, 1992.

Which Way to the Beach?, 1992.

More than Words, 1993.

Summer Love, 1993.

Two Hearts, 1993.

Where the Boys Are, 1993.

Graduation Day, 1994.

College Bound, 1994.

"CYBERSURFERS" SERIES; WITH TED PEDERSEN

Pirates on the Internet, Price Stern Sloan (Los Angeles, CA), 1995.

Cyberspace Cowboy, Price Stern Sloan, 1995.

Ghost on the Net, Price Stern Sloan, 1996.

Cybercops and Flame Wars, Price Stern Sloan, 1996.

■ Sidelights

Mel Gilden's fiction spans a variety of genres. He has written novelizations of scripts from the television program *Beverly Hills 90210* and from the film *The Jungle Book,* adapted from Rudyard Kipling's classic children's books. He is best known, however, for the many science fiction and fantasy parodies he has published. In books such as *The Return of Captain Conquer, Outer Space, and All That Junk, M Is for Monster, Surfing Samurai Robots,* and *Pirates on the Internet,* Gilden has carved a niche for himself as an adult, children's, and young adult author. Critics compare his work to that of Daniel Pinkwater, Douglas Adams, and the Monty Python troupe of actors, and praise Gilden for his bizarre sense of fun. In *The Planetoid of Amazement,* for instance, the strangeness begins with a mother and father who used to work for superheroes. Their son, Rodney Congruent, wishes for his own adventure and follows bizarre instructions that he receives in the mail. "Just check your sense of reality at the door," wrote *School Library Journal* contributor Lyle Blake Smythers in an assessment of the book.

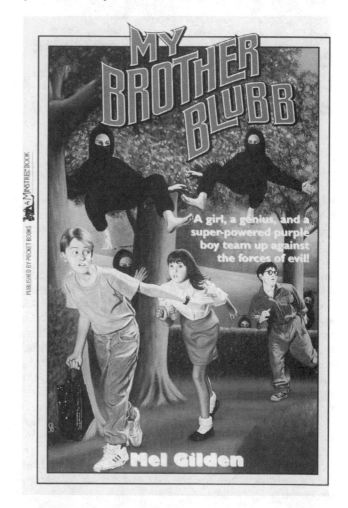

Genius Sidney Agenda creates a morphing blob called Blubb, who teams up with Daphne Trusk to save Sidney from the evil ninjas who have kidnapped him in Mel Gilden's fantasy novel.

In Gilden's sequel to *Outer Space, and All That Junk,*
Myron, Hugo, and Princess return to combat aliens
who use giant pumpkins as time-travel vehicles. (Cover
illustration by Ray Goudey.)

Gilden began his career as a novelist for young adults
with *The Return of Captain Conquer,* "a wonderfully
funny science fiction serial parody," according to Annette Curtis Klause in *School Library Journal,* "that
stays true to its inner logic throughout." It tells of how
Watson Congruent launches a search for his father,
Sherlock, who has disappeared along with the memora-
bilia of the famous TV show that he sells to discriminating fans. The author explores a similar theme in *Harry
Newberry and the Raiders of the Red Drink,* in which
young Harry tries to find the reason why his mother
(possibly the assistant of the comic book superheroine
Tuatara) has been kidnapped by the evil Bonnie Android. "Gilden reels out a series of madcap adventures,
one more wacky than the rest," stated *Booklist* contributor Barbara Elleman.

Gilden's *How to Be a Vampire in One Easy Lesson,* part
of his "Fifth Grade Monster" series intended for
younger readers, tells about an entire classroom consisting of unusual children that are described by *School*
Library Journal contributor Elaine E. Knight as
"straight out of Universal Studios." Featured characters
include C. D. Bitesky, a junior vampire; the Steins,
brother Frankie and sister Elisa; and Howie Wolfner, a
young man with a definite hair problem every full
moon. The class's adventures cover more than fifteen
volumes in the "Fifth Grade Monster" series and
emphasize how the word "monster" can be simply a
descriptive rather than a judgmental term. "Allusions to
classic monster films are everywhere," Knight concluded.

Outer Space, and All That Junk tells of how thirteen-
year-old Myron Duberville discovers that his eccentric
uncle Hugo, chairman of the board of Astronetics
Corporation, is not in fact hallucinating when he claims
that he has discovered aliens in the old junk that is
heaped on city streets. Hugo has collected and modified
an old 1960 Chevrolet Belvedere in order to speed the
extraterrestrial visitors on their way home. Opposed to
Hugo are Pinch and Grinley, who want to remove him
from the board of the company. Myron finds himself
unwillingly roped into cooperating with his uncle's
scheme in order to save both their lives. "Pinkwater
fans," declared a *Kirkus Reviews* contributor, "will revel
in this madcap adventure." In *The Pumpkins of Time,*
Gilden's sequel to *Outer Space, and All That Junk,*
Myron, Hugo, and Myron's cohort Princess return to
combat time-travelling aliens who use giant pumpkins
in their temporal journeys. "Gilden," Klause concluded
in a *School Library Journal* review of *Outer Space, and
All That Junk,* "is becoming a force in his own right."

■ Works Cited

Elleman, Barbara, review of *Harry Newberry and the
Raiders of the Red Drink, Booklist,* June 15, 1989, p.
1821.

Klause, Annette Curtis, review of *The Return of Captain
Conquer, School Library Journal,* September, 1986,
pp. 134-35.

Klause, Annette Curtis, review of *Outer Space, and All
That Junk, School Library Journal,* December,
1989, p. 100.

Knight, Elaine E., review of *How to Be a Vampire in
One Easy Lesson, School Library Journal,* January,
1991, p. 90.

Review of *Outer Space, and All That Junk, Kirkus
Reviews,* October 15, 1989, pp. 1529-30.

Smythers, Lyle Blake, review of *The Planetoid of
Amazement, School Library Journal,* November,
1991, p. 117.

■ For More Information See

PERIODICALS

Booklist, August, 1986, p. 1672; November 1, 1989, p.
563; December 1, 1989, p. 742; October 15, 1994,
p. 426.

Publishers Weekly, December 11, 1987, p. 65; May 11,
1992, p. 62; July 4, 1994, p. 64.

School Library Journal, May, 1989, p. 104; October,
1994, p. 122.

Voice of Youth Advocates, December, 1986, p. 237; October, 1989, p. 212; June, 1990, p. 115; December, 1991, p. 322; February, 1992, p. 382; April, 1992, p. 42; August, 1994, p. 145; December, 1994, p. 286.*

*   *   *

GUEVARA, Susan

■ Personal

Born in Walnut Creek, California; married, husband's name is Blair. *Education:* Graduate of the San Francisco Art Academy; studied painting at the Royal Academy of Fine Art in Belgium.

■ Addresses

Home—San Francisco, CA.

■ Career

Illustrator.

■ Awards, Honors

Pura Belpre award, Association for Library Services to Children (ALSC) and REFORMA (National Association to Promote Library Services to the Spanish-Speaking), 1995, for *Chato's Kitchen.*

■ Illustrator

Ned Miller, *Emmett's Snowball,* Holt (New York City), 1990.

Dian Curtis Regan, *The Class with the Summer Birthdays,* Holt, 1991.

Kathryn Lasky, *I Have an Aunt on Marlborough Street,* Macmillan (New York City), 1992.

Arthur A. Levine, *The Boardwalk Princess,* Morrow (New York City), 1993.

(With others) Margarita Robleda Moguel, *El Carrito de monchito,* Houghton (Boston), 1993.

Aileen Friedman, *The King's Commissioners,* Scholastic (New York City), 1994.

Virginia Haviland, reteller, *Favorite Fairy Tales Told in Italy,* Morrow, 1995.

Gary Soto, *Chato's Kitchen,* Putnam (New York City), 1995, published in Spanish as *Chato y su cena,* Putnam, 1997.

Marion Dane Bauer, *Jason's Bears,* Bridgewater Books (Mahwah, NJ), 1996.

Tony Johnston, *Isabel's House of Butterflies,* Sierra Club Books, 1997.

■ Sidelights

The illustrations of Latina artist Susan Guevara have graced works ranging from traditional tales rooted in the quiet serenity of the Italian countryside to modern stories set in the fast-paced, inner-city Hispanic culture of East Los Angeles. From Virginia Haviland's collected

"No hay problema, *homeboy*", se dijo Chato, y siguió a su nariz hasta la cerca.
Los ojos se le agrandaron al espiar por entre dos tablas a cinco ratones grises del color de las piedras del río.

Los bigotes le vibraron de placer, y de un salto se subió a la cerca para verlos mejor.

Susan Guevara's award-winning illustrations grace Gary Soto's tale of crafty mice who outwit hungry cats trying to lure them to a banquet where they are to be the main course. (From *Chato y su cena,* published in English as *Chato's Kitchen.*)

Favorite Fairy Tales Told in Italy to Chicano writer Gary Soto's award-winning *Chato's Kitchen,* Guevara has reflected and enhanced the vision of many authors of children's books. A student at both the San Francisco Art Academy and Belgium's Royal Academy of Fine Art, she has developed technical skills and creative interpretations that have been praised by reviewers and readers alike.

Guevara's first published illustration project was the 1990 picture book *Emmett's Snowball,* written by Ned Miller. In this story, a young boy begins to make a snowball; with the help of friends and neighbors his efforts eventually result in the largest snowball in the world. Guevara's watercolor and charcoal drawings, which use contrasting warm and cool colors to depict the warmth of friends and neighbors amid the chill of winter, were cited as an "ideal complement to [Miller's] slightly offbeat story" by Denise Anton Wright in *School Library Journal.* In the equally offbeat *The Boardwalk Princess,* Guevara intersperses Arthur A. Levine's lighthearted fairy tale about an evil witch, a magic potion, and a clever young girl with "humorously illustrated ... watercolors loaded with period detail," according to *Booklist* contributor Janice Del Negro. And, in the opinion of Kay Weisman in her review for *Booklist,* Guevara's "brightly colored acrylic paintings add humor" to Aileen Friedman's *The King's Commissioners,* a 1994 story about a king's frustration with simple mathematics.

In *Chato's Kitchen,* written by the acclaimed poet and children's author Gary Soto, a wily cat and his friends decide to lure the small *ratoncitos* (mice) of his barrio home to an untimely end by preparing a bounty of good food. Soon the scent of everything from enchiladas to frijoles fills the air, and the hungry cats extend an invitation to their intended main course, only to be outsmarted in return. Guevara's illustrations for this highly praised though controversial work, which earned her the first Pura Belpre award for illustration, features what a *Publishers Weekly* critic termed "wickedly funny, urban paints" and felines that the critic called "delicious send-ups of *barrio* characters."

In her acceptance speech for the Pura Belpre Award, as recorded in the *Journal of Youth Services in Libraries,* Guevara described the process of illustrating a children's book. "A good story gives me wings," the illustrator explained. "Wings to zoom me in, out, over the character's world.... Wings to carry me someplace worth going, someplace readers might wish to go." She cited as her main task "communicating the ideas and beliefs of a specific world" created by the author, her tools for communicating being "technique, palette, viewpoint, and subject matter." Immersing herself in the world of her characters, Guevara researches movies, books, settings, and other illustrations of the period or place where the story takes place. In the case of *Chato's Kitchen,* her immersion in the culture of the barrio even resulted in a vision: "Tijuana black velvet paintings" would be the inspiration for much of Guevara's work for the book.

■ Works Cited

Review of *Chato's Kitchen, Publishers Weekly,* February 6, 1995, pp. 84-85.

Del Negro, Janice, review of *The Boardwalk Princess, Booklist,* April 15, 1993, p. 1519.

Guevara, Susan, "Pura Belpre Award Acceptance Speech for Illustration 1995," *Journal of Youth Services in Libraries,* spring, 1997, pp. 273-75.

Weisman, Kay, review of *The King's Commissioners, Booklist,* February 15, 1995, p. 1092.

Wright, Denise Anton, review of *Emmett's Snowball, School Library Journal,* February, 1991, p. 73.

■ For More Information See

PERIODICALS

Booklist, January 15, 1993, p. 921.
Horn Book, September-October, 1995, pp. 591-92.
Publishers Weekly, May 3, 1993, p. 308; March 6, 1995, p. 70.
School Library Journal, March, 1993, p. 189; June, 1993, p. 98.

H

DONALD HALL

HALL, Donald (Andrew, Jr.) 1928-

■ Personal

Born September 20, 1928, in New Haven, CT; son of Donald Andrew (a businessman) and Lucy (Wells) Hall; married Kirby Thompson, September 13, 1952 (divorced, 1969); married Jane Kenyon (a poet), April 17, 1972 (died of leukemia, April 22, 1995); children: (first marriage) Andrew, Philippa. *Education:* Harvard University, B.A., 1951; Oxford University, B. Litt., 1953; attended Stanford University, 1953-54.

■ Addresses

Home—Eagle Pond Farm, Danbury, NH 03230. *Agent*—Gerald McCauley Agency, Inc., Box 844, Katonah, NY.

■ Career

Harvard University, Cambridge, MA, junior fellow in the Society of Fellows, 1954-57; University of Michigan, Ann Arbor, 1957-75, began as assistant professor, became professor of English; full-time freelance writer, 1975—. Broadcaster on several British Broadcasting Corporation radio programs, 1959-80; host of *Poets Talking,* a series of television interviews with poets, broadcast nationally on more than eighty stations, 1974-75; has given poetry readings at more than a thousand colleges, universities, schools, and community centers. *Member:* PEN, American Academy and Institute of Arts and Letters.

■ Awards, Honors

Newdigate Prize, Oxford University, 1952, for poem "Exile"; Lamont Poetry Prize, Academy of American Poets, 1955, for *Exiles and Marriages;* Edna St. Vincent Millay Award, Poetry Society of America, 1956; Guggenheim fellowship, 1963-64, 1972-73; *New York Times* Notable Children's Books citation, 1979, for *Ox-Cart Man;* Sarah Josepha Hale Award, 1983, for writings about New England; *Horn Book* Honor List, 1986, for *The Oxford Book of Children's Verse in America;* Lenore Marshall Prize, 1987, for *The Happy Man;* National Book Critics Circle Award for poetry, *Los Angeles Times* Book Prize in poetry, both 1989, both for *The One Day;* named poet Laureate of New Hampshire, 1984-89; 1995—.

■ Writings

FOR CHILDREN

Andrew the Lion Farmer, illustrated by Jane Miller, F. Watts, 1959, illustrated by Ann Reason, Methuen, 1961.

Riddle Rat, illustrated by Mort Gerberg, Warne, 1977.

Ox-Cart Man, illustrated by Barbara Cooney, Viking, 1979.

The Man Who Lived Alone, illustrated by Mary Azarian, Godine, 1984.

(Editor) _The Oxford Book of Children's Verse in America_, Oxford University Press, 1985.

The Farm Summer 1942, illustrated by Barry Moser, Dial, 1994.

I Am the Dog, I Am the Cat, illustrated by Moser, Dial, 1994.

Lucy's Christmas, illustrated by Michael McCurdy, Harcourt Brace, 1994.

Lucy's Summer, illustrated by McCurdy, Harcourt Brace, 1995.

When Willard Met Babe Ruth, illustrated by Moser, Harcourt Brace, 1996.

Old Home Day, illustrated by Emily Arnold McCully, Harcourt Brace, 1996.

The Milkman's Boy, illustrated by Greg Shed, Walker, 1997.

POETRY

Fantasy Poets No. 4, Fantasy Press, 1952.

Exile, Fantasy Press, 1952.

To the Loud Wind and Other Poems, Pegasus, 1955.

Exiles and Marriages, Viking, 1955.

The Dark Houses, Viking, 1958.

A Roof of Tiger Lilies, Viking, 1964.

The Alligator Bride: Poems, New and Selected, Harper, 1969.

The Yellow Room: Love Poems, Harper, 1971.

The Gentleman's Alphabet Book (limericks), illustrated by Harvey Kornberg, Dutton, 1972.

The Town of Hill, Godine, 1975.

A Blue Wing Tilts at the Edge of the Sea: Selected Poems, 1964-1974, Secker & Warburg, 1975.

Kicking the Leaves, Harper, 1978.

The Toy Bone, Boa Editions, 1979.

Brief Lives: Seven Epigrams, William B. Ewart, 1983.

The Twelve Seasons, Deerfield Press, 1983.

Great Day in the Cow's House, illustrated with photographs by T. S. Bronson, Ives Street Press, 1984.

The Happy Man, Random House, 1986.

The One Day, Ticknor & Fields, 1988.

Old and New Poems, Ticknor & Fields, 1990.

The Museum of Clear Ideas, Ticknor & Fields, 1993.

The Old Life, Houghton Mifflin, 1996.

Without, Houghton Mifflin, 1998.

Contributor of poetry to numerous periodicals, including the _New Yorker, New Republic, New Criterion, Kenyon Review, Iowa Review, Georgia Review, Ohio Review, Gettysburg Review, Nation_, and _Atlantic_.

PROSE

String Too Short to Be Saved: Recollections of Summers on a New England Farm (autobiography), illustrated by Mimi Korach, Viking, 1961, expanded ed., Godine, 1979.

Henry Moore: The Life and Work of a Great Sculptor, Harper, 1966.

As the Eye Moves: A Sculpture by Henry Moore, illustrated with photographs by David Finn, Abrams, 1970.

Marianne Moore: The Cage and the Animal, Pegasus, 1970.

The Pleasures of Poetry, Harper, 1971.

Writing Well, Little, Brown, 1974, 9th ed., HarperCollins, 1997.

(With others) _Playing Around: The Million-Dollar Infield Goes to Florida_, Little, Brown, 1974.

(With Dock Ellis) _Dock Ellis in the Country of Baseball_, Coward, 1976.

Goatfoot Milktongue Twinbird: Interviews, Essays, and Notes on Poetry, 1970-76, University of Michigan Press, 1978.

Remembering Poets: Reminiscences and Opinions—Dylan Thomas, Robert Frost, T. S. Eliot, Ezra Pound, Harper, 1978, revised edition published as _Their Ancient Glittering Eyes_, Ticknor & Fields, 1992.

To Keep Moving: Essays, 1959-1969, Hobart & William Smith Colleges Press, 1980.

To Read Literature, Holt, 1980.

The Weather for Poetry: Essays, Reviews, and Notes on Poetry, 1977-1981, University of Michigan Press, 1982.

Fathers Playing Catch with Sons: Essays on Sport (Mostly Baseball), North Point Press, 1985.

Seasons at Eagle Pond, illustrated by Thomas W. Nason, Ticknor & Fields, 1987.

Poetry and Ambition, University of Michigan Press, 1988.

Here at Eagle Pond, illustrated by Nason, Ticknor & Fields, 1990.

Life Work, Beacon Press, 1993.

Death to the Death of Poetry: Essays, Reviews, Notes, Interviews, University of Michigan Press, 1994.

Principle Products of Portugal: Prose Pieces, Beacon Press, 1995.

Contributor of short stories and articles to numerous periodicals, including the _New Yorker, Esquire, Atlantic, Playboy, Transatlantic Review_, and _American Scholar_.

PLAYS

An Evening's Frost, first produced in Ann Arbor, MI, produced Off-Broadway, 1965.

Bread and Roses, produced in Ann Arbor, MI, 1975.

Ragged Mountain Elegies, produced in Peterborough, NH, 1983, revised version published as _The Bone Ring_ (produced in New York at the Theater of the Open Eye, 1986), Story Line, 1987.

EDITOR

The Harvard Advocate Anthology, Twayne, 1950.

(With Robert Pack and Louis Simpson) _The New Poets of England and America_, Meridian Books, 1957.

Whittier, Dell, 1961.

Contemporary American Poetry, Penguin (England), 1962, Penguin (Baltimore), 1963.

(With Pack) _New Poets of England and America: Second Selection_, Meridian Books, 1962.

A Poetry Sampler, F. Watts, 1962.

(With Stephen Spender) _The Concise Encyclopedia of English and American Poets and Poetry_, Hawthorn, 1963.

(With Warren Taylor) _Poetry in English_, Macmillan, 1963.

A Choice of Whitman's Verse, Faber & Faber, 1968.

Man and Boy, F. Watts, 1968.

The Modern Stylists, Free Press, 1968.

American Poetry: An Introductory Anthology, Faber & Faber, 1969.

(With D. L. Emblem) *A Writer's Reader,* Little, Brown, 1969, 8th ed., Longman, 1997.

The Pleasures of Poetry, Harper, 1971.

The Oxford Book of American Literary Anecdotes, Oxford University Press, 1981.

To Read Literature: Fiction, Poetry, Drama, Holt, 1981, 3rd ed., Harcourt, 1992.

Claims for Poetry, University of Michigan Press, 1982.

To Read Poetry, Holt, 1982, revised ed. published as *To Read a Poem,* Harcourt, 1992.

The Contemporary Essay, St. Martin's, 1984, 3rd ed., 1995.

To Read Fiction, Holt, 1987.

(With Pat Corrington Wykes) *Anecdotes of Modern Art: From Rousseau to Warhol,* Oxford University Press, 1990.

Andrew Marvell, *The Essential Marvell,* Ecco, 1991.

Edwin Arlington Robinson, *The Essential Robinson,* Ecco, 1993.

■ Sidelights

Donald Hall is an award-winning poet and essayist who has written children's books that explore many of the same themes as his adult poetry and prose: a longing for past, more bucolic times, a reverence for nature, and an abiding love of baseball. Hall, who lives on the farm in New Hampshire that he visited in summers as a boy, is also noted for the anthologies he has edited and is a popular speaker and reader of his own poems.

Born in 1928, Hall grew up in Hamden, Connecticut, a child of the Great Depression of the 1930s, though not greatly affected by it. The Hall household was marked by a volatile father and a mother who was "steadier, maybe with more access to depths because there was less continual surface," as Hall explained in an essay for *Contemporary Authors Autobiography Series* (*CAAS*). "To her I owe my fires, to my father my tears. I owe them both for their reading." Reading of all sorts went on in the Hall household, and from an early age he learned to value books and reading. "Reading was *good,*" he recalled in *CAAS*. By age twelve, Hall had discovered the poet and short story writer Edgar Allan Poe: "I read Poe and my life changed," he remarked in *CAAS*. He soon set his course on becoming a writer and poet himself, rushing home from school to write in the late afternoon. Another strong influence in Hall's early years was his maternal great-grandfather's farm in New Hampshire, where he spent many summers. The pull of nature became a compulsion in him so strong that decades later he bought that same farm and settled there as a full-time writer and poet.

Hall attended Philipps Exeter Academy and despite early frustrations had his first poem published at age sixteen. He was a participant at the prestigious Bread Loaf Writer's Conference that same year. From Exeter, Hall went to Harvard University, where he was groomed in league with other poets-in-training such as Adrienne Rich, Robert Bly, Frank O'Hara, and John Ashbery; he also studied for a year there with Archibald MacLeish. Looking back in *CAAS,* Hall commented that as a result of those four years in college "some things increased: sophistication, competence, literary knowledge, cynicism. Nothing altered shape or direction; and when I went to Oxford for two years after Harvard, again nothing much altered." At Oxford University in England, Hall became one of the few Americans to win the coveted Newdigate contest for his poem "Exile."

Returning to the United States, Hall spent three years at Harvard and there assembled a book of poetry, *Exiles and Marriages.* In 1957 he took a position as assistant professor of English at the University of Michigan, where he remained until 1975. During those years he wrote volumes of poetry and essays, but Hall had always contemplated returning to the rural paradise that he had found as a youth in New Hampshire. Finally he was in a position to make this a reality, and when his grandmother, who owned Eagle Pond Farm, passed away at age 97, he bought the farm, left teaching, and moved there with his second wife, the poet Jane Kenyon. With one child in college at the time and another having not yet started, the move to New Hampshire was a risky one. Giving up the relative security of a tenured position at Michigan was a difficult decision, "but I did not hesitate, I did not doubt," Hall recalled in *CAAS.* "I panicked but I did not doubt." Since that time, Hall has been earning a living

In Hall's World War II-era story, nine-year-old Peter learns about life on a farm during his stay with his grandparents while his father is in the service. (From *The Farm Summer 1942,* **illustrated by Barry Moser.)**

from his writing and speaking, and children's books have become an increasingly important part of his work.

In 1977, two years after settling at Eagle Pond Farm, Hall published *Riddle Rat,* the story of a rat who tells riddles for the enjoyment and entertainment of his rodent siblings. Riddle Rat learns his riddling skills at school under the watchful eye of Aunt Agatha and from there takes off to dizzying heights of silliness: "What is the tiniest room in the whole World? A mushroom." A *Publishers Weekly* commentator called Hall's story and jokes "dazzling nonsense" and noted that the conundrums "are bound to be cherished by boy and girl readers."

Hall's next children's book established his name in the field. *Ox-Cart Man,* based on an oral fable that Hall also used as inspiration for a separate poem by the same name, is the distillation of a story told to Hall by an older relative when he was a boy. A fable on the cyclical nature of life, *Ox-Cart Man* tells of a New England farmer who, in October, loads his cart with the year's produce to be sold at market. The man sells not only the produce, but also the cart and ox. He stocks up on supplies the family will need for the year and heads home where he begins the process all over again that very night, working on a harness for a young ox while his family is busy sewing and spinning. The illustrator, Barbara Cooney, won a Caldecott Medal for her drawings in what a *Junior Bookshelf* reviewer dubbed a "very original book." Citing the "deceptively simple" text by Hall, the critic continued, "Here is a whole way of life set down and preserved in all its integrity." Zena Sutherland, assessing the book for the *Bulletin of the Center for Children's Books,* noted that "the text has the lulling quality of a bucolic idyll," while Kristi L. Thomas commented in *School Library Journal* that in *Ox-Cart Man,* the author expresses for readers "the

sense that work defines us all, connects us with our world, and we are all rewarded ... in measure of our effort." Mary M. Burns, writing in *Horn Book,* declared that *Ox-Cart Man* is "like a pastoral symphony translated into picture book format," and praised its "stunning combination of text and illustrations."

Hall also used the rural northeast as the setting for his next children's title, *The Man Who Lived Alone.* Having weathered a difficult childhood, the unnamed protagonist of this story settles in the rugged hills of New Hampshire, where he fashions an independent life for himself, growing old: "He kept his beard winter and summer now, because it was easier / and as he got older and older, it grew so long that it covered the darns on his shirt." A *Kirkus Reviews* critic, describing the book as a work that is not "for the faint of heart," observed that Hall "can string together the vagaries of a solitary rustic, from youth to old age, with a folk-ballad rightness that substitutes for a story." Anna Biagioni Hart commented in *School Library Journal,* "Here is a book as sturdy, genuine and beautiful as a Shaker bench." Hart further stated that Hall and the illustrator, Mary Azarian, fill the book with the "rhythm and temperament" of New England life. In an enthusiastic review in the *New York Times Book Review,* Thomas Powers mentioned the "sheer eloquence of economy" in Hall's prose and concluded that *The Man Who Lived Alone* "is a children's book only in the sense that it's the size and shape of a children's book and includes beautiful illustrations ... as children's books are supposed to. I think children will like it. I know I did."

More rural memories are served up in Hall's *The Farm Summer 1942.* In this book, young Peter must spend the summer with his grandparents on their New Hampshire farm when his father is sent off to war and his mother goes to New York. Here Peter learns of life on a farm

Lucy Wells enjoys an eventful summer on a New Hampshire farm in 1910. (From *Lucy's Summer,* written by Hall and illustrated by Michael McCurdy.)

Restless in Blackwater, Fred Bosell married a Lowell girl, and they moved to Ohio.

Once, when he was an old man, he came back for the Fourth of July. He umpired the baseball game between Blackwater's married and single men.

Hall depicts the history of a fictional New Hampshire village over a period of two hundred years in *Old Home Day*. (Illustrated by Emily Arnold McCully.)

and overcomes his initial homesickness to take part in the rhythm of the working day and the seasons. Deborah Stevenson, writing in the *Bulletin of the Center for Children's Books,* noted, "This is an evocative account of daily farm life, gently tidied through backward-looking eyes but still full of interesting detail." Stevenson also remarked that there was "little plot" to the story, and a *Publishers Weekly* critic commented on this as well, stating that the "tale of Peter's separation from his parents seems almost incidental to the collection of nostalgic details." *Horn Book*'s Nancy Vasilakis found that the "evocation of rural America ... brings to vibrant life a period of recent history," and that the illustrations by Barry Moser "add substance and intimacy to the story" to create a picture book that "is an excellent way to introduce a sense of history to children."

Hall and Moser have teamed up on two further titles, *I Am the Dog, I Am the Cat* and *When Willard Met Babe Ruth.* In the former book, Hall lets dogs and cats express their respective world- and self-views, as well as how they see each other, in such observations as, "Cat: The dog amuses me. He cares about what people think!" A *Kirkus Reviews* contributor, calling the book "a delight," found that "Hall's declarations are right on target." Roger Sutton of the *Bulletin of the Center for Children's Books* enjoyed the way "Hall's dialogue contrasts the ways and means of the two pets" as well as their "mock-majestic" statements. *Horn Book*'s Ann A. Flowers lauded both the text and the illustrations of the work and concluded, "The art perfectly accompanies a prose poem that faithfully describes our closest animal companions."

With *When Willard Met Babe Ruth,* Hall was able to indulge his love for baseball, about which he has written several adult books. Young Willard Babson gets to meet

Hall was able to indulge his love for baseball in *When Willard Met Babe Ruth,* the story of a young boy and a famous baseball player whose lives subtly intertwine. (Illustrated by Barry Moser.)

Babe Ruth when he and his father pull the honeymooning Ruth's car out of a New Hampshire ditch. For the next 20 years, the lives of the two subtly intertwine, though at a distance. At the end, Willard's daughter, who is appropriately named Ruth and who has inherited her father's admiration of the player, meets her baseball hero. A critic in *Kirkus Reviews* dubbed the book a "heartfelt piece of Americana from two old pros," while *Booklist* reviewer Bill Ott commented that "both words and pictures draw their energy from the sense of universality they bring to the experience of hero worship."

Hall's evocation of rural and agrarian America also appears in the companion volumes, *Lucy's Christmas* and *Lucy's Summer*. Set in 1909 and 1910 in a New Hampshire farming community, the "Lucy" books recount the seasonal preparations of families of that day. With *Lucy's Christmas,* plans are afoot for a holiday celebration; the scene is rendered in loving detail, allowing readers to "smell the kerosene from the lamps [and] sense the deepness of the woods," according to a writer for *Kirkus Reviews*. Elizabeth S. Watson in *Horn Book* called *Lucy's Christmas* a "charming look back at an early-twentieth-century Christmas," and Roger Sutton, reviewing the title in *Bulletin of the Center for Children's Books,* concluded that the "homespun setting" created by Hall and illustrator Michael McCurdy "makes for pleasant winter daydreams." Based loosely on the stories of Hall's mother's own New Hampshire childhood, the "Lucy" stories continued with *Lucy's Summer,* in which a millinery shop is set up in the front room of the family house and canning is also in progress. A *Publishers Weekly* critic praised Hall's "elegant yet homey imagery" and noted that, while the book does not offer much of a plot, "the fond recollections of each vignette resonate with certain charm." A *Quill and Quire* reviewer stated that this "is a book to pore over often, with text and pictures giving renewed pleasure with every reading."

Hall's nostalgia for the past is also expressed in his *Old Home Day* and *The Milkman's Boy*. The former story traces the history of Blackwater Pond, a small settlement in New Hampshire, from distant geologic times to its bicentennial celebration in 1999. A critic for *Kirkus Reviews* declared that the "lyrical" work acts as "a thorough history of the waxing, waning, and potential rebirth of America's small towns." A *Publishers Weekly* contributor averred that Hall's "eloquent" text and the watercolor graphics of award-winning illustrator Emily Arnold McCully together present "a distinctive, heartfelt portrait of a New Hampshire town." Hall's "soulful narrative," concluded the reviewer, "betrays his deep affection for this region." *The Milkman's Boy,* loosely based on Hall's own childhood, offers what a *Publishers Weekly* critic described as an "inviting glimpse" into the "evolving lives of a turn-of-the-century dairy family."

Hall continues to live and work on his New Hampshire farm, a site which serves as both his abode and an inspiration for much of his work. In addition to writing,

Hall traveled to India twice with his wife, and in 1993, the couple did a book tour together, as well as appearing on stage in a production of *Love Letters*. Tragically, in 1994, Jane Kenyon was diagnosed with leukemia. In the autumn of that year, she underwent a bone marrow transplant. The transplant was successful and the couple returned to New Hampshire in February, 1995, but by spring Kenyon relapsed and died on April 22. Since that time, Hall has appeared at several tributes to his late wife's work, written an afterword to a posthumous collection of Kenyon's poetry, *Otherwise: New and Selected Poems,* and has continued to produce books for children.

■ Works Cited

Burns, Mary M., review of *Ox-Cart Man, Horn Book,* February, 1982, pp. 44-45.

Review of *The Farm Summer 1942, Publishers Weekly,* April 11, 1994, p. 65.

Flowers, Ann A., review of *I Am the Dog, I Am the Cat, Horn Book,* September-October, 1994, p. 577.

Hall, Donald, *Riddle Rat,* Warne, 1977.

Hall, Donald, essay in *Contemporary Authors Autobiography Series,* Volume 7, Gale, 1988, pp. 55-67.

Hall, Donald, *The Man Who Lived Alone,* Godine, 1984.

Hall, Donald, *I Am the Dog, I Am the Cat,* Dial, 1994.

Hart, Anna Biagioni, review of *The Man Who Lived Alone, School Library Journal,* February, 1985, p. 64.

Review of *I Am the Dog, I Am the Cat, Kirkus Reviews,* August 15, 1994, p. 1129.

Review of *Lucy's Christmas, Kirkus Reviews,* October 15, 1994, pp. 1420-21.

Review of *Lucy's Summer, Publishers Weekly,* April 10, 1995, p. 62.

Review of *Lucy's Summer, Quill and Quire,* May, 1995, p. 51.

Review of *The Man Who Lived Alone, Kirkus Reviews,* November 1, 1984, p. 88.

Review of *The Milkman's Boy, Publishers Weekly,* July 14, 1997, p. 83.

Review of *Old Home Day, Kirkus Reviews,* July 15, 1996, p. 1048.

Review of *Old Home Day, Publishers Weekly,* August 12, 1996, p. 82.

Ott, Bill, review of *When Willard Met Babe Ruth, Booklist,* March 15, 1996, p. 1262.

Review of *Ox-Cart Man, Junior Bookshelf,* December, 1980, pp. 283-84.

Powers, Thomas, review of *The Man Who Lived Alone, New York Times Book Review,* January 13, 1985, p. 26.

Review of *Riddle Rat, Publishers Weekly,* June 13, 1977, p. 108.

Stevenson, Deborah, review of *The Farm Summer 1942, Bulletin of the Center for Children's Books,* July, 1994, p. 358.

Sutherland, Zena, review of *Ox-Cart Man, Bulletin of the Center for Children's Books,* February, 1980, p. 110.

Sutton, Roger, review of *I Am the Dog, I Am the Cat, Bulletin of the Center for Children's Books,* December, 1994, p. 129.

Sutton, Roger, review of *Lucy's Christmas, Bulletin of the Center for Children's Books,* October, 1994, pp. 48-49.

Thomas, Kristi L., review of *Ox-Cart Man, School Library Journal,* October, 1979, p. 140.

Vasilakis, Nancy, review of *The Farm Summer 1942, Horn Book,* July-August, 1994, p. 441.

Watson, Elizabeth S., review of *Lucy's Christmas, Horn Book,* November-December, 1994, p. 711.

Review of *When Willard Met Babe Ruth, Kirkus Reviews,* March 1, 1996, pp. 374-75.

■ For More Information See

BOOKS

Children's Books and Their Creators, edited by Anita Silvey, Houghton Mifflin, 1995.

Contemporary Literary Criticism, Gale, Volume 13, 1980, Volume 37, 1986, Volume 59, 1989.

Dictionary of Literary Biography, Volume 5: American Poets since World War II, Gale, 1980.

Fifth Book of Junior Authors and Illustrators, edited by Sally Holmes Holtze, H. W. Wilson, 1983.

PERIODICALS

Booklist, July 15, 1977, p. 1728; June 1, 1994, p. 1816; August, 1994, p. 2051; September 15, 1994, p. 132; September 1, 1996, p. 724.

Bulletin of the Center for Children's Books, March, 1985, pp. 126-27; June, 1996, p. 336; October, 1996, p. 61.

Emergency Librarian, March, 1995, p. 44; January, 1996, p. 55.

Horn Book, May, 1995, pp. 324-25; November, 1996, pp. 724-25.

Kirkus Reviews, July 15, 1997, p. 1111.

Los Angeles Times Book Review, August 4, 1996, p. 11.

School Library Journal, September, 1977, p. 108; September, 1994, p. 101; May, 1996, p. 113; October, 1996, p. 96.

—Sketch by J. Sydney Jones

* * *

HANFF, Helene 1916-1997

OBITUARY NOTICE—See index for *SATA* sketch: Born April 15, 1916, in Philadelphia, PA; died of pneumonia, April 9, 1997, in New York, NY. Screenwriter and author. Hanff dedicated her entire career to writing, first as a manuscript reader for Paramount Pictures and later as a television scriptwriter for Columbia Broadcasting System (CBS) and National Broadcasting Company (NBC). While establishing herself also as a prolific author of children's books, Hanff gained critical and popular acclaim for her 1970 work, *84, Charing Cross Road.* The book originated as a series of letters that Hanff exchanged with an antiquarian bookseller's chief buyer, Frank Doel, and other staff in London. In an effort to further educate herself by reading classic literature, Hanff ordered books from the store, located on Charing Cross Road, and often wrote of her opinions to Doel. She exchanged witty letters with Doel and the staff, and she also sent some goods to them during wartime rationing overseas. The correspondence continued for some twenty years until Doel's death. *84, Charing Cross Road* was later adapted for film, television, and the stage. Hanff ultimately visited the shop herself upon learning of Doel's passing. Her travels were the basis for her later book *The Duchess of Bloomsbury Street.* Hanff initially began pursuing a career in writing in 1938 after winning a Bureau of New Plays fellowship. Later, she gained experience by working with the Theater Guild. She wrote numerous plays, which were never produced, and later described this early part of her career in *Underfoot in Show Business.* Her television work, which flourished in the 1950s, included writing for *Hallmark Hall of Fame* and *The Adventures of Ellery Queen.* From 1978 to 1985 Hanff provided monthly radio broadcasts for the British Broadcasting Corporation's *Woman's Hour.* Her 1992 book *Letter from New York* contained excerpts from those broadcasts. Among her other books were history texts for young readers such as *The Day the Constitution Was Signed* and *The Movers and Shakers.*

OBITUARIES AND OTHER SOURCES:

PERIODICALS

Los Angeles Times, April 13, 1997, p. B3.
New York Times, April 11, 1997, p. B12.
Times (London), April 11, 1997.
Washington Post, April 13, 1997, p. B6.

* * *

HARPER, Jo 1932-

■ Personal

Born January 12, 1932, in Lockney, TX; daughter of J. B. (a farmer and investor) and Melba (Floyd) Harper; married James Lowell Hoggins (marriage ended); children: Josephine M. Harper, James Francis Lowell, De Agon Hoggins. *Education:* Texas Tech University, B.A., 1951, M.A., 1964; doctoral study at Pennsylvania State University, 1970-71; also attended Columbia University, 1977, Escuela Internacional Sampere, Madrid, Spain, 1974, Inter-American University, Saltillo, Mexico, 1978, Cuernavaca Language School, Cuernavaca, Mexico, 1979, and University of Texas at Austin.

■ Addresses

Home—1605 Huge Oaks, Houston, TX 77055. *Agent*—Renee Cho, McIntosh & Otis, Inc., 310 Madison Ave., New York, NY 10017.

■ Career

Librarian at a junior high school in Plainview, TX, 1951-52; first-grade teacher for Spanish-speaking chil-

JO HARPER

dren, Plainview, 1959-60; high school teacher of English, Spanish, and humanities, Plainview, 1964-68; Texas A & I University, Kingsville, instructor in English, 1968-70; Rockingham Community College, Wentworth, NC, instructor in English and Spanish, 1971-77; Armstrong State College, Savannah, GA, assistant professor of English and Spanish, and foreign student adviser, 1977-80; Texas Southern University, Houston, director of intensive English for foreign students, 1980-84; University of Houston, Houston, lecturer in English, 1984-96; Spring Branch Education Center, Houston, teacher of English to at-risk high school students, 1996—. Museum of Fine Arts, senior docent; Houston Arboretum, volunteer; storyteller at local elementary schools.

■ **Writings**

The Harper's Voices—Caves and Cowboys: Family Song Book, illustrated by Robert Boustany, photographs by George R. Jefferson, JCH Press, 1988.
Pals, Potions, and Pixies: Family Songbook, illustrated by Boustany, photographs by Jefferson, JCH Press, 1988.
Jalapeno Hal, illustrated by Jennifer Beck Harris, Simon & Schuster (New York City), 1993.
Outrageous, Bodacious Boliver Boggs!, illustrated by JoAnn Adinolfi, Simon & Schuster, 1996.

Deaf Smith: Scout, Spy, Texas Hero, illustrated by Virginia Rhoeder, Eakin Publications (Austin, TX), 1996.
Bigfoot Wallace: Texas Ranger and Mier Survivor, Eakin Publications, 1997.
The Legend of Mexicatl, Turtle Press (New York), 1998.
Prairie Dog Pioneers, Turtle Press, 1998.

Contributor to magazines and newspapers.

■ **Work in Progress**

John C. C. Hill, a biography of John Christopher Columbus Hill, the youngest member of the ill-fated Mier expedition from the Republic of Texas against Mexico.

■ **Sidelights**

Jo Harper told *Something about the Author* (*SATA*): "I grew up in the Texas Panhandle riding horses, eating jalapeno peppers, and spinning whoppers. I used to go with my grandfather to auctions and bid on cattle as they ran through the ring. When I was seventeen I got my first car and drove to Mexico City. Even though these are miles and years away from me now, the Panhandle and things Mexican still permeate my work. *Jalapeno Hal* and *Outrageous, Bodacious Boliver Boggs!* are Texas tall tales. *Deaf Smith, Bigfoot Wallace,* and *John C. C. Hill* are biographies of Texas heroes. *Caves and Cowboys* and *Pals, Potions, and Pixies* are printed in both English and Spanish. *The Legend of Mexicatl* (also in English and Spanish) is the story of the legendary founder of the Aztecs, and *Prairie Dog Pioneers* is based on a true story about going up the Cap Rock in a covered wagon and living in a dugout on the prairie."

■ **For More Information See**

PERIODICALS

Booklist, October 1, 1993, p. 352.
Children's Book Review Service, Spring, 1996, p. 134.
Horn Book Guide, Fall, 1996, p. 258.
Publishers Weekly, July 26, 1993, p. 70
School Library Journal, March, 1994, p. 198; April, 1996, p. 110.

* * *

HASTINGS, Beverly
See JAMES, Elizabeth

* * *

HAYNES, David 1955-

■ **Personal**

Born August 30, 1955, in St. Louis, MO. *Education:* Macalester College, B.A., 1977; Hamline University, M.A., 1989.

■ Addresses

Home—St. Paul, MN. *Office*—c/o Milkweed Editions, 430 1st Ave. N., Suite 400, Minneapolis, MN 55401.

■ Career

C. V. Mosby Publishing Co., St. Louis, MO, associate editor, 1978-81; schoolteacher in St. Paul, MN, 1981-93; writer, 1993—. Morehead State University, visiting scholar, 1994; Mankato State University, visiting writer, 1994; teacher at Writer's Center, Bethesda, MD, 1994-95, and Hamline University, 1995; Warren Wilson College M.F.A. Program for Writers, faculty member, spring, 1996, and 1997. National Board for Professional Teaching Standards, member of adolescent generalist standards committee, 1990—, teacher in residence, 1994—; Minnesota Humanities Commission, member of advisory committee, Teacher Institute, 1993-94. The Loft, member of board of directors, Regional Writing Center, 1985-89; New Rivers Press, member of board of directors, 1993—.

■ Awards, Honors

Fiction prize from *City Pages,* 1984, for the story "Taking Miss Kezee to the Polls"; winner of the Loft Mentor Series, 1985-86; fellowships from Cummington Community of the Arts, 1986-89, and Ragdale Foundation, 1988-96; winner of the Loft International Residency Series, 1989; winner of Regional Writers Contest, Lake Superior Contemporary Writers, 1989; awards from Virginia Center for the Creative Arts, 1989-95; Best Books for Young Adults, American Library Association, 1994, and Minnesota Voices Project Winner, New Rivers Press, both for *Right by My Side;* Minnesota State Arts Board fellowship, 1995; Haynes was selected as one of *Granta* magazine's Best of the Young American Novelists, 1996; Loft Career Initiative grant, 1996; Friends of American Writers Adult Literary Award for *Somebody Else's Mama.*

■ Writings

FOR YOUNG PEOPLE

Right by My Side (young adult novel), New Rivers Press, 1993.
Business as Usual (West 7th Wildcats 1), Milkweed, 1997.
The Gumma Wars (West 7th Wildcats 2), Milkweed, 1997.

OTHER

Somebody Else's Mama, Milkweed (Minneapolis, MN), 1995.
Heathens, New Rivers Press (Minneapolis, MN), 1996.
Live at Five, Milkweed, 1996.
All American Dream Dolls, Milkweed, 1997.

Contributor to anthologies, including "Breckenridge Hills, 63114" (essay), *Imagining Home,* University of Minnesota Press (Minneapolis), 1995. Also contributor of short stories to periodicals, including *Other Voices, Glimmer Train,* and *Colors.*

■ Adaptations

Two of Haynes's short stories were chosen to be recorded for the "Selected Shorts" program on National Public Radio.

■ Sidelights

An African American short story writer and novelist, David Haynes writes of middle-class, midwestern, blue-collar families with black, not white, faces. "I don't tell the popular narratives, the commercial narratives, that one is supposed to tell as an African American writer, and there is a price to be paid for that," Haynes told Nathalie Op De Beeck in an interview for *Publishers Weekly.* Major publishing houses have urged him to add sex and violence to make his work more marketable, but he has continued to write about ordinary low-income black and white families, rooted in reality but imbued with universal ambitions and hopes.

In David Haynes's second "West 7th Wildcat" story, eleven-year-old Lu struggles to appease his two grandmothers when their visit becomes a war for his attention. (Cover illustration by David Zinn.)

In what a *Kirkus Reviews* critic described as "a funny and cynical coming-of-age novel," Haynes's first book, *Right by My Side,* tells of high school sophomore Marshall Field Finney, whose mother has left him and his father Sam, the local landfill manager. Living in a crackerbox housing development for blacks outside St. Louis, Marshall has ample cause to protest "unfairness," but his case is further aggravated when his lonely father takes up with a series of girlfriends and an overzealous teacher tries to recruit Marshall and his friends as community activists. A *Publishers Weekly* reviewer praised Haynes's "engaging character who tackles fundamental issues such as love, family, and benevolence." In his *Booklist* review, John Mort wrote, "What sets this novel apart is Marshall himself, his kindness, his sanity in an insane world," but above all, Mort goes on to say, it is Marshall's "voice" that is reminiscent of Holden Caulfield's. A *Kirkus Reviews* critic concluded that Haynes's "artful fiction" should appeal to many, "including the savvy YA crowd," particularly for its "gentle mockery of victimology and its smart-mouthed humor." A reviewer for *School Library Journal,* Virginia Ryder, like others, predicted that "Teens will adore this book." Indeed, *Right by My Side* was honored by the American Library Association as one of the Best Books for Young Adults of 1994.

Haynes himself never considered his first book to be young adult literature. Three years after the book was published, in 1996, he told Op de Beeck: "I thought *Right by My Side* was an adult book, and I still think it's an adult book. I always thought the book was about the father, Sam, and when I was writing it that was my intention.... But of course everybody has their own take, and a lot of people happened to resonate with the story of the teenager." In fact, rather than Sam or the angry young protagonist, the author admitted that he identified more with the "gung ho" teacher who tried to inspire her students to action outside the classroom. Haynes is not married and has no children himself, but his years as a classroom teacher, as Op de Beeck points out, "qualify him as an astute chronicler of wisecracking kids and their aggrieved parents."

In his two juvenile books in the West 7th Wildcats series, Haynes directs his tales to an upper elementary audience. *Business as Usual* recounts the hard work and challenges a sixth grade class faces as they focus on how to run a business in their economics unit. In *The Gumma Wars,* eleven-year-old Lu visits museums and stores in twin cities St. Paul and Minneapolis with two grandmothers vying for his attention.

Haynes has also written other novels for adults that feature memorable characters and deal with themes of identity, complex family relationships, and class issues. He has been especially praised for his vivid female characters, notably the feisty Miss Kezee of *Somebody Else's Mama,* and for the humor that pervades all his writing.

■ Works Cited

Mort, John, review of *Right by My Side, Booklist,* February 15, 1993, p. 1037.

Op de Beeck, Nathalie, "David Haynes: A Twin Cities Maverick," *Publishers Weekly,* April 22, 1996, pp. 48-49.

Review of *Right by My Side, Kirkus Reviews,* February 15, 1993, p. 170.

Review of *Right by My Side, Publishers Weekly,* March 1, 1993, p. 53.

Ryder, Virginia, review of *Right by My Side, School Library Journal,* December, 1993, p. 149.

■ For More Information See

PERIODICALS

Los Angeles Times Book Review, September 24, 1995, p. 6.

New York Times Book Review, June 18, 1995, p. 21; May 5, 1996, p. 22.

Publishers Weekly, April 10, 1995, p. 55; February 19, 1996, p. 205; March 18, 1996, p. 60; April 22, 1996, pp. 48-49.

*   *   *

HENEGHAN, James 1930- (B. J. Bond)

■ Personal

Born October 7, 1930, in Liverpool, England; emigrated to Canada in 1957, became a citizen in 1963; son of John (a civil engineer) and Ann (Fitzgerald) Heneghan; children: Ann, Robert, John, Leah. *Education:* Simon Fraser University, British Columbia, B.A., 1971. *Hobbies and other interests:* Jogging, reading, fishing, music, movies, and the theater.

■ Career

Writer and educator. *Member:* West End Writers Society, Canadian Society of Children's Authors, Illustrators, and Performers.

■ Writings

(With Bruce McBay) *Puffin Rock,* illustrated by Vesna Krstanovich, Book Society of Canada, 1980.

(With Bruce McBay, under joint pseudonym B. J. Bond) *Goodbye, Carleton High,* Scholastic-TAB, 1983.

Promises to Come, Overlea House, 1988.

The Case of the Marmalade Cat, illustrated by Carol Wakefield, Scholastic Canada (Richmond Hill, Ont.), 1991.

Blue, Scholastic Canada, 1991.

The Trail of the Chocolate Thief, Scholastic Canada, 1993.

Torn Away: A Novel, Viking, 1994.

The Mystery of the Golden Ring, Scholastic Canada, 1995.

The Case of the Blue Raccoon, Scholastic Canada, 1996.

Wish Me Luck, Farrar, Straus, and Giroux, 1997.

JAMES HENEGHAN

Contributor to periodicals, including *B. C. Runner.*

■ Adaptations

A sound recording of *Torn Away* was produced by CNIB in 1994.

■ Sidelights

An author who also teaches high school and has worked as a police officer in his adopted home of Vancouver, British Columbia, Heneghan is credited with bringing a fresh approach to the genre novel for young adults and primary graders. Addressing such literature as the mystery, the YA novel, the war story, and the science fiction adventure, he writes comic fiction and action-filled stories for younger readers and deeper, more thoughtful books for teenagers; several of his books are set in British Columbia and one begins in his hometown of Liverpool, England. In his works for young adults, the author introduces more realistic, and difficult, problems—such as abandonment and feeling rage—than those resolved by characters in his works for younger readers. In addition, Heneghan's novels often feature episodes critics find are compelling in their fast-paced action and suspense without sacrificing subtleties of characterization or setting.

Heneghan is perhaps best known as the author of *Torn Away,* a young adult novel that has the conflict between Catholics and Protestants in contemporary Belfast as its point of reference. In this work, thirteen-year-old Declan is forced to emigrate to Canada to live with his Uncle Matthew and his family in British Columbia after his father, mother, and sister are killed by the Protestants in war-torn Northern Ireland. Once in British Columbia, Declan, who is intent on going back to Belfast to join the IRA and revenge his family, attempts to smuggle himself on to a plane bound for Scotland before he is brought back to his uncle. Declan gradually warms to his kind relatives and to the beauty of the landscape of British Columbia. After learning that his father was not a hero, but rather an informer who was attempting to protect his wife and unborn child, the boy realizes that violence is a dead end; at the end of the novel, Declan decides to remain in Canada. Reviewers singled out the effectiveness of the author's portrayal of Declan's rage, and the slow evolution of his feelings toward his new family. "What will hold readers," noted Roger Sutton of *Bulletin of the Center for Children's Books,* "is the vivid drama of the scenes in Belfast and Declan's halting, grudging acceptance of Matthew's love.... [We] get a sobering, immediate picture of a country and civil war that would quickly make kids grow up fast." *Booklist* reviewer Hazel Rochman said, "Readers will feel for the desperate boy nearly destroyed by civil war. The best scenes evoke his haunting memories of guns and firebombs and contrast those nightmares with the rich silence of the wilderness and the kindness of community." Barbara Greenwood of *Quill and Quire* called *Torn Away* a "powerful story" and concluded, "Each character, while representing an idea Declan must ponder, is also fully realized and interesting. The author's skillful use of symbols ... to reveal Declan's changing feelings gives depth to the fast-paced and engrossing action."

Blue is a young adult novel that *Quill and Quire* reviewer Jeffrey Canton said "is most certainly innovative" and which "adds a fantastic twist to the traditional boy and dog story." In this work, Ted, an unhappy boy who longs to escape from his home life, is befriended by a blue sheepdog who has crash-landed on earth from outer space and utilizes his telepathic powers to win the boy's affections. Along the way to the story's happy ending, Ted must deal with the death of a beloved pet, handle failure when he does not make the school basketball team, and come to terms with his mother's burgeoning relationship with the owner of their farm. Heneghan returns to the Liverpool of his childhood in *Wish Me Luck,* a young adult novel that revolves around the relationship of twelve-year-old Jamie Monaghan with the new kid in town, Tom Bleeker, the somewhat shady character who is his next-door neighbor. Based on the true story of the sinking of a passenger liner by a German U-boat during World War II, *Wish Me Luck* dramatizes the real-life transportation of British children to Canada when the country became the target of Axis bombs during the war. Although the ocean liner on which the boys are traveling is torpedoed, they are rescued at the end of the story. A reviewer in

Heneghan's historical World War II novel follows Jamie Monaghan, whose parents send him from England to Canada aboard a ship that is doomed to be attacked by a German U-boat. (Cover illustration by Paul Lee.)

Publishers Weekly noted, "Heneghan pulls off a rare achievement: he creates historical fiction that does not depend on historical incidents—even so dramatic an incident as the WW II torpedoing of an ocean liner—for its tension, momentum or purpose." The reviewer concluded, "Because the characters seem so real, the reader shares their shock and horror and breathes in relief at their rescue. Eye-opening and utterly gripping."

With *The Case of the Marmalade Cat* and *The Trail of the Chocolate Thief,* Heneghan created two comic mysteries for readers in the early primary grades featuring Clarice O'Brien, a girl detective who some critics compare to the protagonist of Louise Fitzhugh's *Harriet the Spy*. Along with two of her pals, Sadie and Brick, Clarice sets up a detective agency in Vancouver to solve the small mysteries of their friends and acquaintances, such as missing cats and stolen toys. Writing in *Canadian Materials* about *The Case of the Marmalade Cat,* David H. Elias maintained, "For seven-to-ten year-olds, this book may provide a simple episodic kind of entertainment." *The Trail of the Chocolate Thief* includes a checklist of all the thefts from Sadie's notebook.

Quill and Quire reviewer Ken Setterington predicted, "Young readers will enjoy trying to solve the case along with the detectives.... Once again, Heneghan has created a mystery for middle readers with a fast pace, realistic dialogue, and lots of laughs."

Heneghan once commented that before he turned to writing, "it was photography. I took many pictures of bridges. I don't know why except that they appealed to the eye and heart. Vancouver's Lions Gate Bridge, for example, I shot with a four-by-five Linhof on panchromatic film, using a rising front and red filter on a clear, cold day. The steel girders rise up from the icy waters of Burrard Inlet in silver arches, leaping like salmon into a black sky.

"Perhaps writing is another kind of bridge, a bridge between the writer and his audience, where the writer's perception and vision are used to catch those nuances of light and shade that are a portrait of the human heart."

Heneghan once told *Something about the Author* (*SATA*): "Writing for teenagers started as a joint idea when a colleague and I saw a need for high-interest stories for our own English students who were reading at a low level and who needed motivation to read. Our early stories, unpublished, tried to include characters and settings and situations our students could recognize and identify with.

"I enjoy writing for children, but still regard myself as a beginner. One thing I *have* discovered is that children are tough critics—they know what they like, and only your best will do."

■ Works Cited

Canton, Jeffrey, review of *Blue, Quill and Quire,* February, 1992, p. 34.

Elias, David H., review of *The Case of the Marmalade Cat, Canadian Materials,* September, 1991, p. 220.

Greenwood, Barbara, review of *Torn Away, Quill & Quire,* April, 1994, p. 39.

Rochman, Hazel, review of *Torn Away, Booklist,* February 15, 1994, p. 1072.

Setterington, Ken, review of *The Trail of the Chocolate Thief, Quill & Quire,* October, 1993, p. 41.

Sutton, Roger, review of *Torn Away, Bulletin of the Center for Children's Books,* February, 1994, p. 189.

Review of *Wish Me Luck, Publishers Weekly,* May 5, 1997, p. 211.

■ For More Information See

PERIODICALS

Books in Canada, February, 1980, p. 23.

Canadian Children's Literature, no. 17, 1980, p. 77; fall, 1994, p. 76; September, 1996, p. 65.

Emergency Librarian, March, 1992, p. 58; September, 1994, p. 55.

In Review, January, 1980, p. 41.

Kirkus Reviews, April 15, 1994, p. 557.*

HEWITSON, Jennifer 1961-

■ Personal

Born January 8, 1961, in Riverside, CA; daughter of John (a teacher) and Diane (a teacher) Hewitson. *Education:* Attended Palomar Junior College, 1980-82; California State University, Long Beach, B.F.A., 1984. *Hobbies and other interests:* Traveling, reading, and gardening.

■ Addresses

Office—P.O. Box 231477, Encinitas, CA 92023-1477.

■ Career

Illustrator.

■ Awards, Honors

Communication Arts Annual Award of Excellence, 1987, 1992, 1993; Print Regional Design Award of Excellence, 1987, 1988, 1990, 1991, 1992, 1993, 1997, for various illustrations, encompassing advertising, editorial, packaging, self-promotional materials and personal logos; Merit Award, *Studio* Magazine Annual, Silver Award, Western Art Directors Club, and Don Belding Award, Ad Club of Los Angeles, all 1992.

■ Illustrator

Dorothy and Thomas Hoobler, *A Promise at the Alamo: The Story of a Texas Girl,* Silver-Burdett, 1992.
Evelyn Wolfson, *From Earth to Beyond the Sky: Native American Medicine,* Houghton Mifflin, 1993.
(Reteller) Jacqueline Dembar Greene, *Manabozho's Gifts: Three Chippewa Tales,* Houghton Mifflin, 1994.
Rachel Taft Dixon, *The Witch's Ring,* Hyperion, 1994.
(Compiler) Jane Yolen, *Mother Earth, Father Sky: Poems of Our Planet,* Boyds Mills Press, 1996.
Minfong Ho and Saphan Ros, *Brother Rabbit: A Cambodian Tale,* Lothrop, Lee & Shepard, 1997.

■ Sidelights

Jennifer Hewitson told *SATA:* "I've been drawing all my life and feel lucky to be making my living through my art. My illustrations are used in a variety of forums from editorial and publishing to advertising and packaging— all very different but always about communication of ideas.

I am inspired most by nature and try to foster relationships with environmental organizations and use my art to help them promote appreciation and preservation of our world. The book *Mother Earth, Father Sky* was a real joy to illustrate as it is about the celebration of our planet and therefore close to my heart.

"I love to travel and have managed to take wonderful trips which have inspired and educated me. I've used

JENNIFER HEWITSON

these opportunities to get photo reference shots from the wildlife of Africa to religious ceremonies in Indonesia. When I'm not traveling or drawing I do enjoy gardening, long walks with my dog, and working out at the gym to keep the cobwebs out after those long hours at my table."

Among the books Hewitson has illustrated for children is *Brother Rabbit.* Written by Minfong Ho and Saphan Ros, *Brother Rabbit* is the story of a wily rabbit who plays tricks on everyone around him. He cajoles an elephant into freeing him from a tree stump, tricks a woman out of her basket of bananas, and has a battle of wits with a cranky crocodile. Hewitson's watercolor and scratchboard illustrations, which have been compared to batik textiles and wood cuts, "manage to be both rustic and refreshingly sophisticated, decorative and dynamic," according to a *Publishers Weekly* reviewer. *School Library Journal* contributor Ellen Fader applauded Hewitson's ability to capture the details of village life in Cambodia in her bold single- and double-page spreads that "look great at a distance."

■ Works Cited

Review of *Brother Rabbit, Publishers Weekly,* April 14, 1997, p. 75.
Fader, Ellen, review of *Brother Rabbit, School Library Journal,* May, 1997, p. 120.

■ For More Information See

PERIODICALS

Bulletin of the Center for Children's Books, January, 1994, p. 171.
Horn Book, May-June, 1997, p. 333.
Kirkus Reviews, November 15, 1993, p. 1470.

* * *

HOFFMAN, Mary (Margaret) 1945-
(Mary Lassiter)

■ Personal

Born April 20, 1945, in Eastleigh, Hampshire, England; daughter of Origen Herman (a railway telecommunications inspector) and Ivegh (a homemaker; maiden name, Lassiter) Hoffman; married Stephen James Barber (a social worker), December 22, 1972; children: Sarah Rhiannon, Rebecca Imogen, Jessica Rowena. *Education:* Newham College, Cambridge, B.A., 1967; University College, London, postgraduate diploma in linguistics, 1970. *Politics:* Disillusioned Labour voter/pro animal rights. *Religion:* Anglo-Catholic. *Hobbies and other interests:* Choral singing, cooking, cats, doing the *Times* crossword, old roses.

■ Addresses

Home—28 Crouch Hall Rd., London N8 8HJ, England. *Agent*—Pat White, Rogers, Coleridge & White, 20 Powis Mews, London W11, England.

■ Career

Journalist and author. The Open University, Milton Keynes, England, lecturer in continuing education, 1975-80; reading consultant for British Broadcasting Corporation school television series *Look and Read,* 1977-95; Campaigner for libraries. *Member:* Society of Authors, National Union of Journalists, International Board on Books for Young People (Hans Christian Anderson Medal panelist, 1981, 1987), London Zoological Society (fellow).

■ Awards, Honors

Shortlist, Smarties Book Prize, British Book Trust, for *Nancy No-Size,* 1987, and *Henry's Baby,* 1993; commended, Kate Greenaway Medal, 1991, for *Amazing Grace;* shortlist, Kurt Maschler Award, British Book Trust, 1995, for *Song of the Earth.*

■ Writings

FOR CHILDREN; FICTION

White Magic, Rex Collings (London), 1975.
(With Chris Callery) *Buttercup Buskers' Rainy Day,* illustrated by Margaret Chamberlain, Heinemann (London), 1982.
(With Willis Hall) *The Return of the Antelope,* illustrated by Faith Jacques, Heinemann, 1985.
Beware, Princess!, illustrated by Chris Riddell, Heinemann, 1986.
The Second-Hand Ghost, illustrated by Eileen Browne, MMB/Deutsch, 1986.
King of the Castle, illustrated by Alan Marks, Hamish Hamilton (London), 1986.
A Fine Picnic, illustrated by Leon Baxter, Silver Burdett (Chicago), 1986.
Animal Hide and Seek, illustrated by Baxter, Macdonald, 1986, Silver Burdett, 1987.
The Perfect Pet, illustrated by Baxter, Silver Burdett, 1986.
Clothes for Sale, illustrated by Baxter, Silver Burdett, 1986.
Dracula's Daughter, illustrated by Riddell, Heinemann, 1986.
Nancy No-Size, illustrated by Jennifer Northway, Oxford University Press, 1987.
Specially Sarah, illustrated by Joanna Carey, Methuen (London), 1987.
My Grandma Has Black Hair, illustrated by Joanna Burroughes, Dial (New York), 1988.
Catwalk, illustrated by J. Burroughes, Methuen, 1989.
All about Lucy, illustrated by J. Carey, Methuen, 1989.
Min's First Jump, illustrated by John Rogan, Hamish Hamilton, 1989.
Mermaid and Chips, illustrated by Bernice McMullen, Heinemann, 1989.
Dog Powder, illustrated by Paul Warren, Heinemann, 1989.
Just Jack, illustrated by Carey, Methuen, 1990.
(Editor) *Ip, Dip, Sky Blue,* Collins, 1990.
Leon's Lucky Lunchbreak, illustrated by Polly Noakes, Dent 1991.
The Babies' Hotel, Dent, 1991.
Amazing Grace, illustrated by Caroline Binch, Dial, 1991.
Max in the Jungle, illustrated by Rogan, Hamish Hamilton, 1991.
The Ghost Menagerie, illustrated by Laura L. Seeley, Orchard Books (London), 1993, republished as *The Four-Legged Ghosts,* Dial, 1994.
Henry's Baby, illustrated by Susan Winter, Dorling Kindersley, 1993.
Cyril MC, Viking, 1993.
Bump in the Night, Collins, 1993.
Grace and Family, illustrated by Caroline Binch, Frances Lincoln, 1995, published in the United States as *Boundless Grace,* Dial, 1995.
Trace in Space, Hodder & Stoughton, 1995.
A Vanishing Tail, Orchard Books, 1996.
Quantum Squeak, Orchard Books, 1996.
Special Powers, Hodder & Stoughton, 1997.
A First Bible Storybook, illustrated by Julie Downing, Dorling Kindersley, 1997.
An Angel Just Like Me, illustrated by Cornelius Van Wright and Ying-Hwa Hu, Dial, 1997.
(Editor) *Stacks of Stories,* Hodder, 1997.
Comet, Orchard Books, 1997.
A Twist in the Tail, illustrated by Jan Ormerod, Frances Lincoln, 1998.

Several of Hoffman's books have been translated into Spanish.

FOR CHILDREN; NONFICTION

Whales and Sharks, Brimax, 1986.
(With Trevor Weston) *Dangerous Animals,* Brimax, 1986.
Amazing Mammals Kit, Dorling Kindersley, 1993.
Song of the Earth, illustrated by Jane Ray, Orion, 1995, published in the United States as *Earth, Fire, Water, Air,* Dutton, 1995.
Sun, Moon, and Stars, illustrated by Ray, Orion, 1998, Dutton, 1998.

FOR CHILDREN; "ANIMALS IN THE WILD" SERIES

Tiger, Belitha/Windward, 1983, Raintree, 1984, rev. ed., Belitha/Windward, 1988.
Monkey, Belitha/Windward, 1983, Raintree, 1985, rev. ed., Belitha/Windward, 1988.
Elephant, Belitha/Windward, 1983, Raintree, 1985, rev. ed., Belitha/Windward, 1988.
Panda, Belitha/Windward, 1983, Raintree, 1985, rev. ed., Belitha/Windward, 1988.
Lion, Raintree, 1985.
Zebra, Raintree, 1985.
Hippopotamus, Raintree, 1985.
Gorilla, Raintree, 1985.
Wild Cat, Raintree, 1986.
Giraffe, Raintree, 1986.
Snake, Raintree, 1986.
Bear, Raintree, 1986.
Wild Dog, Raintree, 1987.
Seal, Raintree, 1987.
Antelope, Raintree, 1987.
Bird of Prey, Raintree, 1987.

FOR ADULTS

Reading, Writing, and Relevance, Hodder & Stoughton (London), 1976.
(Under name Mary Lassiter) *Our Names, Our Selves,* Heinemann, 1983.

Contributor to *Times Educational Supplement.* Reviewer for *School Librarian, Guardian, Telegraph* and other periodicals. Author of monthly column in *Mother* (magazine), 1984-87.

■ **Work in Progress**

Women of Camelot, illustrated by Christina Balit; *Three Wise Women; Clever Katya; Virtual Friend.*

■ **Sidelights**

Mary Hoffman is the prolific author of a number of books for elementary-grade readers that take a new slant on interpersonal relationships, many of which have been depicted in stereotypical fashion in books for young children. Confronting such issues as sexism, racism, and discrimination against the elderly by portraying non-traditional characters leading fulfilling lives and coping with prejudice and discrimination in a positive manner, Hoffman is credited with adding a level of sophistication to books for preschool children and beginning readers alike. The bubbly and enthusiastic protagonist of her best-selling *Amazing Grace* provides an example that encourages young children to think beyond stereotypical roles and boundaries in both Hoffman's native Great Britain and the United States, where the book has been equally popular.

Raised in London during the 1950s, Hoffman has vivid memories of her own childhood, during which she claims she didn't give much thought to "all those serious grown-up things" that would later appear in her work. In an essay for *Something about the Author Autobiography Series (SAAS),* she characterized her youth as "the years which made me the person I am now. Whenever I write, I am in touch with the five-year-old or seven-year-old or nine-year-old who is still inside me." Gaining an aptitude for writing and languages and a love of English literature during her school years, Hoffman found herself unsure of her future occupation after graduating from Cambridge University. Working as a tutor and teacher of English, Latin, and Anglo-Saxon, she soon settled in to write a full-length novel. After a year and a half of hard work, during which time Hoffman also accepted work as a book reviewer for the *Times Literary Supplement,* her first novel, *White Magic,* was completed; it was published in 1975.

With one published novel under her belt, Hoffman was determined to pursue a career as a writer. In 1980, after working for five years as a teacher at the Open Universi-

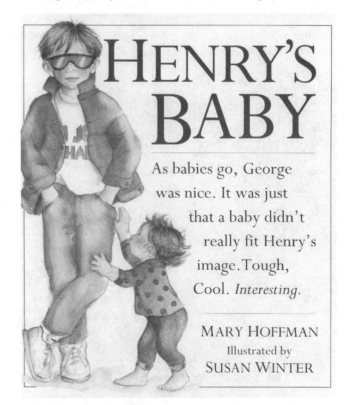

Henry discovers new feelings for his baby brother in Mary Hoffman's story about peer relations and family obligations.

ty, she left her job to become a freelance author of children's literature. As Hoffman characterized that time in her life in _SAAS,_ "the books and articles came thick and fast"—over thirty-five works of fiction or nonfiction bearing her name were published during the 1980s. Among them was the sixteen-volume "Animals in the Wild" series. Each book in the series discusses a particular kind of animal, ranging from antelopes to zebras, and provides an introduction to the animal's habitat, behavior, and the effects of man's interference on the species. "These are sharply conservationist," their author once admitted of the series to _SATA,_ "and I do care very much about the way humans treat animals. (This is not the same as _not_ caring about the way humans treat humans, by the way.) I am a vegetarian myself and have been for [several decades] and I regard fur coats as an ultimate obscenity."

Hoffman's interest in nature has also found an outlet in more recent works, such as 1995's _Earth, Fire, Water, Air,_ as well as in her fiction. _Earth, Fire, Water, Air,_ published in England as _Song of the Earth,_ is a collection of verse, mythology, and ecology reflecting the attitude of primitive cultures and organized around each of the four elements in turn. The work drew praise from _Booklist_ contributor Susan Dove Lempke, who noted that "few books for children attempt the richness of ideas and pictures found here." Noting that Hoffman's research is thorough and her words are "few and well chosen," a _Junior Bookshelf_ contributor hailed the volume as a "rewarding book for parents and children to explore together."

In the mid-1970s, during the height of the feminist movement, Hoffman joined a women's group that

Sun gods are usually male. Because the sun disappears below the horizon at each dusk and rises with the dawn each morning, many people believed in a fiery god who died every night and came back to life every morning. Ra, for example, steered across the heavens in a boat, pursued by a huge crocodile, which seemed to devour the sun at the end of the day. The reappearance of the sun in the morning was a sign that Ra had killed the crocodile once more.

Focusing on the four natural elements, Hoffman explains related legends, tales, and beliefs of various cultures. (From _Earth, Fire, Water, Air,_ illustrated by Jane Ray.)

examined children's books for racism, sexism, ageism, and socio-economic prejudice. As a result, she became very conscious of creating balanced stories, yet realized the importance of remaining "funny, lively, and linguistically inventive." As the author herself once noted in _SATA,_ "propaganda is boring." "In my own books I try for strong and memorable heroines," Hoffman explained, citing her 1986 books _Beware, Princess!_ and _Dracula's Daughter_ as examples. This trend continues in the 1988 picture book _My Grandma Has Black Hair,_ wherein the author creates a whimsical character that is unlike any grandmother known to most of the story-hour crowd in their books, but very recognizable in real life. The young narrator admits that her independent, free-spirited grandma is "a little nutty," but prefers her to the stereotypical white-haired, apron- and slipper-clad, cookie-baking little old lady of most fiction. The granddaughter ultimately recognizes that adoring her family and telling wonderful stories is all that is really important in order to be a wonderful granny. "Children who have nonstereotypical grandmothers should especially relate to this story," noted _Booklist_ reviewer Ilene Cooper.

Many of Hoffman's books for young people are geared toward the preschool crowd, while others provide a fun challenge for beginning readers. A nontraditional approach to family relationships is contained within the illustrated pages of _Henry's Baby._ At first worried that having a baby brother will make him uncool with the group of boys that he wants to join, young Henry Moon finds out that his diaper-clad sibling is actually a novelty. "This picture book demonstrates that having a gentle, nurturing side can be masculine," noted _Five Owls_ contributor Stephen Fraser, praising the volume for addressing the problems of young boys. In the picture book _Nancy No-Size,_ the problems of being the middle child are addressed, in this case within a biracial family where siblings' differences extend beyond personalities to skin color as well.

Among Hoffman's books for slightly older readers, perhaps her most popular story is _Amazing Grace._ Called a "superb picture book to challenge stereotypes" by _School Librarian_ contributor Chris Stephenson, _Amazing Grace_ features a feisty young black protagonist with a love of acting. Grace is determined to land the role of Peter in her elementary school's production of _Peter Pan,_ even though Peter was a boy—and white at that—as Grace's classmates remind her. Reviewer Betsy Hearne lauded the picture book in the _Bulletin of the Center for Children's Books,_ describing the book's main character as "a girl whose love of stories empowers her to overcome race and gender prejudice to do what she dreams." Hearne also noted that Hoffman's _Amazing Grace_ "demonstrates the potency of imagination by being potently imaginative." Hoffman, who based the main character in _Amazing Grace_ on her own childhood, produced a sequel to the story, _Boundless Grace,_ in 1995.

Other books by Hoffman that are designed for beginning readers include several stories involving the otherworld-

In Hoffman's fantasy for young readers, Alex and Carrie learn their pet mouse can magically summon the ghosts of animals who have lived in their home. (From *The Four-Legged Ghosts*, illustrated by Laura L. Seeley.)

ly. *The Second-Hand Ghost*, published in 1986, introduces readers to Lisa, a girl who suddenly finds herself the owner of a small, troubled ghost who has been stitched up inside the pocket of an old jacket. The miniature spirit's search for a way to end his supernatural state and find eternal rest becomes the focus of this humorous tale. In the off-beat *Dog Powder*, a boy named Colin, unable to have a dog of his own due to his landlord's restrictions, is sold a bottle of Dawn-to-Dusk Dog Powder that causes pooches to appear with each shake of the magical dust. Problems arise when too many ephemeral hounds start causing chaos for Colin in this story that a *Junior Bookshelf* reviewer characterized as "charming, skillfully crafted," and "heart-warming." Sprites, spirits, and pets are all combined in Hoffman's *The Four-Legged Ghosts*, in which young Alex Brodie receives a white mouse for his birthday and discovers that the small rodent has the ability to summon forth ghostly pets from years past. "Likable characters, lively

action, and a fresh take" on traditional themes characterize the easy-reader, according to a *Kirkus Reviews* contributor.

On Hoffman's frequent visits to classrooms around her native England to talk to her young fans, children are always curious about her life as a writer. "Why I am a writer is because it's the only thing I am good enough at to do professionally," Hoffman once explained to *SATA*. "I am very lucky to do for a job the thing that I enjoy most. I love everything to do with writing—from buying the paper to proofreading.... You know the way that some people are stage-struck? So much so that they'll even make tea or find props? Well, I'm the same about books—page-struck, perhaps? I can never quite believe that this is what I am, this is really what I do and I am not making it up. It still surprises me every time I look at my bookcases that house my titles."

■ Works Cited

Cooper, Ilene, review of *My Grandma Has Black Hair*, *Booklist*, June 1, 1988, p. 1676.
Review of *Dog Powder*, *Junior Bookshelf*, December, 1989, p. 278.
Review of *The Four-Legged Ghosts*, *Kirkus Reviews*, August 1, 1993, p. 1002.
Fraser, Stephen, review of *Henry's Baby*, *Five Owls*, May/June, 1994, p. 106.
Hearne, Betsy, review of *Amazing Grace*, *Bulletin of the Center for Children's Books*, September, 1992, pp. 3-4.
Hoffman, Mary, essay in *Something about the Author Autobiography Series*, Volume 24, Gale, 1997, pp. 127-43.
Lempke, Susan Dove, review of *Earth, Fire, Water, Air*, *Booklist*, January 1-15, 1996, p. 829.
Review of *Song of the Earth*, *Junior Bookshelf*, April, 1996, pp. 73-74.
Stephenson, Chris, review of *Amazing Grace*, *School Librarian*, November, 1991, p. 140.

■ For More Information See

PERIODICALS

Booklist, September 1, 1993, p. 60; April 15, 1995, p. 1506.
Bulletin of the Center for Children's Books, March, 1988, p. 137; July, 1988, p. 231; January, 1996, p. 162.
Growing Point, January, 1987, p. 4739; November, 1989, p. 5245.
Horn Book, July-August, 1995, p. 450.
Junior Bookshelf, August, 1983, p. 164; October, 1986, p. 186; October, 1991, p. 204; December, 1991, p. 243.
Magpies, March, 1996, p. 33.
Publishers Weekly, September 11, 1987, p. 92; August 2, 1991, p. 72; July 12, 1993, p. 80; May 8, 1995, p. 294; December 18, 1995, p. 54.
School Librarian, February, 1996, p. 20.
School Library Journal, March, 1985, p. 152; December, 1986, p. 123; March, 1987, pp. 145-46; October, 1988, p. 122; December, 1997, p. 93.

HOMEL, David 1952-

■ Personal

Born September 15, 1952, in Chicago, IL; immigrated to Canada; naturalized Canadian citizen; son of Irving Homel and Bernice Isaacs Brenner; married Marie-Louise Gay (a writer and illustrator of children's books); children: Gabriel, Jacob. *Education:* Indiana University, B.A. (with honors), 1975; University of Toronto, M.A., 1976, post-graduate study, 1977. *Hobbies and other interests:* Baseball and travel.

■ Addresses

Home—773 Davaar, Montreal, Quebec H2V 3B3, Canada.

■ Career

Freelance journalist, 1977—; documentary filmmaker and writer. McGill University, teacher, 1982-83; Concordia University, teacher, 1983—. President of Canada's Public Lending Rights Commission, 1990-92. Member of board of directors of Salon du Livre de Montreal, 1984-91. *Member:* PEN, National Writers' Union of Canada, Literary Translators' Association of Canada.

■ Awards, Honors

Hans Christian Andersen Award for excellence in translation from International Board on Books for Young People, 1982, for *The King's Daughter;* Bronze Medal from Hemisfilm Festival, 1984, award for best of category from Hemisfilm Festival, 1985, Bronze Award from Houston International Film Festival, Bronze Plaque from Columbus Film Festival, Bronze Award from New York International Film and Television Festival, and first place from National Educational Film Festival, all for *Visions;* grants from Canada Council, 1988 and 1989-90; finalist for W. H. Smith First Novel Award from Books in Canada, 1989, for *Electrical Storms;* finalist for Governor-General's award for translation, 1989, for *How to Make Love to a Negro;* grant from Ministere es Affaires Culturelles (Quebec), 1991-92; grants from Canada Council, 1991 and 1992-93; award for best paperback fiction from Foundation for the Advancement of Canadian Letters, 1993, for *Rat Palms.*

■ Writings

FOR CHILDREN; TRANSLATOR

Suzanne Martel, *The King's Daughter* (translation of Martel's *Jeanne, fille du roy*), Groundwood Books/ Douglas & MacIntyre (Toronto), 1980.
Monique Corriveau, *A Perfect Day for Kites* (translation of Corriveau's *Le Garcon au cerf-volant*), Groundwood Books/Douglas & MacIntyre, 1981.
Monique Corriveau, *Seasons of the Sea* (translation of Corriveau's *Les Saison de la mer*), Groundwood Books, 1989.

FOR ADULTS; FICTION

Electrical Storms (novel), Random House (Canada), 1988.
Rat Palms (novel), HarperCollins, 1992.

Short fiction represented in anthology *Coup de foudre,* XYZ Editeurs (Montreal), 1993.

NONFICTION

Mapping Literature: The Art and Politics of Translation (essays), Vehicule Press (Montreal), 1988.

Contributor to periodicals, including *Books in Canada, Calgary Herald, Canadian Art, Toronto Globe and Mail, Hungry Mind Review, Montreal Calendar,* and *Toronto Star.*

TELEVISION PRODUCTIONS

(Author of English-language dialogue) *Fils de la liberte,* Radio-Quebec/Antenne 2/Interimage, 1980-81.
Visions (thirteen-part documentary series), Television Ontario, 1981-83.
Visions: The Critical Eye, Television Ontario, 1983.

Also author of *Le Diable dans l'eprouvette* (six-part documentary series), 1985-87; contributor to various Radio-Canada television productions. Story editor for *Realities,* Television Ontario, 1983.

FILM SCRIPTS

Salut, Montreal! (dramatic short), International Cinemedia, 1980.
Bon Appetit! (dramatic short), International Cinemedia, 1980.
Supervising for Results (four-part instructional series), Cinemedia, 1980-81.

TRANSLATOR

Louis Caron, *The Draft Dodger* (translation of Caron's *L'Emmitoufle*), Anansi Press (Toronto), 1980.
Ginette Bureau, *Mona: A Mother's Story* (translation of Bureau's *Mona*), Clarke, Irwin (Toronto), 1981.
Robert Lalonde, *Sweet Madness* (translation of Lalonde's *La Belle epouvante*), General Publishing (Toronto), 1982.
Archambault Prison Theatre Collective, *No Big Deal!* (translation of *Y a rien la!*), Exile Editions (Toronto), 1982.
Robert Marteau, *Mount Royal* (translation of Marteau's *Mont-Royal*), Exile Editions, 1983.
Chrystine Brouillet, *Dear Neighbor* (translation of Brouillet's *Chere Voisine*), General Publishing, 1984.
Jacques Renaud, *Broke City* (translation of Renaud's *Le Casse*), Guernica Editions (Montreal), 1984.
Marc Raboy, *Media and Messages* (translation of Raboy's *Media et mouvements sociaux*), Between the Lines (Toronto), 1984.
Robert Marteau, *Pig-Skinning Day* (translation of Marteau's *Le Jour qu'on a tue le cochon*), Exile Editions, 1984.
Rejean Ducharme, *Ha! Ha!,* Exile Editions, 1986.

Carol Couture and Jean-Yves Rousseau, *The Life of a Document: A Global Approach to Archives and Records Management* (translation of Couture and Rousseau's *Les Archives au vingtieme siecle*), Vehicule Press, 1987.

Suzanne Guy, *Like a Heartbreak* (screenplay; translation of Guy's *C'est comme une peine d'amour*), Les Films du Crepuscule (Montreal), 1987.

Francis Simard, *Talking It Out: The October Crisis from Inside* (translation of Simard's *Pour en finir avec octobre*), Guernica Editions, 1987.

Robert Marteau, *River without End: A Logbook of the Saint Lawrence* (translation of Marteau's *Fleuve sans fin: Journal du Saint-Laurent*), Exile Editions, 1987.

Dany Laferriere, *How to Make Love to a Negro* (translation of Laferriere's *Comment faire l'amour avec un Negre sans se fatiguer*, Coach House Press (Chicago), 1988.

Robert Marteau, *Voyage to Vendee* (translation of Marteau's *Voyage en Vendee*), Exile Editions, 1988.

Real Simard and Michel Vastel, *The Nephew: Making of a Mafia Hitman* (translation of Simard and Vastel's *Le Neveu*), Prentice-Hall (Toronto), 1988.

Monique Begin, *Canada's Right to Health* (translation of Begin's *L'Assurance-Sante au Canada*), Optimum Books (Montreal), 1988.

Daniel Sernine, *Those Who Watch over the Earth* (translation of Sernine's *Organisation Argus*), Black Moss, 1990.

Denis Cote, *The Invisible Empire* (translation of Cote's *La Puissance invisible*), Black Moss, 1990.

Wayne Grady and Maurice Henrie, *The Mandarine Syndrome* (translation of Grady and Henrie's *La Vie secrete des grands bureaucrates*), University of Ottawa Press, 1990.

Dany Laferriere, *Eroshima*, Coach House Press, 1991.

Pierre Bourgault, *Now or Never!* (translation of Bourgault's *Maintenant ou jamais!*), Key Porter Books, 1991.

Clement Marchand, *Vanishing Villages* (translation of Marchand's *Corriers des villages*), Guernica Editions, 1992.

Dany Laferriere, *An Aroma of Coffee* (translation of Laferriere's *L'Odeur du cafe*), Coach House Press, 1993.

Louis Caron and Francois Poche, *Montreal: A Scent of the Islands* (translation of Caron and Poche's *Montreal: Parfum d'isles*), Editions Stanke, 1994.

Dany Laferriere, *Dining with the Dictator* (translation of Laferriere's *Le Gout des jeunes filles*), Coach House Press, 1994.

Dany Laferriere, *Why Must a Black Writer Write about Sex?* (translation of Laferriere's *Cette grenade dans la main du jeune Negre est-elle une arme ou un fruit?*), Coach House Press, 1994.

Daniel Pennac, *Better than Life* (translation of Pennac's *Comme un roman*), Coach House Press, 1994.

Translator and general editor of *Contaminants in the Marine Environment of Nunavik,* Institut National de la Recherche Scientifique/Rawson Academy of Aquatic Science. Also translator of *An Integrated Health Care System* (documentary), National Film Board (Montreal), 1984; *White Justice* (documentary), Informaction (Montreal), 1985; *The Creole Connection* (documentary), Informaction, 1986; *Competing for Space* (documentary), Radio Quebec (Montreal), 1987. Contributor of translated materials to periodicals.

■ Sidelights

David Homel is an American-born Canadian writer who has published novels and has supplied scripts for various television and film productions. In addition, Homel has written the English-language translations for numerous works, including Suzanne Martel's story *The King's Daughter,* for which he won the prestigious Hans Christian Andersen Award for excellence in translation from the International Board on Books for Young People in 1982. Married to the successful children's book author and illustrator Marie-Louise Gay, Homel enjoys traveling two or three months a year with his wife and two children to such places as Greece, southern France, Maine and Georgia, Mexico and California.

Homel comments: "The novel is a means of escape. Self-escape for the writer, who can become other people during the period of writing. Escape for the reader to a place not necessarily better, but at least different from his and her everyday life. My novels are methods of inquiry about the things that keep me awake at night—theological inquiry, questions about American culture—but all of this must happen without an ounce of heaviness.

"Every day of writing must bring a particular kind of twisted joy."*

*   *   *

HONEYCUTT, Natalie 1945-

■ Personal

Born February 5, 1945, in Washington, D.C.; daughter of Linwood Benjamin Honeycutt and Phyllis Arlene Cooley; married Rod Ives; children: Jennifer, Andrew. *Education:* Attended University of Maine and California State University-San Francisco.

■ Addresses

Home and office—P.O. Box 1078, McCloud, CA 96057.

■ Career

Writer.

■ Awards, Honors

Notable Trade Book in the Field of Social Studies, National Council for the Social Studies, 1986, for *The All New Jonah Twist;* Pick of the List, American Booksellers Association (ABA), 1988, for *The Best-Laid Plans of Jonah Twist,* 1991, for *Ask Me Something Easy,*

NATALIE HONEYCUTT

and 1997, for *Twilight in Grace Falls;* Recommended Books for Reluctant Young Adult Readers and Best Books for Young Adults, Young Adult Library Services Association of the American Library Association (ALA), both 1992, and both for *Ask Me Something Easy.* Several of Honeycutt's books have appeared on Master Lists for Young Reader Awards in many different states.

■ Writings

Invisible Lissa, Bradbury Press, 1985.
The All New Jonah Twist, Bradbury Press, 1986.
Josie's Beau, Orchard Books, 1987.
The Best-Laid Plans of Jonah Twist, Bradbury Press, 1988.
Ask Me Something Easy, Orchard Books, 1991.
Juliet Fisher and the Foolproof Plan, Bradbury Press, 1992.
Whistle Home, Orchard Books, 1993.
Lydia Jane and the Babysitter Exchange, Bradbury Press, 1993.
Twilight in Grace Falls, Orchard Books, 1997.
Granville Jones: Commando, Farrar, Straus & Giroux, 1998.

The All New Jonah Twist was translated and published in a Japanese edition, and *Ask Me Something Easy* was published in a Dutch edition.

■ Work in Progress

A picture book for Orchard Books.

■ Sidelights

Natalie Honeycutt is best known as the author of a quartet of books for middle-grade readers, all based in the same third-grade classroom and featuring recurring characters: Jonah Twist, his buddy, Granville, perfect, bossy Juliet Fisher, and the untidy but enthusiastic Lydia Jane. These characters and their adventures have been featured in *The All New Jonah Twist, The Best-Laid Plans of Jonah Twist, Juliet Fisher and the Foolproof Plan,* and *Lydia Jane and the Babysitter Exchange,* the first two of which have earned awards for Honeycutt. The author has also written for both younger and older readers with *Whistle Home,* a picture book, and her award-winning novel *Ask Me Something Easy* for young adults. Honeycutt is credited with fast-moving stories which usually involve multi-layered plots, for her fine delineation of character, and her vivid details which bring her stories to life.

Born in Washington, D.C., Honeycutt was the second of five daughters. She grew up in Bethesda, Maryland, and by the fifth grade she had fallen in love—with reading. "I read *The Secret Garden* and *Call of the Wild,*" Honeycutt reported to *SATA.* "I knew suddenly that magic could be found between the covers of a book, and since then, each time I pick one up, I hope for magic again. Often I am rewarded." Her love of reading did not automatically lead Honeycutt to writing, however. "I remember my astonishment when a high school English teacher told me she thought I was a 'natural writer' and suggested I write something for the school's literary magazine; I was quite sure she'd mistaken me for someone else. Did this woman know something about me that I didn't myself? Perhaps."

It was almost two decades before this teacher's words were heeded. Meanwhile, life intervened: Honeycutt went to college, married and had two children. "I didn't take up writing seriously until I was 35 years old," Honeycutt recalled for *SATA.* "I was, by then, motivated as much out of a deep curiosity about the writing process as by a desire to tell a story. And I think it is this curiosity that has served me best over the ensuing years—that has kept me striving to improve my skills and push the limits of my abilities."

Honeycutt's first novel, *Invisible Lisa,* tells the story of fifth-grader Lissa, who is kind, friendly, likable, and badly wants to join the in-crowd. In her case, that means joining Debra Dobbins's exclusive club. But there is a problem: Lissa has caused embarrassment to the popular Debra on the soccer field, and Debra seeks revenge by manipulating others in the class to ignore Lissa and by ruining Lissa's Indian village social studies project. Through it all Lissa battles to win back the friends that Debra has stolen from her, and when she finally gets into the exclusive club—only to discover it is just a lunch club where members share their food—she is amazed that something so mundane could have occupied so much of her time and attention. In the end, Lissa spiritedly tells Debra off and leaves the club, to be followed by many others. Ilene Cooper, writing in

Booklist, felt that the book was "agreeably written," and that the theme, "which is central to middle-grade experience, should provide some solace for those who are going through a similar situation." *Voice of Youth Advocates* contributor Jean Kaufman commented that she "thoroughly enjoyed this book." Noting the well-drawn main character as well as secondary characters, Kaufman concluded that "these strengths make this one of the better books dealing with peer relations."

Kirkus Reviews called Honeycutt's second novel, *The All New Jonah Twist,* "a humorous, compassionate story that's right on target." With this book, Honeycutt introduces many of the characters who would appear again in later stories. Jonah has a hard time of it: perpetually tardy at home and at school, he also is forgetful. But promised a pet if he gets his act together, Jonah determines to change his ways. He begins well, but soon runs into trouble with a new, and very diminutive, kid in his third-grade room. Granville acts tough because of his size, and secretly tries to win Jonah's friendship. But his unorthodox ways toward friendship simply drive Jonah away initially, then finally win him over. Meanwhile, with the help of his teacher and a kindly elderly neighbor, Jonah proves himself responsible. *Publishers Weekly* dubbed Honeycutt's second novel a "winner," and went on to comment that the book "is full of delightful surprises and enhanced by deft characterizations of adults as well as the children in her large cast." Carolyn Phelan of *Booklist* noted that Honeycutt created, in the character of Jonah, "a sympathetic figure who grows with the help of circumstances, friends, and his own will to change." A *Kirkus Reviews* critic concluded that Jonah "is an unforgettable character, one who we'd like to see again."

For her third book, however, Honeycutt chose an older audience and examined the age-old themes of friendship, honesty, and relations between boys and girls. Set in San Francisco, *Josie's Beau* tells the story of two twelve-year-olds, Josie Pucinski and Beau Finch, who have been friends since childhood. Now they are on the edge of turning that friendship into a first, tentative romance, but this summer there is more in the air than romance. Beau has been saving up for a special skateboard, and that is a slow process. There is also a bully to contend with, Matt Ventura, who takes a special glee in beating up Beau, whose pacifist parents are strongly opposed to fighting. Beau's mother threatens to stop him from buying his skateboard if such fights continue, and when the inevitable occurs, Josie jumps in to help her friend. She tells a lie, that she beat Beau up, to explain his bruises. This causes tensions between the two families, who have lived near each other for years. Finally, caught in the lie, Josie ultimately must tell the truth. "Happily, a little honesty goes a long way toward righting the problem," commented Ilene Cooper in *Booklist.* "True to life and amusing, this very readable novel is right on target for its intended audience." A *Kirkus Reviews* critic agreed, noting that *Josie's Beau* "has a pleasant, easy-to-read style . . . . It is a pleasure to find a contemporary story that holds together and remains interesting without undue melodrama." Zena

Sutherland of *Bulletin of the Center for Children's Books* concluded that "This would be a good read even if it weren't lightened by humor, which it is."

Honeycutt returned to middle-grade readers with *The Best-Laid Plans of Jonah Twist.* In this sequel to *The All New Jonah Twist,* young Jonah has earned his pet, a kitten. But all is not happy at home: It appears the kitten has caused the disappearance of Woz, his older brother's hamster. At school, things are not much better. He and Granville are compelled to take on the class perfectionist and tattletale, Juliet Fisher, as a partner in a report on elephant seals. A third plot revolves around the mysterious disappearance of an elderly neighbor, Mr. Rosetti, whom no one but Jonah seems to miss. Shifting back and forth between plot lines, Honeycutt focuses on Jonah's persistence in finding Woz hidden behind the refrigerator and Mr. Rosetti, in the hospital with a broken hip. Back at school, Juliet is proving a better partner than expected. Her organizational skills come into play, helping them all earn top marks, while Juliet's mother helps to sneak them into the hospital to present Mr. Rosetti with a kitten. *Kirkus Reviews* commented that Honeycutt "deftly blends these mildly unusual

Seventeen-year-old Addie reflects on her father's departure and the subsequent breakup of her family in Honeycutt's poignant novel. (Cover illustration by Larry Raymond.)

events with well-realized, wonderfully authentic characters; kids will also relish the many comic moments." Roger Sutton in *Bulletin of the Center for Children's Books* noted that Honeycutt blends "Jonah's serious and not-so-serious concerns in a natural and appealing way, with Jonah's ingenuous perspective untainted by cuteness," while a *Publishers Weekly* commentator concluded that *The Best-Laid Plans of Jonah Twist* is "humorous and incisive."

Honeycutt reported to *SATA* that she would not recommend her work habits to other prospective writers. "When a book is going well, I often put in a series of eighteen-hour days in front of the word processor. If it's going poorly, I avoid my desk chair for days or weeks at a time. (And please don't imagine that this is time 'off.' I wring my hands every minute.) I always hope to wake up one day and find I've been replaced by someone who puts in a daily four hours at the computer ... come rain, shine or high water." Her particular work schedule does get the job done, however, as Honeycutt has published a book almost every year since her first. Almost three years, however, came between the second Jonah book and Honeycutt's next novel, *Ask Me Something Easy,* an award-winning young adult title. The narrative tells the story of Addie who, after her father leaves, must learn to cope with her distant mother, sensitive younger twin sisters, and a "perfect" older sister. Susan Rosenzweig, writing in *Voice of Youth Advocates,* called *Ask Me Something Easy* a "poignant story of an angry and bitter family break-up, with a chillingly realistic depiction of the terrible toll such events take on parents and children." Now 17, Addie looks back ten years to the break-up of her family. As a result of her father's departure, Addie lost her close bond to her older sister, Dinah, who became the confidante of her deeply wounded mother. Meanwhile, the younger sisters retreat more into themselves, leaving Addie isolated at home. The same isolation happens at school, as well, as Addie's grades take a nose-dive, and Addie only sees her father once after he leaves the family. The one ray of hope is the glimmer of renewal in Addie's closeness to Dinah when the older sister gently scratches a story onto her back to soothe her to sleep. Sutherland of *Bulletin of the Center for Children's Books* observed that this "might be grim were it not so skillfully crafted," while *Booklist*'s Hazel Rochman noted that Honeycutt "writes a clear prose, with a compelling sense of place, a taut buildup of scene, and a fusion of physical and emotional experience." Margaret A. Bush concluded in her *Horn Book* review of the novel that this "powerful, evocative account is a remarkable revelation of the survival of the human spirit."

Two further installments in the world of third-graders followed: *Juliet Fisher and the Foolproof Plan* and *Lydia Jane and the Babysitter Exchange.* In the former, prim and proper Juliet, part of the cast of *The Best-Laid Plans of Jonah Twist,* comes front and center to star in her own novel. Setting out to prove a good example to sloppy Lydia Jane, Juliet is instead ultimately influenced by her messy classmate. Juliet is finicky and near perfect. She is always correct in clothing, manners and

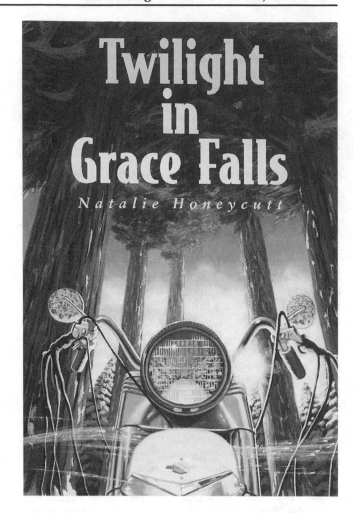

Eleven-year-old Dasie Jenson witnesses the pain and dejection caused by the failing timber industry in her logging town. (Cover illustration by John Ward.)

schoolwork. As her mother is a dietician, she also eats only the right foods. In short, she is in love with order, but one day her teacher, Mrs. Lacey, seats Lydia Jane Bly next to her. The two are polar opposites: Lydia, well-liked by the other students, revels in bright, bright clothing, snacks on junk food, and not only talks during the lesson, but is quite happy to be an average student. Believing Lydia has been sent as a test, Juliet sets about to reform her new deskmate, only to discover that Lydia feels she needs no such help. Jonah and Granville try to help Juliet with alarming and amusing results. They tell Juliet that she must mimic Lydia and then maybe the other girl will see the error of her ways. Instead, Juliet begins to change. Deborah Abbott in *Booklist* noted that Honeycutt "nimbly paints a portrait of Juliet's metamorphosis from caterpillar to stunningly beautiful and happy butterfly," and concluded that this beginning chapter book was "fun, refreshing, and great for reading aloud." Elizabeth Hamilton, writing in *School Library Journal,* commented that "Honeycutt's characters are real and full of comic energy," while *Publishers Weekly* noted the author's sharp "wit" and ended with the hope "that she will include the new and improved Juliet in future stories."

The popular Lydia Jane appears again in Honeycutt's next story, in which she hatches a plan to release herself from the clutches of a cautious babysitter. Blessed with an inquiring mind, Lydia Jane and her sister Gabrielle are held back from experiencing the world by Mrs. Humphrey, who watches them after school. Anything more dangerous than television is off limits for the girls. Ultimately Lydia Jane is successful in finding a new babysitter, a high school student, who is adventurous and curious. Meanwhile, Lydia Jane is also cementing her new friendship with Juliet Fisher. Deborah Stevenson, reviewing the book in *Bulletin of the Center for Children's Books,* commented that "Lydia Jane's doings are spontaneous and funny; her book is full of warmth and freshness that kids will enjoy."

In addition to the picture book, *Whistle Home,* Honeycutt has also written a novel for young readers, *Twilight in Grace Falls.* The result of several years of research and difficult writing and re-writing, *Twilight in Grace Falls* is a "fully realized world" and a "well-written story of a mill town's economic demise," according to a *Kirkus Reviews* critic. A resident of such a town in Northern California, Honeycutt blended personal experience with a sharp eye to tell the story of eleven-year-old Dasie, whose father works in the saw mill which is the town's main source of employment. Dasie's brother Sam leaves the town to join the Navy, an act which ushers in many changes in the life of the family. The lumber mill shuts down, and the men of the town, including Dasie's father, are suddenly out of work. There is also her favorite cousin, Warren, who wants nothing more than to be a logger in Grace Falls and who dies in a motorcycle accident that might well be suicide. *Booklist*'s Rochman, in a starred review, commented on the "elegiac tone to this moving novel," while a *Publishers Weekly* reviewer commented that Honeycutt, writing with "enormous compassion ... captures the spirit of a dying community confronting financial ruin," and concluded that the novel paid "a moving tribute to a disappearing way of life."

Honeycutt has noted that the writing of *Twilight in Grace Falls* took the longest of any her books thus far, with many false starts and re-writes. But challenges are something she seems to thrive on, trying her hand at different genres and styles to stretch her own writing abilities while never losing sight of the fact that at heart her mission is to tell a good story that will capture a reader's attention. "It will come as no surprise," Honeycutt told *SATA,* "that my advice to aspiring writers is to read. Read constantly, and often critically. Nobody should read critically all the time of course—that would spoil the fun! But if you read an especially wonderful book, it can be very constructive to read it a second time while asking yourself, 'How did the writer *do* this?'"

■ Works Cited

Abbott, Deborah, review of *Juliet Fisher and the Foolproof Plan, Booklist,* May 15, 1992, p. 1682.
Review of *The All New Jonah Twist, Kirkus Reviews,* June 1, 1986, p. 864.
Review of *The All New Jonah Twist, Publishers Weekly,* June 27, 1986, p. 90.
Review of *The Best-Laid Plans of Jonah Twist, Kirkus Reviews,* October 1, 1988, p. 1470.
Review of *The Best-Laid Plans of Jonah Twist, Publishers Weekly,* September 9, 1988, p. 135.
Bush, Margaret A., review of *Ask Me Something Easy, Horn Book,* July-August, 1991, p. 463.
Cooper, Ilene, review of *Invisible Lissa, Booklist,* April 1, 1985, p. 1120.
Cooper, Ilene, review of *Josie's Beau, Booklist,* December 1, 1987, p. 634.
Review of *Granville Jones, Publishers Weekly,* February 9, 1998, p. 96.
Hamilton, Elizabeth, review of *Juliet Fisher and the Foolproof Plan, School Library Journal,* July, 1992, p. 59.
Review of *Josie's Beau, Kirkus Reviews,* October 1, 1987, p. 1463.
Review of *Juliet Fisher and the Foolproof Plan, Publishers Weekly,* March 16, 1992, p. 80.
Kaufman, Jean, review of *Invisible Lissa, Voice of Youth Advocates,* October 15, 1985, p. 258.
Phelan, Carolyn, review of *The All New Jonah Twist, Booklist,* May 15, 1986, p. 1397.
Rochman, Hazel, review of *Ask Me Something Easy, Booklist,* June 1, 1991, p. 1868.
Rochman, Hazel, review of *Twilight in Grace Falls, Booklist,* March 15, 1997, p. 1239.
Rosenzweig, Susan, review of *Ask Me Something Easy, Voice of Youth Advocates,* April, 1991, pp. 30-31.
Stevenson, Deborah, review of *Lydia Jane and the Babysitter Exchange, Bulletin of the Center for Children's Books,* September, 1994, pp. 156-57.
Sutherland, Zena, review of *Ask Me Something Easy, Bulletin of the Center for Children's Books,* February, 1991, p. 142.
Sutherland, Zena, review of *Josie's Beau, Bulletin of the Center for Children's Books,* December, 1987, p. 66.
Sutton, Roger, review of *The Best-Laid Plans of Jonah Twist, Bulletin of the Center for Children's Books,* September, 1988, p. 10.
Review of *Twilight in Grace Falls, Kirkus Reviews,* February 15, 1997, p. 300.
Review of *Twilight in Grace Falls, Publishers Weekly,* January 27, 1997, pp. 107-08.

■ For More Information See

PERIODICALS

Bulletin of the Center for Children's Books, October, 1993, p. 47.
Horn Book, January-February, 1994, pp. 64-5.
Horn Book Guide, Fall, 1992, p. 264; Spring, 1994, pp. 38, 77.
Publishers Weekly, August 9, 1993, p. 476; August 23, 1993, p. 72.
School Library Journal, August, 1986, p. 93; December, 1987, p. 86; November, 1988, p. 111; March, 1991, p. 212; November, 1993, p. 84.*

—Sketch by J. Sydney Jones

HOPKINS, Mary R(ice) 1956-

■ Personal

Born September 6, 1956, in Oxnard, CA; daughter of John Forrest (a contractor) and Catherine Powers Birdwell Rice; married Gary Hopkins (a contractor), November 27, 1985; children: Trisha, David. *Education:* Point Loma Nazarene College, B.A. *Religion:* Presbyterian.

■ Addresses

Office—Big Steps 4 U, P.O. Box 362, Montrose, CA 91021. *Electronic mail*—BigSteps @ aol.com.; website—http://maryricehopkins.com

■ Career

Sparrow Records, Brentwood, TX, recording artist; Maranatha! Music, San Juan Capistrano, CA, recording artist; Big Steps Records, Montrose, CA, founder. Presenter of family concerts, under auspices of Big Steps Ministries; works recorded on audio cassettes and videotapes.

■ Writings

HipHipHip Hippopotamus, Crossway (Wheaton, IL), 1996.
Animal Alphabet, Crossway, 1997.

■ Sidelights

Writer-musician Mary R. Hopkins is popular with children, teenagers, and parents at the Family Concerts she performs at summer camps, conferences, and children's ministry conventions. She began her career in the

MARY R. HOPKINS

San Bernardino Mountains as a regular singer/composer. Her songs and stories are geared to build self-esteem, create joy, and nurture faith.

* * *

HOUK, Randy 1944- (Joey Elliott)

■ Personal

Born Dorothea Randolph Houk, September 10, 1944, in Bethlehem, PA; daughter of Robert T. and Dorothea B. (Brush) Houk; married Thomson J. Hudson (an investments manager and executive), September, 1991; stepchildren: T. Blaine, Taylor J. *Education:* Wheaton College, Norton, MA, B.A. *Politics:* Democrat. *Religion:* Episcopalian. *Hobbies and other interests:* Hiking, swimming and snorkeling, skiing, tennis, illustration, gourmet cooking, singing professionally, travel, storytelling.

■ Addresses

Home—Fairfield, CT. *Office*—Benefactory, Inc., 1 Post Rd., Fairfield, CT 06430.

■ Career

Soundworks, Arlington, VA, president; National Public Radio, Washington, DC, director of publishing; Soundprints, Norwalk, CT, founder, president, and chief executive officer; Benefactory, Inc., Fairfield, CT, founder, CEO, president, writer, and illustrator.

■ Awards, Honors

Honor Award, National Parenting Publications, 1997, for *Chessie, the Travelin' Man.*

■ Writings

CHILDREN'S BOOKS (WITH THE HUMANE SOCIETY OF THE UNITED STATES)

Ruffle, Coo, and Hoo Doo, Benefactory (Fairfield, CT), 1993.
Bentley and Blueberry, Benefactory, 1993.
Jasmine, Benefactory, 1993.
Hope, Benefactory, 1995.
Wolves in Yellowstone, Benefactory, 1995.
Chessie, the Travelin' Man, Benefactory, 1997.
Rico's Hawk, Benefactory, 1998.

CHILDREN'S BOOKS; UNDER PSEUDONYM JOEY ELLIOTT

Beezle's Bravery, Soundprints (Norwalk, CT), 1989.
Scout's New Home, Soundprints, 1989.

■ Sidelights

Randy Houk comments: "I was a voracious reader as a child, and I grew up preferring most animals and most children to most adults. As I am basically unmanageable, I've had to build a business that employs me to do

RANDY HOUK

what I love most: writing, illustrating, and reading my stories to children all over the country, which also allows me to travel. My stories are all true stories about living animals. They are intended to teach children core values, especially about animal protection and environmental preservation, in the context of a riveting story that brings the featured animal to life for a young child. Benefactory books are accompanied by plush animals and audiotapes narrated by Tom Chapin. A percentage of all sales goes to the Humane Society of the United States and other nonprofit groups. I am passionate about the work I do, and I hope to do this work until I am a hundred-and-three.

"My mother was a passionate animal devotee. She taught her eight children to be responsible caretakers.

Her love for the earth and all living things has colored all I do. My mother taught me to sew before I was seven, and by the time I was seven, I was selling hand-made doll clothes to the local gift store. Mother must have encouraged us to stick our necks out, for in my family there are four entrepreneurs who have started their own businesses.

"My writing process takes many forms. I write my children's books in rhyme these days. I begin with the research, once the Humane Society of the United States has approved a new subject. After I become very familiar with the habits and habitat of my subject species, I develop an outline for a story. Because the stories are all based on true events, I only need to imagine what could have happened within the basic parameters. Sometimes writing is easy, but sometimes it takes time to find just the right combination of words.

"I cannot remember a time when I did not care enormously about contributing. This rampant idealism has taken a number of forms. With my company, The Benefactory, and the Humane Society of the United States, a number of elements combined as inspiration. First, it came to me in a flash that a book, combined with audiotape and adorable plush animal, could make a story come to life. The animal becomes real to the child; it is not just another wolf, it is the wolf who had pups in Yellowstone last summer. Second, we could be a company that gave something back to aligned nonprofit groups. Third, I could use all the skills I've developed in publishing, entrepreneurship, illustration, writing, and teaching children into one venture. I wanted to stretch myself, grow, and create something of lasting value. This year my book *Chessie, the Travelin' Man* won the National Parenting Publications Honors Award. I'm having a *lot* of fun!"

■ For More Information See

PERIODICALS

Publishers Weekly, December 11, 1995, p. 70; October 20, 1997.
School Library Journal, March, 1994, p. 198; November, 1997, p. 105.

I–J

INGRAMS, Doreen 1906-1997

OBITUARY NOTICE—See index for *SATA* sketch: Born January 24, 1906, in London, England; died July 25, 1997. Author. Ingrams was an authority on the Arab world. She began her studies of socio-economic conditions in Arabia in 1934 when her husband, Harold, was stationed in Aden. She spent a great deal of time researching the lives of Arab women and was responsible for founding a Bedouin Girls' School, the first of its kind. Her first book, *Survey of Social and Economic Conditions in the Aden Protectorate,* was published in 1949 after her return to England. She joined the staff of the British Broadcasting Corp. (BBC) in 1956 as a senior assistant in Arabic Service, a position she held until 1968. Ingrams also lectured extensively and served on the Council for the Advancement of Arab-British Understanding. Her other works include *Palestine Papers, 1917-1922: Seeds of Conflict, Mosques and Minarets, Tents to City Sidewalks,* and *The Awakened: Women of Iraq.* She also served as co-editor of a sixteen-volume work entitled *Records of Yemen 1798-1960.*

OBITUARIES AND OTHER SOURCES:

PERIODICALS

Times (London; electronic), August 11, 1997.

* * *

JAMES, Elizabeth 1942-
(Elizabeth Carroll, Katherine Duval, E. James Lloyd, James Lloyd, pseudonyms; Beverly Hastings, a joint pseudonym)

■ Personal

Born November 5, 1942, in Pittsburgh, PA; daughter of Curtis Blakeslee (a salesman) and Sally (a banker; maiden name, Lloyd) James; married J. David Marks (a motion picture executive), June 24, 1973. *Education:* Colorado College, B.A., 1963; graduate study at University of California, Los Angeles, and California State

ELIZABETH JAMES

College (now University) at Long Beach. *Hobbies and other interests:* Reading, travel, tennis, gardening, and living life.

■ Career

Author. United Air Lines, Los Angeles, CA, stewardess, 1963-65; Otis Productions, Los Angeles, writer and female lead in the motion picture *Born Losers,* 1965-67; freelance writer, 1965—; Sullivan Educational Systems (publisher), assistant director, 1970-72. Consultant to Stanford Research Institute in evaluating Project Follow Through, 1972; Educational Commission of the States, Denver, television programming consultant, 1972-73.

Member of the board of directors, Neighbors of Watts, 1978. _Member:_ Screen Actors Guild, Society of Children's Book Writers and Illustrators, Authors Guild, Women's National Book Association, Mystery Writers of America, PEN, Writers Guild of America (West), Southern California Council on Literature for Children and Young People, Southern California Children's Booksellers Association.

■ **Awards, Honors**

Member of the Year award, Society of Children's Book Writers, 1986.

■ **Writings**

FOR CHILDREN

(With Carol Barkin) _The Simple Facts of Simple Machines,_ illustrated by Daniel Dorn Jr. and Susan Stan, Lothrop, 1975.
(With Barkin) _Slapdash Sewing,_ illustrated by Rita Floden Leydon, Lothrop, 1975.
(With Lee Arthur and Judith B. Taylor) _Sportsmath: How It Works,_ Lothrop, 1975.
(With Carol Barkin) _Slapdash Cooking,_ illustrated by Leydon, Lothrop, 1976.
(With Barkin) _Slapdash Alterations: How to Recycle Your Wardrobe,_ illustrated by Leydon, Lothrop, 1977.
(With Barkin) _Slapdash Decorating,_ illustrated by Leydon, Lothrop, 1977.
(With Barkin) _How to Keep a Secret: Writing and Talking in Code,_ illustrated by Joel Schick, Lothrop, 1978.
(With Barkin) _What Do You Mean by "Average"? Means, Medians, and Modes,_ illustrated by Schick, Lothrop, 1978.
(With Barkin) _How to Grow a Hundred Dollars,_ illustrated by Schick, Lothrop, 1979.
(With Barkin) _How to Write a Term Paper,_ Lothrop, 1980.
(With Barkin) _The Complete Babysitter's Handbook,_ illustrated by Rita Floden Leydon, Wanderer, 1980, revised as _The New Complete Babysitter's Handbook,_ illustrated by Martha Weston, Clarion, 1995.
(With Barkin) _A Place of Your Own,_ illustrated by Lou Jacobs, Jr., Dutton, 1981.
(With Malka Drucker) _Series TV: How a Show Is Made,_ Clarion, 1983.
(With Carol Barkin) _How to Write a Great School Report,_ Lothrop, 1983.
(With Barkin) _The Scary Halloween Costume Book,_ illustrated by Katherine Scoville, Lothrop, 1983.
(With Barkin, under joint pseudonym Beverly Hastings) _Watcher in the Dark,_ Pacer, 1986.
(With Barkin) _How to Write Your Best Book Report,_ illustrated by Roy Doty, Lothrop, 1986.
(With Barkin) _Happy Thanksgiving!,_ illustrated by Giora Carmi, Lothrop, 1987.
(With Barkin) _How to Be School Smart: Secrets of Successful Schoolwork,_ illustrated by Roy Doty, Lothrop, 1988.

(With Barkin) _Happy Valentine's Day,_ illustrated by Martha Weston, Lothrop, 1988.
(With Barkin) _Jobs for Kids: The Guide to Having Fun and Making Money,_ illustrated by Roy Doty, Lothrop, 1990.
(With Barkin) _Sincerely Yours: How to Write Great Letters,_ Clarion (New York), 1993.
(With Barkin) _The Holiday Handbook,_ illustrated by Melanie Marder Parks, Clarion, 1994.
(With Barkin) _Social Smarts: Modern Manners for Today's Kids,_ illustrated by Weston, Clarion, 1996.

"TRANSITION" SERIES; WITH CAROL BARKIN

Are We Still Best Friends?, illustrated by Heinz Kluetmeier, Raintree (Milwaukee, WI), 1975.
Doing Things Together, illustrated by Kluetmeier, Raintree, 1975.
I'd Rather Stay Home, illustrated by Kluetmeier, Raintree, 1975.
Sometimes I Hate School, illustrated by Kluetmeier, Raintree, 1975.

"MONEY" SERIES; WITH CAROL BARKIN

Managing Your Money, illustrated by Santos Paniagua, Raintree, 1977.
What Is Money?, illustrated by Dennis Hockerman, Raintree, 1977.
Understanding Money, illustrated by Hockerman, Raintree, 1977.

NOVELS

(Under pseudonym Katherine Duval) _Ziegfeld: The Man and His Women_ (novelization of screenplay by Joanna Lee), Paradise, 1978.
(With Barkin, under joint pseudonym Beverly Hastings) _Don't Talk to Strangers,_ Jove, 1980.
Secrets, Berkley, 1983.
(With Barkin, under joint pseudonym Beverly Hastings) _Don't Cry, Little Girl,_ Pocket Books, 1987.

OTHER

(Under pseudonym James Lloyd) _Born Losers_ (screenplay), American International, 1967.
(Under pseudonym E. James Lloyd) _Loose Change,_ Willgeorge Productions, 1971.
(With Barkin) _Helpful Hints for Your Pregnancy,_ Fireside, 1984.

Author of other screenplays and television scripts.

■ **Sidelights**

Elizabeth James is the author of several works of juvenile and young adult nonfiction. Curiosity and a vivid recollection of how difficult it was to navigate the middle-school years has guided her choice of subject matter; along with co-author Carol Barkin, James tackles everything from how to deal with arguments in _Are We Still Best-Friends?_ to sporting the latest fashion trends on a budget in _Slapdash Alterations: How to Recycle Your Wardrobe._ "Every experience I have, every place I go, every person I meet, all provide grist for the mill," James once explained to _SATA._

James was born in Pittsburgh, Pennsylvania, in 1942 and attended Colorado College. After graduating in 1963, she decided to spend a few years working as an airline stewardess so that she could see the world. Two years later, she moved to Los Angeles to attend graduate school. There, James told *SATA*, "the magic of the movies beckoned. My first screenplay, *Born Losers*, was produced independently and released by American International Pictures in 1967. It was the first of the 'Billy Jack' films and I played the female lead opposite Tom Laughlin who played Billy Jack."

After the success of her first film, James wrote several other screenplays, as well as a television movie-of-the-week. She also engaged in consulting work for educational film production companies, an experience that inspired her to begin writing for children. Her first book, *The Simple Facts of Simple Machines*, which she co-authored with Carol Barkin, was published in 1975. Containing diagrams and photographs that allow young readers to grasp the fundamental physics that allow machines to operate, the book was praised by reviewers for its straightforward approach. Levers, wedges, pulleys, screws, and the wheel-and-axle are included in a "lucid" text that Zena Sutherland of the *Bulletin of the Center for Children's Books* declared to have "just

THE NEW COMPLETE
BABYSITTER'S
HANDBOOK

by Carol Barkin & Elizabeth James
Illustrated by Martha Weston

James's how-to book about minding children is pocket-sized for easy carrying and reference.

enough repetition to enforce concepts." Shirley A. Smith hailed *Simple Machines* as "one of the best books on machines" in her review for *School Library Journal.* Such praise convinced James that she and Barkin had formed an effective partnership. Their collaboration, which began in 1975, has continued for more than two decades.

Self-improvement is a theme found in many of the Barkin-James duo's books. Academic success is the focus of *How to Be School Smart: Secrets of Successful Schoolwork,* a "cheerful, chatty" primer on study skills, test-taking, and learning styles, according to Irene Close in *Voice of Youth Advocates.* Other books providing techniques to improve school performance include *How to Write Your Best Book Report, How to Write a Term Paper,* and even *Sometimes I Hate School,* a 1975 title that helps young people cope with the stresses of class work.

Social skills are covered in *Sincerely Yours: How to Write Great Letters* and *Social Smarts: Manners for Today's Kids,* the latter written in 1996. *Sincerely Yours* "could do a lot for reviving interest in the art of letter writing" according to *Voice of Youth Advocates* contributor Patricia Gosda. Gosda further praised the volume for its inclusion of a wide variety of sample correspondence, including examples of letters to magazine and newspaper editors, requests for information, and letters to friends and relatives. Although part of the volume also deals with written decorum, handling people face to face is the focus of *Social Smarts.* Telephone manners, making introductions, table manners during fancy dinners, proper behavior as a houseguest, and the like fill the volume. While some criticism was leveled at the volume for its slant toward young women, Jerry D. Flack noted in his *School Library Journal* review that James and Barkin "are to be commended for giving wise counsel for difficult situations." And Stephanie Zvirin observed in *Booklist* that the co-authors go beyond "simply tell[ing] readers how to behave—they usually explain why."

Realizing the importance of knowing some basic mathematic and economic concepts prompted James and Barkin to write several of their nonfiction works. *What Do You Mean by "Average"?,* published in 1978, shows how mean, median, and mode are used in supporting or evaluating data and how these three methods of averaging numbers can generate drastically different "average" results in a data-set. Sutherland of the *Bulletin of the Center for Children's Books* praised the work for highlighting possible "pitfalls" in survey results. Other works focusing on math as it is used in everyday society are collected in James and Barkin's "Money" series: *Managing Your Money, What Is Money?,* and *Understanding Money.* Their *How to Grow a Hundred Dollars* provides young people with basic entrepreneurial skills while, on a lighter note, *How to Keep a Secret: Writing and Talking in Code* applies mathematical concepts to devise ciphers, codes, and number substitutes to make letters to friends and diary entries all but impenetrable to the "enemy."

James and Carol Barkin offer advice to young people on handling several confusing social situations in their handbook on etiquette.

While much of her work with co-author Barkin has been directed toward a pre-teen audience, James has also published several books for older teens. Among these is *A Place of Your Own,* a guide for setting up one's first home away from the parental nest. The book's suggestions, which require little in the way of cash, include creative decorating techniques such as building and refurbishing furniture, basic sewing skills that produce decorative accents, and common-sense tips for dealing with bathrooms, kitchens, and lack of adequate storage. Geared for the most reluctant of readers and equally effective for those for whom English is not a first language, *A Place of Your Own* also includes useful information such as "Where to Get Things," prompting *Voice of Youth Advocates* contributor Joan Jestel to commend the work as "well thought-out." Jestel noted that "the practicality of the projects and accuracy of the instructions are good."

While James took formal writing courses during her college years, she has always maintained that reading, a sound knowledge of the English language, and a broad range of life experiences are most useful to a budding writer. In addition, writers must possess a healthy curiosity, according to the author, because they must be prepared to research information for their books. "Every book requires research," James once explained to *SATA,* "but I find it impossible to write from library research alone. For both fiction and nonfiction I must have some sort of intuitive grasp of the subject matter before I can begin. I need to already know something about the topic, to be interested in that theme or problem, to care about it. If parts of the book are set in locations I'm unfamiliar with, I go there.... I try everything out to make sure it works and that it works by following the directions I've written." And she finds that her methods ultimately prove the old adage "'write what you know.'"

■ Works Cited

Close, Irene, review of *How to Be School Smart: Secrets of Successful Schoolwork, Voice of Youth Advocates,* June, 1988, p. 102.

Flack, Jerry D., review of *Social Smarts: Manners for Today's Kids, School Library Journal,* September, 1996, p. 217.

Gosda, Patricia, review of *Sincerely Yours: How to Write Great Letters, Voice of Youth Advocates,* August, 1993, p. 177.

Jestel, Joan, review of *A Place of Your Own, Voice of Youth Advocates,* April, 1982, pp. 45-46.

Smith, Shirley A., review of *The Simple Facts of Simple Machines, School Library Journal,* May, 1975, p. 57.

Sutherland, Zena, review of *The Simple Facts of Simple Machines, Bulletin of the Center for Children's Books,* July-August, 1975, p. 178.

Sutherland, Zena, review of *What Do You Mean by "Average"?, Bulletin of the Center for Children's Books,* January, 1979, p. 83.

Zvirin, Stephanie, review of *Social Smarts: Manners for Today's Kids, Booklist,* September 1, 1996, p. 122.

■ For More Information See

PERIODICALS

Booklist, May 1, 1978, p. 1432; March 15, 1988, p. 1259; May 1, 1993, p. 1586.

Horn Book, December, 1978, p. 667.

Kirkus Reviews, April 1, 1978, p. 377; July 1, 1996, pp. 968-69.

School Library Journal, April, 1982, pp. 82-83.

*　　　*　　　*

JAQUES, Faith 1923-1997

OBITUARY NOTICE—See index for *SATA* sketch: Surname pronounced "Jakes"; born December 13, 1923, in Leicester, England; died July 12, 1997. Illustrator, educator, author. Jaques was an accomplished illustrator of children's books, providing pictures for such works as Roald Dahl's *Charlie and the Chocolate Factory* and Philippa Pearce's *What the Neighbours Did.* Jaques worked to gain recognition for illustrators, particularly in regard to receiving royalties along with authors for the work. Jaques served with the Women's Royal Naval Service during World War II, becoming a petty officer. In 1950 she began working as a visiting lecturer at the Guildford School of Art in England, followed eventually by a stint at the Hornsey College of Art beginning in 1958. She worked as an illustrator with various firms, including Folio Society Books, Reader's Digest Educational Books, BBC School Publications, and Cape, Heinemann, Methuen, and Penguin. In addition to illustrating the books of others, she created the artwork for books of her own, including *Tilly's House, Frank and Polly Muir's Big Dipper,* and *The Christmas Party.* Her illustrator credits include pictures for reprints of such classics as Louisa May Alcott's *Little Women,* Robert Louis Stevenson's *Treasure Island,* Charles Dickens's *David Copperfield,* Anthony Trollope's *Small House at Allington* and Jane Austen's *Persuasion.* Jaques also illustrated books in "The Apprentices" series by Leon Garfield and other works by noted contemporary authors including Natalie Savage Carlson, Nina Bawden, Roald Dahl, and Allan Ahlberg.

OBITUARIES AND OTHER SOURCES:

PERIODICALS

Times (London; electronic), August 1, 1997.

K

KAY, Jackie
See KAY, Jacqueline Margaret

* * *

KAY, Jacqueline Margaret 1961-
(Jackie Kay)

■ Personal

Born November 9, 1961, in Edinburgh, Scotland; children: one son. *Education:* University of Stirling, B.A. (honors, English), 1983.

■ Addresses

25 Macefin Ave., Manchester M21 7QQ, England. *Agent*—Pat Kavanagh, Peters Fraser & Dunlop, 503/4 The Chambers, Chelsea Harbour, London SW10 OXF, England.

■ Career

Poet and playwright. Writer-in-residence, Hammersmith, London, 1989-91.

■ Awards, Honors

Eric Gregory Award, 1991; Scottish Arts Council Book Award, and Saltire First Book of the Year Award, both 1991, and Forward Prize, 1992, all for *The Adoption Papers;* Signal Poetry Award, 1993, for *Two's Company;* Somerset Maugham Award for *Other Lovers.*

■ Writings

POETRY, AS JACKIE KAY

The Adoption Papers, Bloodaxe (Newcastle upon Tyne, England), 1991.
That Distance Apart (chapbook), Turret (London), 1991.
Two's Company (for children), illustrated by Shirley Tourret, Puffin (London), 1992.
Other Lovers, Bloodaxe, 1993.

Three Has Gone (for children), illustrated by Jody Winger, Blackie Children's Books (London), 1994.

OTHER

Bessie Smith (biography), Absolute, 1997.

Contributor of play *Twice Over* to the collection *Gay Sweatshop: Four Plays and a Company,* edited by Philip Osment, Methuen Drama, 1989; featured in *Penguin Modern Poets,* Vol. 8: *Jackie Kay, Merle Collins, Grace Nichols,* Penguin, 1996. Poems have appeared in *Artrage* and *Feminist Review* and in the collection *Dangerous Knowing: Four Black Women Poets,* Sheba, 1983; short stories have appeared in anthologies *Everyday Matters 2,* 1984, and *Stepping Out,* 1986. The play *Chiaroscuro* is collected in *Lesbian Plays,* edited by Jill Davis, 1987.

■ Sidelights

Jackie Kay is a writer whose "position in English poetry is well nigh unique," according to Christine Pagnoulle in *Contemporary Poets.* This uniqueness is attributed to aspects of her personal life and history that have formed the subject matter of much of her writing. Kay is a Scottish poet who writes in both the Scots dialect and in standard British English. She is also a black woman who was adopted as a child by Caucasian parents and grew up in the predominantly white society of Scotland. In addition, Kay is a lesbian, a fact that influences her plays and adult poetry. Kay's poetry has directly addressed her life in such works as *The Adoption Papers,* an award-winning adult poetry collection that includes a ten-poem sequence rendering of the story of the author's search for her birth mother from three perspectives, that of the child, her biological mother, and her adoptive mother. In her collections of poetry for children *Two's Company* and *Three Has Gone,* Kay takes on the topic of racism, among other experiences from her childhood, in a manner that is considered lighter than her adult works but equally thoughtful and meaningful.

Born in Edinburgh, Scotland, Kay grew up in Glasgow; she discovered her love for poetry through the works of the celebrated Scottish poet Robert Burns. After receiving an honours degree in English from Stirling University, Kay embarked upon a career in England as a writer for the theater as well as for television and radio. Her plays began to be produced by women's theater groups, and she contributed poems and short stories to anthologies and magazines. Her first published book of poetry is *The Adoption Papers,* a work in which Kay tells her own story in verse and gives voices to her two mothers. This sequence, asserted *Booklist* reviewer Pat Monaghan, "should become a feminist classic." The volume, which is noted for the poet's use of rhythm and sound, also includes poems about death, including dying of AIDS; about gay love; and about life in Thatcher-era Britain. Kay's second collection of poetry for adults, *Other Lovers,* is also praised for its use of language. In this work, Kay includes memories of the racism directed at her as a child—a section described by Christine Pagnoulle as "remarkable for dramatic vividness and humor"—as well as a long sequence on relationships; the volume also contains a poem written from the perspective of a sixteen-year-old girl. "Writing is very important to me because is helps me to define what I want to change and why," Kay told the *Bloomsbury Guide to Women's Literature.* The author's writing for adults was characterized by the editors of the *Bloomsbury Guide* as "politically engaged poetry that deals with the interrelationship of race, sexuality and gender in British society."

In her poetry collections for children, Kay focuses on experiences important to her young audience and draws on many of the subjects and issues that she addresses in her adult works. At the center of her poetry for children is the author's evocation of a sensitive child's perceptions of the people and society around her. "A spirited child with a lively imagination she must have been, and that spirit pervades her work," wrote Judith Nicholls in a review of *Three Has Gone* for *Books for Keeps.* In turn, Kay's first collection for children, *Two's Company,* was praised as "a brilliant debut in writing for children," by Morag Styles in *Books for Keeps,* who continued, "There is plenty of fun, pain too, lyrical moments, compassion, but absolutely no sentimentality (the great fault of so many who attempt to write for the young)." In *Two's Company,* Kay writes in blank verse about a variety of childhood experiences, from the pain of divorce to the joys of travel. Imaginary friends are the subject of several poems in the collection, some of which are narrated by Carla, a girl whose parents have separated and who is trying to live with her customary spirit. In *Three Have Gone,* Kay's subjects range from a Gaelic dog who refuses to speak English to childhood betrayal and guilt and the joys and difficulties of living within a family. Writing in *Junior Bookshelf,* D. A. Young said, "Here we have an excellent successor to *Two's Company.* [Kay] continues to delight us with childhood memories crisply retold as if they had happened yesterday." *Books for Keeps* reviewer Judith Nicholls offered similar praise: "Jackie Kay was a well-praised Signal Award winner for *Two's Company* last year.... [*Three Has Gone*] confirms that talent." In addition to her poetry and plays, Kay is the author of an adult biography of

seminal American blues singer Bessie Smith, who is also the subject of a sequence of poems in Kay's volume *Other Lovers.*

■ Works Cited

Buck, Clare, editor, *The Bloomsbury Guide to Women's Literature,* Prentice-Hall, 1992, p. 691.

Monaghan, Pat, review of *The Adoption Papers, Booklist,* March 15, 1992, p. 1332.

Nicholls, Judith, review of *Three Has Gone, Books for Keeps,* September, 1994, pp. 20-21.

Pagnoulle, Christine, essay on Jackie Kay in *Contemporary Poets,* sixth edition, St. James, 1996, pp. 565-66.

Styles, Morag, review of *Two's Company, Books for Keeps,* March, 1993, p. 28.

Young, D. A., review of *Three Has Gone, Junior Bookshelf,* February, 1995, pp. 21-21.

■ For More Information See

PERIODICALS

Books for Keeps, November, 1992, p. 23.
Books for Your Children, autumn, 1994, p. 28.
Junior Bookshelf, August, 1994, p. 135.
School Librarian, May, 1994, p. 70.
Times Educational Supplement, February 19, 1993, p. R2; November 11, 1994, p. R7.
Times Literary Supplement, May 22, 1992, p. 30.

*   *   *

KOMAIKO, Leah 1954-

■ Personal

Born June 1, 1954, in Chicago, IL; daughter of Robert Komaiko (a musicologist); divorced. *Education:* University of Utah, B.A.

■ Addresses

Home—15104 Hamlin St., Van Nuys, CA 91411. *Agent*—Edite Kroll, 12 Grayhurst Park, Portland, ME.

■ Career

Writer. Involved in cause-related marketing projects for corporations and children. Has appeared on the Public Broadcasting Station's *Reading Rainbow. Member:* Society of Children's Book Writers and Illustrators.

■ Awards, Honors

Has received several Children's Choice awards.

■ Writings

PICTURE BOOKS

I Like the Music, illustrated by Barbara Westman, HarperCollins, 1987.

Annie Bananie, illustrated by Laura Cornell, HarperCollins, 1987.

Earl's Too Cool for Me, illustrated by Cornell, HarperCollins, 1988.

My Perfect Neighborhood, illustrated by Westman, HarperCollins, 1990.

Where Can Daniel Be?, illustrated by Denys Cazet, Orchard, 1992.

(Self-illustrated) *A Million Moms and Mine,* L. Claiborne, 1992.

Leonora O'Grady, illustrated by Cornell, HarperCollins, 1992.

Aunt Elaine Does the Dance from Spain, illustrated by Petra Mathers, Delacorte, 1992.

Shoe Shine Shirley, illustrated by Franz Spohn, Delacorte, 1993.

Broadway Banjo Bill, illustrated by Spohn, Delacorte, 1993.

Great-Aunt Ida and Her Great Dane, Doc, illustrated by Steve Schindler, Delacorte, 1994.

Just My Dad and Me, illustrated by Jeffrey Greene, HarperCollins, 1995.

Fritzi Fox Flew in from Florida, illustrated by Thatcher Hurd, HarperCollins, 1995.

On Sallie Perry's Farm, illustrated by Cat Bowman Smith, Simon & Schuster, 1996.

EASY-READERS

Annie Bananie Moves to Barry Avenue, illustrated by Abby Carter, Delacorte, 1996.

Annie Bananie: Best Friends to the End, illustrated by Carter, Delacorte, 1997.

Annie Bananie and the People's Court, Delacorte, in press.

Annie Bananie and the Pain Sisters, Delacorte, in press.

■ Work in Progress

A nonfiction book about aging for adults.

■ Sidelights

Picture-book author Leah Komaiko was raised in a musical environment, and her love of music can be heard weaving its way through the lighthearted verses she writes for young children. "I begin my poems by hearing a rhythm," Komaiko explained in an interview for *Publishers Weekly.* "There's no story unless there's rhythm. Then I do the words." In addition to adding a musical element to her work, the author of such books as *Great-Aunt Ida and Her Great Dane, Doc, Aunt Elaine Does the Dance from Spain,* and *Annie Bananie—Best Friends to the End* characteristically celebrates positive relationships between young children and older adults— grandparents and other elderly people who both entertain and inspire their younger friends. "Komaiko's perky verse ... keeps the story skipping along at a pace precluding any boredom in the audience," noted a *Kirkus Reviews* writer in an assessment of *Great-Aunt Ida and Her Great Dane, Doc,* which pairs the outgoing Ida with her impatient young nephew and shows that age can sometimes outpace youth.

Libby Johnson and her new friend Annie Bananie try to get Libby's canine-hating grandma to kiss Annie's dog in Leah Komaiko's humorous tale of summer amusement. (From *Annie Bananie Moves to Barry Avenue,* illustrated by Abby Carter.)

A student of poetry, Komaiko attended the University of Utah before becoming a children's book author. One of her first stories for young people, 1987's *I Like the Music,* is about a small girl who is entranced by the rhythmic hustle and bustle of the activity she hears from her upstairs apartment window in a city neighborhood. Not only does she like to listen, but she likes to make "city music" too, like the "rapa-tapa-tapa on the hot concrete." Grandmother, on the other hand, dislikes the racket she hears echoing up from the street. Instead, she loves the majestic sounds of classical music and is disappointed that her young companion is less than enthusiastic about their trips together to Symphony Hall. Finally, the local orchestra plans an open-air performance in a nearby park, which allows grandmother and granddaughter to find something they can enjoy together. *I Like the Music* took "a long time," Komaiko admitted to *Publishers Weekly.* "The day I got the words 'shabops-it/On the topsit' (a line that refers to a junk man playing on garbage can lids), I thought I'd died and gone to heaven."

Annie Bananie was introduced to Komaiko's young readers in 1987. Sad after her best friend Annie moves away from the neighborhood, the book's five-year-old narrator remembers all the fun the pair used to have: "Made me brush my teeth with mud, / Sign my name in cockroach blood" were some of the dares the two girls had bonded their close friendship with. New friends will come her way, the newcomer realizes, although Annie will always remain special. Anna Biagioni Hart called the book "a daffy, energetic, and heartfelt celebration of friendship" in a review of *Annie Bananie* for *School Library Journal*. And *Booklist* reviewer Ellen Mandel recommended the book as "therapeutic for youngsters separated from good friends."

The character of Annie Bananie reappears in several books by Komaiko written for older children. In *Annie Bananie Moves to Barry Avenue*, the energetic Annie and her rottweiler Boris enliven the summer vacation of Libby, who has come to Barry Avenue to stay with her terribly unexciting Grandmother Gert. Several more girls from the neighborhood soon join the pair, and soon they have formed a local dog-owner's club. Libby, elected the club's president, has no dog and must fulfill her membership requirement by getting her pet-hating grandmother to warm up to Boris enough to kiss him on his doggy lips. The girls' friendship continues through the start of the new school year in 1997's *Annie Bananie—Best Friends to the End*. Allowed to leave school and have lunch at a friend's home one day, Annie and Libby opt instead for a hamburger at a nearby fast-food restaurant because Libby is embarrassed about her Grandmother Gert; however, their deception is discovered when, back in class, Annie becomes sick and throws up on her friend. While noting that *Annie Bananie—Best Friends to the End* contains a "fast-paced but choppy" narrative, *School Library Journal* reviewer Pamela K. Bomboy recommended it as "an easy read ... for newly independent readers."

While several picture books by Komaiko—including *Leonora O'Grady* and the lighthearted *Great-Aunt Ida and Her Great Dane, Doc*—feature elderly protagonists as their main characters, others present youthful protagonists doing kid stuff under the watchful eye of loving caretakers. In *Earl's Too Cool for Me*, published in 1988, Komaiko pairs what a *Publishers Weekly* reviewer dubbed as "a finger-snapping rhythm" with a main character that is, to the book's young, bespectacled narrator, simply the hippest kid in the neighborhood. *On Sally Perry's Farm* shows how a young girl gains self-confidence as she works alongside friends at an urban-neighborhood farm in a book that a *Publishers Weekly* critic termed "effervescent." A foxy visitor from sunny Florida weaves a warm-weather fantasy in Komaiko's humorous *Fritzi Fox Flew in from Florida*, while in *Just My Dad and Me* a small girl in a close, bustling family fantasizes about spending time alone with her busy but loving father.

In addition to writing children's books, Komaiko has visited young readers at schools and has also developed and produced several programs for children's television. In addition, she is working on both fiction and nonfiction books for adult readers. However, as she told

Publishers Weekly, writing for children remains her favorite occupation.

■ Works Cited

Bomboy, Pamela K., review of *Annie Bananie—Best Friends to the End, School Library Journal*, May, 1997, p. 102.

Review of *Earl's Too Cool for Me, Publishers Weekly*, September 9, 1988, p. 133.

Review of *Great-Aunt Ida and Her Great Dane, Doc, Kirkus Reviews*, January 1, 1994, p. 65.

Hart, Anna Biagioni, review of *Annie Bananie, School Library Journal*, August, 1987, p. 70.

Komaiko, Leah, *Annie Bananie*, illustrated by Laura Cornell, HarperCollins, 1987.

Komaiko, Leah, *I Like the Music*, illustrated by Barbara Westman, HarperCollins, 1987.

Mandel, Ellen, review of *Annie Bananie, Booklist*, June 1, 1987, p. 1523.

Review of *On Sally Perry's Farm, Publishers Weekly*, June 10, 1996, p. 99.

Roback, Diane and Kimberly Olson Fakih, "Flying Starts," *Publishers Weekly*, December 25, 1987, p. 41.

■ For More Information See

PERIODICALS

Booklist, September 15, 1987, p. 150; January 1, 1994, pp. 832-33.

Bulletin of the Center for Children's Books, October, 1987, p. 33; May, 1992, p. 241.

Kirkus Reviews, November 1, 1987, p. 1577; June 1, 1992, p. 720; October 1, 1992, p. 1257; February 15, 1995, p. 227.

Publishers Weekly, October 26, 1992, p. 70; January 9, 1995, p. 63; May 29, 1995, p. 83.

School Library Journal, March, 1988, p. 168; November, 1988, p. 90; April, 1993, p. 98; February, 1997, p. 82.

Teaching and Learning Literature, January-February, 1998, p. 91.

* * *

KOVALSKI, Maryann 1951-

■ Personal

Born June 4, 1951, in New York, NY; daughter of Samuel and Alice (Caputo) Kovalski; married Gregory Sheppard (a commercial film director), August 30, 1976; children: Genevieve F., Joanna E. *Education:* Attended New York School of Visual Arts, 1969-72.

■ Addresses

Home—138 Balmoral Ave., Toronto, Ontario, Canada M4V 1J4. *Office*—14 Monteith St., Ontario, Canada M4Y 1K7.

MARYANN KOVALSKI

■ Career

Author and illustrator. Vickers & Benson Advertising, Montreal, Canada, art director, 1974-75; freelance editorial illustrator, 1975-84; co-owner of Dinsmore Gallery, 1984-85. *Exhibitions:* Dinsmore Gallery, Toronto, 1983; Children's Bookstore, Toronto, 1984; McGill Club, Toronto, 1987; Vancouver Art Gallery, British Columbia, 1988. *Member:* Canadian Society of Children's Authors, Illustrators, and Performers, Writers Union, Society of Illustrators (NY), McGill Club.

■ Writings

SELF-ILLUSTRATED

Brenda and Edward, Kids Can Press, 1984.
The Wheels on the Bus, Little Brown, 1987.
Jingle Bells, Little, Brown, 1988.
Frank and Zelda, Kids Can Press, 1990, published in the U.S. as *Pizza for Breakfast,* Morrow, 1991.
Take Me Out to the Ball Game, Scholastic, 1992.

ILLUSTRATOR

Allen Morgan, *Molly and Mr. Maloney,* Kids Can Press, 1981.
Ted Staunton, *Puddleman,* Kids Can Press, 1983.
Lois Sharon and Bram Sharon, *Mother Goose: Songs, Finger Rhymes, Tickling Verses, Games and More,* Douglas & McIntyre, 1985, Atlantic Monthly, 1986.
Frances Harber, *My King Has Donkey Ears,* Scholastic-TAB, 1986.
Tim Wynne-Jones, *I'll Make You Small,* Douglas & McIntyre, 1986.

Rose Robart, *The Cake That Mack Ate,* Kids Can Press, 1986, Little, Brown, 1987.
Paulette Bourgeois, *Grandma's Secret,* Kids Can Press, 1989, Little, Brown, 1989.
John Green, *Alice and the Birthday Giant,* Scholastic, 1989.
John Green, *Junkpile Jennifer,* Scholastic, 1991.
Rhea Tregebov, *The Big Storm,* Kids Can Press, 1992, Hyperion, 1992.
Rita Golden Gelman, *I Went to the Zoo,* Scholastic, 1993.
David Booth, *Doctor Knickerbocker and Other Rhymes,* Kids Can Press, 1993, Ticknor & Fields, 1993.
Laura Krauss Melmed, *The Marvelous Market on Mermaid,* Lothrop, Lee and Shepherd, 1994.
Sherie Ditch, *Mabel Murple,* Doubleday Canada, 1995.
Margaret Atwood, *Princess Prunella and the Purple Peanut,* Key Porter Books, 1996, Workman, 1996.

Several of Kovalski's books have appeared in French editions as well as in braille. She has also made a sound recording, "Illustrating for Picture Books," for the Canadian Society of Children's Authors, Illustrators and Performers.

■ Sidelights

Maryann Kovalski is an American-born Canadian illustrator and author of children's books noted for her humor and richly detailed, nostalgic drawings. Often employing popular songs or folktales as the centerpiece of her stories, Kovalski has created a series of books around the adventures of the sisters Jenny and Joanna, and their spry grandmother. Familiar songs—"The Wheels on the Bus," "Jingle Bells," and "Take Me out to the Ball Game" are used as the thematic glue for such adventures, and the lyrics as well as musical notations are included in the illustrations. One of Canada's most popular illustrators, Kovalski has also done artwork for many of Canada's best-loved contemporary authors, including Tim Wynne-Jones and Margaret Atwood.

Born in New York, Kovalski was brought up in the Bronx at a time "when kids roamed freely and relatively safely," as she noted in an essay for *Something about the Author Autobiography Series* (*SAAS*). A Catholic, Kovalski experienced the ritual of the church in all its forms throughout the cycle of the year as she was growing up. There were processions through the neighborhood with her altar-boy brothers taking part, and these "ecclesiastical beauty pageants" made a strong impression on the young Kovalski. Raised during the 1950s, she experienced the fears brought on by the Cold War with nuclear attack drills at school, but she also experienced an America of a different epoch, the last of small town and neighborhood America before the restless onslaught and homogenization brought about by television and other mass media. It was a simpler age, when kids played in fire hydrant spray during the steaming summer months and old people leaned on pillows in their windows watching. It is a world lost in reality, but one preserved in many of Kovalski's illustrations.

Kovalski's father, a chimneysweep, played a significant role in her life. Never losing a childish glee at life, he would bring home all manner of strays, from kittens to a pair of chickens. If the bill collectors were being overly persistent, he would go off fishing. From her mother and her mother's sisters grew an early love of storytelling, especially for ghost stories. And from her father's parents Kovalski took great comfort. "I loved going to my grandparent's apartment," Kovalski recalled in *SAAS*. "It was big and clean and smelled of floor wax and furniture polish. The beds were covered in thick quilts which my grandmother made and stuffed herself with the down from the live chickens she chose at the dockside market." From Poland, these grandparents still spoke their old language at family gatherings, still clung to the traditions of another time and place.

Another early influence on Kovalski was books, a never-ending fascination. "I loved picture books even when I was too old for the them," Kovalski wrote in *SAAS*. At ten, the pictures of Jean de Brunhoff for *Babar* still mesmerized her. She spent long hours at the library near her grandparents' apartment, and one particular spring evening she had her family searching the neighborhood for her when she lost all sense of time and returned home after dark. Along with books came a love for drawing. "I knew I wanted to be an artist as far back as I could remember," Kovalski commented. This ambition ran neck and neck with her desire to be a nun, until the habits which nuns wore became less formal and ornate and Kovalski lost interest in that particular career path.

Kovalski's grandparents died when she was just nine years old, leaving a void in the young girl's life. Shortly thereafter, her father moved the family to Florida, hoping to get rich on real estate ventures. But as so often happens with grand plans, things went badly awry. After a few months, the family was on its way back to New York in their overloaded station wagon. Once settled again in the Bronx, Kovalski attended public school for the first time, as the local Catholic school had a long waiting list. Experiencing the feelings of being an outsider, picked on and bullied, Kovalski turned to her drawing and to the library. "One day," she recalled in *SAAS*, "a professional artist came to our school. He wore a beret, just like in the drawings of the artists. He looked over our shoulders as we drew in the art room. I was always so happy in the art room .... He placed his hand on my head and said to my teacher, 'This girl is going to be a famous artist someday.'"

To help make ends meet, Kovalski's mother took a job as an information operator and worked nights. Since Kovalski's father drove a taxi also at night, the children were left on their own, their one boon companion a fluffy white puppy. Slowly, the family finances improved and a new apartment was found, one where Kovalski had a room to herself for the first time. Throughout grade school and into high school, she maintained her dream of becoming an artist. But while art came easily for her, other subjects, especially math and science, were like pulling teeth.

After high school, Kovalski applied to the School of Visual Arts in New York, though family finances seemed to make attendance there little more than a dream. A summertime job at a diner, however, provided enough money for the first term tuition, and that fall, Kovalski entered the art school. At first her progress was slow, aided little by the current vogue for conceptual artworks over traditional watercolors and oils. Her first two years were spent more in having fun and learning about herself than in learning about illustration. But in her third year, a trip to Canada inspired Kovalski.

Returning to New York, she had formulated a plan to live in Montreal and to that end, worked on an animated film which would teach French to children. Planned both as a school-leaving project and a passport to work in Canada, the short animated film was her first concerted effort, involving nearly 3,000 paintings or cells which would present a cartoon cat whose tail enlarged to spell out French words and which would then turn into the image that it had spelled. Though the finished film was far from successful, the discipline of drawing had aided her other work, and upon graduation she won an illustration job with *Harper's* for a story by John Barth. Soon thereafter Kovalski moved to Montreal as planned, though life as a freelance illustrator was not the easiest. She worked in a variety of jobs: creating advertising copy, designing logos, and working on cartoon strips. In Montreal she also met her future husband and, once married, the couple moved to Toronto and began a family.

Kovalski's first excursion into children's books was as an illustrator for the work of others, creating artwork for

Fanciful illustrations by Kovalski underscore the message of Margaret Atwood's tongue-twisting fairy tale in which a self-centered princess finds her future plans destroyed when her looks are spoiled by a magic spell. (From *Princess Prunella and the Purple Peanut*.)

Frank and Zelda wish for a thousand customers a day when their business slackens, but soon find themselves regretting the chaos that results when the wish comes true. (From *Pizza for Breakfast,* written and illustrated by Kovalski.)

Allen Morgan's *Molly and Mr. Maloney* and Ted Staunton's *Puddleman,* both "enjoyable volumes," according to Anne Gilmore in *Quill and Quire.* By 1984, Kovalski had published her own book, *Brenda and Edward,* about two dogs who live "a blissful, contented existence," according to Gilmore, in a cardboard box behind a French restaurant in Toronto—a book inspired by a dog which had gotten onto the Toronto subway one day shortly after Kovalski had moved to that city. One day, Brenda, the female dog of the blissful duo, tries to bring a forgotten lunch to Edward, who works as a night watchdog at a garage. Soon lost, she eventually is hit by a car and is taken away by the driver. Poor Edward is devastated by her mysterious disappearance. Several years later a car comes into his garage with the scent of Brenda on it. Edward gets in and refuses to budge. Taken to the large country estate of the owners of the car, he there finds his long lost Brenda and the two are reunited to live happily in the country together. "Kovalski's soft, sentimental illustrations are a perfect complement to this gentle story," Gilmore concluded in *Quill and Quire.* Bernard Schwartz, writing in *Canadian Children's Literature,* echoed this sentiment, calling *Brenda and Edward* "a tender anthropomorphic story about love, caring, responsibility and faithfulness," and noted that the illustrations "effectively carry the story-

line and depict a wide range of events in city scenes and interior views."

With her 1987 title, *The Wheels on the Bus,* Kovalski introduced the sisters Jenny and Joanna and their resourceful, spunky grandmother. In this story, the three are off on a shopping trip for new winter coats, but get so involved at the bus stop singing the lyrics of the song, "The Wheels of the Bus," that they in fact miss their bus home when it comes. Never mind; Granny takes matters in hand and hails a taxi. Susan Nemeth McCarthy noted in *School Library Journal* that "Kovalski builds a humorous original story around the traditional verse," while *Books in Canada* contributor Mary Ainslie Smith commented on the "wonderful double-decker bus filled with pompous snobs, crying babies, [and] harried parents." Schwartz, writing in *Canadian Children's Literature,* noted Kovalski's "whimsical" illustrations, done mainly in colored pencils and some wash, while Andre Gagnon in *Canadian Materials* called the illustrations "lively and full of small details that children will discover as they read the story." In the main, these illustrations give a rather nostalgic air to the story, depicting a cityscape of an earlier time, and there is a remarkable similarity between the grandmother of the

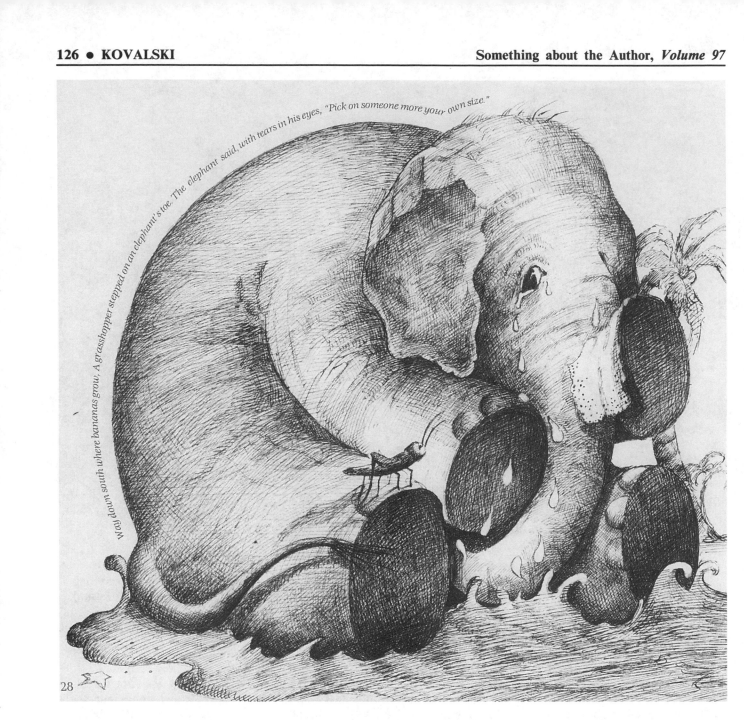

Way down south where bananas grow, A grasshopper stepped on an elephant's toe. The elephant said, with tears in his eyes, "Pick on someone more your own size."

Kovalski's comical illustrations complement the light-hearted verse in David Booth's collection, *Doctor Knickerbocker and Other Rhymes.*

story and Kovalski's Polish grandmother with whom she spent so many memorable hours as a child.

Further adventures of Jenny and Joanna with their grandmother came with *Jingle Bells,* another story employing a popular song at its center. This time the trio is off to New York City for a winter visit and an evening ride in a horse-drawn carriage. With snowflakes falling, the three burst into song, the "Jingle Bells" of the title. At the same time, a runaway horse in Central Park is ultimately stopped by the indomitable grandmother. Peter Carver, reviewing *Jingle Bells* for *Books for Young People,* noted that Kovalski's "magnificently detailed images are rich with colour," and Susan Hepler dubbed the artwork "eyecatching" in *School Library Journal,* concluding that Kovalski "renders events hu-

morously, breaks the black-line borders just as children like to behave outside the boundaries once in a while, and delightfully depicts the snowy nighttime city." *Booklist*'s Denise M. Wilms also noted the cityscapes filled with "snowy good cheer," and added that the "story's effervescence makes it a sure pleaser as an upbeat Christmas tale," while Charles Causley called the book "a lovely, lively tale" in *Times Educational Supplement.*

Kovalski returned to this winning combination of characters and song-based storyline with *Take Me Out to the Ballgame,* in which the sisters are taken to a ball game by their "wacky, fun-loving grandmother," according to *Booklist*'s Bill Ott. While Ott noted what he thought was a "problem with the plot"—just who won the game and why was grandmother climbing the bleachers to catch a balloon at the last pitch?—he concluded that such inconsistencies would be ignored by kids "who'll just go on chuckling at Grandma's goofy antics." Shirley Wilton commented in *School Library Journal* that the book was not so much about baseball as it was about a "grandmother who, despite her girth, her high heels, and red polka-dot dress, is a great sport and good companion at the ball park." Kovalski's illustrations, as usual, are richly detailed in this book, and Sandy Odegard, writing in *Canadian Children's Literature,* noted that *Take Me Out to the Ballgame* is "the sort of picture book you can spend time on pointing out details to your listener."

A picture book for older readers which does not include Jenny and Joanna is *Frank and Zelda,* titled *Pizza for Breakfast* in its U.S. edition. The story of a Depression-era pizza parlor hitting hard times, the book is loosely based on the story, "The Fisherman's Wife." When the factory closes down next door, the pizzeria owned by Frank and Zelda takes it on the chin. But when a customer comes and pays them in wishes, Frank wishes for a thousand cash-paying customers "every day and forever." The reader is reminded to be careful of what he or she wishes for, as the couple are soon inundated by customers, so many that they wish for a larger place. Wishes soon spiral out of control and finally Frank and Zelda wish only that they had never started with all these wishes. Presto: instant quiet in the old pizzeria. Patty Lawlor writing in *Quill and Quire* noted the "droll pen" of this writer-illustrator and concluded punningly that "When it comes to pizzas, Kovalski delivers." Theo Hersh commented in *Canadian Materials* on the "soft, overflowing illustrations [that] emphasize the story's humor," and decided that this "happy story" would be "enjoyed by young children."

Kovalski's illustrations for the work of other writers has been equally rewarding for both her and her audience, adding extra dimensions to the text. As *School Library Journal*'s Kathy Piehl noted in a review of Rita Golden Gelman's *I Went to the Zoo:* "The text makes this a natural for group sharing, but listeners will want to look at the pictures on their own to fully appreciate the antics." Of that same title, *Publishers Weekly* concluded that "Kovalski's funny and friendly soft pencil drawings will entertain presiding adults as well." Kovalski spoke about the role of illustrator in an article by Laurie Bildfell in *Quill and Quire.* "As an illustrator," Kovalski said, "I sometimes feel like I'm directing little movies— I'm totally interpreting the story. If you've got a lousy story, an illustrator can't save it, but if it's a good story, the illustration can really make it sing." Sometimes Kovalski's role goes far beyond that of mere decorator of text. As she once noted for *SATA,* with the manuscript of Rose Robart's *The Cake That Mack Ate,* she actually changed the character of Mack from a little boy to a dog because "it just seemed to make sense."

Reviewers have noted various influences in Kovalski's work. Reviewing her illustrations for David Booth's *Doctor Knickerbocker and Other Rhymes,* Carolyn Phe-lan commented in *Booklist* that "Kovalski's style, sophisticated yet humorous, is reminiscent of Edward Gorey's work," and reviewing that same book for *School Library Journal,* Barbara Chatton noted the same comparison. Reviewing the humorous and rather feminist fairytale, *Princess Prunella and the Purple Peanut,* by the well-known Canadian writer Margaret Atwood, *Publishers Weekly* called Kovalski's illustrations "droll," while Hazel Rochman in *Booklist* noted that her "line-and-watercolor pictures evoke a Marie Antoinette-style palace, with wry images and slapstick action." It is exactly this blend of wry humor and zany images—with both text and illustrations—that make Kovalski's work a favorite with young readers, and that has earned her the reputation of one of the most popular of contemporary Canadian illustrators and writers.

■ Works Cited

Bildfell, Laurie, "Maryann Kovalski," *Quill and Quire,* October, 1988, pp. 8, 10.

Carver, Peter, review of *Jingle Bells, Books for Young People,* October, 1988, pp. 13-14.

Causley, Charles, "Ringing in the New," *Times Educational Supplement,* December 1, 1989, p. 31.

Chatton, Barbara, review of *Doctor Knickerbocker and Other Rhymes, School Library Journal,* September, 1993, p. 238.

Gagnon, Andre, review of *The Wheels on the Bus, Canadian Materials,* March, 1988, p. 57.

Gilmore, Anne, review of *Brenda and Edward, Quill and Quire,* November, 1984, p. 12.

Hepler, Susan, review of *Jingle Bells, School Library Journal,* October, 1988, p. 35.

Hersh, Theo, review of *Frank and Zelda, Canadian Materials,* January, 1991, pp. 27-28.

Review of *I Went to the Zoo, Publishers Weekly,* July 12, 1993, p. 77.

Kovalski, Maryann, *Pizza for Breakfast,* Morrow, 1991.

Kovalski, Maryann, essay in *Something about the Author Autobiography Series,* Volume 21, Gale, 1996, pp. 225-61.

Lawlor, Patty, "In Search of Picture-Book Perfect," *Quill and Quire,* September, 1990, p. 19.

McCarthy, Susan Nemeth, review of *The Wheels on the Bus, School Library Journal,* November, 1987, p. 94.

Odegard, Sandy, "Play Ball," *Canadian Children's Literature,* No. 70, 1993, p. 94.

Ott, Bill, "Rooting for the Home Team," *Booklist,* January 15, 1993, p. 914.

Phelan, Carolyn, review of *Doctor Knickerbocker and Other Rhymes, Booklist,* August, 1993, p. 2052.

Piehl, Kathy, review of *I Went to the Zoo, School Library Journal,* November, 1993, p. 79.

Review of *Princess Prunella and the Purple Peanut, Publishers Weekly,* January 1, 1996, pp. 70-71.

Rochman, Hazel, review of *Princess Prunella and the Purple Peanut, Booklist,* December 15, 1995, p. 703.

Schwartz, Bernard, "Reprise: A Select Group," *Canadian Children's Literature,* No. 60, 1990, pp. 135-37.

Smith, Mary Ainslie, review of *The Wheels on the Bus, Books in Canada,* December, 1987, p. 13.

Wilms, Denise, review of *Jingle Bells, Booklist,* October, 1988, pp. 410-11.

Wilton, Shirley, review of *Take Me Out to the Ballgame, School Library Journal,* April, 1993, p. 112.

■ For More Information See

BOOKS

Children's Literature Review, Volume 34, Gale, 1995, pp. 113-19.

PERIODICALS

Booklist, February, 15, 1991, pp. 1201-02; January 1, 1994, pp. 833-34.

Books in Canada, April, 1991, p. 37.

Canadian Materials, March, 1989, p. 87.

Emergency Librarian, March, 1988, p. 23; March, 1989, p. 21; November, 1991, pp. 51, 59; January, 1995, p. 56.

Five Owls, January-February, 1988, p. 42.

Horn Book, January-February, 1994, pp. 67-68.

New York Times Book Review, March 20, 1988, p. 35.

Publishers Weekly, February 15, 1993, p. 238; July 5, 1993, p. 73.

School Library Journal, January, 1994, p. 100; May, 1996, pp. 94-95.*

—Sketch by J. Sydney Jones

L

LADD, Louise 1943-
(Marion Engle)

■ Personal

Born July 4, 1943, in Montclair, NJ; daughter of Chester R. and Marion C. Ladd; married Calvin Cordulack, 1965-77; married Doug Taylor, 1979; children: (first marriage) Julianne, Christopher, Jeffrey. *Education:* Wellesley College, B.A., 1965. *Politics:* Democrat. *Religion:* Society of Friends (Quakers). *Hobbies and other interests:* Reading, ice skating, acting, gardening, traveling.

■ Addresses

Home and office—27 Bloomfield Dr., Fairfield, CT 06432. *Agent*—Mary Jack Wald, Mary Jack Wald Associates, Inc., 111 East 14th St., Suite 113, New York, NY 10003.

■ Career

Writer. Teacher of the Writers' Workshop, Fairfield University, CT; also taught at Manhattanville College. Actress and producer of the Connecticut Center Acting Ensemble for 19 years; worked for ten years in the children's room at the Darien and Fairfield libraries. Freelance editor. *Member:* Society of Children's Book Writers and Illustrators, National League of American Pen Women, Women Writing the West.

■ Writings

FOR YOUNG ADULTS

A Whole Summer of Weird Susan, Bantam (New York City), 1987.
The Double Fudge Dare, Bantam, 1989.
The Anywhere Ring 1: Miracle Island, Berkley Publishing (New York City), 1995.
The Anywhere Ring 2: Castle in Time, Berkley Publishing, 1995.
The Anywhere Ring 3: Lost Valley, Berkley Publishing, 1996.

LOUISE LADD

The Anywhere Ring 4: Cherry Blossom Moon, Berkley Publishing, 1996.

"DIAMOND DUDE RANCH" SERIES

Call Me Just Plain Chris, TOR Books (New York City), 1998.
The Wrangler's Secret, TOR Books, 1998.
Prize-Winning Horse—Maybe, TOR Books, 1998.
The Perfect Horse, TOR Books, 1998.

Me, My Mare, and the Movie, TOR Books, 1998.
Rodeo! TOR Books, 1998.
Home for Christmas, TOR Books, 1998.
Belle's Foal, TOR Books, 1998.

Also ghostwriter for two popular series, including *The Magic Attic Club,* under the pen name Marion Engle.

OTHER

(Editor with husband Doug Taylor) *Sandy Dennis: A Personal Memoir* (adult biography), Papier-Mache Press (Watsonville, CA), 1997.

■ Work in Progress

Elizabeth/Lilibet, an adult historical novel; *What's a Nice Girl Like Me Doing in a Crime Like This?* an adult suspense novel; a how-to article "From Stage to Page," to be published in Writer's Digest, 1998; and a personal memoir, "Best Friends Forever," to be published in *A Fifth Helping of Chicken Soup for the Soul.*

In this installment of Louise Ladd's "Anywhere Ring" series, Jenny's magic ring transports her to a western adventure set in 1906 Colorado.

■ Sidelights

Louise Ladd comments: "I began to write in my early forties, partly so I could go to work in my bathrobe if I wanted. My husband Doug, a playwright as well as an actor, director, and teacher, encouraged me in spite of my first pathetic attempts at truly awful short stories. One, 'The Magic Umbrella,' written as an assignment for the Institute of Children's Literature, wasn't quite so bad. Bolstered by praise from Doug and my son, I slowly turned it into a novel for middle-grade readers, *A Whole Summer of Weird Susan.* By the time it sold to Bantam Books almost two years later, I was hooked on writing as a lifestyle, a passion, and a source of deep satisfaction.

"Great good fortune guided me to join a workshop led by Jean Mercier, former editor of children's books at *Publishers Weekly,* who praised and red-penciled me into decent prose. All the lucky stars were shining when Mary Jack Wald agreed to represent my work. She has stuck by me through thick and thin and has come up with numerous great ideas just when I needed them most.

"As a person who cannot live without books, I try to write the sort of humorous, adventurous stories I would enjoy if I were a child, in the hope that the joy of reading will be passed on to the growing generation. While I continue to write for the younger audience, I am also working on two adult novels, which I find far easier. Writing for young people requires using very specific and limiting do's and don'ts, while with adults, it is great fun to use any old word I choose, no matter how sophisticated.

"I studied acting for many years, developing an understanding of the creative process. My writing methods are essentially a direct translation of what I learned on stage. Playing a role or writing a scene, I try to allow my characters to behave naturally under fictitious circumstances. Coming up with story ideas is identical to creating improvisations in class, never forgetting the central impelling force: a sense of urgency. The highest compliment of all is when I am told, 'I couldn't put your book down,' especially when adults say it about my novels for kids!

"I approach writing as a job. After all, if I didn't write, I'd have to put on high heels and sit in an office, taking orders from someone else. On days when I face the computer with dread, thinking of the alternative cures writer's block within seconds. Basically I write because I love to create. Who could ask for anything more?"

■ For More Information See

PERIODICALS

Booklist, September 15, 1987, p. 155.
Publishers Weekly, August 28, 1987, p. 80; January 13, 1989, p. 91; March 3, 1997, p. 59.
School Library Journal, May, 1989, p. 110.

LASSITER, Mary
See HOFFMAN, Mary (Margaret)

*   *   *

LAUX, Connie
See LAUX, Constance

*   *   *

LAUX, Constance 1952-
(Connie Deka, Connie Laux, Zoe Daniels)

■ Personal

Born January 21, 1952, in Cleveland, OH; daughter of Stanley J. (a police officer) and Mildred (Parcheta) Deka; married David H. Laux, Jr. (in sales), October 12, 1973; children: Anne, David. *Education:* Cleveland State University, B.A., 1973; also attended Queen's College, Oxford. *Hobbies and other interests:* Gardening, reading.

■ Addresses

Home—3914 Skyview Dr., Brunswick, OH 44212. *Agent*—Laura Peterson, Curtis Brown, Ltd., 10 Astor Pl., New York, NY 10003.

■ Career

Writer. Juvenile Diabetes Foundation, volunteer worker, 1991—. *Member:* Romance Writers of America (chapter president, 1987-90), Novelists, Inc., Ohio Published Authors League.

■ Awards, Honors

Bright Promise was named the "best selling Americana novel of 1993" by *Booklovers;* KISS award, *Romantic Times* Magazine, for *Touched by Magic.*

■ Writings

FOR CHILDREN

R. L. Stine's Ghosts of Fear Street, Book VII: Fright Knight, Pocket Books (New York City), 1996.

"YEAR OF THE CAT" HORROR TRILOGY; FOR YOUNG ADULTS; UNDER PSEUDONYM ZOE DANIELS

The Dream, (Book I), Berkley Publishing (New York City), 1995.
The Hunt, (Book II), Berkley Publishing, 1995.
The Amulet, (Book III), Berkley Publishing, 1995.

"BLOOD MOON" HORROR TRILOGY; FOR YOUNG ADULTS

The Curse, (Book I), Harper (New York City), 1995.
The Fortune Teller, (Book II), Harper, 1995.
The Reckoning, (Book III), Harper, 1996.

CONSTANCE LAUX

OTHER

Twilight Secrets (romance novel), Diamond (New York City), 1992.
(As Connie Deka) *Bright Promise* (romance novel), Diamond, 1993.
Moonlight Whispers (romance novel), Diamond, 1993.
Earthly Delights (romance novel), Zebra Books (New York City), 1995.
Touched by Magic (romance novel), Zebra Books, 1996.
Angel Love (romance novel), Zebra Books, 1996.
Devil's Diamond (romance novel), Topaz Books, 1998.

Work represented in anthologies, including *Angel Love,* Zebra Books, 1996.

■ Work in Progress

Two romance novels, *Shadowlands* and *Diamonds and Desire;* a young adult horror series.

■ Sidelights

Constance Laux comments: "All writing starts with an idea, and ideas come from everywhere. Snatches of conversation, articles in the newspaper, something I see on television—any one of them can start an idea germinating. After I have my idea, I begin my research. That can be especially time-consuming when I am working on a historical romance, but even contemporary stories need research. I generally do enough to get started, then research as I write. As a wise writer once said, all writing is re-writing. My process involves lots of hours slapping sentences into shape, and lots more hours working and reworking. It can take from two months (for a young adult novel) to six months (for a historical romance) for me to complete a book."

■ For More Information See

PERIODICALS

Kliatt, January, 1996, p. 10.
Library Journal, August 1996, p. 57.
Voices of Youth Advocates, August, 1995, p. 145.

*   *   *

DAVID LAVENDER

LAVENDER, David (Sievert) 1910-

■ Personal

Born February 4, 1910, in Telluride, CO; son of Edgar Norfolk and Edith (Garrigues) Lavender; married Martha Bloom, 1933 (deceased); married Mildred Moreland, 1960 (deceased); married Muriel Sharkey, 1990; children: (first marriage) David Garrigues, (second marriage; stepchildren) James Moreland, Judith Moreland Money, Leith Moreland Hollowell; (third marriage; stepchildren) Theresa Sharkey, Robert Sharkey, Miles Sharkey. *Education:* Princeton University, A.B., 1931; Stanford University, graduate study, 1931-32.

■ Addresses

Home—4771 Thacher Road, Ojai, CA 93023.

■ Career

Author and educator. Thacher School, Ojai, CA, member of faculty, 1943-70. Consultant to special collections at the library of the University of California, Santa Barbara, 1982-91, and to the California history section, Oakland Museum, 1983-84. *Member:* American Society of Historians, Southwest National Parks and Monuments Association (board member, 1981-91), Ojai Land Conservancy (board member).

■ Awards, Honors

Commonwealth Club of California medals, 1948, for *The Big Divide,* 1958, for *Land of Giants,* 1975, for *Nothing Seemed Impossible,* and 1989, for *The Way to the Western Sea;* Buffalo Award, New York Westerners, Spur Award, Western Writers of America, and Rupert Hughes Award, Los Angeles Authors Club, all 1954, all for *Bent's Fort;* Guggenheim fellowships, 1961-62, 1968-69; Western Writers of America award, and American Heritage award, both 1965, both for *The Great West;* Award of Merit, American Association for State and Local History, 1968, for *The Rockies;* Award of Merit, California Historical Society, 1980, for outstanding contribution to California history; named Historical Society of Southern California fellow, 1988.

■ Writings

FOR CHILDREN

Trouble at Tamarack, Westminster, 1943.
Mick Maroney, Raider, Westminster, 1946.
Golden Trek, Westminster, 1948.
The Trail to Santa Fe, Houghton, 1958.
The Story of California (textbook), American Heritage (New York City), 1969.
The Santa Fe Trail, Holiday House, 1995.
Snowbound: The Tragic Story of the Donner Party, Holiday House, 1996.
Mother Earth, Father Sky: The Pueblo Indians of the American Southwest, Holiday House, 1998.

ADULT NOVELS

Andy Claybourne, Doubleday, 1946.
Red Mountain, Doubleday, 1963.

NONFICTION

One Man's West, Doubleday, 1943, 2nd ed., 1956.
The Big Divide, Doubleday, 1948.
Bent's Fort, Doubleday, 1954.
Land of Giants: The Drive to the Pacific Northwest, 1750-1950, Doubleday, 1958.
The Story of Cyprus Mines Corporation, Huntington Library, 1962.
Westward Vision: The Story of the Oregon Trail, McGraw, 1963.
The Fist in the Wilderness, Doubleday, 1964.
The Great West, American Heritage, 1965, revised as *American Heritage History of the Great West,* Bonanza Books (New York City), 1982.

Climax at Buena Vista, Lippincott, 1966.

The Rockies, Harper, 1968.

The Great Persuader, Doubleday, 1970.

California: Land of New Beginnings, Harper, 1972.

Nothing Seemed Impossible: William C. Ralston and Early San Francisco, American West (Palo Alto, CA), 1975.

California: A Bicentennial History, Norton, 1976.

(And photographer, with Lee Boltin) *David Lavender's Colorado,* Doubleday, 1976.

Winner Take All: A History of the Trans-Canada Canoe Trail, McGraw, 1977.

The Southwest, Harper, 1980.

Los Angeles, Two Hundred, Continental Heritage (Tulsa, OK), 1980.

The Overland Migrations, Jefferson National Memorial, 1981.

Colorado River Country, Dutton, 1982.

Fort Laramie and the Changing Frontier, National Park Service, 1984.

River Runners of the Grand Canyon, Grand Canyon History Association, 1985.

Images from the Southwest, illustrated by Marc Gaede, Northland (Flagstaff, AZ), 1986.

The Telluride Story, Wayfinder Press (Ouray, CO), 1987.

The Way to the Western Sea: Lewis and Clark across the Continent, Harper, 1988.

(Contributor) *Growing up Western,* Knopf, 1990.

Let Me Be Free: The Nez Perce Tragedy, HarperCollins, 1992.

Author of pamphlets for the National Park Service. Contributor to *Encyclopedia Britannica* and to periodicals, including *Arizona Highways, National Geographic Traveler, New York Times, New York Herald Tribune,* and *Wilderness Magazine.* Author of museum catalogue *California: A Place, a People, a Dream,* Chronicle Books, 1986, for Oakland Museum.

■ Adaptations

Bent's Fort and *One Man's West* were both recorded on audio cassette, Books on Tape, 1986.

■ Work in Progress

The Grand Canyon, a nonfiction book for Holiday House.

■ Sidelights

Born in Colorado and living for many years in his adopted state of California, historian and educator David Lavender has written extensively on the history and geography of the western United States. In books that include *The Way to the Sea: Lewis and Clark across the Continent* and *California: Land of New Beginnings,* as well as numerous publications for the National Park Service and local museums, Lavender has shared his extensive knowledge and enthusiasm for wide open spaces of the West with children and adults alike.

The awe-inspiring beauty of the land serves as the backdrop to several of Lavender's works included in the "Regions of America" series, one of which is *The Rockies,* published in 1968. Against the towering mountain range that stretches northward from Central New Mexico to the Canadian border, Lavender spins a saga that includes Spanish conquistadors, the Gold Rush, the coming of the Iron Horse (railroads), and the growth of modern industry, all of which have been affected by the region's unique landscape. Bitter wars between farmers over water and grazing rights, the rise of the recreation industry, mining operations, and environmental concerns are also issues that play a crucial part in Lavender's broad-ranging history. Through his intimate knowledge of the region of his birth, the author "communicates [his love of the Rockies] to the reader," according to a *Publishers Weekly* reviewer. Lavender's 1972 work, *California: Land of New Beginnings,* similarly focuses on the history of that state as it relates to the landscape. "Lavender lends his history a benevolent perspective despite his acknowledgment of California's ugly patches," noted a *Publishers Weekly* critic, commenting on the author's choice to balance his twelve-decade discussion of the state's cultural richness and Ronald Reagan's governorship with the political scandals of earlier decades and the racial strife that still afflicts many of California's urban areas. In *The Southwest,* Lavender describes the life of peoples living in that region's "harsh, demanding, sun-blasted" land from the prehistoric era to the present. Age-old racial and cultural

Lavender's even-handed account relates the details of the Donner Party's arduous journey west in 1846 which resulted in incidents of cannibalism. (Cover photo by Stephen Trimble.)

In *The Santa Fe Trail,* Lavender describes the main route linking American homesteaders in the west with traders to the east.

conflicts, the advent of statehood, the rise of modern cities, and the threats posed by modern industry figure prominently within the pages of his history of the Southwest region.

In addition to general regional histories, Lavender has published several books that focus on particular events in the history of the western United States. Published in 1988, *The Way to the Western Sea* details the 1804-1806 expedition headed by Meriwether Lewis and William Clark to explore the newly acquired Louisiana Purchase, a former French territory stretching west of the Mississippi River to the Rocky Mountains. Beginning in St. Louis, Missouri, the pair traveled up the Missouri River and down the Columbia River to the shores of the Pacific Ocean—the "Western Sea" of Lavender's title. Detailing the expedition's interaction with the Native American tribes of the region, the volume also reveals the tragic aftermath of the expedition, as Lewis later succumbed to alcoholism, abandoned his friends, and eventually committed suicide. Calling the author's treatment of this subject "suspenseful, moving, [and] detailed," a *Publishers Weekly* reviewer maintained that Lavender "transforms [Lewis and Clark's] schoolbook exploit into the stuff of high adventure and American tragedy."

With passage to the Pacific Ocean opened by Lewis and Clark, the western territories were quickly flooded with settlers in search of a new home. Lavender's 1995 book, *The Santa Fe Trail,* describes the main route linking homesteaders as far west as Santa Fe, New Mexico, with traders to the east. A 775-mile-long pathway beginning in Independence, Missouri, the trail took between seven to ten weeks for a party of settlers to traverse and acted as a lifeline to the West from 1821 until the coming of the railways in the late 1870s. "Lavender chronicles the development of commerce ... clearly explaining the risks travelers faced, as well as the potential for profit that attracted so many traders," noted Kristin Lott, praising the thoroughness of *The Santa Fe Trail* work in her review for *School Library Journal.*

With the arrival of waves of white settlers from the East, thirsty for land and resources, came the gradual displacement of Native American people. In his 1992 work *Let Me Be Free: The Nez Perce Tragedy,* Lavender examines how the nomadic tribe who attempted to befriend early white settlers—including Lewis and Clark, fur traders, and Christian missionaries—was forced to leave the lands of their ancestors through the machinations of self-serving politicians and land speculators that resulted in the "thief treaty" of 1863. Ending with the capture of the mythic Chief Joseph and his band of hold-outs by the U.S. Cavalry after a 1,700-mile march to Canada in 1877, Lavender "offers a tragic tale of a Native American tribe's loss of its land, culture, and identity," according to a *Kirkus Reviews* contributor who praised the extensive collection of photographs included in the volume.

While tragedy would ultimately befall all the Native American tribes, Anglo settlers also endured their share of hardship during the settlement of the West. While harsh winters, Indian attacks, and the likelihood of suffering injury, starvation, or disease made the trip westward in the mid-nineteenth century a risky undertaking, no tragedy has been more compelling to later historians and the general public than that suffered by the ill-fated Donner Party, organized in 1846 by two elderly farmers, Jacob and George Donner. In *Snowbound: The Tragic Story of the Donner Party,* Lavender recounts this often-sensationalized segment of the history of the West, as a wagon train carrying eighty-three settlers became trapped by the onset of winter in an area of the Sierra Nevada that provided them with neither sufficient food nor shelter. Making an effort to downplay the horrific reports of cannibalism in the camp by noting the many acts of heroism that also occurred, Lavender allows readers to "[come] away with a much clearer understanding of the hardships and dangers of crossing the continent by wagon train—*any* wagon train," according to *School Library Journal* contributor Elaine Fort Weischedel. Praising the author's use of primary source materials and numerous photographs, Hazel Rochman noted in *Booklist* that Lavender, "an eminent historian of the west ... combin[es] a vivid narrative with his analysis of what happened and why." "Evenhanded and a bit probing, this is a fascinating account of the human cost in opening the West," added Margaret A. Bush in her review of *Snowbound* for *Horn Book.*

"This job of mine could hardly be better," Lavender once told *SATA.* "I explore the best parts of the American West—backpacking, riding horseback, and sometimes in jeeps or rafting—in order to acquire for my writing a sense of immediacy and reality. Then, as I read what others have said on the subject and as I refine my own thoughts during the process of writing, a new sort of energizing takes over and I find myself looking with new eyes and a new understanding at old scenes, a constant sequence of rediscoveries as it were." Although a prolific writer on the subject of western United States history, Lavender denies tiring of the subject: "No, I don't get tired of the West," he explained to *SATA;* "it is too big and too dynamic, and filled with too many choice inhabitants for that."

■ Works Cited

Bush, Margaret A., review of *Snowbound: The Tragic Story of the Donner Party, Horn Book,* September-October, 1996, pp. 618-19.
Review of *California: Land of New Beginnings, Publishers Weekly,* September 25, 1972, p. 53.
Lavender, David, *The Southwest,* Harper, 1980.
Review of *Let Me Be Free: The Nez Perce Tragedy, Kirkus Reviews,* March 15, 1992, p. 373.
Lott, Kristin, review of *The Santa Fe Trail, School Library Journal,* June, 1995, p. 121.
Rochman, Hazel, review of *Snowbound: The Tragic Story of the Donner Party, Booklist,* June 1-15, 1996, p. 1692.
Review of *The Rockies, Publishers Weekly,* March 11, 1968, p. 46.
Review of *The Way to the Western Sea, Publishers Weekly,* October 14, 1988, p. 54.
Weischedel, Elaine Fort, review of *Snowbound: The Tragic Story of the Donner Party, School Library Journal,* July, 1996, p. 92.

■ For More Information See

PERIODICALS

Booklist, April 15, 1968, p. 970; September 1, 1972, p. 24; November 15, 1988, p. 534.
Kirkus Reviews, October 15, 1988, p. 1511.
New York Times Book Review, May 10, 1970; August 5, 1973.
Publishers Weekly, November 12, 1979, p. 54; March 30, 1992, p. 96.

* * *

LESSEM, Don 1951-

■ Personal

Born December 2, 1951, in New York, NY; son of Lawrence (a dentist) and Gertrude (a psychologist; maiden name, Goldman) Lessem; married Paula Hartstein (a reading specialist), June 8, 1978; children: Rebecca, Erica. *Education:* Brandeis University, B.A.

DON LESSEM

(cum laude) 1973; studies in biobehavioralism, University of Massachusetts—Boston, 1976; Knight Science Journalism fellowship, Massachusetts Institute of Technology, 1988. *Politics:* Anarchist. *Religion:* Jewish. *Hobbies and other interests:* Travel, sports.

■ Addresses

Home and office—84 Moffat Rd., Waban, MA 02168. *Electronic mail*—DinoDonL@aol.com. *Agent*—Al Zuckerman, Writers House, 21 W. 26th St., New York, NY 10010.

■ Career

Writer and consultant. Dinosaur Productions, Waban, president, 1995—; Dinosaur Exhibitions, Waban, MA, president, 1996—. Columnist for *Highlights Magazine.* Writer for and host of television programs *Discovery* and *Nova* for PBS. Technical advisor on films and for theme parks. *Member:* Dinosaur Society (founder), Society of Vertebrate Paleontology, Windsor Club (board member).

■ Awards, Honors

Winner of several National Science Teachers Association Awards for his books for children.

■ Writings

Life Is No Yuk for the Yak: A Book of Endangered Animals, illustrated by Linda Bourke, Crane Russak (New York), 1977.
Aerphobics: The Scientific Way to Stop Exercising (humor), Morrow, 1980.
The Worst of Everything: The Experts' Listing of the Most Loathsome and Deficient in Every Realm of Our Lives, McGraw-Hill, 1988.
(With John R. Horner) *Digging Up Tyrannosaurus Rex,* Crown, 1992.
Kings of Creation: How a New Breed of Scientists Is Revolutionizing Our Understanding of Dinosaurs, illustrated by John Sibbick, Simon & Schuster, 1992, republished as *Dinosaurs Rediscovered: New Findings Which Are Revolutionizing Dinosaur Science,* Touchstone, 1993.
(With John R. Horner) *The Complete T. Rex: How Stunning New Discoveries Are Changing Our Understanding of the World's Most Famous Dinosaur,* Simon & Schuster, 1993.
(With Donald F. Glut) *The Dinosaur Society's Dinosaur Encyclopedia,* Random House, 1993.
The Iceman, Crown, 1994.
Jack Horner: Living with Dinosaurs, illustrated by Janet Hamlin, Scientific American Books for Young Readers (New York), 1994.
Inside the Amazing Amazon: Incredible Fold-Out Cross Sections of the World's Greatest Rainforest, illustrated by Michael Rothman, Crown, 1995.
Ornithomimids, the Fastest Dinosaur, illustrated by Donna Braginetz, Carolrhoda (Minneapolis, MN), 1996.

Raptors! The Nastiest Dinosaurs, illustrated by David Peters, Little, Brown, 1996.
Seismosaurus: The Longest Dinosaur, illustrated by Donna Braginetz, Carolrhoda, 1996.
Troodon, the Smartest Dinosaur, illustrated by Donna Braginetz, Carolrhoda, 1996.
Utahraptor: The Deadliest Dinosaur, illustrated by Donna Braginetz, Carolrhoda, 1996.
Supergiants! The Biggest Dinosaurs, illustrated by David Peters, Little, Brown, 1997.
Bigger than T-Rex, Random House, 1997.
Skeleton Detective, Random House, 1997.
Dinosaur Worlds: New Dinosaurs, New Discoveries, Boyds Mills, 1997.
Dinosaurs to Dodos: Encyclopedia of Extinct Animals, Scholastic, 1998.
All the Dirt on Dinosaurs, Tor, 1998.

■ Work in Progress

Dinosaur Lands (twelve volumes), for Carolrhoda, 1999.

■ Sidelights

Don Lessem told *Something about the Author* (*SATA*), "Dinosaurs are my writing life, at least much of it. My job as I see it is to communicate the latest discoveries of dinosaurs to anyone who gives a hoot, especially kids. I do so via exhibits I build, such as Lost World; writing a column for *Highlights Magazine;* creating CDs for

Don Lessem's biography profiles John R. Horner, chief curator of paleontology at the University of Montana and inspiration for the scientist in *Jurassic Park.* (Cover illustration by Janet Hamlin.)

Microsoft; creating the largest dinosaur charity and its children's newspaper (The Dinosaur Society and *Dino Times*); creating websites of my own (www.gigano tosaurus.com); casting the largest meat-eating dinosaur; advising on theme parks and movies; writing and hosting *Nova* and *Discovery* documentaries; AND writing books.

"While I've also written books on Amazon animals and mummies, I got onto dinosaurs visiting a Montana dig for a newspaper while an MIT science journalism fellow in 1988. I find the new discoveries, the remote locales, the characters who study dinosaurs, and the scavenger hunting that is much of the science to be continually fascinating. Many, at least those under the age of ten, share that interest, fortunately, or I'd be working nights at McDonald's."

Lessem is a science writer for middle graders and humorous books for adults whose engaging style and evident excitement about his topics, coupled with his dedication to providing accurate, accessible information on his subjects, have made his books popular with readers and critics alike. Nicknamed "Dino Don," Lessem is best known for his books on dinosaurs and the scientists who have dedicated their lives to uncovering the mysteries of these long-extinct animals. His first books, including *Life Is No Yuk for the Yak,* in which profiles of endangered species are accompanied by lighthearted limericks and Linda Bourke's cartoon illustrations, often combine science with a humorous approach. The majority of his books outline the history of and current findings about a wide variety of dinosaurs—their discovery, habits, environments, and time periods. In addition to his works about dinosaurs, Lessem is the author of a book on the Amazon rainforest, *Inside the Amazing Amazon,* in which the text augments oversize fold-out illustrations by Michael Rothman that detail plant and animal life in the world's largest rainforest. He is also the creator of *The Iceman,* a book describing the discovery of a five-thousand-year-old mummy in the mountains of Europe and what scientists gleaned from it about the life of prehistoric Europeans, and *Jack Horner: Living with Dinosaurs,* a biography about John R. Horner, the chief curator of paleontology at the University of Montana and the scientific advisor on the film *Jurassic Park* who is also a friend of the author. A writer who studied biobehavioralism at the University of Massachusetts and science journalism at MIT, Lessem is the founder of several dinosaur-related organizations, including the Dinosaur Society, a group for children; Dinosaur Productions; and Dinosaur Exhibitions; he is also a member of the developing committee for the Society of Vertebrate Paleontology.

Notable among Lessem's many books on dinosaurs is *Dinosaur Worlds: New Dinosaurs, New Discoveries,* a work in which several of the most important sites where dinosaur remains have been found are introduced to the reader, who is also given information on the environments, prey, and life cycles of a large number of the creatures. "[This] is a book that report writers and

Dinosaur expert Lessem has penned several books about the extinct creatures, among them his 1997 work centering on the gigantic plant-eating sauropods.

dinophiles won't want to miss," averred Stephanie Zvirin in *Booklist.* Lessem's books on individual dinosaurs include *Raptors! The Nastiest Dinosaurs, Ornithomimids: The Fastest Dinosaur, Troodon: The Smartest Dinosaur, Seismosaurus: The Longest Dinosaur,* and *Utahraptor: The Deadliest Dinosaur,* all part of a series on special dinosaurs published by Carolrhoda in 1996. In these books, Lessem gathers information on the discovery of the fossil remains of each dinosaur type and the paleontologists who found them as well as on how information about their abilities and habits has been deduced from the fossil evidence; in addition, the author speculates about possible evolutionary descendants of his subjects. "Lessem treats a popular topic adeptly, humorously, and with a balance of information that is both relevant and stimulating to read," remarked Olga Kuharets in a review of *Seismosaurus* and *Utahraptor* in *School Library Journal.* In her *Booklist* review of *Ornithominids* and *Troodon,* Frances Bradburn commented that these "finely crafted" books offer "a fascinating look at how paleontologists discover the fossilized remains of these huge beasts." In addition, Lessem's texts are praised by critics for their clarity and organization of a wealth of fascinating material.

Lessem's dedication to introducing children and adults to the lives of the scientists behind the scientific discoveries has yielded such works as *Kings of Creation:*

How a New Breed of Scientists Is Revolutionizing Our Understanding of Dinosaurs and *Jack Horner: Living with Dinosaurs.* In *Kings of Creation,* the author presents an overview of the explosion of new information that has become available over the last three decades, in which the popular image of dinosaurs has been completely revised by a group of scientists who have uncovered signs of intelligence, speed, and nurturing in species previously thought to be stupid, slow, and hostile even to their own offspring. Leading scientists, significant digs, and the new theories are all presented in a work in which Lessem, according to a reviewer for *Publishers Weekly,* "presents a lively sampling of current and significant work on dinosaurs worldwide.... This is the best book on the subject since Robert Bakker's *Dinosaur Heresies* and a treat for buffs." In Lessem's book about Horner, the paleontologist with whom Lessem has written two books and with whom he worked as a consultant on the immensely popular film *Jurassic Park,* the author presents both personal background about Horner and his most famous scientific discoveries. Lessem "writes with zest, showing the determination and excitement that accompanied Horner's explorations," remarked Susan Dove Lempke in *Bulletin of the Center for Children's Books.* Evelyn Tiffany-Castiglioni noted in *Appraisal* that "Lessem's portrayal of Horner feels authentic: a plainspoken, quiet, thoughtful man who is most at home walking on the badlands where dinosaurs walked before him." Writing in the same publication, Patricia Manning maintained that Lessem's writing style in *Jack Horner* is "perfectly tailored to fourth and fifth graders." A reviewer in *Kirkus Reviews* concurred: "[The] book works thanks to Lessem's own enthusiasm for dinosaurs and his impressive knack for writing in kid-speak."

Lessem's books on dinosaurs and paleontologists have garnered widespread praise for their accumulation of a wealth of information on a topic of interest to many children. This information is consistently presented in an attractive, uncluttered format, in prose that critics consider both clear and inspirational, displaying the author's own enthusiasm for his subject. Lessem's books on the scientists whose lives have been dedicated to revising and augmenting what is known about dinosaurs display similar qualities, according to the author's reviewers.

"My aspiration," Lessem told *SATA,* "is to continue providing children with what for so long they have lacked—current and accurate information on new scientific discoveries and the methods behind them in hopes of feeding their mania for dinosaurs and spreading it to all of science as a lifetime interest.

"I'm doing so most recently by not only writing but 'packaging' books, providing illustrators and graphics for publishers, for fifteen children's books in press. I hope to continue as long as dinosaurs are still alive, at least in the imaginations of many of us."

■ Works Cited

Bradburn, Frances, review of *Ornithomimids* and *Troodon, Booklist,* February 15, 1996, p. 1014.
Review of *Jack Horner, Kirkus Reviews,* November 15, 1994, p. 1534.
Review of *Kings of Creation, Publishers Weekly,* March 2, 1992, p. 58.
Kuharets, Olga, review of *Seismosaurus* and *Utahraptor, School Library Journal,* September, 1996, p. 218.
Lempke, Susan Dove, review of *Jack Horner, Bulletin of the Center for Children's Books,* December, 1994, p. 135.
Manning, Patricia, review of *Jack Horner, Appraisal,* winter, 1995, p. 112-13.
Tiffany-Castiglioni, Evelyn, review of *Jack Horner, Appraisal,* winter, 1995, pp. 113-14.
Zvirin, Stephanie, review of *Dinosaur Worlds, Booklist,* November 15, 1996, pp. 583-84.

■ For More Information See

PERIODICALS

Appraisal, winter-spring, 1996, pp. 35-36.
Booklist, April 1, 1992, p. 1419; September 1, 1996, p. 997.
Bulletin of the Center for Children's Books, September, 1994, p. 17.
Kirkus Reviews, May 15, 1994, p. 702; December 1, 1995, p. 1703.
Publishers Weekly, November 4, 1996, p. 78.
School Library Journal, March, 1978, p. 138; July, 1994, p. 111; January, 1996, p. 120; October, 1996, pp. 135-36; September, 1997, p. 232; December, 1997, p. 140.

* * *

LEVIN, Miriam (Ramsfelder) 1962-

■ Personal

Born August 30, 1962, in New York, NY; daughter of Walter (a mechanical engineer) and Ruth (Schwarzschild) Ramsfelder; married Alan Jay Levin (a certified public accountant), July 4, 1985; children: Eric, Jeremy, Rebecca. *Education:* Rutgers University, B.A., 1984. *Religion:* Jewish.

■ Addresses

Home—42-39 Herold Dr., Fair Lawn, NJ 07410. *Electronic mail*—amejr @ juno.com.

■ Career

Teacher, social worker.

■ Writings

In the Beginning, illustrated by Katherine Janus Kahn, Kar-Ben (Rockville, MD), 1996.

Miriam Levin with children.

Contributor to *Bergen Record.*

■ Sidelights

Miriam Levin told *Something about the Author* (*SATA*): "I have always been a writer. No matter what the occasion, I had a poem, letter, or story to accompany it. More importantly, however, I have also always been a reader. I believe that it is this love of books that has enabled me to succeed as an author today. As I read mysteries, love stories, biographies, and best-selling novels, I am also learning about the art of writing. As I read picture books to my children, I listen with a writer's ear to the content and quality of these stories, and I learn. It was the echo of other people's words that convinced me to begin my own writing career.

"Today, I am the mother of three young children, a teacher, and a graduate student pursuing a master's degree in social work. I write whenever I have the opportunity, which unfortunately is not often. Even when I cannot put pen to paper, I am still writing in my head. My first published book, *In the Beginning,* a biblical allegory, was composed in this fashion until I found the time to actually write it out on scraps of paper. I have also written other children's books with biblical themes, as well as books that have more widespread appeal. These are still looking for a publishing house to call home."

■ For More Information See

PERIODICALS

School Library Journal, January, 1997, p. 84.

*   *   *

LILLEY, Stephen R(ay) 1950-

■ Personal

Born September 13, 1950, in Louisiana, MO; son of Forrest T. (a farmer and carpenter) and Darlene (Stephens; present surname, Cearlock) Lilley; married Rebecca J. Schuster (a counselor), June 10, 1972; children: Jacob Stephen, Sariya Desiree. *Education:* University of Missouri-Columbia, B.S., 1972; Northeast Missouri State University (Truman University), M.A., 1976. *Politics:* "Independent voter." *Religion:* Southern Baptist. *Hobbies and other interests:* Reading, hunting, music, shooting, sports acrobatics.

STEPHEN R. LILLEY

■ Addresses

Home—274 Lilley Lane, Elsberry, MO 63343.
Office—Elsberry High School, Elsberry, MO 63343.

■ Career

Schoolteacher in Winfield, MO, 1972-74; Lincoln County Schools, Elsberry, MO, teacher, 1974—. Northeast Missouri State University, adjunct faculty, 1977; Hannibal LaGrange College, adjunct faculty, 1989-92. Jazz musician and trumpet player. *Member:* American Federation of Musicians, Missouri Federation of Parents (president of Elsberry chapter, 1988-91).

■ Awards, Honors

History Feature of the Year Award, *Highlights for Children,* 1990; National Silver Medal, U.S. Sports Acrobatic Federation, 1994; Outstanding History Teacher award, Troy, MO chapter, Daughters of the American Revolution, 1997.

■ Writings

Hernando Cortes, Lucent Books (San Diego, CA), 1996. *The Conquest of Mexico,* Lucent Books, 1997.

Contributor to periodicals, including *Highlights for Children.*

■ Work in Progress

Fighters against Slavery (tentative title), completion expected in 1998.

■ Sidelights

Stephen R. Lilley told *Something about the Author* (*SATA*): "I have always been a reader (I suspect most authors have been). The transition to writing for publication seemed natural enough. Both my mother and grandmother were successful authors, but I just seemed to accumulate rejection slips. Eventually, my sale of two short articles on Congressman Clarence Cannon encouraged me to continue writing. One day while killing time at our family's yard sale, my wife suggested I jot down a short article for publication in *Highlights for Children.* On a discarded computer printout I wrote an anecdote about Alexander the Great, cleaned it up, and submitted it. *Highlights* bought Alexander and two more, introducing me to the wonderful world of children's literature.

"Writing juvenile history gives me a chance to give young people a necessary sense of past, not always an easy thing to do with adolescents. I think it is crucial that juvenile history (and all other history) be accurate and uncompromising. Too often authors and publishers produce trendy, politicized works or write books devoid of moral integrity. The written word is too powerful to squander in this way.

"As for my personal life, I'm a bit of a dabbler. I am a working musician and part-time farmer. For four years I made up half of the oldest sports acrobatic pair in the United States. I enjoy hunting and other outdoor activities. Few things please me as much as a hot meal of game meat and home-grown garden produce. I have encouraged my own children to write, and both have published in magazines. I am most pleased that my wife and children also share the most important thing in my life—my faith in Christ."

■ For More Information See

PERIODICALS

Horn Book Guide, Fall, 1996, p. 371.
School Library Journal, January, 1996, p. 134.

* * *

LITTLEFIELD, Holly 1963-

■ Personal

Born April 6, 1963, in Ohio; daughter of Charles (a counselor) and Marilyn (a university administrator; maiden name, Hughes; present surname, Scamman) Littlefield; married John Enright (a financial analyst), October 22, 1988; children: Patrick, Brennan. *Education:* University of Minnesota-Twin Cities, B.A., 1985, M.A., 1992, and doctoral study. *Hobbies and other interests:* Reading, movies, sailing, making stained glass windows, travel.

■ Addresses

Home—15212 65th Place N., Maple Grove, MN 55311. *Office*—227 Lind Hall, University of Minnesota—Minneapolis, MN 55455. *Electronic mail*—littl009 @ maroon.tc.umn.

■ Career

High school teacher in Osseo, MN, 1985-92; University of Minnesota-Minneapolis, researcher and teacher of composition, 1992—. *Member:* Modern Language Association of America, National Council of Teachers of English, Phi Beta Kappa.

■ Writings

Fire at the Triangle Factory (fiction), illustrated by Mary O'Keefe Young, Carolrhoda (Minneapolis, MN), 1996.
The Colors of Germany (nonfiction), Carolrhoda, 1997.
The Colors of Japan (nonfiction), illustrated by Helen Byers, Carolrhoda, 1997.

■ Work in Progress

Children of the Trail West, a nonfiction about wagon trains, *Colors of Ghana,* and *Colors of India.*

Holly Littlefield with Steve.

■ Sidelights

Holly Littlefield told *Something about the Author* (*SATA*): "I really love the challenge of writing for children. When I was a child I read constantly, and I would like to think that I am writing the kinds of books that I would have enjoyed then and that my own children will one day like. I also like to do the research that goes with writing these books. So much of history is about what the adults did and said. I try to find and tell the children's stories."

■ For More Information See

PERIODICALS

AJL Newsletter, February-March, 1997, p. 13.
Booklist, August, 1996, p. 1900.
Notes from the Windowsill, July, 1996.
School Library Journal, October, 1996, p. 122.

*   *   *

LLOYD, Alan
See LLOYD, A(lan) R(ichard)

*   *   *

LLOYD, A(lan) R(ichard) 1927-
(Alan Lloyd)

■ Personal

Born February 22, 1927, in London, England; married Daphne Chaffe; children: one son. *Education:* Attended Kingston School of Art.

■ Addresses

Agent—c/o HarperCollins, 77-85 Fulham Palace Road, London W6 8JB, England.

■ Career

Jersey Evening Post, journalist; freelance magazine writer; full-time writer, 1962—. *Military service:* British Army, Royal Fusiliers.

■ Writings

FANTASY NOVELS; "KINE" SERIES

Kine, St. Martin's Press (New York), 1982, Hamlyn (Feltham, England), 1982; also published in England as *Marshworld,* Arrow (London), 1990.
Witchwood, Muller (London), 1989.
Dragonpond, Muller, 1990, published as *Dragon Pond,* Arrow, 1991.

OTHER NOVELS

The Last Otter, illustrated by Douglas Hall, Hutchinson (London), 1984, published in the United States as *The Boy and the Otter,* Holt, Rinehart, and Winston, 1985.

The Farm Dog, Hutchinson Century (London), 1986.
Wingfoot, Grafton (London), 1993.

NONFICTION; AS ALAN LLOYD

The Drums of Kumasi, Longman (London), 1964.
The Making of the King 1066, Holt, Rinehart, 1966, published in England as *The Year of the Conqueror,* Longman, 1966.
The Spanish Centuries, Doubleday, 1968.
Franco, Doubleday, 1969, Longmans (Marlow, England), 1970.
The King Who Lost America: A Portrait of the Life and Times of George III, Doubleday, 1971, published in England as *The Wickedest Age: The Life and Times of George III,* David and Charles (Newton Abbot, Devon), 1971.
The Maligned Monarch: A Life of King John of England, Doubleday, 1972, published in England as *King John,* David and Charles, 1973.
The Zulu War, 1879, Hart-Davis, MacGibbon (London), 1973.
Marathon: The Story of Civilizations on Collision Course, Random House (New York), 1973, Souvenir Press (London), 1974.
The Scorching of Washington: The War of 1812, David and Charles, 1974, R. B. Luce (Washington, D.C.), 1975.
The Tares Report on the Last Days of Pompeii, Souvenir, 1975.
The War in the Trenches, David McKay (New York), 1976, Hart-Davis MacGibbon, 1976.
Destroy Carthage: The Death Throes of an Ancient Culture, Souvenir, 1977.
The Great Prize Fight, Coward McCann and Geoghegan (New York), 1977, Cassell (London), 1977.
The Hundred Years War, Hart-Davis, MacGibbon, 1977.
The Gliders: The Story of the Wooden Chariots of World War II, Battery Press, 1982.

FICTION; AS ALAN LLOYD

The Eighteenth Concubine, Hutchinson, 1972.
Trade Imperial, Coward McCann and Geoghegan, 1979.

■ Sidelights

A. R. Lloyd is an English author of fiction and nonfiction for young people and adults who is noted for writing books that are both action-oriented and reflective. As Alan Lloyd, he writes informational books on historical events from world and British history as well as biographies of historical figures and historical novels; as A. R. Lloyd, he creates animal fiction that blends fantasy and reality and is praised for its depiction of English flora and fauna as well as for its ecological message and for the beauty of its prose. In his nonfiction Lloyd has covered such events as the Punic Wars, the last days of Pompeii, the Hundred Years War, the War of 1812, and the Zulu War of 1879; he has also written about the campaigns of the Western Front in World War I and the wooden glider planes used in World War II, and has profiled the controversial English kings John and George III as well as Spanish general Francisco

Franco. As a writer of fiction, Lloyd is well known for his fantasy series about Kine, a weasel who defends and preserves his community against predatory animals, as well as for *The Last Otter (The Boy and the Otter),* a novel about how a young otter—the last of his race—is helped to return to his river home by a nameless runaway. In both *The Last Otter* and the "Kine" series, Lloyd makes his animals anthropomorphic by giving them speech and other human characteristics, attributes that have received a mixed reception from critics. However, Lloyd is commended for his accurate descriptions of the Kentish countryside; for his expressive, sympathetic characterizations; for his lyrical prose; and for his exciting narratives.

Set on the marshlands of Kent, England, *The Last Otter* describes how the otter Lut is saved from extinction by the care of his human friend, who finds the otter a mate and watches his cubs. Both the animal and the boy are attempting to live freely in nature. However, each of them is being pursued—the boy by the local child care department and the otter by human poachers; Lut is also harassed by Fingertaker, a fierce old otter, and Esox, a pike. With the help of a reclusive landowner and an elderly boatman, the boy—who is shot by the poachers—enables Lut to start a new family and thus carry on his race. "A well-written story that is both moving and thought-provoking," wrote Mary L. Adams in *Voice of Youth Advocates.* A reviewer in *Publishers Weekly* called *The Last Otter* an "intensely stirring novel" and added, "Lloyd's compassionate, memorably lyrical prose evokes the primeval beauty of this terrain, and the splendor of every creature found there." Shirley Toulson of *British Book News* claimed that Lloyd's book will be compared with two other classic English novels about otters, Henry Williamson's *Tarka the Otter* and Gavin Maxwell's *Ring of Bright Water,* because, like them, it "relentlessly confronts the urban reader with the slower, alien rhythms of the natural world."

Lloyd's next novel, *The Farm Dog,* is set during World War II and features Zac, a mysterious mongrel who materializes out of the Kentish bog in order to help farmer Wif Tuck with his ratting and herding. Zac stays with Wif and his family through their daily struggles as they try to keep their farm solvent during the war; as the story progresses, the dog shows, in the words of *School Library Journal* contributor Annette DeMeritt, "steadfastness, courage, and heart." At the end of the story, Zac disappears into the bog as the war nears its end, and Wif tracks him to the place from which he initially emerged—a downed German bomber. Calling *The Farm Dog* a "dog story that also tells a story of human life," DeMeritt noted that dog lovers will appreciate the "spare prose" and "vivid characters."

In the "Kine" series, Lloyd describes how the native animals of a peaceful woods and marsh, led by a brave weasel and his companions, fight for their territory against malicious invaders. In the first story, *Kine* (also published as *Marshworld*), the villains routed by the heroic Kine are minks; in the third adventure, *Dragon-pond* (also published as *Dragon Pond*), Kine battles a giant polecat, an evil owl, and a nasty ferret in order to keep his home safe. In this story, which depicts Kine's last hurrah, the courageous weasel receives assistance from his weasel friends as well as from a rook, two thrushes, and a shrew. A *Kirkus Reviews* critic noted, "Anglophilic adults will appreciate Lloyd's mesmerizing tribute to the beauties and hidden ways of the flora and fauna of woods, streams, ponds, and fields."

■ Works Cited

Adams, Mary L., review of *The Boy and the Otter, Voice of Youth Advocates,* December, 1985, pp. 320-21.

Review of *The Boy and the Otter, Publishers Weekly,* May 10, 1985, p. 221.

DeMeritt, Annette, review of *The Farm Dog, School Library Journal,* March, 1987, p. 178.

Review of *Dragon Pond, Kirkus Reviews,* July 1, 1991, p. 814.

Toulson, Shirley, review of *The Last Otter, British Book News,* November, 1984, p. 689.

■ For More Information See

PERIODICALS

Books and Bookmen, March, 1985, p. 35.
Fantasy Review, June, 1985, p. 29.
Guardian Weekly, July 21, 1985, p. 22.
Kirkus Reviews, May 1, 1985, p. 387; January 1, 1987, p. 11.
New York Times Book Review, May 29, 1966, p. 7.
Publishers Weekly, January 21, 1983, p. 70.
Times Literary Supplement, May 17, 1966, p. 220; May 28, 1970, p. 584; June 9, 1972, p. 652; December 27, 1974, p. 1471; May 6, 1977, p. 554.*

—Sketch by Gerard J. Senick

*   *   *

LLOYD, E. James
See JAMES, Elizabeth

*   *   *

LLOYD, James
See JAMES, Elizabeth

M

MACKAY, Claire 1930-

■ Personal

Born December 21, 1930, in Toronto, Ontario, Canada; daughter of Grant McLaren (an accountant) and Bernice (a secretary and bereavement counselor; maiden name, Arland) Bacchus; married Jackson F. Mackay (an economist, chemical engineer, and jazz musician), September 12, 1952; children: Ian, Scott, Grant. *Education:* University of Toronto, B.A. (with honors), 1952; postgraduate studies in social work, University of British Columbia, 1968-69; University of Manitoba, Certificate in Rehabilitation Counseling, 1971. *Avocational interests:* Bird-watching, collecting dictionaries.

■ Addresses

Home and office—6 Frank Crescent, Toronto, Ontario M6G 3K5, Canada.

■ Career

Polysar Corporation, Sarnia, Ontario, library assistant in research department, 1952-55; Plains Hospital (now Wascana Hospital), Regina, Saskatchewan, medical social worker, 1969-71; United Steelworkers, Toronto, Ontario, research librarian, 1972-78; freelance researcher and writer, 1978—. Writer-in-the-School, John Wanless School, Toronto, 1986; Writer-in-the-Library, Toronto and Borough libraries, 1987. Trustee, judge, and juror for various literature and arts competitions. Consultant and editor, Houghton Mifflin Canada, 1986-91. *Member:* International PEN, International Board on Books for Young People (Canadian section), Canadian Authors Association, Writers Union of Canada, Canadian Society of Children's Authors, Illustrators, and Performers (CANSCAIP; founding member; secretary, 1977-79; president, 1979-81), Children's Book Centre (board member, 1985-89), Writers' Development Trust, Friends of the National Library of Canada, Children's Literature Round Table of Toronto, Town of York Historical Society.

■ Awards, Honors

Writing grants from Ontario Arts Council, 1980, 1983, 1984, 1985, 1986, and 1989; second prize, *Toronto Star* short story contest, 1980, for "Important Message: Please Read"; Ruth Schwartz Foundation Award for best children's book, 1982, for *One Proud Summer;* honorable mention, Children's Literature Prize competition, Canada Council, 1982; Canadian Authors Association, Vicky Metcalf Award, 1983, for body of work for children, and Vicky Metcalf Short Story Award, 1988, for "Marvin and Me and the Flies"; notable book

CLAIRE MACKAY

selection, Canadian Library Association, 1987, for *Pay Cheques and Picket Lines: All about Unions in Canada,* and 1990, for *The Toronto Story;* Award of Excellence competition, Parenting Publications of America, honorable mention in column/regular feature category, 1989, and first prize in column/humor category, 1990; finalist in Mr. Christie Book Award, 1990, and City of Toronto Book Awards, 1991, both for *The Toronto Story;* Civic Award of Merit, City of Toronto, 1992.

■ Writings

FOR CHILDREN

Mini-Bike Hero, Scholastic, 1974, rev. ed., 1991.
Mini-Bike Racer, Scholastic, 1976, rev. ed., 1991.
Exit Barney McGee, Scholastic, 1979, rev. ed., 1992.
(With Marsha Hewitt) *One Proud Summer* (historical novel), Women's Educational Press, 1981.
Mini-Bike Rescue, Scholastic, 1982, rev. ed., 1991.
The Minerva Program, James Lorimer, 1984, Houghton, 1992.
Pay Cheques and Picket Lines: All about Unions in Canada, Kids Can Press, 1987, rev. ed., 1988.
The Toronto Story, Annick Press, 1988.
Touching All the Bases: Baseball for Kids of All Ages, illustrated by Bill Slavin, Boardwalk Books/Scholastic, 1994.
(With Jean Little) *Bats about Baseball,* illustrated by Kim LaFave, Viking, 1994.
Laughs: Funny Stories Selected by Claire Mackay, Tundra Books, 1997.

Some of Mackay's works have been published in French, Swedish, Japanese, and Norwegian.

OTHER

Contributor to *Canadian Writers' Guide,* and *Writers on Writing.* Contributor of articles, speeches, short stories, poetry and book reviews to periodicals, including *Canadian Children's Literature, Canadian Women's Studies, Chatelaine, Writers' Quarterly, Quill and Quire, Toronto Star,* and *Globe and Mail* (Toronto). Editor of *CANSCAIP News,* 1978-83, associate editor, 1983-85. Author of "Women's Words," a monthly feminist column in *Steel Labour,* 1975-78, and of regular column in *Kids Toronto,* 1986-93.

■ Work in Progress

A novel about a radical family in the Great Depression; an alphabet book in verse.

■ Adaptations

One Proud Summer has been opted for film by Les Productions Barbara Schrier, Inc., Montreal, Quebec; *Pay Cheques and Picket Lines: All about Unions in Canada* has also been opted for film.

■ Sidelights

Claire Mackay is a Canadian writer of fiction and nonfiction for young adults and juvenile readers. Her popular titles include *Mini-Bike Hero* (and its two sequels), *Exit Barney McGee, One Proud Summer, The Minerva Program,* and the nonfiction work *Pay Checks and Picket Lines: All about Unions in Canada.* The winner of numerous awards for her writing, Mackay is also active away from her writing desk, visiting schools and libraries all across Canada and speaking with thousands of children who have read her books. Qualities of Mackay's fiction that endear her to young readers are the use of story lines to which young readers can relate and characters who tend to be misfits or outlaws who make important steps toward maturity during the course of the story. Increasingly, Mackay's writing has taken a nonfiction turn, with publication of *The Toronto Story* in 1988 and *Touching All the Bases* in 1994. Such titles are not dry recitations of fact, but employ inventive formats and quirky facts that Mackay, a researcher, manages to unearth.

Born in Toronto in 1930, Mackay was a child of the Great Depression. Her father lost his job the year she was born, and he would not get another steady job until Mackay was ten. Those early years were ones of constant moves; the family relocated ten times in as many years. The loss of his ability to provide for the family sent Mackay's father looking for solutions: "One was alcohol, the other was communism," Mackay wrote in an essay for *Something about the Author Autobiography Series* (*SAAS*). Throughout the 1930s, the entire family was involved in the cause of communism; young Mackay and her mother delivered illegal leaflets in the dark of night, "creeping through the sleeping streets of Toronto like spies," according to Mackay in *SAAS*. For Mackay at the time, communism was not a dirty word. "In those terrible years of the Dirty Thirties, when poverty destroyed the lives of so many, we thought that if you weren't a Communist, you were either a rich and ruthless exploiter of the masses, or you were abysmally stupid, several sandwiches short of a picnic." This upbringing influenced the course of her future life. Though she eventually came to see communism through other than rose-colored glasses, she did study economics and political science in college and continues to be involved in labor matters. Her father's other answer to his problems, however, had less benign consequences for the family. For Mackay growing up, it was almost as if she did not have a father at times, for he was a binge drinker until he finally discovered Alcoholics Anonymous when Mackay was eighteen. Increasingly, support of the family rested on the shoulders of the mother.

Mackay took refuge in books as a youngster. "Reading became my passion, my escape, my obsession, my solace in times of trouble," she wrote in *SAAS*. "I don't think I exaggerate when I say reading became my vocation." She read widely and indiscriminately, everything from children's books to works of science and philosophy. By the time she was eight, Mackay was reading twenty books a week. Some of her reading included traditional children's classics, such as *Black Beauty, The Jungle Book,* and *Little Women,* but she also tackled more mature books such as the novels of Dickens, the mysteries of Sherlock Holmes, the gore of *Frankenstein*

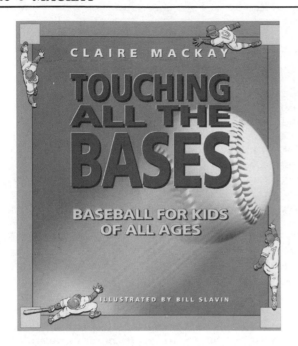

Mackay, a baseball enthusiast, collects facts and stories about the game in this 1994 book.

and *Dracula,* and even works by Karl Marx and Sigmund Freud. Her one favorite childhood book, *Og, Son of Fire,* featured a stone-age protagonist, a misfit boy and a quiet revolutionary, who eventually is given the gift of transmitting fire to his people. "Why did I love Og so?" Mackay questioned herself in *SAAS.* "The answer isn't far to seek. I was Og.... I dreamed Og dreams of quest and discovery, of impossible bravery."

Another refuge for Mackay was school, though she did not have an auspicious start, having to repeat kindergarten. But her skill with words ultimately made school work easy for her. From some teachers she learned a

love for poetry, from others a pure love of learning. She reached the eighth grade by the age of eleven. In high school she finally found a social niche, when she was placed in a class of bright children grouped together because of their IQ scores. She worked on the school newspaper and did well in English and other languages. After high school, Mackay won a scholarship that helped her attend the University of Toronto where she majored in political science. It was also at the university that she met her future husband, whom she married in 1952, the year of their graduation. A chemical engineer, Mackay's husband was sent all over Canada for his work. An early stint in Sarnia, Ontario, saw Mackay working as a research assistant in the library of a government-owned rubber and plastics company, a job close to her heart, for she had begun working in libraries when she was ten. When she became pregnant, Mackay left the job and for the next thirteen years devoted herself to motherhood, raising three boys.

During this time, Mackay returned to university to pursue studies in social work; she also pursued her early dream of writing, spurred on by teachers at college. At first, she wrote only poetry, following Jonathan Swift's famous dictum, as she pointed out in *SAAS,* that "'Proper words in proper places make the true definition of style.'" The family moved to British Columbia for a time and then back eastward to Saskatchewan, where Mackay worked in social services in a hospital. Reaching age forty, Mackay resolved to turn her vague dreams of writing into reality; it was now or never.

It helped that her youngest son was searching for a book in the local library on mini-bikes and could find nothing. He asked his mother to write one for him. "Until that moment, writing for children and young people had never once crossed my mind," Mackay noted in *SAAS.* "I thought poetry, or elegant and

Nana must be making jokes on purpose. Ryder decided to throw her a curve.

"Nana, I think I might like to be a deep sea diver like your friend Marlin."

Nana had a comeback ready. "What a great sinker!" she said.

Ryder gets frustrated while trying to discuss his future with his baseball-obsessed grandma in Mackay's *Bats about Baseball*, cowritten with Jean Little and illustrated by Kim LaFave.

sophisticated short stories.... I did *not* think about writing a book about a boy and a mini-bike. But that's what I wrote." The result—after painstaking rewrites—was a manuscript entitled *Mini-Bike Hero,* but still her son was not satisfied, for this did not look like a book one found at a library. So Mackay sent her book off to Scholastic, and the book was subsequently published in 1974. It now looked very much like those found at the library, but with one big difference: *Mini-Bike Hero* sold out its first print run of 45,000 copies in the first four months, and it and its two sequels have sold over half a million copies.

Mini-Bike Hero features a twelve-year-old protagonist, Steve MacPherson, who is in love with mini-bikes. However, he must conceal this love from his father, who lost his own brother in a motorcycle accident and is fervently against the two-wheelers. Secretly Steve pursues his new hobby, breaking the rules of the adult world to satisfy his own needs. He earns money for the forbidden bike and learns all about biking from a local mechanic. But on his first ride, Steve gets far more than he bargained for, rescuing several local Indian people in a storm and riding injured to fetch the police. Though Vicki Wright, reviewing the novel in *Canadian Children's Literature,* found that the passage wherein Steve saves the native people depicted them as stereotypes, she also felt that Steve "is a fine model ... a highly likeable superhero." Told from the child's perspective, the novel is almost totally free of depictions of adult supervision. Explaining the novel's popularity with young readers, Wright pointed out that it is the young protagonist who is in charge here; it is Steve "who functions as an adult, and who is indeed superior to the adults with whom he interacts." Wright also commented on the lack of "preaching, the uncomplicated characterization," and the "abundant" action in this escapist book.

Fan letters soon came pouring in, requesting a sequel, a wish echoed by Mackay's publishers. Ultimately Mackay complied, dedicating the second mini-bike adventure, *Mini-Bike Racer,* to the first young boy who had written her a fan letter. This second book continues the adventures of the trio of friends introduced in *Mini-Bike Hero:* Steve MacPherson, Kim Chambers, and Julie Brennan. Recovering from the injuries incurred at the end of the first adventure, Steve soon loses the friendship of his buddy, Kim. Julie takes his place, becoming Steve's riding buddy. An early adventure involves Steve's being held as a hostage during the hold-up of the local cycle repair shop. Thereafter Steve and Julie prepare for a big race in which he will meet his ex-friend Kim as a new rival. But Steve encounters more trouble when he stumbles onto the robbers' hideout and is captured by them. His subsequent rescue resolves the plot threads, bringing his old friend back to him. While many reviewers found this sequel to be less novel than the original, N. B. Johnson, writing in *The World of Children's Literature,* commented that "Mackay does have some knowledge of motorcycle and mini-bike racing and uses that to good advantage." Wright, in *Canadian Children's Literature,* concluded that Mackay

"must know that there are countless readers who hope that both Julie and Steve will ride again."

In fact, Mackay once again received enough fan mail—many this time from girls—to encourage her to a third title in the series, *Mini-Bike Rescue,* which appeared in 1982. In this book, Julie is sent from her Saskatchewan home in the summer to work at her aunt's motel in Ontario. Expecting a boring summer away from her Suzuki, Julie is pleasantly surprised when she soon finds herself astride a bike and having adventures ranging from robberies and forest fires to a rescue at the edge of a cliff. Reviewing the book in *Quill and Quire,* Linda Granfield noted that the use of jargon, action, and adult-adolescent confrontations would "appeal to the pre-adolescent."

In between the second and third mini-bike books, Mackay wrote two other novels as well as a weekly column for a union's monthly newspaper. In 1978 she began writing full-time. The next year she published *Exit Barney McGee,* the story of a boy who runs away to Toronto, partly to escape his mother's new husband, and partly to locate his own biological father, whom he ultimately finds is a down-at-the-heel alcoholic. "I wanted to say something about alcoholism," Mackay explained in *SAAS.* "I wanted to get across somehow that alcoholics, no matter that the world sees them as weak rejects and throwaways, are still fully human and capable of deep emotion, even heroism." Jean Blair Simms, reviewing the novel in *Canadian Children's Literature,* found the attempt successful. "In this novel ... you suffer the agonies of a parent who loses a son; and you are deeply touched along with Barney, at the startling condition of alcoholics," Simms wrote. Sandra Burke-Pidhurskyj noted in *In Review* that the story "is a realistic novel that tackles difficult problems facing a teenager" and also commented that the book "moves at a fast pace" and "is quite dramatic and believable." Writing in *Canadian Literature,* Lynn Wytenbroek called the novel "both engaging and moving."

Mackay teamed up with the writer Marsha Hewitt to write a historical treatment of a strike at a Canadian textile factory, *One Proud Summer.* Set in 1946, the book is the story of men, women, and children who went on strike for one hundred days, as told from the viewpoint of a thirteen-year-old striker, Lucie La Plante. Eva Martin, writing about the book in *In Review,* thought it was "an excellent portrayal of an important summer in a young girl's life." Another girl on the cusp of womanhood is Minerva, the protagonist of Mackay's 1984 *The Minerva Program.* An outcast at school, Minerva begins to find her niche with computers when she is falsely accused of tampering with grades through the school's computer system. Her search for vindication is the engine of this novel which is marked, as Jean Little noted in *Canadian Children's Literature,* by "suspense, surprise, humour, an engaging heroine ... a mysterious villain, dialogue so real that its author has to be an inveterate eavesdropper on today's kids, an ingenious plot satisfyingly resolved, and ... a computer." Writing this book, Mackay indulged in her love for names: Each of the characters' names is a code for that person. Minerva, for example, is the Roman goddess of wisdom, which Mackay noted in *SAAS* is "the message in the book ... that we need wisdom in this new world of high technology."

Since the mid-1980s, Mackay's work has taken a nonfiction turn, which has resulted in a trio of books popular with young and old alike. *Pay Cheques and Picket Lines* is the story of unions in Canada; its good reception was aided by the fact that it came out in the middle of a teachers' strike. Mackay's penchant for research and interesting, quirky historical facts is evident in this book which Eva Martin called "well organized and stimulating" in *Books for Young People*. The popularity of this book brought a publisher to Mackay to write a history of Toronto to be published on the two-hundredth anniversary of the settling of the city. *The Toronto Story* is full of anecdotes and narrative drive and finds an audience with children and adults, just as does Mackay's *Touching All Bases: Baseball for Kids of All Ages*. Pat Steenbergen in *Canadian Materials* emphasized this in a review of the latter book: "Claire Mackay has written a book that will be enjoyed by both fans and casual observers of the game of baseball."

Mackay continues to maintain a busy schedule of writing and speaking. In *SAAS* she summed up her career: "My life as a writer for young people, although it didn't begin until I was forty-one years old, has brought me great riches. Not in dollars, I hasten to add, but in friendship, in travel, in that invigorating sense of renewed hope that comes with talking to kids."

■ Works Cited

Burke-Pidhurskyj, Sandra, review of *Exit Barney McGee, In Review,* February, 1982, pp. 45-46.
Granfield, Linda, review of *Mini-Bike Rescue, Quill and Quire,* May, 1983, p. 12.
Johnson, N. B., review of *Mini-Bike Racer, The World of Children's Literature,* fall, 1997, pp. 26-27.
Little, Jean, "Talent In, Talent Out," *Canadian Children's Literature,* No. 43, 1986, pp. 47-48.
Mackay, Claire, essay in *Something about the Author Autobiography Series,* Vol. 25, Gale, 1997, pp. 195-212.
Martin, Eva, review of *One Proud Summer, In Review,* February, 1982, p. 39.
Martin, Eva, review of *Pay Cheques and Picket Lines, Books for Young People,* December, 1987, p. 7.
Simms, Jean Blair, "Journeying to Maturity," *Canadian Children's Literature,* No. 20, 1980, pp. 67-69.
Steenbergen, Pat, review of *Touching All the Bases, Canadian Materials,* November-December, 1994, pp. 224-25.
Wright, Vicki, review of *Mini-Bike Hero* and *Mini-Bike Rescue, Canadian Children's Literature,* No. 7, 1977, pp. 36-38.
Wytenbroek, Lynn, "Raw vs. Clever," *Canadian Literature,* fall-winter, 1993, pp. 172-73.

■ For More Information See

BOOKS

Canadian Books for Children: A Guide to Authors and Illustrators, edited by Jon Stott and Raymond Jones, Harcourt Brace, 1988.
Children's Literature Review, Vol. 43, Gale, 1997.
Gertridge, Allison, *Meet Canadian Authors and Illustrators: 50 Creators of Children's Books,* Scholastic Canada, 1994.
Twentieth-Century Children's Writers, St. James Press, 1995.

PERIODICALS

Books in Canada, August-September, 1984, p. 32; April, 1988, p. 36, June 1997, p. 35.
Canadian Children's Literature, No. 54, 1989, pp. 26-30; No. 64, 1991, pp. 6-25, 80-81.
Emergency Librarian, December, 1987, pp. 59-64; March, 1988, p. 26; May, 1988, p. 56; January, 1991, p. 52; January, 1992, p. 60; January, 1994, pp. 45, 56; May, 1994, p. 45; January, 1995, p. 56; March, 1995, p. 17.
Maclean's, December 7, 1987, p. 56.
Quill and Quire, November, 1990, p. 13.
School Librarian, August, 1987, p. 255.
School Library Journal, August, 1995, p. 125.
Times Educational Supplement, May 24, 1991, p. 24.

—Sketch by J. Sydney Jones

* * *

MARSDEN, John 1950-

■ Personal

Born September 27, 1950, in Melbourne, Victoria, Australia; son of Eustace Cullen Hudson (a banker) and Jeanne Lawler (a homemaker; maiden name, Ray) Marsden. *Education:* Mitchell College, diploma in teaching, 1978; University of New England, B.A., 1981.

■ Addresses

Home—Box 139, Newstead, Victoria 3462, Australia.

■ Career

Geelong Grammar School, Geelong, Victoria, Australia, English teacher, 1982-90; writer, 1991—; primary school teacher, c. 1995—. Worked at various jobs, including truck driver, hospital worker, and delivery person, c. 1968-77.

■ Awards, Honors

Children's Book of the Year award (Australia), 1988, Premier's Award (Victoria), 1988, Young Adult Book Award (New South Wales), 1988, Christopher Award, 1989, and Notable Book, American Library Association, 1989, all for *So Much to Tell You...*; Writers' Fellowship, Australia Council, 1993; Australian Muticultural Children's Book Award and New South Wales Talking

JOHN MARSDEN

Book Award, both for *Tomorrow, When the War Began...;* New South Wales Talking Book Award, for *The Dead of Night.*

■ Writings

So Much to Tell You..., Walter McVitty, 1988, Little, Brown, 1989.
The Journey, Pan Australia, 1988.
The Great Gatenby, Pan Australia, 1989.
Staying Alive in Year 5, Pan Australia, 1989.
Out of Time, Pan Australia, 1990.
Letters from the Inside, Pan Australia, 1991, Houghton Mifflin, 1994.
Take My Word for It, Pan Australia, 1992.
Looking for Trouble, Pan Australia, 1993.
Cool School, Pan Australia, 1995.
Dear Miffy, Pan Macmillan, 1997.

Also author of *Creep Street,* 1996; *Checkers,* 1996; and *Norton's Hut,* illustrated by Peter Gouldthorpe, 1996.

"TOMORROW, WHEN THE WAR BEGAN" SERIES

Tomorrow, When the War Began, Pan Australia, 1993, Houghton Mifflin, 1995.
The Dead of Night, Pan Australia, 1994, Houghton Mifflin, 1997.
The Third Day, the Frost, Pan Australia, 1995, published as *The Killing Frost,* Macmillan, 1995.
Darkness, Be My Friend, Pan Australia, 1996.
Burning for Revenge, Macmillan, 1997.

OTHER

Everything I Know about Writing (nonfiction), Heinemann Australia, 1993.
So Much to Tell You: The Play, Walter McVitty, 1994.

Also editor of *This I Believe* (essays), 1996, and *For Weddings and a Funeral* (poetry), 1996.

■ Sidelights

"I'd have to say that when I finished school I didn't have much understanding of life," John Marsden admitted in an autobiographical essay for *Something about the Author Autobiography Series* (*SAAS*). Marsden, the well-known author of books about adolescents, spent many years after finishing school drifting from job to job and seeking his true vocation. He eventually became a teacher, thereby developing a solid understanding of the language, morality, and character of his teenage students. Marsden's experience, coupled with his writing skill, has resulted in several well-received novels for young adults.

A native of Australia, Marsden debunked some of the myths of his native land in his *SAAS* essay: "Growing up in Australia wasn't a matter of kangaroos, surfboards, and the wild outback. Not for me, anyway. My childhood was spent in the quiet country towns in the green southern states of Victoria and Tasmania. It was peaceful, secure, and often very boring." Marsden's father managed a bank, a responsibility he held for forty-eight years. This had a marked yet contrary effect on the young Marsden. He related: "Perhaps one of the things I've done in my adult life is to react against that kind of commitment. At the latest count I've had thirty-two different jobs."

Growing up in small Australian towns during the 1950s gave Marsden experiences that were quite different from children in urban America during the same era. In Marsden's village, ice was still delivered to people for their iceboxes, cooking was mainly done on stoves powered by fuel, and no one he knew owned a television set. "I first saw television when I was ten years old. In our small Tasmanian town an electrical shop brought in a TV and put it in their window, for the wedding of Princess Margaret. On the great day the whole town gathered in front of the shop and the set was switched on. All we saw was 'snow'—grey and white static, with a few figures vaguely visible through the murk," Marsden wrote in *SAAS.*

Marsden was too infatuated with literature to care if his family had a television. "I read and read and read," he commented to *SAAS.* "When I ran out of books for boys I read the girls' books.... Some days, I'd borrow three titles (the maximum allowed) from the town library, read them, and get them back to the library by five o'clock, in time to exchange them for three more before the library shut. I'd become a speed reader without really trying!" Marsden also found another pastime that was to help him with his later writing. "My favourite game was to draw a town layout on the driveway with chalk and use little model cars to bring the town to life. Perhaps that's how I first became used to creating and living in imaginary worlds."

Marsden became such a lover of books that by the time he was in grade three, he had memorized *The Children of Cherry Tree Farm*. His teacher would use him when she wanted to take a break. "She'd have me stand up in front of the class and recite the next chapter to the other kids ... from memory. She'd go off to the staff room and leave me there. I loved it! Maybe that's where I got my first taste of the power of storytelling."

That school year was also a difficult one for Marsden. His teacher would fly into rages and yell at the children. She believed in corporal punishment and would cane the children for the slightest disobedience. Each Friday the teacher would give the class a ten-question quiz; if a student failed to answer at least seven questions correctly, he was beaten. "Recently I met up with a girl who'd been in that class with me," Marsden related. "As she talked about those Friday tests she started to tremble with the memories. At the age of forty-four she was still haunted by her grade three days." When Marsden was promoted to the next grade, he was rewarded in two ways: his teacher was much more nurturing, and she saw in him the seeds of a writer, letting him edit the school paper. "This was my first taste of publication," he told *SAAS*. "It was a heady experience. Seeing my name in print, having people—even adults—reacting to and commenting on what I'd written was powerful stuff."

At the age of ten, Marsden moved with his family to the large city of Sydney. Having mainly grown up in country towns, Marsden was fascinated with his new experience. "I thought Sydney was huge and exotic, and wildly exciting," Marsden commented. "I spent my first week collecting bus tickets, to the amusement of the staff in the hotel where we stayed. Riding on the escalators was as good as Disneyland."

Marsden's parents enrolled him at The King's School, a prestigious private school that was run like a military establishment. There was very little Marsden liked about the place, from the stuffy uniforms to the military drills they were required to perform. He also felt out of touch with happenings in the world. "The rest of the Western world was embarking on a decade of drugs, free love, and the Beatles, but at King's boys continued to salute their teachers, drill with rifles for hours every week, and stand to attention when speaking to prefects." Marsden spent his time in somewhat subversive activities: he wrote short books with plots that were stolen from famous mystery novels, distributed his underground newspaper about new rock bands, and read books under his desk during class.

At the time, Marsden found that there was very little literature written for adolescents. He read adult literature but was quite taken aback by his first reading of J. D. Salinger's *Catcher in the Rye,* a classic coming-of-age story that was—and still is—controversial. The book "had me gasping for breath," Marsden commented in

SAAS. "I'd never dreamt you were allowed to write like that.... For the first time I was reading a genuine contemporary teenage voice. If I've had any success at capturing teenage voices on paper, it's because of what I learnt at the age of fifteen from J. D. Salinger."

School had very little settling influence on Marsden; he continued being a rebel despite the conservative atmosphere. "I began to question everything: religion, education, law, parenting. All the institutions and customs that I'd been taught to accept unquestioningly," he related to *SAAS*. It is of little surprise that when Marsden graduated from King's he had not received any military awards or promotions. He did, however, win some academic prizes, including one for an essay on poets of World War I.

After graduating, Marsden enrolled at the University of Sydney, but soon lost interest in his studies and dropped out. He then tried his hand at many exotic jobs. He told *SAAS* that some of his employment included "collecting blood, looking after a mortuary at nights, working in a side-show, being a night clerk in the casualty department of Sydney Hospital, and guarding Australia's oldest house from vandals." Marsden's interest in these occupations, however, generally waned rather quickly. "Once I mastered a job I got bored with it and started restlessly looking for the next challenge. Maybe that was a reaction to the boredom of my early life and the tedium of most of my years in schools."

Marsden continued to write and submitted a novel to a publisher that was rejected. He drifted from job to job, yet somehow succeeded in finishing the first year of a law school course. However, he slipped into a deep depression and ended up in a psychiatric institution, where he met a fourteen-year-old girl who would not speak to anyone. Marsden wondered about this, and on the girl's last day at the institution he got to talk to her. The girl's plight became the inspiration for Marsden's novel *So Much to Tell You....*

At the age of twenty-seven, bored with his latest promotion to a desk job at a delivery company, Marsden saw a newspaper advertisement about teaching classes and decided to apply. "I'd always had a vague idea that I might enjoy [teaching], but then I'd had the same vague ideas about other jobs and they hadn't worked out.... From the very first day, however, I knew I'd found my vocation." Marsden soon had a position teaching at Geelong Grammar School, a very famous Australian school. After several years of teaching, Marsden was encouraged to resume writing.

Marsden told *SAAS* that during a school holiday "I sat down and started to write. I made two decisions that turned out to be critical. One was to use the diary format, the other was to aim it at teenage readers. These two decisions seemed to free me to write more fluently than before. I worked in an intensity of emotion, a state that I often slip into when writing." On the very last day of his vacation, Marsden finished the book. He sent it off to a variety of publishers but received only negative responses. Luckily, a chance meeting with a bookseller helped Marsden get the manuscript into the right hands.

So Much to Tell You... focuses on a mute girl who is sent to a special boarding school rather than a psychiatric hospital. The girl has been physically scarred in an accident. Readers get to know her through her diary entries, where her secrets are gradually revealed: her father scarred her with acid that was meant to injure her mother. One of the girl's teachers is able to break into her silent world, and at the end of the novel, there is the hope that she will begin coming out of her isolation. The book caught on quickly and soon became an Australian best-seller. "A good proportion of the first print run was bought by my students, who were smart enough to know how to improve their grades in English," Marsden joked.

Reviews of *So Much to Tell You...* were favorable. Jo Goodman, writing in *Magpies,* declared that the book was "a riveting first novel which grips the reader from the start," adding: "I found the observation and the

WINNER OF AUSTRALIA'S
1988 BOOK OF THE YEAR AWARD
John Marsden

So Much
To
Tell You

She could never
talk again.
Not after what
happened....

"Unique and
affecting."
Booklist

FAWCETT JUNIPER
0-449-70374-6

Marsden's award-winning novel chronicles the emotional recovery of an abused teenage girl who is mute until a teacher breaks into her silent world.

characters authentic, the suspense gripping, and the slow and subtle revelation of the truth both painful and illuminating." *School Library Journal* contributor Libby K. White asserted: "Marsden is a master storyteller." I. V. Hansen, commenting in *Children's Literature in Education,* claimed that the novel offers "a moving story, tragic, simple, generous, tender. It is the kind of novel that seems to come from nowhere, yet we know it has been with us all the time."

In *The Journey,* Marsden built a fable around adolescent coming-of-age rituals. In this tale, a society sends its adolescents on a journey of self-discovery; the youths return with seven stories of experience and enlightenment. The local council then judges whether the stories are suitable enough to allow the youths to pass into adulthood. Margot Nelmes commented in *Reading Time* that "this is a rare book, fortifying to the spirit, gripping, and worthy of reading more than once."

Marsden turned to lighter works with the publication of *The Great Gatenby* and *Staying Alive in Year 5. The Great Gatenby* is about the popular but reckless Erle Gatenby, who causes trouble wherever he goes. *Staying Alive in Year 5* offers one boy's perspective on his class's experience with an unusual teacher named Mr. Merlin. Halina Nowicka in *Reading Time* termed *Staying Alive* "a really good, humorous story."

Marsden's *Letters from the Inside* and *Dear Miffy* have evoked controversy. *Letters from the Inside* centers around two girls, Mandy and Tracy, who have become pen pals. After a few exchanges of letters, Tracy reveals that she is actually serving time in a maximum security prison. Mandy admits that her brother is quite violent, and the end of the novel alludes to the fact that Mandy might have been attacked by him. In *Reading Time,* Ashley Freeman called *Letters from the Inside* a "compelling story, which totally involves the reader." Other critics were alarmed by the manner in which Marsden presented the subject of domestic violence. Elizabeth Gleick contended in the *New York Times Book Review* that the book "might be faulted for one reason and one reason alone: it offers not the palest glimmer of hope." *Dear Miffy,* which features a jacket notice warning that "Contents may offend some readers," has engendered a similar reaction. In this novel, institutionalized teenager Tony, who comes from a broken home and a working-class environment, writes to his girlfriend Miffy, a beautiful girl from a wealthy and very troubled family. Tony's letters, which are never mailed, recount their relationship from its turbulent beginnings through its tragic conclusion. *Dear Miffy* is filled with violence, sex, and profanity set against a backdrop of corruption, injustice, and dysfunctional families. Discussing the controversy surrounding the work in *Horn Book,* Karen Jameyson wrote: "In inevitable parallel with the U.S. discussion about *The Chocolate War,* [critics] point out that the shades of gray in this book are so dark as to be unrealistic. Surely no life can be so dismal; surely no group of characters can be so totally lacking in redeeming features; surely no slice of life can be so void of ... hope." Others commentators have rallied to Marsden's

TOMORROW, WHEN THE WAR BEGAN

John Marsden

When a group of teenagers return from a camping trip and find their town under siege, they organize a strike against the invaders. (Cover photo by Will Hillenbrand.)

support, commending his forthright treatment of difficult subjects and his capacity to endow his protagonists with an authentic teenage voice.

Marsden has also written a series of adventure stories about a world ruled by children. "One of my childhood fantasies had been of a world without adults, a world in which the adults had magically disappeared and the kids were left to run the place," Marsden wrote in *SAAS*. Out of this fantasy came a series of novels that centered around an invasion of Australia. The first book in the series, *Tomorrow, When the War Began,* is about a group of teenagers who go on a camping trip in the bush. On their return they realize that everyone in their town has been captured, and they must fend for themselves. Quickly, the group organizes to resist the invaders, blowing up a lawn mower to kill one soldier. *The Dead of Night* and *The Third Day, the Frost* furthers the story of the teenagers as the war in their country continues. Reviewing the former for *Voice of Youth Advocates,* Alice F. Stern commented: "If you hope for a plot with any closure, you will not find it here. What you will find is a strong adventure story, a little romance, and an excellent psychological study." *Horn Book* reviewer

Jennifer M. Brabander praised *The Dead of Night* as "riveting," citing favorably the depth of Marsden's characters and adding: "Thoughtful explorations of the nature of fear, bravery, and violence—natural conversations during wartime—add depth and balance to the edge-of-the-seat action and intense first-person narration."

Writing these books became an obsession for Marsden. "I realised that when I was halfway through [the first novel] that one book would not be enough to tell the story. The scenario was just too big for one volume.... As I wrote the second book, ... I began to realise that two wouldn't be enough either. With some reluctance I came to the conclusion that there would have to be a third one," Marsden related in *SAAS*. Even after this "trilogy" was complete, Marsden wasn't satisfied. He has also finished a fourth and fifth book in the series, *Darkness, Be My Friend* and *Burning for Revenge,* and there are plans for two more.

"I imagine I'll always be writing, all my life, because there is something within me that needs to tell stories," Marsden related to *SAAS*. Marsden returned to teaching school after taking several years off to write full-time. "The other passion of my life is the preservation of life," Marsden commented in *SAAS*. "The older I get, the more disturbed I get by the wanton destruction of other creatures by humans.... I hope I continue to improve in my treatment of my fellow creatures, be they animal or vegetable."

■ **Works Cited**

Brabander, Jennifer M., review of *The Dead of Night, Horn Book,* September-October, 1997, p. 575-76.

Freeman, Ashley, review of *Letters from the Inside, Reading Time,* Volume 35, number 4, 1991, p. 32.

Gleick, Elizabeth, review of *Letters from the Inside, New York Times Book Review,* November 13, 1994, p. 29.

Goodman, Jo, review of *So Much to Tell You...,* *Magpies,* March, 1988, p. 30.

Hansen, I. V., "In Context: Some Recent Australian Writing for Adolescents," *Children's Literature in Education,* September, 1989, pp. 151-63.

Jameyson, Karen, "Contents May Offend Some Readers," *Horn Book,* September-October, 1997, pp. 549-52.

Marsden, John, autobiographical essay in *Something about the Author Autobiography Series,* Volume 22, Gale, 1996, pp. 169-85.

Nelmes, Margot, review of *The Journey, Reading Time,* Volume 33, number 2, 1989, p. 28.

Nowicka, Halina, review of *Staying Alive, Reading Time,* Volume 33, number 4, 1989, p. 24.

Stern, Alice F., review of *The Dead of Night, Voice of Youth Advocates,* February, 1998, p. 387.

White, Libby K., review of *So Much to Tell You...,* *School Library Journal,* May, 1989, p. 127.

■ For More Information See

BOOKS

Children's Literature Review, Volume 34, Gale, 1995, pp. 140-51.
Twentieth-Century Young Adult Writers, St. James, 1994, pp. 423-24.

PERIODICALS

Booklist, October 15, 1994, p. 420; April 15, 1995, p. 1493.
Bulletin of the Center for Children's Books, November, 1997, p. 92.
Carousel, summer, 1996.
Horn Book, September-October, 1989, p. 630; September, 1995, pp. 634-39.
Junior Bookshelf, June, 1996, pp. 128-29.
Magpies, April, 1989, pp. 20-22; September, 1990, pp. 5-9.
Pandemonium, Volume 1, issue 1, March, 1996.
Publishers Weekly, August 4, 1997, p. 75.
Quill and Quire, January, 1990, p. 18.
Reading Time, Number 4, 1989, pp. 4-6; Number 1, 1994, pp. 36-37; August, 1997, p. 32; November, 1997, p. 35.
School Library Journal, January, 1997, p. 37.
Voice of Youth Advocates, December, 1994, p. 276; August, 1995, p. 162.

*   *   *

MARSHALL, Janet (Perry) 1938-

■ Personal

Born May 26, 1938, in New Haven, CT; married Colin Marshall (a lawyer), May 6, 1961; children: Gordon, Andrew, Elizabeth, Jennifer. *Education:* Studied fine arts at the Hartford Art School, University of Hartford. *Hobbies and other interests:* Reading, traveling, antiquing, painting.

■ Addresses

Home and office—36 Bradley Hill Rd., Hingham, MA 02043.

■ Career

Author and illustrator.

■ Awards, Honors

Children's Choice Award, International Reading Association, 1996, for *Look Once, Look Twice.*

■ Writings

SELF-ILLUSTRATED PICTURE BOOKS

My Camera: At the Zoo, Little, Brown, 1989.
My Camera: At the Aquarium, Little, Brown, 1989.
Ohmygosh My Pocket, Boyds Mills (Honesdale, PA), 1992.

JANET MARSHALL

Look Once, Look Twice, Houghton Mifflin, 1995.
Banana Moon, Greenwillow, 1998.

ILLUSTRATOR

Dee Dee Duffy, *Barnyard Tracks,* Boyds Mills, 1992.
Molly Manley, *Talkaty Talker: Limericks,* Boyds Mills, 1994.
Dee Dee Duffy, *Forest Tracks,* Boyds Mills, 1996.
Molly Manley, *Lola Tortola,* Macmillan Carribean, 1998.

■ Sidelights

Marshall is an author and illustrator of concept books for preschoolers whose works challenge young readers to look more closely at the world around them. In these picture books, which feature intriguingly rendered papercuts in bold, vibrant colors and simple texts, Marshall seeks to enhance children's sense of abstraction. The author/artist characteristically uses the guessing game format to introduce her young audience to such concepts as the patterns found in nature and the animals found at the zoo. Praised for the design of her books as well as for the composition of her pictures, Marshall offer works that are considered both educational and entertaining. She has stated that she most enjoys depicting animals, and in *My Camera: At the Aquarium* and *My Camera: At the Zoo,* the artist has devised texts in which toddlers are introduced to a variety of animals, first in unusual close-up pictures that reduce the animals to mere color and pattern, and then in more conventional form on succeeding pages. Marshall has illustrated all

There once was an artist named Nellie,
Who painted her cottage with jelly,
And then on one shutter
She spread peanut butter
And slid down the stairs on her belly.

Marshall uses cut paper designs to illustrate Molly Manley's picture-book collection of eleven limericks. (From *Talkaty Talker.*)

her projects with cut paper, a media that adds bold color and intriguing visual impact to the design of each book.

In *My Camera: At the Zoo* and *My Camera: At the Aquarium*, Marshall uses her illustrations to represent photographs taken by a child and renders close-ups of parts of various animals followed by a portrait of the complete animal on the succeeding page, a method inspiring her young audience to guess the identity of each. "Marshall's illustrations pull readers through the book," claimed Susan Scheps in her review of *My Camera: At the Zoo* in *School Library Journal.* In a *School Library Journal* review of *My Camera: At the Aquarium*, Phyllis G. Sidorsky maintained: "The illustrations have a pared-down, childlike simplicity, with colors that are intense and vivid. This type of book has been done successfully with photographs; here it works with equal success through imaginative illustrations." Mary M. Burns's review of the same title in *Horn Book* likewise concluded that "this exercise in perception is as appealing for its exciting graphics as for its content."

In *Look Once, Look Twice*, Marshall relies upon a technique similar to the one she uses in her *My Camera* books. In this work, each letter of the alphabet is rendered with a close-up of a pattern that gives a clue to the animal, bird, insect, flower, fruit, vegetable, or other element of nature revealed on the following page. "Marshall achieves the effect of a peekaboo book without ever putting cutting tool to page . . . . [The] rich colors and intriguing patterns in the beautifully pro-

duced book . . . will tantalize kids," observed Stephanie Zvirin in *Booklist.* Writing in *Bulletin of the Center for Children's Books*, Susan Dove Lempke concurred: "The book's design and its clean cutout illustrations stand out, especially because of the care taken to match the facing pages." Marshall also executed both the art and the story for *Ohmygosh, My Pocket*, a picture book in which a rhyming text tells the story of a boy deciding what to put in his pocket to take to school; his choice is his jauntily attired pet frog. According to Lori A. Janick in *School Library Journal*, this is an "attractively packaged book with a variety of creative uses."

Marshall contributed her vividly colored cut-paper illustrations to Molly Manley's *Talkaty Talker*, a collection of limericks about animals and people in silly situations. "The brightness and scale of the illustrations make the book suitable for group sharing," remarked Meg Stackpole in *School Library Journal.* In *Barnyard Tracks* and *Forest Tracks*, author Dee Dee Duffy introduces youngsters to the sounds of several animals and the sights of their tracks, accompanied by Marshall's cut-paper graphics. In a *Publishers Weekly* review of *Forest Tracks*, the critic observed that Marshall's illustrations "are deeply hued, sharply detailed and, in their stylized allusions to flora and fauna, redolent of forest life."

Marshall told *Something about the Author* (*SATA*): "As an illustrator (and sometimes author) of children's picture books, I strive for qualities that children demonstrate in their own art work—spontaneity, imagination, and a daring use of shape and color. I try to use abstraction as much as possible for I feel children have a very sophisticated understanding of it. I love to have them guess and imagine what might be happening and I love to surprise them. As an artist, I have worked with many different media and subject matter—woodcuts, pen and ink, and oils. I have done landscapes, portraits, still life, etc. Above all, I love illustrating animals. I love working with cut paper because with it I can achieve bright, crisp images and a lot of flexibility."

■ Works Cited

Burns, Mary M., review of *My Camera: At the Aquarium, Horn Book,* November, 1989, p. 762.
Review of *Forest Tracks, Publishers Weekly,* May 13, 1996, p. 74.
Janick, Lori A., review of *Ohmygosh, My Pocket, School Library Journal,* February, 1993, p. 76.
Lempke, Susan Dove, review of *Look Once, Look Twice, Bulletin of the Center for Children's Books,* April, 1995, pp. 281-82.
Scheps, Susan, review of *My Camera: At the Zoo, School Library Journal,* July, 1989, p. 73.
Sidorsky, Phyllis G., review of *My Camera: At the Aquarium, School Library Journal,* October, 1989, p. 91.
Stackpole, Meg, review of *Talkaty Talker, School Library Journal,* March, 1994, pp. 217-18.
Zvirin, Stephanie, review of *Look Once, Look Twice, Booklist,* February 1, 1995, p. 1007.

■ For More Information See

PERIODICALS

Bulletin of the Center for Children's Books, April, 1995, pp. 281-82.
Horn Book, May-June, 1995, pp. 326-27.
Publishers Weekly, February 27, 1995, p. 103.
School Library Journal, April, 1995, p. 126; July, 1996, p. 58.

*   *   *

McCUTCHEON, John 1952-

■ Personal

Born August 14, 1952, in Wausau, WI; son of Donald (in sales) and Clarice (a social worker; maiden name, Abts) McCutcheon; married Parthy Monagan (an AIDS worker), August 11, 1978; children: Will, Peter. *Education:* St. John's University, Collegeville, MN, graduated (summa cum laude). *Religion:* Society of Friends (Quakers). *Hobbies and other interests:* Community organizing, fly fishing, baseball.

■ Addresses

Office—1025 Locust Ave., Charlottesville, VA 22901.
Agent—JoLynne Worley, 215 West 53rd St., Kansas City, MO 64112-2815.

JOHN McCUTCHEON

■ Career

Professional concert musician and composer. Virginia Organizing Project, president of administrative committee. *Member:* American Federation of Musicians (president of local 1000); National Writers Union.

■ Awards, Honors

Two Grammy Award nominations from the National Academy of Recording Arts and Sciences, three Indy Award from NAIRD, seven Parent's Choice Gold Medals, and other awards for musical recordings.

■ Writings

Water from Another Time, Hal Leonard, 1989.
Stone by Stone, Hal Leonard, 1995.
Happy Adoption Day! (songs), illustrated by Julie Paschkis, Little, Brown (Boston, MA), 1996.

RECORDINGS; COMPOSER, ARRANGER, AND/OR PERFORMER

Barefoot Boy with Boots On, Front Hall (Vorheesville, NY), 1980.
Fine Times at Our House, Greenhays, 1982.
Howdjadoo, Rounder, 1983.
Winter Solstice, Rounder, 1984.
John McCutcheon's Hammer Dulcimer Repertoire Tape, Homespun Tapes (Woodstock, NY), 1985.
(With Si Kahn) *Signs of the Times,* Rounder, 1986.
Step by Step, Rounder, 1986.
Gonna Rise Again, Rounder, 1987.
Water from Another Time, Rounder, 1989.
What It's Like, Rounder, 1990.
Family Garden, Rounder (Cambridge, MA), 1993.
Between the Eclipse, Rounder, 1994.
John McCutcheon's Four Seasons: Summersongs, Rounder, 1995.

Sprout Wings and Fly, Rounder, 1997.
Bigger Than Yourself, Rounder, 1997.
(With Tom Chapin) *Doing Our Job,* Rounder, 1997.

Audio recordings include *Mail Myself to You,* 1991; *Rainbow Sign,* 1992; and *John McCutcheon's Four Seasons: Wintersongs,* 1996; video recordings include *Teddy Bear,* 1996. *Rainbow Tales* and *Rainbow Tales Too!* were both produced by Rounder in 1997.

■ Work in Progress

The Gospel According to Joe; continuing *John McCutcheon's Four Seasons,* an audio recording series.

■ Sidelights

John McCutcheon told *Something about the Author* (*SATA*): "I was raised on the straightforward folk music of Woody Guthrie and the plain-spoken stories of my midwestern family. These have led me to a career (if that's what I can call it) in composing songs and stories about real people for real people. It is nothing fancy. Some people call my work political. That's okay, I guess; the worst thing that can happen to politics, or music, is to turn it over to the professionals. I just keep writing and singing and talking—and learning, as I did from Woody, not to forget what you stand for or who you stand with. That can happen in a children's song or a fiddle tune or a song from the day's headlines. It is like a little slice of life."

■ For More Information See

PERIODICALS

Booklist, December 1, 1996, p. 667.
Kirkus Reviews, July 15, 1996, p. 1058.
Publishers Weekly, August 5, 1996, p. 440.
School Library Journal, November, 1996, p. 88.

* * *

McDONALD, Mercedes 1956-

■ Personal

Born January 11, 1956; daughter of Robert B. (an artist and landscape architect) and Marjorie M. (a registered nurse and art gallery owner) McDonald; married Michel Rouhani (an attorney), April 4, 1985. *Education:* Atlanta College of Art, B.F.A., 1980; attended California College of Arts and Crafts, 1982-83; San Francisco Art Institute, M.F.A., 1987. *Hobbies and other interests:* Cats.

■ Addresses

Home and office—4349 Cahuenga Blvd. #10S, Toluca Lake, CA, 91602.

MERCEDES McDONALD

■ Career

Freelance illustrator. California College of Arts and Crafts, San Francisco, adjunct professor of illustration, 1989-95.

■ Awards, Honors

Award from *Communication Arts,* 1990, for a feature article.

■ Writings

(Illustrator) Marguerite M. Davol, *How Snake Got His Hiss: An Original Tale,* Orchard Books (New York City), 1996.
(Illustrator) Anne A. Johnson, *Smoothies: Twenty-Two Frosty Fruit Drinks,* Klutz Press, 1997.

Contributor to magazines, including *Communication Arts.*

■ Work in Progress

Writing and illustrating a children's book; a series of pastels featuring cats.

■ Sidelights

Mercedes McDonald told *Something about the Author* (*SATA*): "I am a fine artist lucky enough to make a career out of art. I started doing illustration while in graduate school, and I love what I do. Illustration allows me time (not much) to pursue my fine art, and I love having my studio at home. In my spare time, I try to do outdoor activities such as hiking and horseback riding. Also, since I love cats, I try to devote time to animal rescue; my niche is the care and feeding of orphan kittens. I also enjoy finding collectibles and odd junk at flea markets. I try to have fun with my art, and hopefully that shows in the work."

* * *

MELNIKOFF, Pamela (Rita)

■ Personal

Born in London, England; daughter of David and Yetta (Spiegel) Melnikoff; married Edward Harris (a doctor), March 29, 1970. *Education:* Attended North London Collegiate School. *Religion:* Jewish.

■ Addresses

Office—c/o *The Jewish Chronicle,* 25 Furnival St., London EC4AIJT, England.

■ Career

The Jewish Chronicle, London, England, reporter and feature writer, 1960-70, film critic, 1970-96. *Member:* The Society of Authors, PEN, The Guild of Jewish Journalists.

■ Awards, Honors

Golden Pen Award, Jewish Education Committee of New York, 1962, for the children's play *The Ransomed Menorah;* Greenwood Prize, the Poetry Society of Great Britain, for an individual poem.

■ Writings

The Ransomed Menorah (play), performed at the Joan of Arc Theater, New York, 1962-63.
The Star and the Sword, illustrated by Hans Schwarz, Vallentine Mitchell, 1965, Crown, 1968.
Plots and Players: The Lopez Conspiracy (young adult novel), illustrated by Ted Bernstein, Blackie, 1988, Peter Bedrick, 1989.
Prisoner in Time: A Child of the Holocaust (young adult novel), Blackie, 1992.

Also author of the libretto for "Heritage," a cantata with music by Cyril Ornadel that was performed by the Alyth Choral Society and had its premiere in London in 1993; the libretto for an opera based on the story of Jacob and Esau with music by David Fligg. Author of several prize-winning poems, many of which have been anthologized. The story *The Star and the Sword* has been translated into German.

■ Work in Progress

A history of Jewish film.

■ Sidelights

Pamela Melnikoff told *Something about the Author* (*SATA*): "I am not exclusively a children's writer. In addition to my children's books and play, I have written

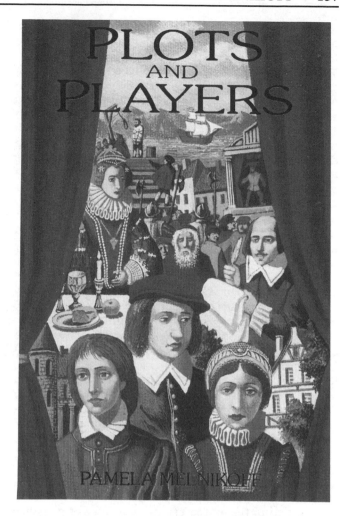

When prejudice leads to accusations of attempted murder against the Jewish physician to Queen Elizabeth, three children fight to save the doctor's life in Pamela Melnikoff's historical novel. (Cover illustration by Michael Iofin.)

the following: the libretto of a cantata, the libretto of an opera on the theme of Jacob and Esau, and individual prize-winning poems. I started writing as a child, and was first published at the age of eight."

As a writer for young people, Melnikoff is the creator of historical novels that characteristically feature Jewish protagonists and real-life historical figures and incidents. Her first book, *The Star and the Sword,* is a story directed to middle graders that the author based on her children's play *The Ransomed Menorah.* Melnikoff sets her book—an adventure tale with historical underpinnings—in medieval England, where a massacre of Jews in Lymford has orphaned twelve-year-old Benedict and his ten-year-old sister Elvira. The children set out on foot to find an uncle whom they hardly know; on their quest, they become friends with Robin Hood and help Sir Edward de Bourg, a Crusader who is an ally of Robin's, on a secret mission to deliver ransom money to the queen in London in order to aid King Richard. A reviewer in *The Booklist and Subscription Books Bulletin* praised Melnikoff's first effort, in which "pathos and humor are blended in [a] lively tale of medieval adventure."

Two decades later, Melnikoff produced her first historical novel for young adults with *Plots and Players*. In this work, the author draws upon the historical event known as the Lopez Conspiracy, in which Queen Elizabeth's Jewish physician, Dr. Rodrigo Lopez, was implicated in a struggle for power in the royal court and wound up convicted of spying for Spain and trying to poison the queen, crimes for which he paid with his life. Melnikoff also draws her background from experiences particular to England's Jews at the time who, feared and hated by the Christian populace, were forced to hide their identities for fear of persecution. *Plots and Players* revolves around Robin Fernandez, a twelve-year-old Jewish boy whose parents fled the Inquisition in Portugal, and his younger brother and sister. The three youngsters have come to know Dr. Lopez and, like him, to secretly continue to practice their Jewish religion though they have officially converted to Christianity. Through this connection with the endangered Lopez, the children encounter Queen Elizabeth herself, as well as William Shakespeare, whose *Merchant of Venice* is believed to have been influenced by the Lopez Conspiracy. When Robin's sister Frances makes an impassioned plea to the queen to revoke Lopez's sentence, the monarch implicitly confirms his innocence, and Robin convinces Shakespeare to recast Shylock as a more sympathetic character. "Melnikoff has taken a dramatic event in history and created a gripping novel for young readers," wrote *School Library Journal* contributor Renee Steinberg, who also noted that the book offers its audience "a background to the all too extensive history of prejudice and its ramifications." *Booklist* reviewer Ellen Mandel asserted, "The author weaves details into a colorful tapestry.... [An] unusual amalgamation of fact and fantasy." A reviewer in *Junior Bookshelf* maintained that *Plots and Players* is "an exciting story which does not make the mistake of 'white-washing' the evils of the age." This book, predicted Margaret W. Ferguson in the *New York Times Book Review,* "will have a special appeal to any child who has encountered, or is about to encounter, Shakespeare in the schoolroom...." Calling the novel a "valuably educational fantasy," Ferguson concluded that *Plots and Players* gives a "provocative and perhaps inspirational revision of history."

Melnikoff is also the author of *Prisoner of Time,* a book for teenagers in which she incorporates fantasy elements for the first time in her stories. In this novel, Jan Weiss, a twelve-year-old Jew living in Prague in the early 1940s, witnesses the deportation of his family to the Nazi concentration camps, and goes into hiding in the attic of family friends. While visiting a Jewish cemetery, he finds a golden bird in the tomb of legendary Rabbi Loewe that transports him back to the Prague of the sixteenth century, where the rabbi—with Jan's help—constructs a golem from clay to save the Jews from persecution. Upon his return to his own time, Jan is picked up by the Nazis and transported to the death camps; although Jan attempts to return to the 1500s, his amulet is stolen in the camps, and his fate seems certain.

As was the case with her earlier books, Melnikoff's novel was praised for its effective incorporation of accurate historical details. *School Librarian* reviewer Angela Lepper called *Prisoner of Time* a "moving story of horror and hope, of depravity and kindness." A critic in *Junior Bookshelf* noted that Melnikoff writes her novel as an "unbiased recorder of possible lives of a few of the one-and-a-half million Jewish children" who disappeared over fifty years ago. The reviewer concluded, "*Prisoner in Time* is an absorbing book even though many readers, perhaps most, will from its beginning anticipate a fateful conclusion. It is still hard to put it down."

■ Works Cited

Ferguson, Margaret W., review of *Plots and Players, New York Times Book Review,* May 21, 1989, p. 34.

Lepper, Angela, review of *Prisoner in Time, School Librarian,* November, 1992, p. 159.

Mandel, Ellen, review of *Plots and Players, Booklist,* July, 1989, pp. 1905-06.

Review of *Plots and Players, Junior Bookshelf,* December, 1988, p. 308.

Review of *Prisoner in Time, Junior Bookshelf,* December, 1992, p. 258.

Review of *The Star and the Sword, Booklist and Subscription Books Bulletin,* March 15, 1969, p. 838.

Steinberg, Renee, review of *Plots and Players, School Library Journal,* July, 1989, p. 83.

■ For More Information See

PERIODICALS

Kirkus Reviews, April 15, 1989, p. 627.

Times Educational Supplement, November 25, 1988, p. 31; February 19, 1993, p. R7.

Voice of Youth Advocates, October, 1989, p. 214.

*   *   *

MOHR, Nicholasa 1938-

■ Personal

Born November 1, 1938, in New York, NY; daughter of Pedro and Nicolasa (Rivera) Golpe; married Irwin Mohr (a clinical child psychologist), October 5, 1957 (deceased); children: David, Jason. *Education:* Attended Art Students' League, 1953-56, Taller de Grafica, Mexico City, 1958, New School for Social Research, c. 1957, Brooklyn Museum of Art School, 1964-66, and Pratt Center for Contemporary Printmaking, 1967-70.

■ Addresses

Home—727 President St., Brooklyn, NY 11215.

■ Career

Fine arts painter in New York, California, Mexico, and Puerto Rico, 1952-62; printmaker in New York, Mexi-

NICHOLASA MOHR

co, and Puerto Rico, 1963—; teacher in art schools in New York and New Jersey, 1967—. Art instructor, Art Center of Northern New Jersey, 1971-73; writer in residence, MacDowell Colony, Peterborough, NH, 1972, 1974, and 1976; artist in residence, New York City public schools, 1973-74; lecturer in Puerto Rican studies, State University of New York at Stony Brook, 1977; conducted and developed specialized Hispanic children's book program, Newark, NJ, 1980-81; distinguished visiting professor at Queens College of the City University of New York, 1988-91; writer in residence, Richmond College (American International University), London, England, 1994-95; visiting scholar at numerous schools, universities, and institutions, including University of San Francisco, 1990, and National Book Foundation, 1992. Lecturer in creative writing for various educator, librarian, student, and community groups. Head creative writer and co-producer of videotape series *Aqui y Ahora* (title means "Here and Now"). Member of New Jersey State Council on the Arts; member of board of trustees, and consultant, of Young Filmmakers Foundation; consultant on bilingual media training for Young Filmmakers/Video Arts. *Member:* Authors Guild, Authors League of America.

■ Awards, Honors

Outstanding book award in juvenile fiction, *New York Times,* 1973, Jane Addams Children's Book Award, Jane Addams Peace Association, 1974, citation of merit for book jacket design, Society of Illustrators, 1974, and *School Library Journal*'s "Best of the Best 1966-78" citation, all for *Nilda;* outstanding book award in

teenage fiction, *New York Times,* 1975, Best Books, *School Library Journal,* 1975, and National Book Award finalist for "most distinguished book in children's literature," 1976, all for *El Bronx Remembered;* Best Books, *School Library Journal,* Best Books for Young Adults, American Library Association, and Notable Trade Book in the Field of Social Studies, National Council for the Social Studies and Children's Book Council (NCSS-CBC), all 1977, all for *In Nueva York;* Notable Trade Book in the Field of Social Studies, NCSS-CBC, 1980, and American Book Award, Before Columbus Foundation, 1981, both for *Felita;* commendation from the Legislature of the State of New York, 1986, for *Rituals of Survival: A Woman's Portfolio;* Notable Trade Book in the Field of Social Studies, NCSS-CBC, 1986, for *Going Home.* Honorary doctorate of letters, State University of New York at Albany, 1989, Edgar Allan Poe Award, Bronx Historical Society, 1990, Association of Hispanic Arts Award, 1993, Nicholasa Mohr Reading Room, New York Public Library-Sedgewick Branch, beginning 1994, Lifetime Achievement Award, National Conference of Puerto Rican Women, 1996, and Hispanic Heritage Award, Hispanic Heritage Foundation, 1997, all for body of work.

■ Writings

FOR YOUNG PEOPLE

(Self-illustrated) *Nilda* (novel), Harper, 1973, 2nd edition, Arte Publico, 1986.

(Self-illustrated) *El Bronx Remembered: A Novella and Stories,* Harper, 1975, 2nd edition, Arte Publico, 1986.

In Nueva York (short stories), Dial, 1977.

(Self-illustrated) *Felita* (novel), Dial, 1979.

Going Home (novel; sequel to *Felita*), Dial, 1986.

All for the Better: A Story of el Barrio (part of "Stories of America" series), illustrated by Rudy Gutierrez, Raintree Steck-Vaughn, 1992.

Isabel's New Mom, Macmillan, 1993.

The Magic Shell, illustrated by Rudy Gutierrez, Scholastic, 1994.

The Song of el Coqui and Other Tales of Puerto Rico, illustrated by Antonio Martorell, Viking, 1995.

Old Letivia and the Mountain of Sorrows/La Vieja Letivia y el Monte de los Pesares, illustrated by Rudy Gutierrez, Viking, 1996.

OTHER

Aqui y Ahora (teleplay), Film Video Arts, 1975.

Inside the Monster (radio play), Film Video Arts, 1981.

Rituals of Survival: A Women's Portfolio (adult fiction), Arte Publico, 1985.

In My Own Words, Simon and Schuster, 1994.

Also author, with Ray Blanco, of *The Artist,* a screenplay. Illustrator of *Hispanic Temas,* edited by Hilda Hidalgo and Joan McEniry, 1985. Contributor of stories to textbooks and anthologies, including *The Ethnic American Woman: Problems, Protests, Lifestyles.* Contributor of short stories to *Children's Digest, Scholastic Magazine,* and *Nuestro.* Member of board of contributing editors, *Nuestro.*

■ Work in Progress

A children's novel.

■ Sidelights

Nicholasa Mohr draws upon her own childhood and adolescence to create novels and short stories that offer realistic and uncompromising portraits of life in New York City's Puerto Rican barrio. Her first book, *Nilda,* for instance, contains many autobiographical elements as it presents the story of a young girl struggling to mature and succeed despite living with poverty and prejudice. Nilda's drive to become an artist mirrors Mohr's own career, which has taken her from creating noteworthy paintings and prints to writing critically acclaimed novels and stories.

Mohr was born in El Barrio in Spanish Harlem to Puerto Rican parents who had moved to New York City during the Depression. She was the youngest child and only girl, so "growing up in a household with six older brothers, and being part of a family who still held old-fashioned Puerto Rican concepts about the male and female role, was often a struggle for me," Mohr related in an essay. She was expected to help more with the housework, and had less freedom to go out with friends. She spent much of her time at home, and occupied herself by drawing and painting.

Art had been an important part of Mohr's life ever since she was a young child. "From the moment my mother handed me some scrap paper, a pencil, and a few crayons, I discovered that by making pictures and writing letters I could create my own world ... like 'magic,'" Mohr related. "In the small crowded apartment I shared with my large family, making 'magic' permitted me all the space, freedom, and adventure that my imagination could handle." Mohr's artistic talents also made her stand out in school, where teachers and classmates would admire her drawings—even if some of them were otherwise prejudiced against her because she was Hispanic.

Drawing and painting comforted Mohr when times were difficult. Her father had died when she was only eight, and her mother struggled to support the family even though she was often ill. Her determination to provide for her children and her frequent words of encouragement to her daughter motivated Mohr. She died before Mohr started high school, however, and the young artist was left with an aunt who was distant and concerned more with her own family than with caring for her orphaned niece. Despite this lack of support, Mohr continued excelling in her artistic studies, inspired by her mother's instructions to keep a close hold on her talent: "My mother, who died in poverty, managed to leave me a rich legacy," the artist related in her essay. This legacy gave Mohr "the strength to continue to follow my own star, even under the worst of circumstances."

A guidance counselor's prejudice almost thwarted Mohr's further education. It was time to select which one of New York City's specialized high schools might best serve Mohr, and her counselor decided that a Puerto Rican girl didn't need an academic education. Although she was one of the most talented artists in her class, Mohr was selected to attend trade school to learn sewing skills. "I remember pleading with [the counselor] to let me at least apply to a better high school," the author recalled. "Her response was that Puerto Rican women were by nature good seamstresses. Therefore, I should follow a natural career and be able to earn a living after graduation." Mohr was lucky and found a school that had a major in fashion illustration; there she was at least able to practice drawing, although she found the repetitious nature of illustrating fashion designs tedious.

After graduation, Mohr attended the Arts Students' League in New York City, where she could study painting and drawing in earnest. Working her way through art school, Mohr intended to save enough money to eventually study art in Europe. But her reading in the local library had drawn her to the work of Mexican muralists and artists such as Diego Rivera, Jose Clemente Orozco, and Frida Kahlo. By the time she had enough money to study abroad, she decided to go to Mexico City. There she saw firsthand the strong,

BY NICHOLASA MOHR
ILLUSTRATIONS BY RUDY GUTIERREZ

When he moves from the Dominican Republic to strange, cold New York City, Jaime Ramos finds solace in the conch shell given to him by his great-uncle.

powerful artwork which had impressed her, especially in the way the paintings made strong personal and political statements without using propaganda. "In a profound way their work spoke to me and my experiences as a Puerto Rican woman born in New York," the artist said in her autobiographical essay. "The impact was to shape and form the direction of all my future work."

After returning to New York, Mohr entered classes at the New School for Social Research, where she met her future husband. She continued polishing her extremely revealing, almost story-like, artistic style. "My experiences were developed in my work," Mohr explained to Paul Janeczko in *From Writers to Students.* "You could see them in my figurative work and the way I use colors. Sometimes I told a story through the visual interpretation and, hopefully, evoked feelings from the viewer." The artist elaborated in her essay: "Instead of just rendering literal scenes ... or becoming aesthetically abstract and interpreting my mastery of techniques, my prints and painting were filled with bold figures, faces, and various symbols of the city. These symbols were numbers, letters, words, and phrases ... a kind of graffiti."

The graffiti-like elements of Mohr's art especially appealed to one of her collectors, a publishing executive. Through Mohr's art agent, he asked if she would be willing to try her hand at writing. The artist was reluctant at first, but her agent soon convinced her that a story of a young Puerto Rican girl could fill a gap in children's literature. "When I was growing up, I'd enjoyed reading about the adventures of many boys and girls, but I had never really seen myself, my brothers, and my family in those books," she wrote in her essay. "We just were not there.... Finally, I agreed to write fifty pages of short stories doing the best I could."

Through hard work and perseverance Mohr produced several stories based on her childhood experiences in the barrio. Much to her disappointment and puzzlement, the publisher turned them down. Her agent explained that because there were no tales of gangs, sex, drugs, and crime, the work didn't seem to be genuine. Mohr was angered by his stereotyping, as she related: "I knew then that I did not exist for him as the person I really was, but rather as the model for a Puerto Rican female protagonist who would be featured in a sensational book that he fantasized would net us a fortune." Disillusioned, Mohr put her manuscript aside and returned to her artwork.

A short time after, however, Mohr met Ellen Rudin, editor-in-chief at HarperCollins, who agreed to review her stories even though she was more interested in Mohr as an illustrator. Rudin soon offered Mohr a contract, and the artist set out to write her first novel. Accompanied by eight illustrations and a jacket by the author, *Nilda* was published in 1973 and gave Mohr a new perspective on her creativity. "It was almost like a catharsis, the first book," Mohr told Janeczko. "I was even thinking of going into sculpture, but all of a sudden I found a medium where I was really comfortable. I could draw a picture with words, and it was extremely stimulating and eye-opening.... Everything I [had] done as an artist [was] transferable to a new craft."

In *Nilda,* the author portrays a Puerto Rican girl as she grows from a child to a teenager during the years of World War II. At home, young Nilda is faced with her family's struggle to survive poverty, while outside that loving circle she is confronted with prejudice from teachers, social workers, police, and classmates. But the novel is not merely a catalog of the problems Nilda encounters; it also describes her experiences at a summer camp, her discovery of a secret garden, and the pleasure she finds in inventing stories and drawing pictures. The entire novel is related "through a child's vision—questioning, resigned, furious, joyful," Edith Blicksilver comments in *Biographical Directory of Hispanic Literature in the United States.* The result is "a powerful story of the hardships of being Puerto Rican and of the barriers facing women," Myra Pollack Sadker and David Miller Sadker state in *Now upon a Time.*

While many children's books have attempted to explore the problems of poor, minority children, *New York Times Book Review* contributor Marilyn Sachs observes that "few come up to 'Nilda' in describing the crushing humiliations of poverty and in peeling off the ethnic wrappings so that we can see the human child underneath." But Miguel A. Ortiz faults the book as undramatic, due to its superficial characters; Nilda "seems to

The tales in Mohr's collection represent the three ancestral peoples of Puerto Rican culture: the indigenous Tainos, the Africans, and the Spaniards. (From *The Song of el Coqui and Other Tales of Puerto Rico,* illustrated by Antonio Martorell.)

be living through events which have no effect on her," he writes in *The Lion and the Unicorn.* Other reviewers, however, praise Mohr for her characterization; Sachs notes that "what makes the book remarkable is the richness of detail and the aching sense of a child's feelings." "There is no pity here, for the author is too much aware of the humanity of her characters and of the other implications of pity to be in any way condescending," Donald B. Gibson comments in *Children's Literature. Nilda,* he concludes, is "what I would call a significant book, a touchstone by which others may be judged."

El Bronx Remembered, Mohr's second book, is a collection of stories set in Nilda's New York City neighborhood, after the war. The narratives vary from stories of teenagers dealing with death, prejudice, and feelings of embarrassment, to the tale of an elderly Jewish man who is befriended by a Puerto Rican family. *El Bronx Remembered* also contains such potentially controversial topics as teenage pregnancy and homosexuality; one story, "Herman and Alice," tells of the doomed marriage between a pregnant teenager and an older homosexual man. Despite such weighty topics, however, Mohr also shows the optimism and humor of the neighborhood, and "her stories focus upon the universal emotions of pride, nostalgia, hope, love, and fear with Chekovian narrative skill," Blicksilver writes.

"In her earlier outstanding novel *Nilda,* it was apparent that if any author could make you hear pulses beating from the pages, Nicholasa Mohr was the one," Sachs similarly remarks. "In *El Bronx Remembered,* she has done it again." The critic continues: "If there is any message at all in these stories, any underlying theme, it is that life goes on. But Nicholasa Mohr is more interested in people than in messages." The reviewer notes that the stories are without "complicated symbolism . . . , trendy obscurity of meaning . . . hopeless despair or militant ethnicity. Her people endure because they are people." "Much has been written about Spanish-speaking communities, but it is rare to find such delicate insight combined with such deliberate detail," Anne M. Flynn maintains in a *Best Sellers* review. "Miss Mohr has the ability to describe quite commonplace situations, dissect them, relate them to the reader, and then allow her interpretations to be savored." "At their best," Paul Heins notes in *Horn Book,* "the short Chekhov-like narratives reveal universal emotions hovering beneath an urban, ethnic casing." A critic for the *Bulletin of the Center for Children's Books* agrees, concluding that Mohr's characters "ring true, having both universality and the special quality of the vitality and warmth of the Puerto Rican community."

In Nueva York is similar to *El Bronx Remembered* in that it contains several stories and novellas set in the Puerto Rican neighborhoods of New York City. *In Nueva York,* however, features several recurring characters: Old Mary, a fiftyish woman whose search for a better life on the mainland often led to heartache; her sons, one of whom she hasn't seen since she left Puerto Rico; and a bedraggled alley cat. Mohr's characters have many problems, often battling "rats, dirt, junkies, street gangs, ruthless landlords, hostile building inspectors, greedy politicians, prejudiced teachers, and racist police," as Blicksilver summarizes. Nevertheless, the critic adds, "they are sustained through their crises by family and community support, by their religious faith, and by loving concern for their children. They do more than survive—they fight back."

In populating the neighborhood of *In Nueva York,* "Mohr creates a remarkably vivid tapestry of community life as well as of individual characters," Zena Sutherland writes in her *Bulletin of the Center for*

Mohr's original folktale relates the trials of Old Letivia, a healer who tries to tame the forces of nature in the Puerto Rican rain forest. (From *Old Letivia and the Mountain of Sorrows,* illustrated by Rudy Gutierrez.)

Children's Books review. The critic adds: "Tough, candid, and perceptive, the book has memorable characters, resilient and responsive, in a sharply-etched milieu." Georgess McHargue, however, faults the stories as "too obviously intended as slice-of-life fiction" with unrealistic characters, as she states in the *New York Times Book Review*. But because many individuals appear in more than one story, Aileen Pace Nilsen suggests in *English Journal*, "the effect is an intimate look into the most interesting parts of several people's lives without the artificial strain of having them all squeezed into a single plot." The result, she continues, is "an excellent book to help people see beyond the stereotypes." "Mohr's characters are warm and believable," Jack Forman similarly notes in *School Library Journal*, "and she succeeds admirably in involving readers in what happens to them."

Mohr turns to a younger audience in *Felita*, a novel about a young girl whose parents move to a more upscale area in hopes of providing a better life for their children. But Felita is unhappy in their new home; she misses her old friends, and prejudice intrudes when her new friends are kept away by their parents and her family is harassed by neighbors. When the family returns to the old neighborhood, Felita is happy again, but she must still confront problems with school and classmates. With the aid of her grandmother, Felita begins to readjust. "The episodic story is usually engaging," Denise M. Wilms writes in *Booklist*, "and Felita's presence is lively and strong."

Mohr continues Felita's story in the 1986 novel *Going Home*. Now eleven years old, Felita has her first boyfriend and is looking forward to a trip to Puerto Rico with her parents. These happy events have a downside, however, for her friends are jealous of Vinnie, her new sweetheart, and her vacation in Puerto Rico is marred by homesickness and the taunts of local children. Felita gradually makes friends, however, and by the time the summer is over she is sad to leave.

Going Home is "a charming sequel to the author's *Felita*," Sutherland claims in *Bulletin of the Center for Children's Books*. The author's narration "is colloquial and exuberant, and Mohr has a particularly sharp eye for the friendships (as well as the downright meanness) of pre-teen girls." As Wilms writes in another *Booklist* review, *Going Home* "is deftly written and lively—an enjoyable story for any reader." "Felita is a vivid, memorable character, well realized and well developed," Christine Behrmann remarks in *School Library Journal*. "It is a pleasure to welcome her back."

In *The Magic Shell*, Jaime moves from the Dominican Republic to New York City. Jaime's great-uncle gives him a large conch shell as a going-away gift and instructs Jaime to listen to the shell when he becomes homesick. Jaime gets used to the different climate, makes friends, and finds it difficult to leave his new home to go back to the Dominican Republic for a visit. "Jaime is convincingly caught between two cultures," writes Marilyn Long Graham of *School Library Journal*, adding that "this upbeat story flows well with a good mixture of imagination and reality." *Bulletin of the Center for Children's Books* critic Roger Sutton praises Mohr's "affectionate portrait" of Jaime, and notes that the book is "pleasant, cozy, and easy to read."

Although Mohr's works have enjoyed popularity with teenagers, "I don't write for young people, per se," she related to Janeczko. "I write for people. Some of them are young and some of them are old. I don't like this division that young people sort of have a place; they're people," the author continued. Nevertheless, she is pleased that her work appeals to younger readers, "because I feel that's part of life, that's part of being alive. But good writing is writing that someone picks up and says, 'Okay, I want to go on with this, not because it's for a teenager or adolescent, but because the writer is saying something that I want to get involved with.'"

Folktales often have an appeal for people of all ages. In her book *The Song of el Coqui and Other Tales of Puerto Rico,* Mohr tells three stories which exemplify the different cultures of Puerto Rico. One story features Haracan, the god of storms worshipped by the indigenous Tainos. Another story tells about a guinea hen who comes to Puerto Rico on a slaveship from Africa, and the last story is about a mule who is brought from Spain to work in a labor camp. The mule, along with a slave, escapes and lives in freedom. The book, illustrated by Antonio Martorell, is described by *School Library Journal* reviewer Maria Redburn as "a book that combines storytelling and artistry to convey the richness of a land's people."

Mohr shares another piece of her cultural heritage in *All for the Better: A Story of El Barrio,* a biography of the community activist Evalina Lopez Antonetty. The story, which focuses on Evalina's childhood, tells readers how at age eleven, Evalina traveled alone from Puerto Rico to New York during the Depression, and how she became increasingly involved in the Spanish community of New York and eventually founded the United Bronx Parents Group. Roger Sutton of the *Bulletin of the Center for Children's Books* thinks that the writing "is a tad tepid and adulatory," but Linda Greengrass says in *School Library Journal* that "the language in this well-written biography is rich, flavored with Spanish words, and yet relatively easy to read."

Although Mohr found writing a way to heighten the artistic energies she had previously expressed through painting, she has no plans to abandon it for yet another creative outlet. "I see fiction as an art form which I don't see myself leaving," the author revealed to Janeczko. "As a writer I have used my abilities as a creative artist to strengthen my skills and at the same time in small measure have ventured to establish a voice for my ethnic American community and our children," Mohr explained in her essay. But more important to her is retaining that "magic" that using her imagination brought her as a young child—that ability her mother instructed her to hold on to at all costs. "Because of who I am," Mohr concluded, "I feel blessed by the work I do, for it permits me to use my talents and continue to 'make magic.' With this 'magic' I can recreate those deepest of personal memories as well as validate and celebrate my heritage and my future."

■ Works Cited

Behrmann, Christine, review of *Going Home, School Library Journal*, August, 1986, p. 105.

Blicksilver, Edith, "Nicholasa Mohr," *Biographical Directory of Hispanic Literature in the United States*, edited by Nicolas Kanellos, Greenwood Press, 1989, pp. 199-213.

Review of *El Bronx Remembered, Bulletin of the Center for Children's Books*, June, 1976, p. 161.

Flynn, Anne M., review of *El Bronx Remembered, Best Sellers*, December, 1975, p. 266.

Forman, Jack, review of *In Nueva York, School Library Journal*, April, 1977, p. 79.

Gibson, Donald B., "Fiction, Fantasy, and Ethnic Realities," *Children's Literature*, Volume 3, 1974, pp. 230-234.

Graham, Marilyn Long, review of *The Magic Shell, School Library Journal*, October, 1995, p. 138.

Greengrass, Linda, review of *All for the Better: A Story of El Barrio, School Library Journal*, May, 1993, p. 118.

Heins, Paul, review of *El Bronx Remembered, Horn Book*, February, 1976, p. 57.

Janeczko, Paul, interview with Nicholasa Mohr, in *From Writers to Students: The Pleasures and Pains of Writing*, edited by M. Jerry Weiss, International Reading Association, 1979, pp. 75-78.

McHargue, Georgess, review of *In Nueva York, New York Times Book Review*, May 22, 1977, p. 29.

Mohr, Nicholasa, *Something about the Author Autobiography Series*, Volume 8, Gale, 1989, pp. 185-194.

Nilsen, Aileen Pace, review of *In Nueva York, English Journal*, February, 1978, p. 100.

Ortiz, Miguel A., "The Politics of Poverty in Young Adult Literature," *The Lion and the Unicorn*, fall, 1978, pp. 6-15.

Redburn, Maria, review of *The Song of el Coqui and Other Tales of Puerto Rico, School Library Journal*, August, 1995, p. 137.

Sachs, Marilyn, review of *Nilda, New York Times Book Review*, November 4, 1973, pp. 27-28.

Sachs, Marilyn, review of *El Bronx Remembered, New York Times Book Review*, November 16, 1975.

Sadker, Myra Pollack, and David Miller Sadker, *Now upon a Time: A Contemporary View of Children's Literature*, Harper, 1977, pp. 210-230.

Sutherland, Zena, review of *In Nueva York, Bulletin of the Center for Children's Books*, July-August, 1977, p. 178.

Sutherland, Zena, review of *Going Home, Bulletin of the Center for Children's Books*, May, 1986, p. 178.

Sutton, Roger, review of *All for the Better: A Story of El Barrio, Bulletin of the Center for Children's Books*, July/August, 1993, p. 353.

Sutton, Roger, review of *The Magic Shell, Bulletin of the Center for Children's Books*, December, 1995, pp. 134-35.

Wilms, Denise M., review of *Felita, Booklist*, December 1, 1979, p. 559.

Wilms, Denise M., review of *Going Home, Booklist*, July, 1986, p. 1615.

■ For More Information See

BOOKS

Children's Literature Review, Volume 22, Gale, 1991.

PERIODICALS

Lion and the Unicorn, April, 1987, pp. 116-21.

* * *

MOLINA, Silvia 1946-

■ Personal

Born October 11, 1946, in Mexico City, Mexico; daughter of Hector Perez Martinez (a writer) and Maria Celis Campos; married Claudio Molina Torres (a geologist), December 18, 1970; children: Silvia Veronica, Claudia Molina Perez. *Education:* Universidad Automa de Mexico, B.A. (literature).

■ Addresses

Home—Manantial 109, Pedregal de San Angel, 01900 Mexico, D.F. *Office*—Oaxaca 1, San Jeronimo Aculco, 10700 Mexico, D.F.

■ Career

Writer. Ediciones Corunda (a publishing house), Mexico, manager. *Member:* Sociedad General Escritores Mexicanos, Asociacion de Escritores de Mexico.

■ Awards, Honors

Xavier Villaurrutia Prize, 1977, for the novel *La manana debe seguir gris (Gray Skies Tomorrow)*; Children's Literature Prize, 1992, for *Mi familia y la Bella Durmiente cien anos despues*.

■ Writings

FOR CHILDREN

El papel (title means "The Paper"), Editorial Patria (Mexico), 1985.

El algodon, Editorial Patria, 1987.

Los cuatro hermanos (title means "The Four Brothers"), Ediciones Corunda (Mexico), 1988.

La creacion del hombre, Editorial Trillas (Mexico), 1989.

La leyenda del sol y de la luna, Editorial Trillas, 1991.

Los tres corazones (title means "The Three Hearts"), Ediciones Corunda, 1992.

Mi familia y la Bella Durmiente cien anos despues (title means "Sleeping Beauty and My Family, One Hundred Years After"), Ediciones Corunda, 1993.

NOVELS

La manana debe seguir gris, Joaquin Mortiz (Col Del Valle, Mexico), 1977, published as *Gray Skies Tomorrow,* Plover Press (Kaneohe, HI), 1993.

Ascension Tun, Martin Casillas (Mexico), 1981.

La familia vino del norte (title means "The Family Came from the North"), Cal y Arena (Mexico), 1988.

Imagen de Hector (title means "Hector's Image"), Cal y Arena, 1990.

Contributor to the book *El Hombre equivocado* (title means "The Mistaken Man"), Joaquin Mortiz, 1988.

SHORT STORIES

Lides de estano (title means "Tin Fights"), Universidad Autonoma Metropolitana, Col. Molinas de Viento (Mexico), 1984.

Dicen que me case yo (title means "They Say I Should Marry"), Cal y Arena, 1989.

Un hombre cerca (title means "A Man Around"), Cal y Arena, 1992.

Several of Molina's stories have been translated into English, French, and German.

ESSAYS

Leyendo en la tortuga, Martin Casillas, 1981.

A vuelta de correo, Universidad Automa de Mexico, 1988.

Campeche, punta del ala del pais, Direccion General de Publicaciones del Consejo Nacional para la cultura y las Artes (Mexico), 1991.

■ Sidelights

In her books for children, Silvia Molina has been praised for her simple, well-paced narratives that explain the making of paper, the development of cotton, or the legends of ancient Mexico. The author comments: "I have been asked on many occasions why most of my characters are women. It turns out that I am a woman and that I base my characters on my own experience. That is something that comes out naturally in my writing, something that I pour out on to the blank page with the idea of discovering myself, of finding what there is of me in the beings I observe, and above all, what I don't have and thus what I envy.

"When I write I discover, surprised, that within me I have an unpostponable desire to be another woman, a different woman, a woman who . . . I will perhaps never be. I am filled with an inevitable desire to make up what I am not, to be able to be what I would like, a desire which will only be fulfilled in the act of writing.

"That is why the women in whom I am searching for myself are brave; they are not afraid of change, nor do they stop time. In my characters I learn to see myself without fear, without pity, crudely. I learn to accept myself full of feelings which have no other place than in these beings into whom I break; I learn to experience passion, to recognize my miseries and smallness."

■ For More Information See

PERIODICALS

Booklist, March 1, 1987, p. 1061; June 1, 1993, p. 1867.

Horn Book, March-April, 1990, p. 228.*

N

NIX, Garth 1963-

■ Personal

Born 1963, in Melbourne, Australia. *Education:* University of Canberra, B.A., 1986. *Hobbies and other interests:* Traveling, fishing, bodysurfing, book collecting, reading, and films.

■ Addresses

Home—Sydney, Australia. *Electronic mail*—garthnix @ ozemail.com.au.

■ Career

Author and publisher. Gotley Nix Evans Pty. Ltd., Sydney, Australia, marketing communications consultant. Worked for the Australian government; worked also in a bookstore and as a sales representative, publicist, and senior editor in the publishing industry. *Military service:* Served four years in the Australian Army Reserve.

■ Awards, Honors

"Books in the Middle: Outstanding Titles" selection, *Voice of Youth Advocates,* 1996, for *Sabriel,* and 1997, for *Shade's Children;* Notable Book designation, American Library Association (ALA), for *Sabriel;* Best Books for Young Adults, ALA, for both *Sabriel* and *Shade's Children;* Best Fantasy Novel, Best YA Novel, Aurealis Awards for Excellence in Australian Speculative Fiction, 1995, for *Sabriel.*

■ Writings

Very Clever Baby's Ben Hur: Starring Freddy the Fish as Charlton Heston, Nix Books (Sydney), 1988.
Very Clever Baby's First Reader: A Simple Reader for Your Child Featuring Freddy the Fish and Easy Words, Nix Books, 1988.
The Ragwitch, Pan Books (Sydney), 1990, Tor, 1995.

GARTH NIX

Very Clever Baby's Guide to the Greenhouse Effect, Nix Books, 1992.
Sabriel, HarperCollins, 1995.
Shade's Children, Allen & Unwin (St. Leonard's, New South Wales), 1997, HarperCollins, 1997.
The Calusari ("X Files" Series) HarperCollins, 1997.

Also author of short stories and co-author of shows for dinner theater.

■ **Sidelights**

Australian writer Garth Nix is earning a reputation in fantasy circles for his engaging and finely detailed fiction for young adults. At the same time, he is a humorist who has written three "Very Clever Baby" books—parodies of an easy reader, the greenhouse effect, and the movie *Ben Hur* featuring Freddy the Fish—that are not yet available outside of his homeland. Nix, who grew up in Canberra, earned a bachelor's degree in professional writing from the University of Canberra before beginning a career in the publishing industry. In 1991, he became a senior editor with HarperCollins Australia. Since then, Nix has traveled through Eastern Europe, the Middle East and Asia, and established a marketing communications agency, Gotley Nix Evans Pty Ltd. He left Gotley Nix Evans in 1998 to concentrate on his writing career.

Sabriel, a young adult novel that is, in the words of *School Library Journal* contributor John Peters, "a vividly imagined fantasy," is the first of Nix's works to receive acclaim in the United States. Sabriel is a young woman who has been trained by her father, Abhorsen, a necromancer who, unlike others of his trade, is skilled at putting uneasy souls to rest instead of calling them to life. Sabriel is in her last year of boarding school when she receives Abhorsen's necromancing tools and sword and realizes that her father's life is in danger—he has left the Land of the Living. Sabriel leaves the safety of her school to return to the Old Kingdom, which her father was supposed to protect, in order to rescue him. As she travels to the world beyond the Land of the Living to the Gates of Death, Sabriel is joined by Mogget, a powerful being in the form of a cat who has acted as her father's servant, and a young prince named Touchstone, whom she has brought back from the dead. With their help, Sabriel battles her way past monsters, beasts, and evil spirits until she finally reaches her father, "only to lose him permanently in the opening rounds of a vicious, wild climax," as Peters explained. However, Sabriel—whom critics acknowledge as an especially sympathetic heroine—realizes that she is her father's successor and that the future of the Old Kingdom depends on her. Peters concluded, "This book is guaranteed to keep readers up way past their bedtime." "Rich, complex, involving, hard to put down," claimed a critic in *Publishers Weekly,* who added that the novel "is excellent high fantasy." *Booklist* reviewer Sally Estes, who compared *Sabriel* favorably to English writer Philip Pullman's fantasy *The Golden Compass,* stated, "The action charges along at a gallop, imbued with an encompassing sense of looming disaster.... A pageturner for sure." Writing in the *Horn Book Magazine,* Ann A. Flowers commented: "The story is remarkable for the level of originality of the fantastic elements ... and for the subtle presentation, which leaves readers to explore for themselves the complex structure and significance of the magic elements." According to a critic for *Voice of Youth Advocates, Sabriel* is "one of the best fantasies of this or any other year."

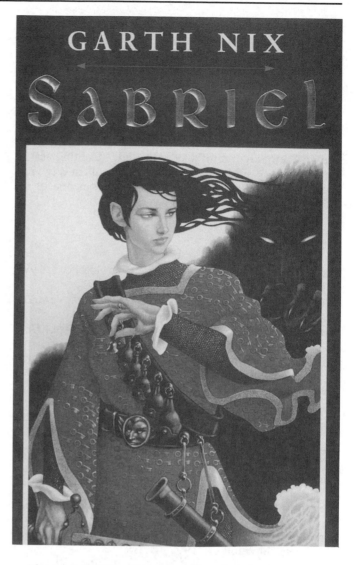

After severe trials, Sabriel realizes her destiny as the heir to her father's legacy as a necromancer in Garth Nix's suspenseful fantasy novel. (Cover illustration by Leo and Diane Dillon.)

Shade's Children is a science fiction novel for young adults that, according to a *Publishers Weekly* critic, "tells essentially the same story" as *Sabriel,* with its "desperate quest by a talented few." In this book, however, a psychic young boy, Gold-Eye, runs to escape the evil Overlords who use the body parts of children for their own insidious purposes. The novel is set in a future time when the earth has been taken over by the terrible aliens, who have destroyed everyone over fourteen; the only adult presence is Shade, a computer-generated hologram. Gold-Eye joins a group of teenagers who, working from Shade's submarine base, fight the Overlords. In addition to battling the aliens, the young people must deal with betrayal and with losing half their group; however, they learn about their special talents and achieve victory through their sacrifices. The *Publishers Weekly* reviewer concluded that while *Shade's Children* "lacks some of the emotional depth of Nix's first work, it will draw (and keep) fans of the genre." According to a critic in *Kirkus Reviews,* the book "combines plenty of comic-book action in a sci-fi setting to produce an exciting read.... [An] action-adventure with uncommon appeal outside the genre." Ann A. Flowers of *Horn Book* praised Nix's characterization of his young protagonists, adding: "The author leaves the reader to draw many conclusions from scattered evidence, hence capturing and holding the audience's attention all the way to the bittersweet ending. Grim, unusual, and fascinating." *Reading Time* contributor Kevin Steinberger similarly enthused: "Exciting action, cracking pace and absorbing intrigue, all in a vividly imagined world, marks *Shade's Children* as one of the best adolescent reads of the year."

■ Works Cited

Estes, Sally, review of *Sabriel, Booklist,* October 1, 1996, p. 350.

Flowers, Ann A., review of *Sabriel, Horn Book,* January-February, 1997, pp. 64-65.

Flowers, Ann A., review of *Shade's Children, Horn Book,* September-October, 1997, pp. 576-77.

Nix, Garth, comments in *www.ozemail.com.au/±garth-nix/garthnix.html.*

Peters, John, review of *Sabriel, School Library Journal,* September, 1996, p. 228.

Review of *Sabriel, Publishers Weekly,* October 21, 1996, p. 84.

Review of *Sabriel, Voice of Youth Advocates,* June, 1997.

Review of *Shade's Children, Kirkus Reviews,* August 15, 1997, pp. 1309-10.

Review of *Shade's Children, Publishers Weekly,* June 16, 1997, p. 60.

Steinberger, Kevin, review of *Shade's Children, Reading Time,* November, 1997, p. 35.

■ For More Information See

PERIODICALS

Australian Book Review, September, 1996, p. 63.

Bulletin of the Center for Children's Books, December, 1996, p. 146; November, 1997, p. 95.

*   *   *

NOBLE, Marty 1947-

■ Personal

Born March 19, 1947, in Berkeley, CA; daughter of Morton and Helen Noble; children: Eric Gottesman. *Education:* "Self-taught." *Religion:* Unitarian. *Hobbies and other interests:* Hiking, yoga, meditation, travel.

■ Addresses

Home and office—4710 Sam Peck Rd., No. 1077, Little Rock, AR 72212.

Marty Noble illustrates this retelling of *Rapunzel,* adapted from Lucy Crane's translation of the cherished Brothers Grimm fairy tale.

■ Career

Artist and illustrator. Teacher of marketing art and silk painting. Owner of a silk screen business, 1974-76; art teacher at a school in Ojai, CA, 1978; designer and manufacturer of dolls, 1979-81; Angel Light Creations (candle manufacturer), owner; work exhibited at galleries in California and represented in private collections.

■ Illustrator

Karen Pandell, *By Day and by Night* (poems), H. J. Kramer, 1991.

Rapunzel: Full-Color Sturdy Book, Dover (Mineola, NY), 1996.

Angels and Cherubs Iron-on Transfer Patterns, Dover, 1996.

Angels Stained Glass Coloring Book, Dover, 1996.

Beauty and the Beast Stained Glass Coloring Book, Dover, 1996.

Little Mermaid Stained Glass Coloring Book, Dover, 1996.

John Robbins, *In Search of Balance,* also published as *The Awakened Heart: Finding Harmony in a Chang-*

ing World, edited by Ann Mortifee, revised edition, H. J. Kramer, 1997.
Ballet Stained Glass Coloring Book, Dover, 1997.
Peter C. Asbjornsen, *East o' the Sun and West o' the Moon and Other Fairy Tales,* Dover, 1997.
Goldilocks and the Three Bears Sticker Storybook, Dover, 1997.
Little Red Riding Hood Sticker Storybook, Dover, 1997.
Medieval Designs Iron-on Transfer Patterns, Dover, 1997.
Mythical Creatures, Dover, 1997.
Ready-to-Use Angel Illustrations, Dover, 1997.
Twelve Days of Christmas Stickers, Dover, 1997.
Ugly Duckling Sticker Storybook, Dover, 1997.
Velveteen Rabbit Sturdy Book, Dover, 1997.

OTHER

Contributor of articles and cover illustrations to magazines, including *Ventura County, Surface Design Journal, American Artist, Monthly Aspectarian, Connecting Link,* and *Creative Crafts.* Creator of illustrations for greeting cards, calendars, posters, limited edition prints on plates and paper, puzzles, and other products.

■ **Work in Progress**

A series of Asian women and "Angel Doll" for Franklin Mint.

■ **For More Information See**

PERIODICALS

American Artist, February, 1988, p. 40.

✶   *   *

NUTT, Ken 1951- (Eric Beddows)

■ **Personal**

Born November 29, 1951, in Ontario, Canada. *Education:* Attended York University, Toronto, Ontario, 1970-72.

■ **Career**

Illustrator. *Exhibitions:* Nutt's work has been shown by the Gallery Stratford, 1990, and the Vancouver Art Gallery, 1988-1990, and is represented in the Osborn Collection in Toronto, Ontario, and the National Library of Canada in Ottawa.

■ **Awards, Honors**

Children's Book of the Year citation, International Order of the Daughters of the Empire (IODE), 1983, Amelia Frances Howard-Gibbon Award, Canadian Association of Children's Librarians (CACL), and Ruth Schwartz Children's Book Award, Ontario Arts Council, both 1984, all for *Zoom at Sea;* Amelia Frances Howard-Gibbon Award, 1986, for *Zoom Away;* runner-up, Book of the Year for Children, Canadian Library

KEN NUTT

Association, 1987, and Honor List for Illustration in Canada citation, International Board on Books for Young People, 1988, both for *The Emperor's Panda;* Honor Book, *Boston Globe-Horn Book* Illustration Award, 1988, for *Joyful Noise;* Children's Book of the Year citation, IODE, 1988, runner-up, Amelia Frances Howard-Gibbon Award, CACL, and Elizabeth Mrazik-Cleaver Picture Book Award, Canadian Children's Book Centre, both 1989, all for *Night Cars;* Notable Books citation, American Library Association, 1992, for *Who Shrank My Grandmother's House?;* Governor General's Award for Illustration, Canada Council, 1996, for *The Rooster's Gift.* Recipient of grants for book illustration from the Ontario Arts Council in 1981 and 1985.

■ **Illustrator**

Tim Wynne-Jones, *Zoom at Sea,* Douglas & McIntyre, 1983, HarperCollins, 1993.
Wynne-Jones, *Zoom Away,* Douglas & McIntyre, 1985, HarperCollins, 1993.
Paul Fleischman, *I Am Phoenix: Poems for Two Voices,* Harper & Row, 1985.

AS ERIC BEDDOWS

David Day, *The Emperor's Panda,* Dodd, Mead, 1986.
Dennis Hasley, *The Cave of Snores,* Harper & Row, 1987.
Paul Fleischman, *Joyful Noise: Poems for Two Voices,* Harper & Row, 1988.
Teddy Jam, *Night Cars,* Orchard Books, 1989.
Paul Fleischman, *Shadow Play,* Harper & Row, 1990.

Barbara Juster Esbensen, *Who Shrank My Grandmother's House? Poems of Discovery,* HarperCollins, 1992.

Tim Wynne-Jones, *Zoom Upstream,* HarperCollins, 1994.

Pam Conrad, *The Rooster's Gift,* HarperCollins, 1995.

■ Sidelights

Ken Nutt is an award-winning Canadian illustrator of children's books who also illustrates under the name of Eric Beddows. Nutt is known for his black and white pencil drawings which demonstrate "a strong handling of light and shadow, composition and form," according to Julie Corsaro in *Booklist.* Nutt has also opted for a full and brilliant palette in such later works as *The Rooster's Gift,* which earned him the Governor General's Award for Illustration from the Canada Council in 1996.

Nutt was born in a small town in the Canadian province of Ontario. He first came into contact with the great works of children's book illustrators through the encyclopedias his parents bought at the local grocery, one volume per week. In these volumes he discovered the work of Gustave Dore, Arthur Rackham, Rockwell Kent, and even William Blake. Known as the student who could draw when he was growing up, Nutt found his place in the social hierarchy of school by drawing campaign posters for student body elections and helping plan the decorations for school dances. After graduating from high school, Nutt attended Toronto's York University for two years, studying painting and drawing. After these two years, he felt he was accomplished enough to go out on his own in the field of art. When his friend, writer Tim Wynne-Jones, asked him to illustrate a children's book, Nutt realized that he had never even considered the possibility of book illustration. "Oddly,"

Nutt reported in *Seventh Book of Junior Authors and Illustrators,* "for all my love of the great illustrators of the past, I had never thought of drawing pictures for a book myself."

That situation changed drastically after the success of *Zoom at Sea,* the first book for which Nutt provided pictures. In this story, the playful cat, Zoom, short for Wynne-Jones's family cat Montezuma, won the hearts of critics and, most importantly, young readers. His adventures with his friend Maria, who transforms her home into an ocean so as to fulfill Zoom's sea-loving fantasy, were perfectly complemented by Nutt's pencil drawings, according to numerous reviewers. Award committees added to the favorable response, and Nutt's career as an illustrator looked promising. Nutt collaborated with Wynne-Jones on all three of the "Zoom" titles, which include *Zoom Away* and *Zoom Upstream.* With *Zoom Away,* the feline and Maria go searching for the elusive Uncle Roy at the North Pole—the transformed attic of Maria's house. Mary Lou Budd, writing in *School Library Journal,* noted that the story "captures and keeps the readers' attention from beginning to end with its action-packed narrative and accompanying pencil illustrations." Budd also noted that Nutt's method of shadowing his back-and-white pictures "gives each one a photographic look." With the final title in the series, *Zoom Upstream,* the fearless feline follows a mysterious trail through a bookshelf to join his friend Maria on another search for Uncle Roy, this time in ancient Egypt. Ilene Cooper wrote in *Booklist* that "Beddows' wonderful pencil illustrations detail the ensuing adventure," going on to call the pictures "wildly imaginative and full of minute particulars." A meticulous researcher, Nutt actually went to Egypt for the last title and spent a great deal of time making his way through tombs and the insides of pyramids. Floating

In his award-winning illustrations for Pam Conrad's *The Rooster's Gift,* Nutt (as Eric Beddows) employs full color panoramic paintings to complement the story of an egocentric rooster who thinks his crow causes the sun to rise.

down the Nile, he did his first rough sketches for *Zoom Upstream.*

Another fruitful collaboration for Nutt has been with the writer Paul Fleischman, with whom he has teamed up on two prize-winning books of poems for children, *I am Phoenix: Poems for Two Voices,* about birds, and the Newbery Medal-winning *Joyful Noise: Poems for Two Voices,* a book of verse which describes the characteristics of a variety of insects. Nutt has also illustrated Fleischman's story *Shadow Play,* about a visit to a county fair by a brother and sister who become entranced by a shadow puppet theater presentation of "Beauty and the Beast."

Other noteworthy titles illustrated under the name Beddows include *The Emperor's Panda,* about a poor young shepherd boy, Kung, who becomes the emperor of China with the help of the magical Master Panda, and the collection of poems, *Who Shrank My Grandmother's House? Poems of Discovery.* In 1996, Nutt illustrated Pam Conrad's *The Rooster's Gift,* an effort that earned him the prestigious Governor General's Literary Award for Illustration in Canada. In Conrad's story, the gift in question is the rising of the sun, for which Rooster takes credit. But one day, oversleeping, Rooster is surprised and dismayed to discover the sun has gotten up without his call. In *Publishers Weekly,* a reviewer noted that "Beddows eschews his characteristic black-and-white drawings in favor of dazzling full-color paintings that both support and extend the story," while Martha V. Parravano, writing in *Horn Book,* commented that "Beddows depicts, in curving lines and soft colors, the changing seasons in the pastoral landscapes rolling out below the chicken coop." Michael Cart concluded his *Booklist* review of *The Rooster's Gift* by praising "Beddows' gently humorous treatment of character, visual pacing, and impressive command of color and light."

Increasingly, Nutt has become Eric Beddows as the illustrator of children's books, the name he has used in book credits since 1986. But Nutt still loves to simply paint for himself. As he explained in *Seventh Book of Junior Authors and Illustrators,* he has many interests beyond book illustration. "I like math and physics and building mathematical models," he noted. Another favorite pastime for the illustrator is paleontology and the collection of fossils, with a specialty in invertebrates. However, "no dinosaurs," as he added that one day he would like to illustrate a fossil book with not one dinosaur featured.

■ Works Cited

Budd, Mary Lou, review of *Zoom Away, School Library Journal,* February, 1994, pp. 92-93.

Cart, Michael, review of *The Rooster's Gift, Booklist,* September 15, 1996, pp. 245-46.

Cooper, Ilene, review of *Zoom Upstream, Booklist,* June 1, 1994, p. 1846.

Corsaro, Julie, review of *Zoom Away, Booklist,* January 1, 1994, p. 834.

Nutt, Ken, "Eric Beddows," autobiographical essay in *Seventh Book of Junior Authors and Illustrators,* edited by Sally Holmes Holtze, H. W. Wilson, 1996, pp. 23-25.

Parravano, Martha V., review of *The Rooster's Gift, Horn Book,* November-December, 1996, pp. 721-22.

Review of *The Rooster's Gift, Publishers Weekly,* September 9, 1996, pp. 82-83.

■ For More Information See

PERIODICALS

Children's Book Watch, June, 1993, p. 1.

Emergency Librarian, May-June, 1993, pp. 68-71.

Quill and Quire, October, 1985.

School Library Journal, August, 1994, p. 148; December, 1994, p. 104.

—Sketch by J. Sydney Jones

O

OKE, Janette 1935-

■ Personal

Surname pronounced "oak"; born February 18, 1935, in Champion, Alberta, Canada; United States citizen born abroad; daughter of Fred G. (a farmer) and Amy M. (Ruggles) Steeves; married Edward L. Oke (a professor), May 13, 1957; children: Terry L., Lavon C., Lorne D., Laurel J. *Education:* Mountain View Bible College, diploma, 1957. *Religion:* Missionary Church.

JANETTE OKE

■ Career

Writer. Canadian Bank of Commerce, Champion, Alberta, teller and ledger keeper, 1952-54; National Bank & Trust Co., South Bend, IN, proofreader and book-keeper, 1957-58; Adlake, Elkhart, IN, mail clerk, 1958-59. Also worked as treasurer of Mountain View Bible College, office worker at Reimer Industries, and loan officer and teller at Royal Bank of Canada, all in Didsbury, Alberta. *Member:* Women's Missionary Society.

■ Awards, Honors

Gold Medallion Award, Evangelical Christian Publication Association, 1983, for *Love's Long Journey;* D.H.L., Bethel College, Mishawaka, IN, 1987; President's Award, Evangelical Christian Publishers Association, 1992, in recognition of contribution to Christian fiction.

■ Writings

Love Comes Softly, Bethany House (Minneapolis), 1979.
Love's Enduring Promise, Bethany House, 1980.
Once upon a Summer, Bethany House, 1981.
Hey, Teacher, Bethel Publishing (Elkhart, IN), 1981.
Love's Long Journey, Bethany House, 1982.
Spunky's Diary, Bethel Publishing, 1982.
When Calls the Heart, Bethany House, 1983.
Love's Abiding Joy, Bethany House, 1983.
Quiet Places, Warm Thoughts, Bethel Publishing, 1983.
New Kid in Town, Bethel Publishing, 1983.
Love's Undying Legacy, Bethany House, 1984.
The Prodigal Cat, Bethel Publishing, 1984.
When Comes the Spring, Bethany House, 1985.
The Impatient Turtle, Bethel Publishing, 1986.
When Breaks the Dawn, Bethany House, 1986.
When Hope Springs New, Bethany House, 1986.
The Winds of Autumn, Bethany House, 1987.
Janette Oke: My Favorite Verse, Accent Books (Denver), 1987.
Love's Unfolding Dream, Bethany House, 1987.
Winter Is Not Forever, Bethany House, 1988.

Love Takes Wing, Bethany House, 1988.
The Father Who Calls, Bethany House, 1988.
Spring's Gentle Promise, Bethany House, 1989.
The Father of Love, Bethany House, 1989.
Love Finds a Home, Bethany House, 1989.
Maury Had a Little Lamb, Bethel Publishing, 1989.
The Calling of Emily Evans, Bethany House, 1990.
Julia's Last Hope, Bethany House, 1990.
Father of My Heart, Bethany House, 1990.
Trouble in a Fur Coat, Bethel Publishing, 1990.
Roses for Mama, Bethany House, 1991.
A Woman Named Damaris, Bethany House, 1991.
This Little Pig, Bethel Publishing, 1991.
They Called Her Mrs. Doc, Bethany House, 1992.
The Measure of a Heart, Bethany House, 1992.
A Bride for Donnigan, Bethany House, 1993.
Heart of the Wilderness, Bethany House, 1993.
The Faithful Father, Bethany House, 1993.
Pordy's Prickly Problem, Bethel Publishing, 1993.
Too Long a Stranger, Bethany House, 1994.
Who's New at the Zoo, Bethel Publishing, 1994.
Janette Oke's Reflections on the Christmas Story, Bethany House, 1994.
The Bluebird and the Sparrow, Bethany House, 1994.
A Gown of Spanish Lace, Bethany House, 1995.
The Red Geranium, Bethany House, 1995.
The Canadian West Saga, Inspirational Press (New York City), 1995.
Drums of Change: The Story of Running Fawn, Bethany House, 1996.
(With T. Davis Bunn) *Return to Harmony,* Bethany House, 1996.
Nana's Gift, Bethany House, 1996.
(With Bunn) *Another Homecoming,* Bethany House, 1997.
The Tender Years, Bethany House, 1997.
The Matchmakers, Bethany House, 1997.
Spunky's First Christmas, Bethany House, 1997.

■ Adaptations

A video of *Spunky's First Christmas* has been made available by Tyndale Family Video, 1997; *When Calls the Heart* was produced as a musical with text by David Landrum and music by Orpha Galloway.

■ Sidelights

Janette Oke's popular romance and historical novels combine fast-moving plots with a strong Christian faith. The combination has proven successful. Oke's novel *A Gown of Spanish Lace,* an adventure set in the old West and featuring a God-fearing young woman named Ariana, sold over 250,000 copies, "more than the latest novels by Jackie Collins, John Irving or James Michener," according to Martha Duffy in *Time.*

Although she has written romances for young adults, children's titles, and novels of contemporary family problems, Oke is best known for her Christian fiction about turn-of-the-century life on the American prairie, a series of works for Bethany House that began with the publication of *Love Comes Softly* in 1979. Oke once

commented: "My interest in writing the type of material that I have comes from a personal interest in that era of our history, and a feeling that little had been written with a Christian slant on the time period." A reviewer for *A Closer Look* states that Oke's readers "have followed her strong characters as they discover God's grace in different historical settings." Oke has begun a new "Prairie Legacy" series which focuses on the children of the primary protagonists from the earlier works. *The Tender Years* is a coming-of-age story exploring fourteen-year-old Virginia's struggles with adolescent angst and peer pressure. "Young adult readers looking for a novel of faith and optimism will enjoy Virginia's story," maintained *Voice of Youth Advocates* contributor Judy Sasges. Another of Oke's historical novels, *Drums of Change,* features a Blackfoot girl named Running Fawn who struggles to grow into adulthood at a time when the lives of her people are changing dramatically. "Based on actual events, this book serves as a history lesson as well as providing a good read," noted *Voice of Youth Advocates* contributor Susan Dunn, who added: "The religious overtones are there, but not so much as to offend non-Christian readers. All in all, a fine story from an already popular author."

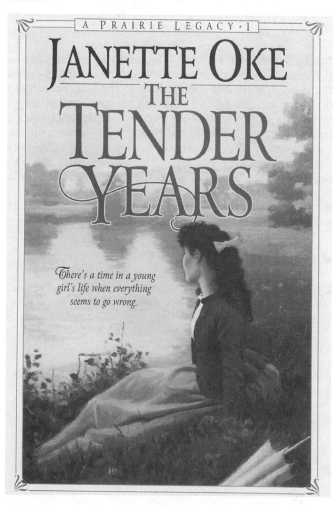

A PRAIRIE LEGACY ● 1

JANETTE OKE
THE TENDER YEARS

There's a time in a young girl's life when everything seems to go wrong.

As fourteen-year-old Virginia matures, she discovers that making the right decision isn't always easy.

Love is a constant theme in Oke's upbeat novels. She explained: "Society is searching for a deeper, more committed type of lasting love. Letters from readers have confirmed this. The love relationship is desired, whether it is between a boy and his grandfather, a husband and his wife, or a boy and girl." Oke's novel *Nana's Gift* tells of the self-sacrificing love shared by a married couple and their children and grandchildren. Duncan has promised his wife Lizzie a pearl necklace, but it is not until their thirty-fifth wedding anniversary that he can deliver on his promise. After Duncan passes away, Lizzie allows younger girls in the family to wear the pearls on their wedding days, "to remind them that marriage takes love," as Oke writes in the story. A *BookPage* critic commented: "Oke stirs the emotions of readers in this moving story of love across generations."

In 1996 Oke teamed with fellow Christian writer T. Davis Bunn to write *Return to Harmony,* the story of girlhood friends who drift apart as they grow older. Bethan marries a local minister while Jodie, after losing her mother to polio, devotes herself to studying biochemistry. The two girls not only follow different paths in life, they also develop differing views of God. Bethan retains her faith while Jodie, because of her mother's death, has doubts. "Jodie eventually discovers that science and religion can coexist," John Mort writes in *Booklist,* "and the friends are reconciled."

Marty Sanchez in *A Closer Look* remarks on the creative differences between the two coauthors: "Oke is noted for strong emotional connections to readers through the ordinary details of her characters' lives, while Bunn builds his stories with more attention to description and intricate plots." Oke and Bunn were aware of the differences in their approach to fiction. But, Oke tells Sanchez, "we were surprised and pleased with the way the story idea began coming together." Sanchez finds that in *Return to Harmony,* "Oke and Bunn remind us that the true harmony of friendship exists with God at the center."

■ Works Cited

Duffy, Martha, "The Almighty to the Rescue," *Time,* November 13, 1995, p. 105.
Dunn, Susan, review of *Drums of Change, Voice of Youth Advocates,* October, 1996, p. 212.
Mort, John, "Christian Fiction," *Booklist,* September 1, 1996, p. 65.
Review of *Nana's Gift, A Closer Look,* December, 1996.
Sanchez, Marty, review of *Return to Harmony, A Closer Look,* August, 1996.
Sasges, Judy, review of *The Tender Years, Voice of Youth Advocates,* February, 1998, pp. 388-89.

■ For More Information See

BOOKS

Logan, Laurel Oke, *Janette Oke: A Heart for the Prairie,* Bethany House, 1993.

PERIODICALS

Booklist, August, 1995, p. 1911; March 15, 1996, p. 1220.
Library Journal, September 1, 1996, p. 164.
School Library Journal, August, 1995, p. 157.
Voice of Youth Advocates, April, 1983, p. 40; October, 1988, p. 183; October, 1995, p. 222.

* * *

O'KELLEY, Mattie Lou 1908-1997

OBITUARY NOTICE—See index for *SATA* sketch: Born March 30, 1908, in Banks County, GA; died July 26, 1997, in Decatur, GA. Artist and author. Although she did not begin painting until the age of sixty, O'Kelley quickly established a reputation as a folk artist whose vivid style captured nostalgic scenes of rural life in the South. She began painting to help ease the pain of an illness. O'Kelley grew up on her family's farm and attended school through the ninth grade. Thereafter, she worked in a series of jobs, including cook, seamstress, and waitress. Upon her retirement in 1968, O'Kelley took up painting and so impressed art dealer Robert Bishop with her work that he helped introduce her pictures to museum professionals and art buyers. Her paintings included scenes of the Georgian countryside and featured gardens, animals, barns, and other folksy subjects. O'Kelley also moved briefly to New York City, turning her talents to urban settings. However, she longed to return to Georgia and finally settled in Decatur. She wrote several books, including *Circus* and *From the Hills of Georgia: An Autobiography in Paintings.* She also illustrated Ruth Yaffe Radin's *A Winter Place.* Her work was featured in calendars and on a cover of *Life* Magazine.

OBITUARIES AND OTHER SOURCES:

PERIODICALS

New York Times, July 31, 1997, p. B6.

* * *

O'LEARY, Patsy B(aker) 1937-

■ Personal

Born September 23, 1937, in North Carolina; daughter of Alton P. (a photographer) and Ethel (in business; maiden name, Leary) Baker; married Denis L. O'Leary (an entrepreneur), 1962 (divorced, 1979); children: Linda O'Leary-Allen. *Education:* East Carolina College (now University), B.S., 1959; California State University, Northridge, M.A., 1979. *Politics:* Independent. *Religion:* Methodist. *Hobbies and other interests:* Reading, antiques, auctions, art, "learning new things."

■ Addresses

Home—310 Baytree Dr., Greenville, NC 27858. *Agent*—Barrie Van Dyck, Barrie Van Dyck Agency, Inc., 217 Spruce St., Philadelphia, PA 19106.

PATSY B. O'LEARY

■ Career

Worked for the film industry in creative development, casting, and production, and as a secretary, 1959-79; freelance writer, 1979—. Pitt Community College, instructor in creative writing, 1980—; East Carolina University, lecturer in English, 1980-81, and Communications, 1990-95; conducted writing seminars. *Get Smart* (television series), worked as assistant to the producer. *Member:* National Writers Union, Poets and Writers, North Carolina Writers Network, Georgia Writers, Inc., Southeastern Writers Association.

■ Awards, Honors

First place award, Council of Authors and Journalists, 1981, for journalism for the article "Missy" and for novel-in-progress for "The Homeplace" (published as *With Wings as Eagles*), 1982, for journalism for the article "Keeper of the Flame" and for novel-in-progress for "Angel Wings," and 1983, for the inspirational poem "Phoenix"; first place award, Tar Heel Writer's Roundtable, 1984, for the short story "A Voice Heard in Ramah." An award was established in O'Leary's honor by her Creative Writing students at Pitt Community College in 1989.

■ Writings

With Wings as Eagles (novel), Houghton (Boston, MA), 1997.

■ Work in Progress

A novel.

■ Sidelights

Patsy B. O'Leary told *Something about the Author* (*SATA*): "*With Wings as Eagles* started out as a short story written for a class in California, where I was working on my master's degree. At a 1980 writer's conference in Georgia, author Shirley Rousseau Murphy told me, 'This needs to be a book!' I worked on it sporadically, then finally took time off from work and lived on savings until it was finished."

Set in rural North Carolina during the Great Depression, *With Wings as Eagles* examines racism, injustice, and economic hardship through the eyes of its twelve-year-old protagonist, Bubba Harkins. Bubba "learns what love and friendship are all about in this probing, deliberately paced debut," noted a *Kirkus Reviews* critic, who added that O'Leary's "explorations of race, friendship, and Bubba's inner turmoil show unusual insight." *School Library Journal* contributor Sylvia V. Meisner praised O'Leary's "finely drawn characters," calling the novel "a well-constructed, memorable story."

"For me," O'Leary continued to *SATA*, "the characters, though fictional, are very real, as is the setting. North Carolina has always had a special hold on my heart. When I was small, we would travel to visit my mother's family at Lowland, North Carolina. Such things as electricity and running water were late coming to that area, so I got a taste of what an earlier time had been like. In the book, I wanted to capture that way of life to show what a pivotal change World War II brought.

"Of course, there were also family stories. Adults loved to swap reminiscences, and we children listened as if to background music while we played, never realizing we were absorbing our own history, or that someday we would tell those tales to our own children ... or use them as bases for scenes in a book!

"I have always enjoyed writing, but I was late coming to it professionally. As a child, I was fortunate in having good teachers and lots of encouragement from family and friends. Sometimes, in fact, I say I was 'born and praised' in North Carolina! My years of studying drama and working in the film industry with some really excellent writers also gave me a good foundation, as did my writing teachers when I returned to California State University, Northridge, for my master's degree.

"In 1979 I came home to North Carolina and have been a freelance writer and teacher ever since. I am still learning, and what I learn, I try to pass on. For new writers, I would say: study, read, treasure your mentors (as I do Shirley), but most of all, write. The best way to learn to write is still ... to write. A lot."

■ Works Cited

Meisner, Sylvia V., review of *With Wings as Eagles,* *School Library Journal,* December, 1997.
Review of *With Wings as Eagles, Kirkus Reviews,* September 1, 1997.

P

PALMER, Kate Salley 1946-

■ Personal

Born in Orangeburg, SC. *Education:* University of South Carolina, B.A., Elementary Education, 1968.

■ Career

Greenville News, Greenville, SC, editorial page cartoonist, 1975-84; Field Newspaper Syndicate (later, News

KATE SALLEY PALMER, self-portrait.

America Syndicate), nationally syndicated cartoonist, 1981-86. Author and illustrator of children's books, 1988—. Speaker at numerous schools, libraries, writer's conferences, reading conferences, teacher's conferences, art museums, and conventions. *Exhibitions:* Anderson Art Center, 1995. *Member:* Association of American Editorial Cartoonists.

■ Awards, Honors

Freedoms Foundation Principal Award, 1981, for editorial cartooning.

■ Illustrator

David G. Cannon, *Hey, Bubba: A Metaphysical Guide to the Good 'Ol Boy,* Peachtree Publishers, 1990.
(And author) *A Gracious Plenty,* Simon & Schuster, 1991.
Diane Johnston Hamm, *How Many Feet in the Bed?,* Simon & Schuster, 1991.
Laurence Pringle, *Octopus Hug,* Boyds Mills Press (Honesdale, PA), 1993.
Mesa Somer, *Night of the Five Aunties,* A. Whitman (Morton Grove, IL), 1996.
Dr. Louis Vine, *Training Problem Dogs: Advice From a Leading Veterinarian on How to Remedy Canine Behavior Problems,* TFH Publications (Neptune, NJ), 1997.
Judith Ross Enderle and Stephanie Gordon Tessler, *Upstairs,* Boyds Mills Press, in press.

"READING RECOVERY" SERIES; ALL PUBLISHED BY KAEDEN CORPORATION

Fishing, 1992.
Gifts For Dad, 1992.
It's Football Time, 1993.
Let's Play Basketball, 1993.
Family Soccer, 1995.
Baseball Fun, 1995.
The Big Fish, 1996.

Illustrations completed for three upcoming "Reading Recovery" books for Kaeden Corporation: *The Puck, My Brother Wants to Be Like Me,* and *Jobs.*

■ Work in Progress

A novel about a girl athlete in the South and a novel about a family of women who write a book together.

■ Sidelights

Kate Salley Palmer told *Something about the Author* (*SATA*): "As a writer and illustrator, I often find myself talking to groups of teachers and/or students about being a writer/illustrator—and fielding questions on how to 'handle' the creative student in the classroom.

"When I was a political cartoonist, my audiences were more angry, more challenging—the questions more pungent. Sometimes, I miss the hostility of those former groups. Writing for children is a more tranquil undertaking (not as many death threats); but, at the same time, there's not the same adrenalin rush—I feel like a high-wire performer who has taken a desk job.

"Not to say that writing isn't rewarding. It's just that the audiences—and the colleagues—take some getting used to; teachers' groups and writers' conferences are a far cry from cartoonists' conventions.

"For instance, teachers and other writers are often surprised when I theorize that being a 'creative' child is not necessarily considered to be a *good* thing, until you grow up and write a book.

"While that creative child is in someone's *classroom,* he's as welcome as a lopsided load in the washing machine: he makes a nerve-eating racket, demands constant attention, and generally exists to create chaos. Almost all cartoonists understand this. Most writers don't.

"Writers, for the most part, are high achievers who made good grades in school, did their work neatly and

A babysitting dad invents affectionate horseplay to distract his squabbling children in this 1993 picture book.

handed it in on time. They were identified early and encouraged, or guided throughout their school years.

"Meanwhile, future cartoonists were defacing their books, their desks, the walls, and anything else they could get their hands on. They drew odd pictures of the teachers and other students. They hardly ever knew what the assignment was: when they did, they got it wrong. Their grades were awful; they refused to 'live up to their potential'; they were regarded as lazy, disruptive and rebellious. They are my people.

"I am proud to represent them in a fine publication such as this one."

Octopus Hug, written by Laurence Pringle and illustrated by Palmer, is an imaginative romp between a father and two small children when Mom goes out for the evening. Dad begins with an octopus hug and proceeds with a series of roughhouse-type games that delight the children. The book presents an African-American father in a positive and engaging light. Louise L. Sherman noted in *School Library Journal* that Palmer's spritely illustrations "add to the lively feeling of the text."

In addition to her many illustrations for books written by others, Palmer has both written and illustrated *A Gracious Plenty.* Exploring the relationship of a maiden great-aunt to her family, Palmer creates a warm portrait of someone who is loved, revered, and lives a full life even though she does not have a husband or children. Palmer's full-color illustrations enhance the gentle story. A *Kirkus Reviews* critic remarked that the illustrations, done in soft pencil, "pungently evoke the scene and amiable character" of this heartwarming book.

■ Works Cited

Review of *A Gracious Plenty, Kirkus Reviews,* July 1, 1991, p. 866.
Review of *Octopus Hug, Publishers Weekly,* October 4, 1993, p. 79.
Sherman, Louise L., review of *Octopus Hug, School Library Journal,* January, 1994, p. 97.

■ For More Information See

PERIODICALS

Kirkus Reviews, September 1, 1993, p. 1150.
Publishers Weekly, October 4, 1997, p. 79.
School Library Journal, September, 1991, pp. 238-39.*

* * *

PATERSON, A(ndrew) B(arton) 1864-1941 (The Banjo)

■ Personal

Born February 17, 1864, in Narrambla, New South Wales, Australia; died in 1941; married Alice Walker, 1903; children: one son, one daughter. *Education:*

Attended University of Sydney, entered in the Roll of Solicitors.

■ Career

Writer. War correspondent for the *Sydney Morning Herald* and *Melbourne Argus* during Boer War, 1899-1901; *Sydney Morning Herald,* China correspondent, 1901, English correspondent, 1902; *Evening News,* Sydney, editor, 1903-06; *Town and Country Journal,* Sydney, editor, 1906-08; *Sydney Sportsman,* editor, 1921-30; *Smith's Weekly,* freelance journalist, c. 1930-33. *Wartime service:* Australian Hospital, Boulogne, Ambulance Driver, 1914-15; served in the British Red Cross Centre and Remount Service in Egypt and Palestine, 1916-18; became Major.

■ Awards, Honors

Named Commander, Order of the British Empire, 1939; Picture Book of the Year Award, Children's Book Council of Australia, 1971, for *Waltzing Matilda,* and 1975, for *The Man from Ironbark.*

■ Writings

VERSE

The Man from Snowy River and Other Verses, Angus & Robertson (Sydney, Australia), 1895.
Rio Grande's Last Race and Other Verses, Angus & Robertson, 1902.
Saltbush Bill, J. P. and Other Verses, Angus & Robertson, 1917.
Rio Grande and Other Verses, Angus & Robertson, 1921.

FOR CHILDREN

The Animals Noah Forgot, Endeavour Press (Sydney), 1933.
Waltzing Matilda, illustrated by Desmond Digby, Collins (Sydney), 1970, Holt (New York), 1972.
Mulga Bill's Bicycle, illustrated by Kilmeny and Deborah Niland, Collins, 1973.
Man from Ironbark, illustrated by Quentin Hole, Collins, 1974.
A Bush Christening, illustrated by Quentin Hole, Collins, 1976.

FICTION

An Outback Marriage, Angus & Robertson, 1906.
Three Elephant Power and Other Stories (short stories), Angus & Robertson, 1917.
The Shearer's Colt, Angus & Robertson, 1936.

OTHER

(Editor) *The Old Bush Songs,* E. W. Cole (Melbourne), 1905.
The Collected Verse of A. B. Paterson, Angus & Robertson, 1921.
Happy Dispatches (semi-autobiographical), Angus & Robertson, 1934.

The World of "Banjo" Paterson: His Stories, Travels, War Reports, and Advice to Racegoers, edited by Clement Semmler, Angus & Robertson, 1967.

Singer of the Bush, A. B. (Banjo) Paterson: Complete Works, 1885-1900, (with introduction by grand-daughters Rosamund Campbell and Phillipa Harvie), Lansdowne Press (Sydney), 1983.

Song of the Pen, A. B. (Banjo) Paterson: Complete Works, 1901-1941, (with introduction by Rosamund Campbell and Phillipa Harvie), Lansdowne Press, 1983.

Also author of many radio plays in *The Land of Adventure* series, c. 1930s.

■ Adaptations

"The Man from Snowy River" was adapted as a motion picture of the same name by Twentieth Century-Fox, 1982.

■ Sidelights

A popular poet at the turn of the century, A. B. Paterson is known for his romantic and humorous portrayal of the Australian bush, or inland wilderness. Unlike his contemporary Henry Lawson, with whom he is often compared, Paterson did not emphasize the harsh conditions of bush life, but rather wrote of its beauty and the fortitude of those who lived there. Paterson is also the reputed author of the lyrics for "Waltzing Matilda," a popular song that has become Australia's unofficial national anthem. Although his authorship of these lyrics has been questioned, Paterson is nonetheless celebrated for his important role in the development of a sense of national identity among Australians.

Paterson grew up on a sheep farm in the bush country of New South Wales, Australia. He was educated in Sydney, but spent much of his free time on his father's farm, where he developed a deep love of the bush. While in Sydney, he lived with his grandmother, who was an established poet of the time. Paterson studied law and began practicing in Sydney, but all the while he was writing poetry. His first poems appeared under the pseudonym "The Banjo," taken from the name of a racing horse. During 1892, Paterson's view on life in the bush was challenged by several other poets, most notably Lawson, who contended that Paterson's writings were sentimental and overly romantic and believed that they did not tell the true story of the bush. The debate raged on for a while until Paterson decided to end it with a conciliatory poem.

Upon the release of Paterson's first collection of verse, *The Man from Snowy River and Other Verses,* in 1895, his popularity soared. "The first edition ... sold out in the week of publication; it went through four editions in six months and it still outsells any other volume of Australian poetry ever published," claims the *Oxford Companion to Australian Literature.* The title poem became Australia's national narrative poem. Paterson wrote several other books of verse that became extremely popular.

Paterson, however, had a yen for adventure that overtook his need for stability. During the Boer War, he left his comfortable legal practice and became a correspondent for two newspapers, the *Sydney Morning Herald* and *Melbourne Argus.* After the war, he continued his work as a journalist and later became a magazine editor. Indulging his love for the bush, he purchased land for grazing in Coodravale, on the upper Murrumbidgee River in 1908. He lived the life of a gentleman farmer

While A. B. Paterson's authorship of the famous folksong "Waltzing Matilda" has been questioned, this picture-book adaptation of his verse won the prestigious Book of the Year Award from the Children's Book Council of Australia in 1971. (From *Waltzing Matilda,* illustrated by Desmond Digby.)

for several years until the advent of World War I. As he had done with the Boer War, Paterson covered the great conflict as a correspondent. He was unable to get close to the front lines, however, so he enlisted in the Remount Service, a branch of the military that supplied horses to Australian forces in the Middle East.

After the war, Paterson returned to Sydney and lived there for the rest of his life. He continued writing verse and also completed novels and short stories. There is some controversy over Paterson's claim of authorship of "Waltzing Matilda." Several critics claim that Paterson stole the song from an English march and the lyrics from a folksong. Some people were found to testify that they had heard the song before Paterson claimed he had written it in 1895. To further complicate the matter, Paterson did not publish the lyrics until 1917. Frederick T. Macartney defended Paterson's authorship in *Meanjin,* contending that "discussion of the origin of 'Waltzing Matilda' has become the Australian equivalent, in its tinpot way, of the Shakespeare-Bacon controversy, now fortunately exhausted by its own vacuity. Our little local puddle could be left to evaporate in the same way but for being stirred up."

Vance Palmer, writing in the *Legend of the Nineties,* commented: "What distinguished Paterson's verse ... was a touch of the folk element. It is hard to analyse, this sense of a voice rising out of the anonymous mass, but it lifts his work above ... other more skilful balladists, and preserves its original freshness."

■ Works Cited

Macartney, Frederick T., *Meanjin,* December, 1964, pp. 386-413; June, 1967, pp. 211-15, 359-63.
Oxford Companion to Australian Literature, Oxford University Press (Melbourne, Australia), 1985, pp. 548-50.
Palmer, Vance, *The Legend of the Nineties,* Melbourne University Press, 1954, pp. 109-30.

■ For More Information See

BOOKS

Authors of Books for Young People, Third edition, Scarecrow Press (Metuchen, NJ), 1990.
Coombes, Archie James, *Some Australian Poets,* Books for Libraries Press, 1970, pp. 77-86.
Great Writers of the English Language, St. Martin's (New York), 1979, pp. 756-58.
Green, H.M., *A History of Australian Literature, Pure and Applied: 1789-1923,* Vol. I, Angus & Robertson, 1961.
Oxford Companion to Twentieth Century Poetry, p. 412.
Semmler, Clement, editor, introduction to *The World of "Banjo" Paterson: His Stories, Travels, War Reports, and Advice to Racegoers* by A. B. Paterson, Angus & Robertson, 1967, p. v-xii.
Twentieth-Century Literary Criticism, Volume 32, Gale (Detroit, MI), 1989, pp. 368-83.

PERIODICALS

Australian Literary Studies 5, October, 1971, 190-95.
Australian Quarterly, June, 1967, pp. 71-78.
Booklist, April 1, 1992, p. 1454.
Horn Book Magazine, November-December, 1991, pp. 768-69.*

*   *   *

PECK, Richard (Wayne) 1934-

■ Personal

Born April 5, 1934, in Decatur, IL; son of Wayne Morris (a merchant) and Virginia (a dietician; maiden name, Gray) Peck. *Education:* Attended University of Exeter, 1955-56; DePauw University, B.A., 1956; Southern Illinois University, M.A., 1959; further graduate study at Washington University, 1960-61. *Politics:* Republican. *Religion:* Methodist.

■ Addresses

Home—155 East 72nd St., New York, NY 10021. *Office*—c/o Dial/Penguin, 375 Hudson St., New York, NY 10014. *Agent*—Sheldon Fogelman, 10 East 40th St., New York, NY 10016.

■ Career

Southern Illinois University at Carbondale, instructor in English, 1958-60; Glenbrook North High School, Northbrook, IL, teacher of English, 1961-63; Scott, Foresman

RICHARD PECK

Co., Chicago, IL, textbook editor, 1963-65; Hunter College of the City University of New York and Hunter College High School, New York City, instructor in English and education, 1965-71; writer, 1971—. Assistant director of the Council for Basic Education, Washington, DC, 1969-70; English-Speaking Union fellow, Jesus College, Oxford University, 1973; lecturer. *Military Service:* U.S. Army, 1956-58; served in Stuttgart, Germany. *Member:* Authors Guild, Authors League of America, Delta Chi.

■ **Awards, Honors**

Child Study Association of America's Children's Book of the Year citations, 1970, for *Sounds and Silences,* 1971, for *Mindscapes,* and 1986, for *Blossom Culp and the Sleep of Death;* Writing Award, National Council for the Advancement of Education, 1971; Edgar Allan Poe Award runner-up, Mystery Writers of America, 1974, for *Dreamland Lake;* Best Books, American Library Association (ALA), 1974, for *Representing Super Doll,* 1976, for *Are You in the House Alone?,* and 1977, for *Ghosts I Have Been;* Notable Book citations, ALA, 1975, for *The Ghost Belonged to Me,* and 1985, for *Remembering the Good Times;* Friends of American Writers Award (older category), 1976, for *The Ghost Belonged to Me;* Edgar Allan Poe Award for best juvenile mystery novel, 1976, and Author's Award, New Jersey Institute of Technology, 1978, both for *Are You in the House Alone?;* School Library Journal's Best Books of the Year citations, 1976, for *Are You in the House Alone?,* 1977, for *Ghosts I Have Been,* and 1985, for *Remembering the Good Times;* New York Times Outstanding Book of the Year citation, 1977, for *Ghosts I Have Been;* Illinois Writer of the Year, Illinois Association of Teachers of English, 1977; School Library Journal's Best of the Best 1966-1978, for *Dreamland Lake* and *Father Figure;* Books for the Teen Age, New York Public Library, 1980, for *Pictures That Storm inside My Head,* 1981, for *Ghosts I Have Been,* and 1982, for *Are You in the House Alone?* and *Close Enough to Touch;* Best Books for Young Adults, ALA, 1981, for *Close Enough to Touch,* 1985, for *Remembering the Good Times,* 1987, for *Princess Ashley,* and 1995, for *The Last Safe Place on Earth;* School Library Journal's Best Books for Young Adults citations, 1981, for *Close Enough to Touch,* 1983, for *This Family of Women,* and 1985, for *Remembering the Good Times;* ALA's Young Adult Services Division's Best of the Best Books 1970-1983, for *Are You in the House Alone?* and *Ghosts I Have Been;* Margaret Edwards Young Adult Author Achievement Award, ALA, and the National Council of Teachers of English/ALAN Award for outstanding contributions to young adult literature, both 1990; University of Southern Mississippi Medallion, 1991; Empire Award, New York Library Association, 1997.

■ **Writings**

NOVELS; FOR YOUNG ADULTS

Don't Look and It Won't Hurt, Holt, 1972.
Dreamland Lake, Holt, 1973, Dell, 1990.
Through a Brief Darkness, Viking, 1973.

Representing Super Doll, Viking, 1974.
The Ghost Belonged to Me, Viking, 1975.
Are You in the House Alone? (with teacher's guide), Viking, 1976.
Ghosts I Have Been (sequel to *The Ghost Belonged to Me*), Viking, 1977.
Father Figure, Viking, 1978.
Secrets of the Shopping Mall, Delacorte, 1979.
Close Enough to Touch, Delacorte, 1981.
The Dreadful Future of Blossom Culp (sequel to *Ghosts I Have Been*), Delacorte, 1983.
Remembering the Good Times, Delacorte, 1985.
Blossom Culp and the Sleep of Death, Delacorte, 1986.
Princess Ashley, Delacorte, 1987.
Those Summer Girls I Never Met, Delacorte, 1988.
Voices after Midnight, Delacorte, 1989.
Unfinished Portrait of Jessica, Delacorte, 1991.
Bel-Air Bambi and the Mall Rats, Delacorte, 1993.
Love and Death at the Mall, Delacorte, 1994.
The Last Safe Place on Earth, Delacorte, 1995.
Lost in Cyberspace, Dial, 1995.
The Great Interactive Dream Machine, Dell, 1996.
Strays Like Us, Dial, 1998.

Audio cassette versions of Peck's young adult books include *The Ghost Belonged to Me,* Live Oak Media, 1976, *Don't Look and It Won't Hurt* (filmstrip with cassette), Random House, and *Remembering the Good Times* (cassette), Listening Library, 1987.

FOR CHILDREN

Monster Night at Grandma's House, illustrated by Don Freeman, Viking, 1977.

ADULT NOVELS

Amanda/Miranda (Literary Guild selection; Reader's Digest Condensed Book Club selection), Viking, 1980.
New York Time, Delacorte, 1981.
This Family of Women, Delacorte, 1983.
London Holiday, Viking, 1998.

EDITOR

(With Ned E. Hoopes) *Edge of Awareness: Twenty-five Contemporary Essays,* Dell, 1966.
Sounds and Silences: Poetry for Now, Delacorte, 1970.
Mindscapes: Poems for the Real World, Delacorte, 1971.
Leap into Reality: Essays for Now, Dell, 1972.
Urban Studies: A Research Paper Casebook, Random House, 1973.
Transitions: A Literary Paper Casebook, Random House, 1974.
Pictures That Storm inside My Head (poetry anthology), Avon, 1976.

OTHER

(With Norman Strasma) *Old Town, A Complete Guide: Strolling, Shopping, Supping, Sipping,* 2nd edition, [Chicago], 1965.
(With Mortimer Smith and George Weber) *A Consumer's Guide to Educational Innovations,* Council for Basic Education, 1972.

(With Stephen N. Judy) *The Creative Word 2,* Random House, 1974.

(Contributor) Kenneth L. Donelson and Alleen Pace Nilsen, *Literature for Today's Young Adults,* Scott, Foresman, 1980.

(Contributor) Donald R. Gallo, editor, *Sixteen: Short Stories by Outstanding Young Adult Writers,* Delacorte, 1984.

(Contributor) Donald R. Gallo, editor, *Visions: Nineteen Short Stories by Outstanding Writers for Young Adults,* Delacorte, 1987.

Write a Tale of Terror, Book Lures, 1987.

(Contributor) Donald R. Gallo, editor, *Connections: Short Stories by Outstanding Writers for Young Adults,* Delacorte, 1989.

Anonymously Yours (autobiography), Silver Burdett, 1991.

Author of column on the architecture of historic neighborhoods for the *New York Times.* Contributor of poetry to several anthologies. Contributor of poems to *Saturday Review* and *Chicago Tribune Magazine.* Contributor of articles to periodicals, including *American Libraries, PTA Magazine* and *Parent's Magazine.*

■ Adaptations

Television movies based on his books include *Are You in the House Alone?,* CBS, 1977, *Child of Glass* (based on *The Ghost Belonged to Me*), Walt Disney Productions, 1979, and *Father Figure,* Time-Life Productions, 1980. Cineville Production Company bought the film rights for *Don't Look and It Won't Hurt* in 1991 and released an adaptation as *Gas Food Lodging,* 1992.

■ Sidelights

Richard Peck is an award-winning author of young adult novels that explore contemporary issues such as peer pressure, single parenting, rape, censorship, suicide, and the death of a loved one. In his two dozen YA titles, Peck has carved out a position for himself as a realistic writer who talks to teen readers on their own terms, imbuing them with a sense of self-confidence and empowerment. Titles such as *Don't Look and It Won't Hurt, Are You in the House Alone?, Father Figure* and *The Last Safe Place on Earth* have won awards, accolades from educators, and a large YA readership.

But Peck also has a lighter side, and has written a series of historical novels for junior high readers, his "Blossom Culp" books, that delve into the supernatural. Peck, dubbed "the renaissance man of contemporary young adult literature" by Patrick Jones in *Children's Books and Their Creators,* additionally has written humor, mystery, and horror YA novels as well as adult novels, and his books are often used in schools. As popular a speaker as he is a writer, Peck—a one-time teacher himself—travels thousands of miles annually to schools across the nation.

Born on April 5, 1934, in Decatur, Illinois, Peck grew up in what he described in a *Publishers Weekly* interview

with Jean Mercier as "in *middle* Middle America." The tranquil life of Peck's childhood has informed much of his fiction: the local park, the kids he knew in grammar and high school, and the old-timers who stopped by his father's filling stations telling stories with a refinement brought on by years of experience. From such characters, Peck experienced his first glimmer of literary style; from his father he acquired an early love of cars and also of Mark Twain.

"From my father I learned nostalgia as an art form," Peck explained in an essay for *Something about the Author Autobiography Series* (*SAAS*). "I fell on Mark Twain's stories of middle-American boyhood because they merged with my dad's memories." Peck's father was a country boy who had come to urban America, like so many others of his generation. But the Peck household still had the atmosphere of another time, with fresh game brought home from Dad's hunting expeditions and fresh produce from the family garden. The extended Peck family of aunts, uncles and grandparents all later found a home and voice in Peck's fiction. An only child

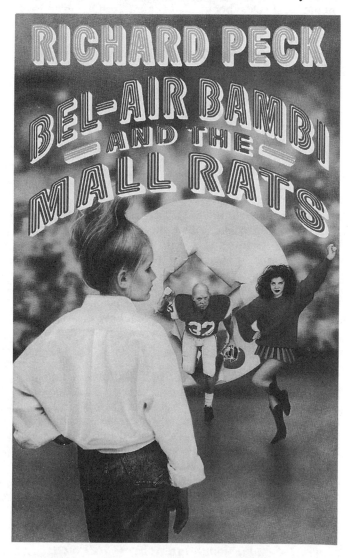

After Bambi Babcock moves to Hickory Fork from Los Angeles, she refuses to be intimidated by the town gang.

for part of his youth, Peck was greatly influenced by this household full of adults who took the time to read to him and tell him stories of the old days. Growing up during the Second World War, Peck was also influenced by the propaganda of war, of the posters warning against loose lips and of kamikaze and blitzkrieg attacks. A memorable teacher in high school managed to impress on him the importance of subject matter for his writing, and after winning a scholarship, he was off to DePauw University in Greencastle, Indiana.

"I entered college with the full complement of late-adolescent complexes," Peck wrote in *SAAS*. "For one thing, I had this secret itch to be a writer, though I wouldn't have admitted any such long shot. Instead, I planned to be a teacher, which seemed to be my nearest approach to the written word." Peck studied his junior year in England, at Exeter University, and it was an experience that helped to open the world for him. "Every late adolescent should be cut out of the pack to find out who he is," Peck noted in *SAAS*. This cutting off from the herd, opting out of peer pressure, is a major theme in Peck's books. Returning to DePauw, Peck graduated the next year and was promptly inducted into the army. "As it turned out," Peck commented in *SAAS*, "I learned at least as much from the two years of army as from two years in college, and it even took me back to Europe." In the military, Peck's educational background helped, and he found himself writing company reports as well as ghost-writing sermons for chaplains of all denominations.

After his two years in the army, Peck went on to graduate school at Southern Illinois University. He cut his teaching teeth as an assistant in college classes, and upon earning his degree he spent two years instructing at the college level. But Peck's original plan was to teach high school English, which he did, starting with a position at Glenbrook North High School in Northbrook, Illinois, a suburb of Chicago. This suburban setting found its way into several of Peck's later novels, but for the time, the idea of writing for a living still seemed impossible to the young English teacher. For a decade Peck vacillated between teaching and textbook editing, until one day in 1971 when he decided to give up both and go into writing.

"I wasn't being allowed to teach as I'd been taught," Peck recalled in *SAAS*. "I turned in my gradebook and my pension plan one May day in 1971 and went home to write a novel." His years of teaching came in handy for such a task, for he had identified an audience and had also learned that kids read not to be educated but "to be reassured, to be given hope," as Peck noted in *SAAS*. His first novel was based on incidents experienced by close friends of his who took in unwed mothers. Peck decided to tell the story of one such young woman, not from the point of view of the unwed mother, but from that of a younger sister. The result was *Don't Look and It Won't Hurt*. When Carol's older sister Ellen gets pregnant, Carol wants to reassure her that somebody in the family still loves her. Letty Cottin Pogrebin, writing in *New York Times Book Review*,

Peck's novel focuses on Todd, a teenager whose previously tranquil community is shaken when a group of parents try to censor books held by the school library.

described the book as a "textured story" and that through "the insightful eyes of the middle child we come to understand the complex forces that lead to the eldest girl's pregnancy." *Children's Book Review Service* noted that "This successful first novel ... will touch girls with its honesty and sensitivity."

For his second title, Peck went back in time and place to the dilapidated amusement park near his childhood home. *Dreamland Lake* tells the story of Flip and Brian during their thirteenth year as they experience the attempts of an inept teacher to involve them in poetry and discover a hero in the local swimming teacher. But when they find the corpse of a tramp in the nearby woods, mystery seems to be abroad. Their attempts to make this common death into a mystery, however, eventually lead to real tragedy in a book that *Kirkus Reviews* described as "invariably reminiscent of *A Separate Peace*." Alice H. Yucht, writing in *School Library Journal*, was enthusiastic about the novel: "Beautifully told, the story has just enough foreshadowing to heighten the sense of impending doom. Everything rings true—the dialogue, the minor characters, as well as Flip and Brian." Writing in *Bulletin of the Center for Children's Books,* Zena Sutherland dubbed *Dreamland Lake* a "subtle and provocative novel."

Peck's third novel is a suspense story set partly in England, involving the kidnapping of the sixteen-year-old daughter of a big time crook by a rival gang. Sutherland noted in *Bulletin of the Center for Children's Books* that *Through a Brief Darkness* is a "suspense story that has good pace and construction," while A. R. Williams in *Junior Bookshelf* concluded: "It is such a good novel that one feels like reading it all over again once one has reached the end." With *Representing Super Doll,* Peck introduced a wholesome farm girl who is suddenly thrown together with the local beauties at her new high school and eventually accompanies one of them to New York City for the Miss Super Doll contest. But when one of the contestants falls ill, the farm girl is asked to take her place. "Peck's writing is admirable," Sutherland commented in a review of the novel for *Bulletin of the Center for Children's Books.* "It has vitality and flow, vivid characterizations and dialogue."

With his fifth novel, Peck introduced one of his most engaging and popular characters, Blossom Culp. And with her, Peck also traveled back in time to the early twentieth century. In *The Ghost Belonged to Me,* and its sequels, *Ghosts I Have Been, The Dreadful Future of Blossom Culp,* and *Blossom Culp and the Sleep of Death,* Peck created a heroine for younger readers. With a tip of the hat to his long-time favorite author, Mark Twain, Peck, in the first novel of the series, laid out a journey of discovery for young Alex Armsworth, his classmate Blossom Culp, and eighty-five-year-old Uncle Miles, as they set out to lay the ghostly spirit of a wandering soul, Inez Dumaine, to rest. A reviewer for the *Times Literary Supplement* noted that "there are more witty asides on each page than in the whole of many British books." Blossom makes a return in the award-winning *Ghosts I Have Been,* in which she discovers that she has even stronger second sight than her friend Alexander, when she is transported aboard the Titanic as it is sinking. Betsy Hearne concluded in *Booklist* that the book was an "outrageous sequence of events charmed together by skillful wordwork," and Glenda Broughton in *Children's Book Review Service* called *Ghosts I Have Been* a "thoroughly engrossing story." The third book in the sequence, *The Dreadful Future of Blossom Culp,* has Blossom time-traveling into the modern world of computers and befriending a boy named Jeremy in a novel that "is perfect for the ten- to fourteen-year-old audience to which it is directed," according to Carl B. Yoke writing in *Fantasy Review. Voice of Youth Advocates* contributor Gayle Keresey noted that the story "skillfully blends contemporary scenes with the past, assuring that the novel will not become quickly out-dated." The fourth book in the series, *Blossom Culp and the Sleep of Death,* finds Blossom and Alexander aiding the ghost of an Egyptian princess by finding her mummy. "As fresh and funny as any in the series," noted a *Bulletin of the Center for Children's Books* commentator, who added:

"A well-crafted, extrasensory mystery with mischievous scenes of high appeal."

Perhaps the book that earned Peck the most notoriety of all his titles is *Are You in the House Alone?,* the story of a rape and its aftermath, told from the victim's point of view. As Alix Nelson noted in the *New York Times Book Review,* Peck's purpose was "to show how rape victims are further victimized by society and the law." Though Nelson objected to the "melodramatic" manner of telling the story, the reviewer felt that "Mr. Peck ought to be congratulated for connecting with, and raising the consciousness of, his target audience on a subject most people shun." A reviewer for *Kliatt* commented that "Peck has created a moving drama full of suspense.... It is first of all a successful novel, but in the reading, one examines the crime of rape in all its emotional and legal complexities." Though some critics found the topic too extreme for young readers, most regarded Peck's work a powerful educational tool. It is used regularly in schools and has been published with an instructor's guide for classroom use.

Though Peck eschews the label of issue writer, he has tackled other difficult teen problems, supplying always

Sixth-grader Josh and his friend Aaron use a computer to travel back in time and repair Josh's family life. (Cover illustration by Broeck Steadman.)

In this second novel about Josh and his techno-whiz friend Aaron, the boys turn a computer into a wish-granting device, but find they have little control over the outcome. (Cover illustration by Broeck Steadman.)

and foremost a story, and secondarily a theme. *Father Figure* deals with the loss of a loved one and the search for meaningful family relationships. When seventeen-year-old Jim Atwater's mother kills herself to avoid the ravages of cancer, he and his younger brother, Byron, are left without a family, their father having deserted them years earlier. The two are eventually reunited with their father in Florida, however, and learn important lessons about getting by and taking people as they are. *Publishers Weekly* called *Father Figure* "the best [book] of many that have won [Peck] honors, and assuredly one of the best for all ages in many a moon," and Peck himself once dubbed it "my best book" in *School Library Journal.* With *Close Enough to Touch,* Peck dealt with teen romance, from the point of view of a young boy whose girlfriend dies, and who ultimately learns to love another. *Voice of Youth Advocates* contributor Mary K. Chelton noted that the book was "highly recommended with Kleenex."

Remembering the Good Times is a novel about teen suicide which a *Publishers Weekly* critic called Peck's "best book so far," adding: "Peck says he hopes parents will read the novel. We hope everyone will." In *Princess*

Ashley, Peck explored the world of teen friendship and manipulation. A *Kirkus Reviews* commentator noted that "Peck deftly captures the evolving concerns of fifteen- and sixteen-year-olds—their speech, anxieties, and shifting relationships with parents and peers," while Denise A. Anton in *School Library Journal* concluded that *Princess Ashley* "is a must for both high school and public library collections." *Unfinished Portrait of Jessica* deals with divorce and both a daughter's disillusionment with the father whom she has idolized and her ultimate reconciliation with her mother. Hazel Rochman praised the novel in *Booklist,* noting that "Peck's beautifully polished sentences hold passionate yearning, and his wit turns brand names into metaphor and reveals difficult truths in the cliches of popular culture." Peck also deals with the fundamentalist Christian right, censorship, and with a community learning to pull together in *The Last Safe Place on Earth,* "a highly topical tale," according to *Publishers Weekly.*

Peck also has a lighter side, writing of discovery in *Those Summer Girls I Never Met,* time-travel in *Voices after Midnight,* southern California brats in *Bel-Air Bambi and the Mall Rats,* and cyberspace in the humorous companion novels, *Lost in Cyberspace* and *The Great Interactive Dream Machine.* Of the first title in the latter two-book series written for juveniles, *Publishers Weekly* commented that "Amiable characters, fleet pacing and witty, in-the-know narration will keep even the non-bookish interested." Janice Del Negro, reviewing *The Great Interactive Dream Machine,* echoed these sentiments, noting that "Peck's humor and pacing keeps the boys—and the reader—moving right along."

In all these works of various genres, Peck has featured adolescents dealing with the major issue of finding their own way in the world, of making that first awkward step toward maturity and independence. Peck's female protagonists display the same degree of independence and resiliency as their male counterparts. In the end, Peck is conservative in what he hopes his YA titles accomplish. As he told Roger Sutton in a *School Library Journal* interview, "I don't know what books can do, except one point is that I wish every kid knew that fiction can be truer than fact, that it isn't a frivolous pastime unless your reading taste is for the frivolous. I wish they knew that being literate is a way of being successful in any field. I wish they all wanted to pit their own experience against the experiences they see in books. And I wish they had to do a little more of that in order to pass class in school. But in books you reach an awful lot of promising kids who write back good literate letters and give you hope. So that's the hope I have."

■ Works Cited

Anton, Denise A., review of *Princess Ashley, School Library Journal,* August, 1987, p. 97.
Review of *Are You in the House Alone?, Kliatt,* winter, 1978, p. 4.

Review of *Blossom Culp and the Sleep of Death, Bulletin of the Center for Children's Books,* April, 1986, pp. 155-56.

Broughton, Glenda, review of *Ghosts I Have Known, Children's Book Review Service,* December, 1977, p. 39.

Chelton, Mary K., review of *Close Enough to Touch, Voice of Youth Advocates,* October, 1981, pp. 36-37.

Del Negro, Janice M., review of *The Great Interactive Dream Machine, Bulletin of the Center for Children's Books,* November, 1996, p. 109.

Review of *Don't Look and It Won't Hurt, Children's Book Review Service,* October, 1972, p. 14.

Review of *Dreamland Lake, Kirkus Reviews,* June 15, 1973, p. 648.

Review of *Father Figure, Publishers Weekly,* July 17, 1978, p. 168.

Review of *The Ghost Who Belonged to Me, Times Literary Supplement,* March 25, 1977, p. 348.

Hearne, Betsy, review of *Ghosts I Have Known, Booklist,* October 1, 1977, p. 300.

Jones, Patrick, "Richard Peck," *Children's Books and Their Creators,* edited by Anita Silvey, Houghton Mifflin, 1995, pp. 512-14.

Keresey, Gayle, review of *The Dreadful Future of Blossom Culp, Voice of Youth Advocates,* December, 1983, p. 280.

Review of *The Last Safe Place on Earth, Publishers Weekly,* December 19, 1994, p. 55.

Review of *Lost in Cyberspace, Publishers Weekly,* September 4, 1995, p. 70.

Mercier, Jean, "*PW* Interviews: Richard Peck," *Publishers Weekly,* March 14, 1980.

Nelson, Alix, "Ah, Not to Be Sixteen Again," *New York Times Book Review,* November 14, 1976, p. 29.

Peck, Richard, "The Genteel Unshelving of a Book," *School Library Journal,* May, 1986, pp. 37-39.

Peck, Richard, essay in *Something about the Author Autobiography Series,* Volume 2, Gale, 1986, pp. 175-86.

Pogrebin, Letty Cottin, review of *Don't Look and It Won't Hurt, New York Times Books Review,* November 12, 1972, pp. 8, 10.

Review of *Princess Ashley, Kirkus Reviews,* May 1, 1987, pp. 723-24.

Review of *Remembering the Good Times, Publishers Weekly,* May 17, 1985, p. 118.

Rochman, Hazel, review of *Unfinished Portrait of Jessica, Booklist,* September 15, 1991, p. 137.

Sutherland, Zena, review of *Dreamland Lake, Bulletin of the Center for Children's Books,* January, 1974, pp. 83-84.

Sutherland, Zena, review of *Representing Super Doll, Bulletin of the Center for Children's Books,* November, 1974, p. 51.

Sutherland, Zena, review of *Through a Brief Darkness, Bulletin of the Center for Children's Books,* March, 1974, pp. 116-17.

Sutton, Roger, "A Conversation with Richard Peck," *School Library Journal,* June, 1990, pp. 36-40.

Williams, A. R., review of *Through a Brief Darkness, Junior Bookshelf,* October, 1976, p. 283.

Yoke, Carl B., "Third in Series Maintains High Standard," *Fantasy Review,* August, 1984, p. 50.

Yucht, Alice H., review of *Dreamland Lake, School Library Journal,* November, 1973, p. 53.

■ For More Information See

Children's Literature Review, Volume 15, Gale, 1988, pp. 146-66.

Gallo, Donald R., *Presenting Richard Peck,* Twayne, 1989.

Twentieth-Century Young Adult Writers, St. James Press, 1994.

PERIODICALS

Booklist, April 15, 1992, p. 1521; June 1, 1992, p. 1768; September 1, 1993, p. 62; May 1, 1994, p. 1611; January 15, 1995, p. 913; October 15, 1995, p. 402; September 1, 1996, p. 131.

English Journal, October, 1991, p. 96; April, 1992, p. 85; November, 1992, p. 96.

Publishers Weekly, October, 18, 1991, p. 64; August 16, 1993, p. 105; September 2, 1996, p. 131.

School Library Journal, May, 1992, p. 147; September, 1993, p. 234; October, 1994, p. 49; April, 1995, p. 154; September, 1995, p. 202; September, 1996, p. 206.

Wilson Library Bulletin, June, 1990, p. 180; December, 1993, p. 116.

—Sketch by J. Sydney Jones

* * *

PINKNEY, John

■ Personal

Born in Gillingham, Kent, England; son of William (an army officer) and Joan Gwendoline (a stenographer; maiden name, McFarlane) Pinkney; married Maggie Miller (a book editor); children: Robin Kirsten, Matthew Damien. *Education:* Attended University of Melbourne. *Politics:* "Center." *Religion:* "No formal religion."

■ Addresses

Home—Victoria, Australia. *Agent*—Tim Curnow, Curtis Brown (Australia), Sydney, Australia.

■ Career

Journalist. *Sun News-Pictorial,* Melbourne, Australia, columnist and feature writer; *Age,* Melbourne, television critic and columnist; *TV Week,* feature writer; *Australian,* columnist and feature writer; also author of logic puzzles for daily newspapers. Television writer; creator of Australian children's paranormal drama series *Number Seven Dream Street* and *The Curse on Tompkin's Timeglass;* radio broadcaster and producer of such weekly programs as *The Truth behind Flying Saucers* and *Do You Believe in Ghosts?*

JOHN PINKNEY

■ **Awards, Honors**

Shared, with two other plays, best stage play award from Elizabethan Theatre Trust and General Motors Holden, for "The Hateful Face in the Mirror;" best horror film award, Asian Film Festival, 1979, for *Thirst.*

■ **Writings**

FOR CHILDREN

The Key and the Fountain, illustrated by Sandra Laroche, Walter McVitty Books (Glebe, New South Wales), 1985.

Sherlock Q. Jones' Casebook of Puzzles, Riddles & Muddles, illustrated by Gillian Brailsford, Five Mile Press (Balwyn, Victoria, Australia), 1991.

More Puzzles, Riddles & Muddles from Sherlock Q. Jones' Casebook, illustrated by Gillian Brailsford, Five Mile Press, 1991.

Kids' Book of 2-Minute Puzzles, 4 vols., illustrated by Faith Richmond, Five Mile Press, 1992.

Puzzles, Riddles & Muddles, Book 3: Sherlock Q. Jones Trapped in Time, illustrated by Gillian Brailsford, Five Mile Press, 1992.

Puzzles, Riddles & Muddles, Book 4: Sherlock Q. Jones in Strange Lands, illustrated by Gillian Brailsford, Five Mile Press, 1992.

The Big Book of Puzzles, Riddles & Muddles (includes *Sherlock Q. Jones' Casebook of Puzzles, Riddles & Muddles, More Puzzles, Riddles & Muddles from Sherlock Q. Jones' Casebook,* and *Puzzles, Riddles & Muddles,* Books 3 and 4), illustrated by Gillian Brailsford, Five Mile Press, 1992.

Mazeworld: The Incredible Maze Journey, illustrated by Tracey Moroney, Five Mile Press, 1993.

Inside the Crystal: The Astonishing Mazeworld Journey, illustrated by Tracey Moroney, Five Mile Press, 1994.

Twice upon a Time, Lothian Books (Port Melbourne, Victoria), 1996.

OTHER

Murgatroyd's Mind-Stretchers, Longman Australia (Croydon, Victoria), 1970.

Thirst, Circus Books (Melbourne, Australia), 1979.

(With Leonard Ryzman) *Alien Honeycomb: The First Solid Evidence of UFOs,* illustrated with photographs by Justin Oakley, Pan Books (Sydney, Australia), 1980.

Think (puzzles), Sun Books (Melbourne, Australia), 1980.

Think Again (puzzles), Sun Books, 1980.

Wordgames: 203 Fun-Packed Puzzles to Stretch Your Wordpower, Sun Books, 1980.

The Great Australian Book of Puzzles, illustrated by Faith Pinkney, Currey O'Neil (South Yarra, Victoria), 1982.

Also author of the stage play "The Hateful Face in the Mirror"; author of several hundred episodes for Australian television series, including *Bellbird, Homicide,* and *Division Four.*

■ **Work in Progress**

A paranormal thriller for adults; research on unidentified flying objects (UFOs); creating anagrams and logic problems.

R

REEDER, Carolyn 1937-

■ Personal

Born November 16, 1937, in Washington, DC; daughter of Raymond and Pauline Owens; married Jack Reeder; children: David, Linda. *Education:* American University, B.A., M.Ed. *Hobbies and other interests:* Reading, gardening, swimming, hiking, cross-country skiing, bicycling.

■ Addresses

Office—P.O. Box 419, Washington, VA 22747.

■ Career

Writer. Former elementary school teacher.

■ Awards, Honors

Scott O'Dell Historical Fiction Award, Scott O'Dell Foundation, Child Study Children's Book Award, Bank Street College, Notable Children's Book, American Library Association (ALA), all 1989, Jefferson Cup Award, Virginia Library Association, Notable Children's Book for the Language Arts, National Council of Teachers of English, and Jane Addams Children's Book Award Honor Book, Jane Addams Peace Institution, all 1990, all for *Shades of Gray;* Joan G. Sugarman Children's Book Award, Washington Independent Writers Legal and Educational Fund, 1993, and Honor Book, Hedda Seisler Mason Award, 1995, both for *Moonshiner's Son.*

■ Writings

HISTORICAL NOVELS FOR CHILDREN

Shades of Gray, Macmillan, 1989.
Grandpa's Mountain, Macmillan, 1991.
Moonshiner's Son, Macmillan, 1993.
Across the Lines, Macmillan, 1997.
Foster's War, Scholastic, 1998.

NONFICTION; WITH HUSBAND, JACK REEDER

Shenandoah Heritage: The Story of the People before the Park, Potomac Appalachian Trail Club, 1978.
Shenandoah Vestiges: What the Mountain People Left Behind, Potomac Appalachian Trail Club, 1980.
Shenandoah Secrets: The Story of the Park's Hidden Past, Potomac Appalachian Trail Club, 1991.

CAROLYN REEDER

Also contributor to *You Have Seen Our Faces: Stories about America,* Scott, Foresman, 1993.

■ Sidelights

Carolyn Reeder is an author of historical novels for young readers. Set mainly in Virginia, her books deal with events from the Civil War—in the novels *Shades of Gray* and *Across the Lines*—to prohibition and the Great Depression, as seen in *Moonshiner's Son* and *Grandpa's Mountain,* respectively. Her books are noted for their strong story lines, realistic characters, and meticulous research, as witnessed from her very first award-winning title, *Shades of Gray.*

Born and raised in Washington, D. C., Reeder had no intention of becoming a writer. An early reader, she always had her "nose stuck in a book," as she noted in an autobiographical sketch on her website home page. Though she worked on college newspapers from junior high school through college, Reeder never saw writing as a primary career goal. "From the summer I was twelve, and taught a neighborhood child to read—he had never learned, even though he was almost nine—I knew I'd be a teacher," Reeder commented on her home page. Earning her degree from American University, that is exactly what she did, teaching fourth, fifth, and sixth grade as well as reading classes.

Later, however, married with two children, Reeder began working together with her husband at night on writing projects. Devoted hikers and campers, the Reeders wrote three nonfiction titles together about their favorite place for hiking, the Shenandoah National Park. Soon, however, her husband's busy schedule kept him from further collaborative efforts, and Reeder continued on her own, researching and writing historical novels. "I decided to try my hand at fiction and write for young people because I knew that kids love a good story," Reeder explained.

For her first fiction book, *Shades of Gray,* Reeder chose the period just after the Civil War. But for twelve-year-old Will Page, the pain of the war is still very present. His father and brother were killed by Northern soldiers, his two sisters died of diphtheria and his mother from grief. Now he has to go live with relatives he has never met, including Uncle Jed who refused to fight for the Confederacy. In a new home, Will has to learn how to fit in with his farm family and work alongside his uncle who he thinks is a coward, as well as face three local bullies who make his life miserable. In the end, Will is finally able to understand that neutrality is not cowardice, and that in fact it took tremendous courage for his uncle refuse to fight. In *Kirkus Reviews,* a critic remarked that "Believable characters and well-placed incident keep the reader going here ... and a good feel for time and place makes [Will's] story memorable." *Horn Book*'s Nancy Vasilakis commented that "the author's unforced, naturalistic prose style will engage middle-grade readers as will the novel's well-developed, amiable characters and its solid moral grounding." Zena Sutherland, writing in *Bulletin of the Center for Chil-*

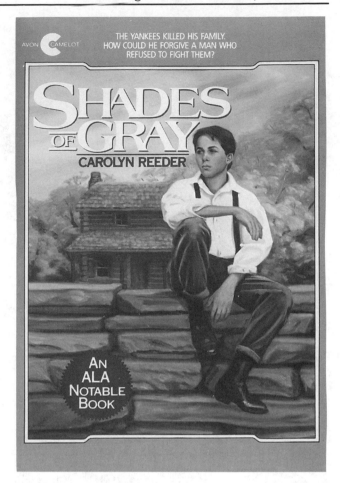

THE YANKEES KILLED HIS FAMILY. HOW COULD HE FORGIVE A MAN WHO REFUSED TO FIGHT THEM?

AVON CAMELOT

SHADES OF GRAY

CAROLYN REEDER

AN ALA NOTABLE BOOK

A winner of several awards, Reeder's historical novel focuses on twelve-year-old Will, a Civil War orphan who finally understands that his uncle's pacifism is not cowardice.

dren's Books, called *Shades of Gray* "an excellent first novel."

Initially Reeder only wrote during vacation times, but soon she found that she wanted to write during the school year as well. For her second novel, *Grandpa's Mountain,* she went forward in time to the 1930s of the Great Depression as witnessed by eleven-year-old Carrie who makes her annual summer visit to relatives in Virginia's Blue Ridge Mountains. But this summer is different; her secure summer vacation is disrupted by government plans to buy out her grandparents' home and include it in a new national park. But Carrie's grandpa assures her that he was born on his land and intends to die there and that he will fight the government all the way. Though in the end her grandfather loses the fight, young Carrie learns the value of fighting for what one believes in. A contributor to *Kirkus Reviews* concluded that Carrie "learns that relations mean more than locations, and that losing may not be so bad if you have tried as hard as you can." Margaret A. Bush, writing in *Horn Book,* commented that Reeder "has given careful thought to her historical setting and the configuration of human responses to loss," and concluded that "the novel strikes many chords while exploring the relationships among family, neighbors, and strangers."

Prohibition is the historical setting for Reeder's third novel, *Moonshiner's Son,* the story of twelve-year-old Tom who works with his father distilling moonshine—illegal liquor—in the remote Blue Ridge Mountains of Virginia. Tom wants to follow in his father's footsteps, but when a preacher moves into the area and starts speaking about the evils of alcohol, things become complicated for the youth. Such complications increase when the preacher informs law officers of the forbidden brew and when the preacher's strong-willed daughter, Amy, begins to figure in Tom's life. "Adroitly, Reeder sets up her story to explore some complex issues," noted a critic in *Kirkus Reviews,* concluding that *Moonshiner's Son* was another excellent work from Reeder, "with strong, memorable characters and a compelling plot, an unusually thoughtful and well-crafted historical novel of these mountain people." *Horn Book*'s Elizabeth S. Watson noted that children will discover "as much about honesty, honor, and generosity as they will learn about ... American history," while in *Publishers Weekly* a reviewer observed that "the reader is drawn into the story, and Tom's concerns seem very real."

Reeder returns to the Civil War era for *Across the Lines,* a story told alternately from the points of view of two boys, one white, one black. Edward and his family are forced to flee to nearby Petersburg when the Union Army takes over their plantation. But Simon, the slave who had been Edward's life-long companion, stays behind. Free now, Simon attaches himself to the Union army, working at a variety of jobs to earn his keep. When the army besieges Petersburg, Simon and Edward face the hardships of war on opposite sides of the siege lines in their separate struggles to understand the meaning of courage and of freedom. In a starred review of *Across the Lines, Booklist* critic Carolyn Phelan stated that "there are few Civil War books for children that explore the reality of war or the subtlety of race relations as sensitively as this involving novel." A critic writing for *Kirkus Reviews* described the book as a "powerful, moving story of friendship, loss, and courage."

Foster's War, Reeder's first book with a setting other than Virginia, is a World War II home front novel. During the months following Pearl Harbor, eleven-year-old Foster Simmons changes from a social misfit to the undisputed leader of the kids in his San Diego neighborhood as they work for the war effort and play war games in the vacant lot near their school. Things change at home, too, as Foster's domineering father becomes an air raid warden, his mother volunteers for the Red Cross, and his big brother Mel is sent overseas.

Reeder drew on her earliest classroom memories and both her own World War II memories and those of her friends in writing *Foster's War.* "It was our war, too," she explained. Each of Reeder's historical novels focuses on real problems of adolescents and uses factual and geographical background to enrich the story. Reeder has, with further book publications, been able to give up teaching and devote full time to writing. Said Reeder, "It's wonderful to have all the time I need to research and write my historical novels and still have time to do the other things I enjoy."

■ Works Cited

Review of *Across the Lines, Kirkus Reviews,* March 15, 1997, p. 467.

Bush, Margaret A., review of *Grandpa's Mountain, Horn Book,* November-December, 1991, pp. 738-9.

Review of *Grandpa's Mountain, Kirkus Reviews,* October 1, 1991, p. 1291.

Review of *Moonshiner's Son, Kirkus Reviews,* June 1, 1993, p. 726.

Review of *Moonshiner's Son, Publishers Weekly,* May 24, 1993, p. 88.

Phelan, Carolyn, review of *Across the Lines, Booklist,* April 1, 1997, p. 1331.

Reeder, Carolyn, comments on home page, www.reeder books.com, April 2, 1997.

Review of *Shades of Gray, Kirkus Reviews,* October 1, 1989, p. 1480.

Sutherland, Zena, review of *Shades of Gray, Bulletin of the Center for Children's Books,* January, 1990, pp. 119-20.

Vasilakis, Nancy, review of *Shades of Gray, Horn Book,* March-April, 1990, p. 203.

Watson, Elizabeth S., review of *Moonshiner's Son, Horn Book,* September-October, 1993, p. 601.

■ For More Information See

BOOKS

Seventh Book of Junior Authors and Illustrators, Wilson, 1996, pp. 263-64.

PERIODICALS

Booklist, June 1, 1993, p. 1816; April 1, 1997, p. 1331.

Bulletin of the Center for Children's Books, December, 1991, p. 103; September, 1993, pp. 22-23.

Publishers Weekly, February 9, 1998, p. 96.

School Library Journal, June, 1992, p. 51; May, 1993, p. 128.

Voice of Youth Advocates, February, 1990, p. 347; August, 1993, p. 157.

—*Sketch by J. Sydney Jones*

* * *

RENDON, Marcie R. 1952-

■ Personal

Born March 2, 1952, in Minnesota; children: Rachael, Simone, Awan.

■ Addresses

Office—c/o Belleville, 308 Prince St., St. Paul, MN 55101. *Electronic mail*—MRendon703@aol.com.

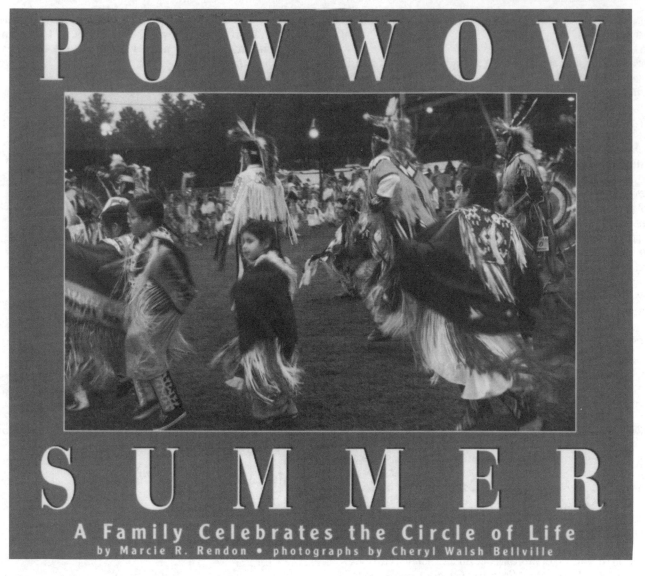

POWWOW SUMMER

A Family Celebrates the Circle of Life
by Marcie R. Rendon • photographs by Cheryl Walsh Bellville

Marcie R. Rendon describes the rituals of a powwow through the experiences of the Downwind family, who belong to the Anishinabe tribe.

■ Career

Writer. Mentor and leader of various writing workshops in Minneapolis, MN, 1994—. *Member:* White Earth Anishinabe, Native Arts Circle, Intermedia Arts, Mystery Writer's Group, Playwrights Center.

■ Awards, Honors

Loft Inroads Writers of Color Award for Native Americans, The Loft, 1990; Mentorship Award for Performing Artists, Intermedia Arts, 1992; Beyond P.R. grant, Center for Arts Criticism, 1994; Critics' Travel grant, Center for Arts Criticism, 1994; Many Voices Multicultural Collaboration grant, Playwrights Center, 1995; WARM Mentorship award, Women's Art Registry of Minnesota, 1995; grant, COMPAS Community Art Program, 1995; Emerging Artists grant, Intermedia Arts, 1995-96; Jerome fellowship, Playwrights Center, 1996-97; Best Dramatic Short Film, American Indian Film Festival, 1996, for *Looks into the Night;* Notable Children's Trade Book in the Field of Social Studies, National Council for the Social Studies and Children's Book Council, 1997, for *Powwow Summer.* Received numerous writing residencies.

■ Writings

Powwow Summer: A Family Celebrates the Circle of Life, photographs by Cheryl Walsh Bellville, Carolrhoda (Minneapolis, MN), 1995, Lerner, 1996.

Other works include a privately printed poetry chapbook, *Dreaming into Being,* and two nonfiction books, *Native Models for Business Success,* Minnesota Junior Achievement Project and *Beyond Survival: Applying for Grants/Awards/Fellowships,* Native Arts Circle (Minneapolis, MN). Work represented in anthologies, including *The Colour of Resistance,* Sister Vision Press; *A Gathering of Spirit,* Firebrand Books; and *Every Woman Has a Story,* Haymarket Press.

OTHER

(With Valerie RedHorse) *Looks into the Night* (screenplay; based on a story by Lorraine Norrgard), American Film Institute, 1995.

Bring the Children Home (play), first produced by the Child's Play Theater in collaboration with Pillsbury House Theater, 1996.

"A Place in the Sun," a song in *InnerCity Opera,* Great American History Theater, St. Paul, MN, 1996.

Outside In, Inside Out (play; based on a story by Peg Wetli), for CLIMB Theater, St. Paul, 1997.

Author of a column on Native sobriety, *Lac Du Flambeau Tribal Press,* 1994. Contributor of articles, poems, and reviews to magazines and newspapers, including *Parenting, Colors, Dreams and Visions, Present Time, Four Directions, Fireweed: A Feminist Quarterly, Womenstruggle,* and *Runner.* Newsletter editor, *Native Arts Circle;* editor of "News Briefs," *Native City News.*

■ Work in Progress

A children's book comparing the lives of two multi-generational families (one Hmong, the other Norwegian), who market produce at the St. Paul Farmer's Market, for Carolrhoda; editing an anthology by women of color, for Spinsters Ink; writing a Frances Densmore play, for Great American History Theatre.

■ Sidelights

Marcie R. Rendon told *Something about the Author* (*SATA*): "With all my writing I try to give hope—hope to Native young people that their histories and stories will not be forgotten, hope to other Native writers that they, too, can be published, hope to poor persons, women, children, persons of color that they, too, can follow their dreams."

■ For More Information See

PERIODICALS

Booklist, July, 1996, p. 1826.
School Library Journal, October, 1996, p. 138.

* * *

RILEY, James A. 1939-

■ Personal

Born July 25, 1939, in Sullivan County, TN; married Dorothy Taylor, October 14, 1960; children: Joshua D., Jubal W. *Education:* East Tennessee State University, B.S., 1961, M.A., 1966; Nova University, Ed.S., 1982. *Religion:* Baptist.

■ Addresses

Home—Rockledge, FL.

■ Career

Writer. Television appearances include *Safe at Home Plate,* 1993, and *A League Second to None,* 1994. *Member:* Society for American Baseball Research.

■ Awards, Honors

Society for American Baseball Research, MacMillan Research Awards, 1990, 1994.

■ Writings

The All-Time All-Stars of Black Baseball, TK Publishers (Cocoa, FL), 1983.

Dandy, Day, and the Devil, TK Publishers, 1987.

Negro World Series of 1942, TK Publishers, 1989.

(Editor) *Black Baseball Journal,* TK Publishers, 1990.

Too Dark for the Hall, TK Publishers, 1991.

(With Renwick W. Speer) *The Hundred Years of Chet Hoff: A Special Tribute to His Life and Baseball Career & a Celebration of His 100th Birthday, May 8th, 1991,* TK Publishers, 1991.

The Biographical Encyclopedia of the Negro Baseball Leagues, Carroll & Graf, 1994.

James A. Riley

One of several books James A. Riley has written about the history of African Americans in baseball, *The Negro Leagues* documents a period of nearly a century, from 1868 to 1960.

(With Buck Leonard) *Buck Leonard, The Black Lou Gehrig: The Hall of Famer's Story in His Own Words,* Carroll & Graf, 1995.

(With Monte Irvin) *Monte Irvin: Nice Guys Finish First,* Carroll & Graf, 1996.

The Negro Leagues, Chelsea House, 1996.

Contributor to books, including *Insiders Baseball,* Scribner, 1983, and *The Ballplayers,* Random House, 1990. Contributor to baseball magazines.

■ Work in Progress

The Chronological Encyclopedia of the Negro Baseball Leagues, for Carroll & Graf; *The Statistical Encyclopedia of the Negro Baseball Leagues,* Carroll & Graf; research on statistics of the Negro leagues.

■ Sidelights

Author James A. Riley documents the lives and careers of African-American baseball players. In his several books on the subject, through interviews and archival sources, he paints a vivid picture of life in the Negro leagues. A reviewer in *Booklist* hails Riley's *Biographical Encyclopedia of the Negro Baseball Leagues* as "a landmark publication in the fields of baseball history and African American history." Citing more than just statistics and other such facts, Riley includes fascinating anecdotal material about both well-known and long-forgotten players. *School Library Journal* contributor Richard Klein insists that "students interested in lesser-known personalities from pre-1946 won't find a better guide" than Riley's encyclopedia. Riley furthers his study in *The Negro Leagues,* an ambitious reference that spans the years 1868 to 1960. *School Library Journal* reviewer Tom S. Hurlburt commends the accuracy and sheer numbers of players and teams discussed in *The Negro Leagues,* adding that the volume is "attractively designed." The careers of Ray Dandridge, Leon Day, and Willie Wells—three superstars from the old Negro baseball league, are spotlighted in *Dandy, Day, and the Devil. Booklist* reviewer Wes Lukowsky asserts that the book offers "a fine supplementary resource for collections where interest in baseball history is high."

■ Works Cited

Review of *The Biographical Encyclopedia of the Negro Baseball Leagues, Booklist,* June 1 & 15, 1994, p. 1866.

Hurlburt, Tom S., review of *The Negro Leagues, School Library Journal,* February, 1997, p. 123.

Klein, Richard, review of *The Biographical Encyclopedia of the Negro Baseball Leagues, School Library Journal,* November, 1994, p. 138.

Lukowsky, Wes, review of *Dandy, Day, and the Devil, Booklist,* March 1, 1988, p. 1090.

■ For More Information See

PERIODICALS

Booklist, January 1, 1995, p. 793.

New York Times Book Review, April 7, 1996, p. 16.

School Library Journal, September, 1995, p. 236.*

*   *   *

RODDA, Emily 1948-
(Jennifer Rowe)

■ Personal

Real name Jennifer Rowe; born in New South Wales, Australia, in 1948; children: one girl, three boys.

■ Addresses

Home—Sydney, Australia.

■ Career

Editor, Angus & Robertson publishers; editor, *Australian Women's Weekly;* writer of children's books and adult crime fiction.

■ Awards, Honors

Book of the Year, Younger Readers Award, Children's Book Council of Australia (CBCA), 1985, for *Something Special,* 1987, for *Pigs Might Fly,* 1989, for *The Best-Kept Secret,* 1991, for *Finders Keepers,* and 1994, for *Rowan of Rin;* Ipswich Festival of Children's Literature, Bilby Award, 1995, for *Rowan of Rin;* Honour Book, Book of the Year, Younger Readers, CBCA, 1997, for *Rowan and the Keeper of the Crystal.*

■ Writings

FOR CHILDREN

Something Special, illustrated by Noela Young, Angus & Robertson, 1984, Holt, 1989.

Pigs Might Fly, illustrated by Noela Young, Angus & Robertson, 1986, published in the U.S. as *The Pigs Are Flying,* Greenwillow, 1988.

The Best-Kept Secret, illustrated by Noela Young, Angus & Robertson, 1988, Holt, 1990.

Finders Keepers, illustrated by Noela Young, Omnibus Books, 1990.

Crumbs!, illustrated by Kerry Argent, Omnibus Books, 1990.

The Timekeeper, illustrated by Noela Young, Omnibus Books, 1992.

Rowan of Rin, Omnibus Books, 1993.

Rowan and the Travellers, Omnibus Books, 1994.

Power and Glory, illustrated by Geoff Kelly, Allen & Unwin, 1994.

Yay!, illustrated by Craig Smith, Omnibus Books, 1996.

Rowan and the Keeper of the Crystal, Omnibus Books, 1996.

Rodda has also written or co-authored two dozen books in the Scholastic series, "Teen Power, Inc."; editor of anthologies, *Love Lies Bleeding, More Poems to Read to Young Australians,* and *She's Apples: A Collection of Winning Stories for Young Australians.*

OTHER; AS JENNIFER ROWE

The Commonsense International Cookery Book, Angus & Robertson, 1978.

Eating Well in Later Life, Angus & Robertson, 1982.

Grim Pickings, Allen & Unwin, 1988.

Murder by the Book, Allen & Unwin, 1989.

Death in Store, Allen & Unwin, 1991, Doubleday, 1993.

The Makeover Murders, Allen & Unwin, 1992, Doubleday, 1993.

Stranglehold, Allen & Unwin, 1993, Bantam, 1995.

Lamb to the Slaughter, Allen & Unwin, 1996, Bantam, 1996.

■ Sidelights

Emily Rodda, the pen name of an Australian writer for children, is a five-time winner of the Children's Book Council of Australia's Children's Book of the Year Award. Her books, including *Something Special* and *Pigs Might Fly,* employ eccentric humor as well as elements of fantasy, mystery, and fairy tale. Ghost-story as well as time-travel motifs also find their way into many of Rodda's plots. This highly popular Australian author has penned a successful fantasy series employing

In her sequel to *Finders Keepers,* Emily Rodda follows Patrick as he again travels to an alternate world across the Barrier, only this time he must save both worlds from destruction. (Cover illustration by Noela Young.)

the young boy Rowan in his adventures amid magic and dragons, a series that has spawned numerous chat-rooms on the Internet. Additionally, Rodda helped launch an adventure/mystery series for young readers for Scholastic, Australia. "Teen Power, Inc." includes some two dozen titles, half of them written by Rodda herself, others co-authored. Writing under her real name, Jennifer Rowe, she has also produced adult mysteries as well as cookbooks.

Born in New South Wales, Rodda worked as an editor at both an Australian publishing house and at a woman's magazine before turning her hand to juvenile fiction. She chose her grandmother's maiden name as a pseudonym to write children's fiction, because at the time of her first publication, her publisher, Angus & Robertson, was also her employer. Rodda's first novel, *Something Special,* was an attempt to document her daughter's growth, and with four children, Rodda had a lot of material at hand for subsequent titles. Aimed at primary graders, *Something Special* tells the story of a little girl, Samantha, who becomes involved in her mother's rummage sale. Set in contemporary times and with a realistic setting, the book nonetheless contains an element of fantasy: Samantha and her friend, Lizzie, become involved with the spirits of the former owners of the clothing donated for the sale.

At the sale, Sam's friend Lizzie leaves the stall for a while. Sam takes a short nap and is surprised by a quartet of spirits who are admiring their donated clothes. Upon Lizzie's return, these visitors have gone and she suspects they were just a dream of Sam's, but the next day one of them actually returns in the flesh to reclaim a favorite "second skin," a tartan dressing gown he has had for years. Ron Morton, writing in *Books for Your Children,* noted that "This is a well written book. . . . Its strength is perhaps its warm, embracing dialogue," and concluded that though the "essence" of the story was fantasy, "there is still something quite believable about what happened." *Books for Keeps* called the book a "thought-provoking and eerie tale" which "catches quite brilliantly the dash, excitement and movement of the preparations" for the sale. Writing about the U.S. edition, a *Kirkus Reviews* critic commented that the book was an "unusual story, beautifully structured and simply but gracefully told," while *School Library Journal* contributor Elisabeth LeBris noted that the book "is told in a light tone with lots of dialogue."

With this first book, Rodda won the Australian Children's Book of the Year Junior Award, one of the most prestigious prizes in Australia, which not only helped sales of the initial title, but also had reviewers and readers alike awaiting a second book. Rodda commented in an interview in *Magpies* that "I was astounded and surprised because I hadn't held out the faintest hope of actually winning. . . . As a child I had always wanted to be a writer; now maybe I really was one." Rodda also noted in the interview, however, that "second books are much harder to pull off than first ones."

In Rodda's video game-inspired picture book, a young protagonist moves to higher levels, battling a series of menacing opponents. (From *Power and Glory,* illustrated by Geoff Kelly.)

Rodda's second book, *Pigs Might Fly,* is a lighthearted fantasy that employs mystery and magical travel to another world. Rachel, about age seven, is in bed with a cold and longs for some excitement to break up her boring days. A picture drawn by a sign-painting friend of her father's is meant to cheer Rachel up, but leads to much more radical results. The picture shows Rachel riding a unicorn in her pajamas while pigs fly overhead. Soon Rachel finds herself on the unicorn while actual pigs are playing in the sky. Left at the door of a peasant couple who insist on calling her Grace, Rachel soon discovers that what is transpiring is known locally as a flying pig storm. The peasants think that Rachel has come from "Outside," a rare event that has also initiated the pig storm. Rachel stays in this fabulous land a day and a half, filled with anxiety about how she will get back home, but she eventually *does* return through the aid of a rhyme discovered at the library. Many reviewers have noted the parallels in the book to *Alice's Adventures in Wonderland* as well as to *The Wizard of Oz,* though Rodda's tale is much shorter and far less complex than either of those two. Howard George, in *Reading Time,* commented that Rodda's second novel was "bound to be a great success with young readers" because "only people with a sense of the ridiculous can appreciate unlikely events." George concluded that "this is a finely crafted book" and that "the humour used is never slapstick nor banal." Reviewing the U.S. edition, published as *The Pigs Are Flying!,* Karen P. Smith commented in *School Library Journal* that this is "an engaging fantasy for beginning fans of the genre," while Karen Jameyson called the story a "comfortable swirl of suspense, adventure, and amusing characters" in *Horn Book. Books for Keeps* concluded its review by stating that *Pigs Might Fly* is a "beautifully unfolded tale from an illuminating, fresh-voiced writer." Award committees agreed with the reviewers, for this second book also earned a Children's Book of the

Year Award from the Children's Book Council of Australia.

Rodda stuck with fantasy for her third title, *The Best-Kept Secret,* which features a magical carousel ride. When this carousel comes to town, the residents all find reasons why they should take a ride on it into the future, including young Joanna, who rescues a boy lost in the future. None of the characters who take the magic ride realize that they are at crossroads in their lives; Joanna has just learned she is to become a big sister. Rescuing the young boy in the future, then, is an unconscious acceptance of this new role. Gerald Haigh, reviewing the book in the *Times Educational Supplement,* noted that Rodda's story "is subtle and layered, and pricks at the emotions in all sorts of ways." *Kirkus Reviews* dubbed it a "deceptively simple tale" and a "charmingly original, neatly structured story," while *School Library Journal* contributor Joanne Aswell concluded *The Best-Kept Secret* an "amusing, optimistic chapter book fantasy to read alone or aloud."

Rodda's first male protagonist appears in her fourth book, *Finders Keepers,* a longer and more sophisticated juvenile novel than any that she had heretofore written. Rodda herself has characterized the book as being special not only for the use of a boy as the central character, but also for the fact that she used "family relationships as a background to the fantasy," as she explained in *Reading Time.* When Patrick takes part in a novel interactive quiz game on his television, he has no idea he will pass through the "Barrier" separating his reality from the "Other Side," but that in fact is exactly what happens. Patrick becomes a Finder of all those things people misplace day to day. His prize is a computer he has been longing for. As Laurie Copping commented in *Reading Time,* the story moves at "a rapid pace, fantasy and reality interchanging so rapidly

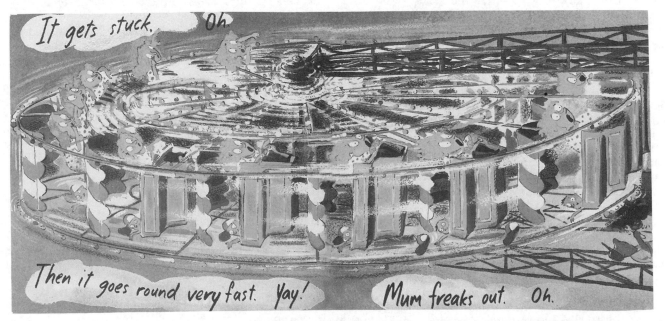

Rodda's zany picture book *Yay!* **follows Jason and his family through a frenzied day at Crazy Family Fun World amusement park. (Illustrated by Craig Smith.)**

that sometimes the reader may wonder whether or not they are experiencing the real or the unreal." *Publishers Weekly* also noted the "lightning speed" at which Rodda kept her story going, and concluded that the book was "an uncommonly satisfying read."

Patrick re-appears in *The Timekeeper,* a sequel to *Finders Keepers* in which he is once again summoned through the Barrier, this time to prevent the destruction of worlds on both sides. Obstacles make his mission all the harder, and Rodda blends elements of computer technology to create "an action-filled fantasy with warm, believable depictions of family relationships," according to Anne Connor in *School Library Journal.* A *Kirkus Reviews* commentator called *The Timekeeper* an "engaging light fantasy."

Rodda has also used the contemporary world of high tech in other books for young readers, including *Crumbs!* and the picture book, *Power and Glory.* The successive competency levels of a video game form the core of the latter title, which Carolyn Phelan dubbed an "unexpected pleasure" in a starred *Booklist* review. John Sigwald, writing in *School Library Journal,* called *Power and Glory* a "big, bold, colorful and cartoony quest for control over electronic nemeses," while *Kirkus Reviews* noted the "clever analogies" Rodda made between the witch, goblin, and ogre of the video game and family members of the boy who is playing the game. "Rodda builds up a throbbing rhythm that approximates the intensity of the play," observed *Publishers Weekly* of this "rousing" picture book.

Far afield from the techno world of the 1990s are Rodda's series of novels about the adventures of Rowan, two of which have been honored by the CBCA. The first title in the series, *Rowan of Rin,* tells the magical story of the village of Rin, where the locals awake one morning to discover that their source of water, a nearby stream, has slowed to a mere trickle. As the days pass, matters get worse, and the stream has almost totally dried up. The villagers depend on this stream to water their animals, the "bukshah," which can no longer get to the water. Something must be done: The villagers agree that someone must travel up the Mountain, an eerie and frightening place, to find out what the problem is. The Wise Woman provides the villagers with a map along with a guiding chant, but it is only the boy who tends the bukshah, Rowan, who can figure out the meaning of the map. Rowan sets out on his quest with six others, braving obstacles including a dragon, until he reaches the top of the Mountain and is able to restore the stream to life. In the process, Rowan also saves the life of his protector, Strong John. *Horn Book*'s Karen Jameyson called the novel a "quest adventure of the highest order" and a "riveting fantasy." Jameyson also noted that Rodda's characters "step off the page as individuals." *Magpies* contributor Joan Zahnleiter commented that the "text is very visual, sparkling with vivid imagery. It would lend itself to an exciting TV production." Rodda has written two further titles in the series, *Rowan and the Travellers* and *Rowan and the Keeper of the Crystal.*

Rodda, who normally works on her writing at night, is a firm believer in a tight plot. Her books may all employ fantasy, but not at the expense of economy of detail. "I love things that all tie up and in fact I find things that don't very irritating if they're that type of book," Rodda noted in a *Magpies* interview. "The kind of book that I regard as an adventure or a fantasy or whatever, I think that deserves a good, neat ending.... There's no little clue that doesn't have a meaning.... Maybe it's a response to the general messiness of life, but I find it very satisfying."

■ Works Cited

Aswell, Joanne, review of *The Best-Kept Secret, School Library Journal,* January, 1991, pp. 79-80.

Review of *The Best-Kept Secret, Kirkus Reviews,* May 15, 1990, p. 802.

Connor, Anne, review of *The Timekeeper, School Library Journal,* October, 1993, p. 128.

Copping, Laurie, review of *Finders Keepers, Reading Time,* No. IV, 1990, p. 25.

Review of *Finders Keepers, Publishers Weekly,* October 18, 1991, p. 64.

George, Howard, review of *Pigs Might Fly, Reading Time,* No. 3, 1987, p. 66.

Haigh, Gerald, "Daredevils," *Times Educational Supplement,* February 17, 1989, p. B28.

Jameyson, Karen, review of *The Pigs Are Flying!, Horn Book,* November-December, 1988, p. 784.

Jameyson, Karen, "News from Down Under," *Horn Book,* November-December, 1993, pp. 778-80.

LeBris, Elisabeth, review of *Something Special, School Library Journal,* January, 1990, pp. 106, 108.

Morton, Ron, review of *Something Special, Books for Your Children,* Spring, 1985, p. 11.

Phelan, Carolyn, review of *Power and Glory, Booklist,* April 15, 1996, p. 1441.

Review of *Pigs Might Fly, Books for Keeps,* March, 1989, p. 18.

Review of *Power and Glory, Kirkus Reviews,* February 15, 1996, p. 299.

Review of *Power and Glory, Publishers Weekly,* May 6, 1996, p. 81.

Rodda, Emily, *The Pigs Are Flying!,* Greenwillow, 1988.

Rodda, Emily, *Something Special,* Holt, 1989.

Rodda, Emily, *Finders Keepers,* Omnibus, 1990.

Rodda, Emily, interview, *Magpies,* July, 1990, pp. 19-21.

Rodda, Emily, CBCA acceptance speech, *Reading Time,* No. IV, 1991, p. 5.

Sigwald, John, review of *Power and Glory, School Library Journal,* May, 1996, p. 97.

Smith, Karen P., review of *The Pigs Are Flying!, School Library Journal,* September, 1988, pp. 185-86.

Review of *Something Special, Books For Keeps,* September, 1986, p. 23.

Review of *Something Special, Kirkus Reviews,* November 1, 1989, p. 1597.

Review of *The Timekeeper, Kirkus Reviews,* October 1, 1993, p. 1278.

Zahnleiter, Joan, review of *Rowan of Rin, Magpies,* November, 1993, p. 31.

■ For More Information See

BOOKS

Children's Literature Review, Volume 23, Gale, 1994, pp. 207-13.

Helbig, Alethea K., and Agnes Regan Perkins, *Dictionary of Children's Fiction from Australia, Canada, India, New Zealand, and Selected African Countries,* Greenwood Press, 1992.

PERIODICALS

Booklist, September 1, 1990, p. 52; January, 1997, p. 768.

Books for Keeps, March, 1989, p. 18; January, 1996, p. 10.

Bulletin of the Center for Children's Books, November, 1993, p. 97.

Emergency Librarian, March, 1989, pp. 25, 27, 47; March, 1991, p. 51; March, 1993, p. 17.

Growing Point, January, 1989, p. 5088.

Junior Bookshelf, April, 1988, p. 94; April, 1993, p. 78.

Publishers Weekly, June 9, 1997, p. 46.

Reading Time, February, 1997, pp. 14-15, 35; August, 1997, pp. 9-10.

School Librarian, November, 1996, p. 172.*

—Sketch by J. Sydney Jones

* * *

ROWE, Jennifer
See RODDA, Emily

* * *

RUURS, Margriet 1952-

■ Personal

Born December 2, 1952, in the Netherlands; daughter of H. Bodbyl and W. Bodbyl-Schut; married Kees Ruurs (a parks and recreation manager), 1972; children: Alexander, Arnout. *Education:* Simon Fraser University, master's of education program. *Hobbies and other interests:* Gardening, traveling, hiking, camping, writing educational materials, and spending time at home with her children.

■ Addresses

Home—R3, Poplar Drive C16, Armstrong, British Columbia, V0E 1B0, Canada. *Electronic mail*—ruurs @ junction.net.

■ Career

Writer and educator. Teaches creative writing enrichment and conducts writing workshops for children in various schools and by e-mail, conducts workshops at Okanagan (B.C.) University College, conducts storytime at Okanagan Regional Libraries. Former chairperson of the board in her local school district. Speaker at children's literature and technology conferences.

MARGRIET RUURS

■ Awards, Honors

Storytelling World Awards, International Reading Association National Convention, "Tellable" Stories for Ages 4-7, honor title, 1997, for *Emma's Eggs.* "Our Choice Catalogue" selection, Canadian Children's Book Centre, for *A Mountain Alphabet* and *Emma's Eggs.*

■ Writings

Apenkinderen, Leopold, 1982.

Fireweed (picture book), illustrated by Roberta Mebs, Burns & Morton (Whitehorse, Yukon, Canada), 1986.

Big Little Dog, illustrated by Marc Houde, Penumbra (Waterloo, Ontario), 1992.

The R.C.M.P (nonfiction), KGR Learning Aides, 1992.

On the Write Track! A Guide to Writing, Illustrating and Publishing Stories (adult nonfiction), Pacific Educational Press (Vancouver, B. C.), 1993, Orca, 1996.

A Mountain Alphabet (picture book), illustrated by Andrew Kiss, Tundra Books of Northern New York, 1996, Tundra Books (Toronto), 1996.

Emma's Eggs (picture book), illustrated by Barbara Spurll, Stoddart Kids (Toronto), 1996.

Also author of *Spectacular Spiders,* Integrated Activities for Primary Classrooms, Pacific Edge Publishing. *Big Little Dog* was published in Braille by CNIB in 1994. Contributor of articles and poems to numerous magazines.

TRANSLATIONS

Judith Viorst, *Alexander and the Terrible, Horrible, No Good, Very Bad Day,* Leopold, 1985.

■ Work in Progress

Emma and the Coyote, a sequel to *Emma's Eggs,* for Stoddart; *Teachers for Sale,* a children's novel; a collection of poetry; research into the influence of technology on the reading and writing of children.

■ Sidelights

Born in the Netherlands, Margriet Ruurs has lived in many places, including California, Oregon, Northern Alberta, and the Yukon; currently, she and her family reside in British Columbia. A teacher of creative writing, she is best known as the creator of picture books that characteristically combine a lighthearted approach with a reverence for nature; she is also the author of fiction for middle graders and nonfiction for children and adults. Ruurs is perhaps most widely recognized as the creator of *A Mountain Alphabet,* an alphabet book in alliterative text that is set in the Canadian Rockies and is structured as a hike through the mountain ranges. The book is illustrated by Andrew Kiss, a well-known oil painter of wildlife, who provides twenty-six pictures that each emphasize a letter of the alphabet. Both the text and the art represent the variety of plant and animal life to be found in the Rockies; Ruurs includes both an introduction and an appended alphabet to provide further information about the scenes depicted. Critics noted that not all the items beginning with a particular letter were mentioned in the text, though all are listed in the back of the book; this, along with the hidden letter itself, is considered an invitation to young readers to closely examine each illustration. "[This] book will help young readers to explore this ecosystem," maintained Barbara Chatton in *School Library Journal.* Chatton added, "While this title provides a valuable resource, it will need adult intervention to help youngsters 'read' the pictures so that they can get the most out of it." *Quill and Quire* reviewer Janet McNaughton concurred: "Some picture books find their real audience with adults who have a special affinity with the subject matter. *A Mountain Alphabet* may well be one of those."

In *Emma's Eggs,* Ruurs tells a humorous story while displaying her knowledge and love of animal life. In this picture book, the author features a mixed-up hen who notices what the humans on her farm are doing with her eggs (for example, scrambling them for eating, or decorating and hiding them for an Easter egg hunt), and tries to accommodate them by herself scrambling her eggs or hiding them. Eventually, however, Emma realizes exactly what her eggs are for. "The story is well written," averred Bridget Donald in *Quill & Quire.* "The narrative descriptions and dialogue convey the energy of Emma's human-like ambitions while preserving a strong sense of her chicken nature." In addition to her picture books, Ruurs is the author of *Big Little Dog,* the story of a boy and his sled dog that is, according to *Quill and Quire* reviewer Fred Boer, "told simply and effectively,

with both drama and suspense." Ruurs is also the author of an informational book on the Royal Canadian Mountain Police and an instructional book on how to get published; she is also a poet and has translated a popular children's book by Judith Viorst into Dutch.

Margriet Ruurs told *Something about the Author* (*SATA*): "Nothing is more fun than playing with words! I started writing stories and poems when I was in grade one. I wrote lots of stories and, thank goodness, my mom kept the scribblers with the poems I wrote when I was little.

"Reading, too, was my favorite pastime. I still read several books a week. I have books in my living room, books in my family room, books in my bedroom, and even books in my bathroom!

"Writing *A Mountain Alphabet* seems easy when you flip through the book now, but it took me almost two years to get the words just right, to say exactly what I wanted to say about life in the mountains. And I hope you have as much fun as I did trying to find all the hidden objects and letters in the book's illustrations!

"I like picture books. I read lots of them and do storytime in the public library every week. I was, therefore, thrilled when *Emma's Eggs* was awarded the 1997 Honor Title by the Storytelling World Awards.

"I love writing poetry. English is my second language and so it was hard for me to write poetry for a while but now I write poetry in both Dutch and English and do some translating as well.

"I teach lots of creative writing workshops in elementary schools and enjoy encouraging kids to write and read as much as they can. When I was little I thought that all authors were either very old or dead.... Now I like telling kids that they, too, can be authors. Being an author means you get to create lots of stories and use your imagination all the time. You have to keep your eyes and ears open for all the stories around. But it also means doing lots of rewriting and editing. That can be hard work but also does improve the final story, so it's worth it!

"I love being home and creating stories—first in my head and eventually on the computer. But I also enjoy traveling to schools and libraries to meet the kids who read my books. A book sitting on the shelf is just cardboard and paper, but a book in the hands of a reader comes to life! I write the stories but you make the book a book by reading it!"

■ Works Cited

Boer, Fred, review of *Big Little Dog, Quill and Quire,* May, 1993, p. 34.

Chatton, Barbara, review of *A Mountain Alphabet, School Library Journal,* February, 1997, pp. 97-98.

Donald, Bridget, review of *Emma's Eggs, Quill & Quire,* August, 1996, p. 42.

McNaughton, Janet, review of *A Mountain Alphabet,*
    Quill and Quire, December, 1996, pp. 36-37.

■ For More Information See

PERIODICALS

Books for Young People, June, 1987, p. 6.
Books in Canada, May, 1993, p. 31.
Canadian Materials, October, 1993, p. 184; January,
    1994, p. 11.

S–T

SALVADORI, Mario (George) 1907-1997

OBITUARY NOTICE—See index for SATA sketch: Born March 19, 1907, in Rome, Italy; came to the United States, 1939; naturalized U.S. citizen, 1944; died June 25, 1997, in Manhattan, NY. Engineer, educator, author. Salvadori was a successful structural engineer who made the study of architecture accessible to inner-city youths. Working with the New York Academy of Sciences, he taught the principles of building construction to Harlem and South Bronx junior-high students. Born in Italy, Salvadori first taught at the University of Rome from 1933 to 1938, eventually escaping Fascist rulership in 1939 to come to the United States. In America, Salvadori first worked for the Lionel Corporation as a time and motion engineer. In 1940 he began a lengthy association with Columbia University in New York City, first as a lecturer and ultimately as a professor of civil engineering and architecture. In 1975 he became a professor emeritus of architecture and the James Renwick Professor Emeritus of Civil Engineering at Columbia. In addition to his duties as an educator, he served as vice-president of the Industrial Products Trading Corporation from 1939 to 1942, as a consultant to the Manhattan Project from 1942 to 1944, and as consulting engineer to the firm of Paul Weidlinger. In 1962 he began three years as vice-president of Advanced Computer Techniques Corporation and in 1963 he became a partner with Weidlinger Associates, where he was named honorary chairperson in 1991. His work with junior-high students began in 1975. That year also saw the establishment of the Salvadori Educational Center on Built Environment, which he chaired until 1991, becoming honorary chairperson in 1993. During his career Salvadori also found time to write. Among his books are *The Mathematical Solution of Engineering Problems, Numerical Methods in Engineering* (with Melvin L. Baron), *Differential Equations in Engineering Problems* (with Ralph J. Schwarz), *Structure in Architecture* (with Robert Heller), *Structural Design in Architecture* (with Matthys Levy), *Statics and Strength of Structures* (with Jeremiah Eck and Giuseppe de Campoli), *Why Buildings Stand Up: The Strength of Architecture,* and a children's book, *Building: The Fight Against Gravity,* which received an award for children's nonfiction from the New York Academy of Sciences and a *Boston Globe-Horn Book* Award, both in 1980. In addition, Salvadori translated verse by Emily Dickinson into the Italian language.

OBITUARIES AND OTHER SOURCES:

PERIODICALS

New York Times, June 28, 1997, p. 28.

* * *

SAVAGE, Jeff 1961-

■ Personal

Born March 9, 1961, in Oakland, CA; son of Dick (a high school teacher) and Nancy (a high school secretary; maiden name, Johnson) Savage; married Nancy Conroy, August 20, 1994; children: Taylor. *Education:* University of California at San Diego, B.A., 1988. *Hobbies and other interests:* Reading, golfing, skiing, hiking, karate, flying airplanes, reading to children, school appearances.

■ Addresses

Home and office—17 Winestone Ct., Napa, CA 94558. *Electronic mail*—JSavagex @ ix.netcom.com.

■ Career

San Diego Union-Tribune, San Diego, CA, sportswriter/reporter, 1984-92; children's author, 1993—.

■ Awards, Honors

First place award, San Diego Press Club, 1992, for Best Sports Writing; Children's Choice Award, International Reading Association-Children's Book Council, 1995, for *Thurman Thomas, Star Running Back;* Honor Book, *Voice of Youth Advocates,* 1996, for *Gold Miners of the Wild West.*

JEFF SAVAGE

■ Writings

"SPORTS GREAT" SERIES

Sports Great Jim Abbott, Enslow, 1993.
Sports Great Karl Malone, Enslow, 1995.
Sports Great Brett Favre, Enslow, 1998.
Sports Great Juwan Howard, Enslow, in press.

"TAKING PART" SERIES

Kristi Yamaguchi: Pure Gold, Dillon, 1993.
Whitney Houston, Dillon, in press.

"SPORTS REPORTS" SERIES

Cal Ripken, Jr.: Star Shortstop, Enslow, 1994.
Thurman Thomas: Star Running Back, Enslow, 1994.
Deion Sanders: Star Athlete, Enslow, 1996.
Emmitt Smith: Star Running Back, Enslow, 1996.
Junior Seau: Star Linebacker, Enslow, 1997.

"WORKING OUT" SERIES

Aerobics, Crestwood (Parsippany, NJ), 1995.
Karate, Crestwood, 1995.
Running, Crestwood, 1995.
Weight Lifting, Crestwood, 1995.

"TRAILBLAZERS OF THE WILD WEST" SERIES

Cowboys and Cow Towns of the Wild West, Enslow, 1995.
Gold Miners of the Wild West, Enslow, 1995.
Gunfighters of the Wild West, Enslow, 1995.

Pioneering Women of the Wild West, Enslow, 1995.
Pony Express Riders of the Wild West, Enslow, 1995.
Scouts of the Wild West, Enslow, 1995.

"THE ACHIEVERS" SERIES

Julie Krone: Unstoppable Jockey, Lerner, 1996.
Andre Agassi: Reaching the Top Again, Lerner, 1997.
Barry Bonds: Mr. Excitement, Lerner, 1997.
Grant Hill: Humble Hotshot, Lerner, 1997.
Mike Piazza: Hard-Hitting Catcher, Lerner, 1997.
Tiger Woods: King of the Course, Lerner, 1997.
Paul Kariya: Hockey Magician, Lerner, 1998.
Drew Bledsoe, Lerner, in press.
Eric Lindros: Center of Attention, Lerner, in press.
Mia Hamm: Soccer Superstar, Lerner, in press.

"RACE CAR LEGENDS" SERIES

Motorcycles, Chelsea House, 1997.

"ACTION EVENTS" SERIES

Demolition Derby, Crestwood (Parsippany, NJ), 1997.
Drag Racing, Crestwood, 1997.
Monster Trucks, Crestwood, 1997.
Mud Racing, Crestwood, 1997.
Supercross Motorcycle Racing, Crestwood, 1997.
Truck and Tractor Pullers, Crestwood, 1997.

"FUNDAMENTAL SPORTS" SERIES

Fundamental Strength Training, Lerner, 1998.

"SPORTS TOP 10" SERIES

Top 10 Basketball Point Guards, Enslow, 1997.
Top 10 Basketball Power Forwards, Enslow, 1997.
Top 10 Football Sackers, Enslow, 1997.
Top 10 Professional Football Coaches, Enslow, 1998.
Top 10 Aggressive Inline Skaters, Enslow, in press.
Top 10 Heisman Trophy Winners, Enslow, in press.

"SPORTS ISSUES" SERIES

A Sure Thing? Sports and Gambling, Lerner, 1997.

OTHER

Demolition Derby, photographs by Larry Buche, Capstone, 1995.
Monster Truck Wars, photographs by David and Beverly Huntoon, Capstone, 1995.
Mud Racing, Capstone, 1995.
Truck and Tractor Pulling, Capstone, 1995.
A Career in Professional Sports, photographs by Peter Ford, Capstone, 1996.
Careers in Sports, Capstone, 1996.
In-Line Skating Basics, Capstone, 1996.
Motocross Cycles, Capstone, 1996.
Racing Cars, Capstone, 1996.
Wrestling Basics, Capstone, 1996.

■ Work in Progress

A series on superstar baseball and softball techniques; a series on olympic sports; several biographies.

■ Sidelights

Jeff Savage told *SATA:* "I remember the precise moment I became a writer. It happened in ninth grade English. The big assignment for the semester was to write a collection of poems. For weeks I toiled nightly beneath a bedlight glow to make my words and lines dance and sing and flow. I enjoyed this crafting process and enthusiastically handed in my work in the form of a book. Then came the day for our graded poems to be returned. I was seated in the far corner of the room. I remember the whispers and giggles of classmates over their marks as I was handed my book. I opened the cover to find my grade. *F.* No explanation, just a fat *F* in red pen across the page. *F* as in floored. Though shy as a boy I mustered enough courage to approach my teacher after class. "Those poems weren't yours," she said. "They were too good. You copied them." I went home confused. Then I grew angry. After class the next day I challenged my teacher to prove that I copied the poems. "Prove that you didn't," is all she said. Then she raised my grade to a *C.* C as in compromise, I guess. On my walk home that day I was struck by a thought. If my teacher guessed my poems were copied, if she gauged them to be professionally done, then as a writer I must be pretty good. That *C* grade took on a fresh look. It stood for confidence. And from that moment on—future career.

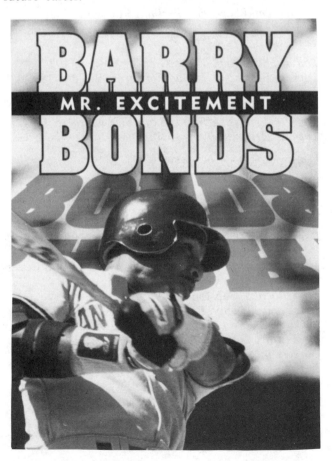

In his sports biography, Savage chronicles the life of all-star outfielder Barry Bonds.

"Though I am a person of varied interests, my writing has focused mainly on sports. I have tilled other fields, such as my series on trailblazing the West, but sports is my flower garden. It is a natural outgrowth of my interest in playing and following sports as a boy, and I've deliberately carried it into my career (first as sports editor for my college newspaper, next as a sports features writer for the *San Diego Union-Tribune,* now as a children's author). I prefer children as my audience because, like my wife, Nancy, who works hard as a special education teacher, I adore them.

"I have been told that a specialty of mine is painting a scene. That's good, because along with careful, concise writing, that is my plan. Certainly a biographer must be a recorder of events, but sports is filled with dates, scores, standings, and statistics, and it's easy to get lost in the jumble. I prefer tucking the numbers into the corners and bringing the characters out front, trying to flesh them out so that readers can feel them breathe and hear them laugh and cry. I commit a generous share of pages to childhood years to provide readers common ground. Thorough research is needed elsewhere; here I use the advantage exclusive to contemporary biographees—peer interviews. I like to talk with as many people as I can."

Savage's commitment to bringing young people closer to their sports heroes is evident in his "Sports Reports" and "Sports Achievers" series. The "Sports Reports" series includes the books *Thurman Thomas: Star Running Back* and *Cal Ripken, Jr.: Star Shortstop.* These works discuss the professional and personal lives of their subjects while highlighting their outstanding achievements. Savage also organizes statistics and facts about each player into "understandable charts and tables," noted *Voice of Youth Advocates* contributor Mary Anne Nichols. To add more depth to the series, Savage quotes people who are associated with the athletes. The author's research provides a "fairly substantial amount of information," according to reviewer Tom S. Hurlburt of *School Library Journal.* Hurlburt added that for students interested in sports biographies, Savage's books should be given "strong consideration."

The "Achievers" series includes books such as *Julie Krone: Unstoppable Jockey* and *Barry Bonds: Mr. Excitement.* This series is similar to "Sports Reports" in that it covers statistics and facts about the athletes. In addition to the basic information, Savage shares individual challenges that each sports star faced and overcame, such as prejudice and sexism. *School Library Journal* contributor Blair Christolon asserted that the "Sports Achievers" series "will be appreciated by readers who want to know just a bit more" about their favorite athletes. Acknowledging the athletes' past difficulties as stepping stones to their success is "inspiring," maintained Laura Tillotson of *Booklist.*

Savage takes on a different perspective in books like *Drag Racing, Demolition Derby,* and *Truck and Tractor Pullers.* These books are part of the author's "Action Events" series in which he re-creates the excitement of

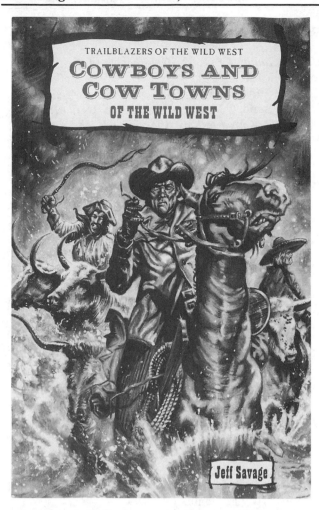

TRAILBLAZERS OF THE WILD WEST
COWBOYS AND COW TOWNS OF THE WILD WEST

Jeff Savage

Savage presents a vivid picture of the Wild West through the experiences of cowboys, gunslingers, ranchers, and businessmen. (Cover illustration by Paul Daly.)

motorsports. Savage relays the experiences of drivers, car designers, and team members for those who desire a realistic view of the powerful vehicles and competitions. In a review of *Drag Racing, Mud Racing,* and *Supercross Motorcycle Racing, School Library Journal* contributor Patricia Manning said that "Savage's writing style ranges from lively to competent sports-page reportage ... exactly what novices to both the sport featured and to reading for pleasure are likely to enjoy." *School Library Journal* contributor Ann G. Brouse, reviewing *Demolitian Derby, Monster Trucks,* and *Truck and Tractor Pullers,* noted that Savage's integration of behind-the-scene activities gives motorsports fans a "better understanding of the effort and preparation that go into the competitions they enjoy."

Another subject of interest to Savage is the "Wild West." The author's "Trailblazers of the Wild West" series includes *Cowboys and Cow Towns of the Wild West* and *Gold Miners of the Wild West.* Savage captures the livelihood of the old frontier in presenting readers with historical events, famous gunslingers (e.g., Billy the Kid), the lifestyle of cowboys, and major contributions from African Americans and women. *School Library*

Journal contributor Rosie Peasley praised Savage's series as "well written, well organized, and packed with information." A *Voice of Youth Advocates* reviewer concluded that with Savage's engaging facts "individual readers can pursue any number of fascinating pathways."

"I once heard a prominent publisher at a convention say, 'Don't be prolific. Write one book a year, two at the most,'" Savage continued to *SATA.* "Great advice for some. Not me. I've been conditioned by a decade of newspaper work to pitch into projects in this manner: investigate, write with passion, polish up, print. I'm most comfortable that way. In fact, the deliberate pace of book publishing took some getting used to, with my first editor practicing great patience with my weekly progress inquiries ('Is it still in galleys?' 'Is it still at the printer?' 'Where is it now?'). Only recently have I settled into the rhythm of book publishing. I'm not yet producing at the rate I'd like, but I'm getting closer. With each book my aim is to outdo the last. Bruce Brooks once wrote to me: 'Keep reading and writing,' suggesting inseparability, and I have learned it is so. Reading completes writing. I am grateful just to be in this wonderful business having a try."

■ **Works Cited**

Brouse, Ann G., review of *Demolition Derby, Monster Trucks,* and *Truck and Tractor Pullers, School Library Journal,* February, 1997, p. 98.

Christolon, Blair, review of *Julie Krone: Unstoppable Jockey, School Library Journal,* September, 1996, p. 217.

Review of *Gold Miners of the Wild West, Voice of Youth Advocates,* August, 1996, p. 151.

Hurlburt, Tom S., review of *Cal Ripken, Jr.: Star Shortstop, School Library Journal,* February, 1995, p. 109.

Manning, Patricia, review of *Mud Racing* and *Supercross Motorcycle Racing, School Library Journal,* February, 1997, p. 124.

Nichols, Mary Anne, review of *Thurman Thomas: Star Running Back, Voice of Youth Advocates,* October, 1994, p. 228.

Peasley, Rosie, review of *Cowboys and Cow Towns of the Wild West, School Library Journal,* February, 1996, p. 110.

Tillotson, Laura, review of *Julie Krone: Unstoppable Jockey, Booklist,* August, 1996, p. 1899.

■ **For More Information See**

PERIODICALS

Booklist, April 15, 1996, pp. 1435-36.
Kirkus Reviews, June 1, 1995, p. 786.
School Library Journal, February, 1994, p. 117; August, 1994, p. 158; October, 1995, p. 151; January, 1996, p. 125; February, 1997, p. 124.

SNYDER, Bernadette McCarver 1930-

■ Personal

Born December 6, 1930, in Long Island, NY; daughter of William C. (in business) and Hazel (Davids) McCarver; married John W. Snyder (a federal civil servant), September 28, 1963; children: Matthew J. *Education:* Attended Washington University, St. Louis, MO. *Politics:* Conservative. *Religion:* Roman Catholic.

■ Addresses

Home and office—1201 Cheverly Ct., St. Louis, MO 63146-4625.

■ Career

Writer. Worked as television writer and producer in advertising and marketing, Nashville, TN, and St. Louis, MO; writer and narrator of public service radio pieces for Missionary Oblates, 1985—. Public speaker.

■ Writings

Graham Crackers, Galoshes, and God: Everywoman's Book of Cope and Hope, Liguori Publications (Liguori, MO), 1982, revised edition, 1995.

BERNADETTE McCARVER SNYDER

The Kitchen Sink Prayer Book, Liguori Publications, 1984.

More Graham Crackers, Galoshes, and God, Liguori Publications, 1985.

Heavenly Hash: A Tasty Mix of Mother's Meditations, Our Sunday Visitor (Huntington, IN), 1985.

Merry Mary Meditations, Liguori Publications, 1987.

(With Hazelmai McCarver Terry) *Cycle C: Decorating for Sundays and Holy Days,* Twenty-Third Publications (Mystic, CT), 1988.

(With Terry) *Cycle A: Decorating for Sundays and Holy Days; Themes, Homily Suggestions, Activities,* Twenty-Third Publications, 1989.

365 Fun Facts for Catholic Kids, Liguori Publications, 1989.

150 Fun Facts Found in the Bible: For Kids of All Ages, illustrated by Chris Sharp, Liguori Publications, 1990.

(With Terry) *Cycle B: Decorating for Sundays and Holy Days,* Twenty-Third Publications, 1990.

The Fun Facts Dictionary: A World of Weird and Wonderful Words, illustrated by Chris Sharp, Liguori Publications, 1991.

That's Life! Featuring the Wit and Wisdom of Bernadette McCarver Snyder, Liguori Publications, 1991.

115 Saintly Fun Facts: Daring Deeds, Heroic Happenings, Serendipitous Surprises for Kids of All Ages, Liguori Publications, 1993.

Painting Rainbows with Broken Crayons: 101 Prayers for Teachers, Parents, and Other Caretakers, Ave Maria Press (Notre Dame, IN), 1995.

Mildew, Mudpies, and Miracles: Gleeful Glimpses into the Whirl of a Woman's World, Charis/Servant Publications (Ann Arbor, MI), 1995.

Have You Ever Seen an Elephant Sneeze? A Zany Zooful of God's Creatures, illustrated by James Richter, Ave Maria Press, 1996.

Have You Ever Heard a Hummingbird Hum? A Colorful Cavalcade of God's Feathery Friends, illustrated by Richter, Ave Maria Press, 1997.

Saintly Celebrations and Holy Holidays: Easy and Imaginative Ideas to Create Your Own Catholic Family Traditions, 1997.

Regular columnist, *Our Sunday Visitor,* 1982—.

■ Sidelights

Bernadette McCarver Snyder told *Something about the Author (SATA):* "My career was in advertising and marketing, with an occasional sale of a humor article. It had never occurred to me to consider writing anything inspirational until I worked in the advertising department of a publishing house that published inspirational books. I decided to try a humorous inspirational book and have since had more than twenty of them published."

SOBOTT-MOGWE, Gaele 1956-

■ Personal

Born April 24, 1956, in Australia; daughter of Allan (in business) and Gladys Sobott; children: Lorato, Thara, Latif.

■ Addresses

Home—London, England. *Office*—c/o Heinemann, Halley Court, Jordan Hill, Oxford OX2 8EJ, England. *Electronic mail*—sobottmogwe @ msn.com.

■ Career

Writer.

■ Writings

FOR CHILDREN; FICTION

The Magic Pool, Heinemann (Oxford, England), 1991.
Thara and the Cassipoohkaman, Baobab Press (Harare, Zimbabwe), 1992.
Speckled Eggs, illustrated by Helen Wilson, Longman (Harlow, England), 1993.
Weird Wambo, Heinemann (Oxford), 1994.
Tumelo and the Blue Birds, Heinemann (Oxford), 1995.
Mare's Aunt, illustrated by Steve Jobson, Longman, 1995.
Tickles, Heinemann (Oxford), 1997.

Children's work represented in anthologies, including *The River That Went to the Sky,* edited by Mary Medlicott, Kingfisher Larousse (London, England), 1995.

OTHER

Colour Me Blue (adult novel), Heinemann (Portsmouth, NH), 1995.

Work represented in anthologies, including *Fishwives and Fabulists,* edited by Daphne Glazer, Manutius Press (Liverpool, England), 1995. Contributor to periodicals, including *Staffrider, Tok, Big Issue, Bete Noir, Journal of Gender Studies,* and *Wasafiri.*

■ Work in Progress

A novel set in southern Africa; a bio-bibliographical study of black South African women writers.

*   *   *

SOENTPIET, Chris K. 1970-

■ Personal

Name is pronounced *soon-pete;* born January 3, 1970, in Seoul, Korea; son of Hariette Orr (self-employed); married Rosanna, May 22, 1995. *Education:* Pratt Institute, B.F.A., 1992.

■ Addresses

Home and office—327 Washington Ave., Brooklyn, NY 11205. *Agent*—Rosanna Soentpiet, 327 Washington Ave., Brooklyn, NY 11205. *Electronic mail*—soentpiet @ aol.com.

■ Career

Illustrator and author. Active presenter at schools and organizations.

■ Awards, Honors

Pick of the List, American Booksellers Association, 1995, Top One Hundred Titles, New York Public Library, 1995, Notable Children's Trade Book in the Field of Social Studies, National Council for the Social Studies (NCSS), 1995, Notable Books, *Smithsonian Magazine,* 1995, all for *The Last Dragon;* Children's Book of the Year Award, and Teacher's Choice, both from International Reading Association, Top 10 Children's Books, *Chicago Tribune,* Notable Books, American Library Association, Top 25 Picks for Youth, *Black History,* Notable Books for a Global Society Award, International Reading Association, Pick of the List, American Booksellers Association, and Book Links Salutes a Few Good Books, all 1996, all for *More Than Anything Else;* Gold Medalist, Society of Illustrators,

CHRIS K. SOENTPIET

Notable Children's Trade Book in the Field of Social Studies, NCSS, Pick of the List, American Booksellers Association, Notable Books, *Smithsonian Magazine,* Notable Children's Books for a Global Society, International Reading Association, Best Books, *San Francisco Chronicle,* all 1996, all for *Peacebound Trains.*

■ Writings

SELF-ILLUSTRATED PICTURE BOOKS

Around Town, Lothrop, Lee & Shepard, 1994.

ILLUSTRATOR

Susan Miho Nunes, *The Last Dragon,* Clarion, 1995.
Marie Bradby, *More Than Anything Else,* Orchard, 1995.
Haemi Balgassi, *Peacebound Trains,* Clarion, 1996.
Cynthia Rylant, *Silver Packages,* Orchard, 1997.
George Ella Lyon, *A Sign,* Orchard, 1998.
Eve Bunting, *So Far from the Sea,* Clarion, 1998.

■ Work in Progress

Silence in the Mountains, to be published by Orchard Books, a story of a Lebanese family immigrating to the United States; *Gift from Korea,* for Lothrop, Lee & Shepard; illustrations for Thomas Barron's *Where's Grandpa?,* for Philomel.

■ Sidelights

Chris K. Soentpiet told *SATA:* "In November 1978, at the age of eight, I was adopted with my older sister from Korea to live with an American family in Hawaii. I went from being the youngest sibling of my Korean family to becoming a middle child of my American family. Two years ago, I had the opportunity to visit my Korean brothers and sisters for the first time since I was adopted nineteen years ago. It was an emotional and happy reunion. (Currently I am writing a story about my adoption to America.)"

Soentpiet is a children's book illustrator and author whose paintings have been praised as warm, detailed, and lively. Critics have highlighted the expressive qualities of Soentpiet's portrayals of people—especially in the faces of the characters in Haemi Balgassi's *Peacebound Trains,* a tale of a young Korean girl waiting for the return of her mother. Still others emphasize the liveliness of the artist's detailed settings—particularly in his own *Around Town* and in the illustrations for Susan Miho Nunes's *The Last Dragon,* both of which are said to display the energy of their urban settings. Soentpiet was born in Korea and educated in the United States, where he was befriended by children's book illustrator Ted Lewin, whose style is considered to have influenced the young artist.

As Soentpiet told *SATA:* "With encouragement and guidance from my good friend, author and illustrator

Cities have hydrants for hot summer days.

In his first picture book, Soentpiet vividly portrays summer in the city through the eyes of a young girl and her mother. (From *Around Town,* written and illustrated by Soentpiet.)

Ted Lewin, I took my portfolio along with some original paintings around New York City. The first ten publishers I visited did not have work for me, until I stepped into the office of Lothrop, Lee and Shepard. They gave me my first opportunity to illustrate and author a children's picture book: *Around Town.*"

In *Around Town,* "lively, ... realistic paintings, splashed with sunlight and color ... celebrate life in the city," according to Hazel Rochman, who reviewed the publication for *Booklist.* The accompanying narrative describes the sights and sounds of a big city as experienced by a young girl and her mother. "This vibrant, exuberant tour of New York City ... will delight children," maintained Janet M. Bair in *School Library Journal.* Likewise, the play of emotions across Peter Chang's face in Soentpiet's illustrations for Susan Miho Nunes's *The Last Dragon* "light up the book," according to *School Library Journal* contributor Margaret A. Chang. Together the author and artist convey Peter's initial discouragement at being left in his great-aunt's home for the summer in Chinatown, as well as his growing excitement as he finds an old ten-person dragon in a shop window and sets about enlisting the aid of various Chinatown residents to help repair it. Critics praised Soentpiet's richly detailed watercolor illustrations, which "are warm, colorful, and full of details unique to Chinatown," Leone McDermott concluded in her review in *Booklist.*

Equally well received were the illustrations for Marie Bradby's *More Than Anything Else,* a fictionalized account of the young Booker T. Washington's struggle to learn to read. The artist "makes the most of lantern, candle, and hearth-lit settings," remarked Elizabeth Bush in *Bulletin of the Center for Children's Books,* "casting deep shadows around the finely individuated features of his characters." In a similar vein, *Quill & Quire* critic Joanne Schott observed that Soentpiet's striking images of lamp-lit characters is reflective of a theme of the book—that literacy, like light, can illuminate the darkness of the mind.

In *Peacebound Trains,* Soentpiet's illustrations again reflect the strong emotions of his characters as he depicts the sadness of Sumi, who watches the trains go by her home in South Korea, waiting for her mother to return from a stint in the army. She is comforted by her grandmother, who tells the heartrending story of the train that separated her own husband from his wife and family as he remained behind to defend the family home from the communist invasion of Seoul years before. "The richly colored illustrations are splashed with light, and convey the unfolding drama," remarked Cynthia K. Richey in *School Library Journal.* Critics praised the unusual combination picture book-chapter book for the information its pictures and text yield about the civil war in Korea as well as the hardships of life during wartime in general.

Soentpiet has contributed the illustrations to several award-winning picture books, garnering praise for the care with which he conveys the emotional lives of his characters. In addition, the detail with which the illustrator paints scenes from New York City in his *Around Town,* of Chinatown in *The Last Dragon,* of the Reconstruction-era South in *More Than Anything Else,* and of the South Korean countryside in *Peacebound Trains,* is considered a valuable extension of the information provided in the texts of these books.

■ Works Cited

Bair, Janet M., review of *Around Town, School Library Journal,* May, 1994, p. 104.

Bush, Elizabeth, review of *More Than Anything Else, Bulletin of the Center for Children's Books,* October, 1995, p. 47.

Chang, Margaret A., review of *The Last Dragon, School Library Journal,* May, 1995, p. 93.

McDermott, Leone, review of *The Last Dragon, Booklist,* May 1, 1995, p. 1580.

Richey, Cynthia K., review of *Peacebound Trains, School Library Journal,* January, 1997, p. 75.

Rochman, Hazel, review of *Around Town, Booklist,* April 1, 1994, p. 1457.

Schott, Joanne, review of *More Than Anything Else, Quill & Quire,* October, 1995, p. 47.

■ For More Information See

PERIODICALS

Bulletin of the Center for Children's Books, October, 1996, p. 48.

Horn Book, September-October, 1995, pp. 586-87.

Kirkus Reviews, March 15, 1994, p. 404; August 1, 1996, p. 1146.

Publishers Weekly, March 7, 1994, p. 70.

*   *   *

THOMAS, Rob

■ Personal

Education: Attended University of Texas at Austin. *Hobbies and other interests:* Performing with rock bands, playing basketball and other sports.

■ Addresses

Home—Austin, TX. *Agent*—Jennifer Robinson, Peter Miller & Association Literary and Film Management, Los Angeles, CA.

■ Career

Author. Teacher of high-school journalism. Channel One (news show for teenage students), Los Angeles, CA, staff member. *Member:* Society of Children's Book Writers and Illustrators, Austin Writer's League.

■ Writings

Rats Saw God, Simon & Schuster, 1996.
Slave Day, Simon & Schuster, 1997.

ROB THOMAS

Doing Time: Notes from the Undergrad (short stories), Simon & Schuster, 1997.
Satellite Down, Simon & Schuster, 1998.

Contributor of a short story entitled *Pet Stories* to *Seventeen* magazine.

■ Work in Progress

A four book series called "The Gifted" for Simon & Schuster.

■ Sidelights

Even as a high school journalism teacher and part-time musician, Rob Thomas always knew he was going to be a writer one day—just as soon as he found the time. "Writing a book was always sort of this mountain out there in my future that I was going to climb someday," Thomas told Joel Shoemaker in a *Voice of Youth Advocates* interview. Eventually disciplining himself to write a page of manuscript every morning, Thomas was able to complete his first novel, *Rats Saw God,* before he was thirty. That book's success with teen readers prompted Thomas to increase his output to three pages a day—and quit his day job to become a full-time writer.

Rats Saw God finds high school senior Steve York on a downslide. He could care less about school—and his future—since learning that the girl who had captured his heart was actually having an affair with one of the teachers at school. Halfway through his junior year in Texas, when he first discovers the truth, Steve begins to do drugs and hang out with the wrong crowd; his grades plummet and he ends the year by bailing out altogether and going to California. Returning to school the following September, Steve is offered a deal by a concerned guidance counselor: if the disillusioned, rebellious teen is willing to chronicle the events leading up to his current self-destructive state in a one-hundred-page story, he can earn back missing English credits needed for graduation. Steve's story provides readers with an understanding of his change in attitude: His parents divorce and his mother leaves, relations with his emotionally distant father deteriorate, and then he falls in love with Dub in a Dadaist club at school, only to stumble upon the secret relationship between her and one of Steve's favorite teachers, Mr. Waters.

While noting that the length of *Rats Saw God* may turn away some readers, *Horn Book* contributor Lauren Adams maintained that Steve's "typically adolescent struggles are related with funny, self-mocking sarcasm and lots of one-liners ... that make for an entertaining and engaging read." Praising Thomas's ear for teen-speak, a *Publishers Weekly* critic noted that the author's "sharp descriptions of cliques, clubs and annoying authority figures will strike a familiar chord." Writing in *Bulletin of the Center for Children's Books,* reviewer Deborah Stevenson claims Thomas's "tone and atmosphere" will attract readers, going on to say, "wisecracking Steve tells his story with an authentically adolescent shallow glibness."

Thomas's second book, *Slave Day,* encompasses a single twelve-hour period during which both student council members and teachers are auctioned off to students as a way to earn money for functions at a Texas high school. On this particular "Slave Day," African-American student Keene Davenport decides to "buy" popular class president Shawn Greeley. Shawn, a school basketball star, is also black; while Keene participates in the fundraiser to demonstrate how it demeans blacks, Shawn has a different perspective, prompted in no small part by his desire to maintain his student-council presidency in the next election. Differing points of view about the school tradition are also expressed by the six other narrators of Thomas's third novel, which follows a number of crises occurring that day at Robert E. Lee High School, including a rape attempt, a computer break-in by the class nerd, and a host of other activities characterized by a *Kirkus Reviews* critic as "scary, sobering, hilarious, and triumphant." *Slave Day*'s "vernacular language and ironic plot twists drive the story," commented Shoemaker in his *Voice of Youth Advocates* review, "while character development is complete enough to show that most characters, even the cruel and shallow ..., have some redeeming qualities."

Slave Day was inspired by Thomas's own experience while teaching journalism in a high school in Austin, Texas, where most of the student body was African American. The decision to include within his novel the first-person viewpoint of two blacks rather than just one allowed Thomas to explore contrasting views of racism and other social issues in the book. "I would have been much more nervous had I written from only one black character's perspective," Thomas explained to Shoemaker. "Then, I'm afraid whatever that character was like, it would have been seen as my take on what all African Americans sound/behave like. If I had just had

In Thomas's irreverently funny novel, cynical teenager Steve York recapitulates the heartbreak and disillusionment of his junior year in high school. (Cover illustration by Chris Raschka.)

Shawn in the book, or Keene, *that* would have been scary."

Satellite Down is Thomas's attempt to answer the question he phrased to Shoemaker: "What would happen if a teenaged boy was handed everything he dreamed of and then discovered most of what he grew up believing was a lie?" In this novel, Patrick Sheridan leaves his small Texan town for an internship in Los Angeles with Classroom Direct, a national television network for schools. While in Los Angeles, Patrick's education takes an unforeseen turn when he discovers his co-workers' corrupt journalistic ethics. Disillusioned with his experience in television, he decides to leave for Northern Ireland, afraid of what he has uncovered. Thomas has also written *Doing Time: Notes from the Undergrad,* a collection of humorous short fiction about school-related experiences shared by many young adults. His novels and short stories continue to explore the issues of adolescence and early adulthood in a sometimes quirky but always humorous fashion.

The characters in Thomas's books are so vivid that many of his readers come away believing that the outrageous plot twists have at their heart things that the author has actually experienced. And many readers write to ask Thomas which of his characters reflects his own personality. "I purposely made Steve York my opposite," the author explained to Shoemaker, referring to the protagonist of *Rats Saw God.* "First of all, Steve was, and possibly is, much smarter than me. He would have loathed me," Thomas admitted, noting that, unlike his protagonist, he was active in both sports and school clubs and got along "terrifically" with his parents. "I dug high school," the novelist maintained, which may explain why writing for young adults has become Thomas's full-time occupation.

■ Works Cited

Adams, Lauren, review of *Rats Saw God, Horn Book,* July-August, 1996, p. 471.

Review of *Rats Saw God, Publishers Weekly,* June 10, 1996, pp. 100-01.

Shoemaker, Joel, "Rats Saw Rob: An Interview with Rob Thomas," *Voice of Youth Advocates,* June, 1997, pp. 89-91.

Shoemaker, Joel, review of *Slave Day, Voice of Youth Advocates,* June, 1997, p. 91.

Review of *Slave Day, Kirkus Reviews,* February 15, 1997, p. 306.

Stevenson, Deborah, review of *Rats Saw God, Bulletin of the Center for Children's Books,* May, 1996, p. 317.

■ For More Information See

PERIODICALS

Booklist, June 1-15, 1996, p. 1704.

Publishers Weekly, February 17, 1997, p. 220.

V–W

VULTURE, Elizabeth T.
See GILBERT, Suzie

* * *

WILLIAMS, Dorothy
See WILLIAMS, Marcia (Dorothy)

* * *

WILLIAMS, Marcia (Dorothy) 1945-
(Dorothy Williams)

■ Personal

Born August 8, 1945, in England; daughter of Martin Innes Gregson (an army officer and farmer) and Joan Alexander Carnwath (a writer); married Tudor Williams, February 21, 1976 (separated); children: Araminta Scarfe, Rufus Williams. *Education:* Educated in England and Switzerland. *Hobbies and other interests:* Animals, reading, travel, food, friends, and film.

■ Addresses

Home—London, England. *Office*—Walker Books, Ltd., 87 Vauxhall Walk, London SE11 5HJ, England.

■ Career

Freelance writer and illustrator of children's books, 1986—.

■ Writings

SELF-ILLUSTRATED

The First Christmas, Random House, 1987.
The Amazing Story of Noah's Ark, Walker Books (London), 1988.
When I Was Little, Walker Books, 1989.
Jonah and the Whale, Random House, 1989.
Not a Worry in the World, Walker Books, 1990, Crown, 1991.

MARCIA WILLIAMS

Joseph and His Magnificent Coat of Many Colors, Walker Books, 1990, Candlewick Press, 1992.
Greek Myths for Young Children, Walker Books, 1991, Candlewick Press, 1992.
(Reteller) Miguel de Cervantes, *Don Quixote,* Candlewick Press, 1993.
(Reteller) *Sinbad the Sailor,* Candlewick Press, 1994.
(Reteller) *The Adventures of Robin Hood,* Candlewick Press, 1995.
King Arthur and the Knights of the Round Table, Candlewick Press, 1996.
(Reteller) *The Iliad and the Odyssey,* Candlewick Press, 1996.

■ Work in Progress

A book on William Shakespeare's plays; a book of Monsters; a book of Dragons.

■ Sidelights

Picture-book author and illustrator Marcia Williams is a writer by tradition as well as by inclination. The daughter of a writer, Williams grew up with books readily available and saw firsthand the discipline need-ed to successfully write for a living. Now a popular author and illustrator, British-born Williams has brought the classic stories she recalls from her own childhood to life for young children: from Sinbad the Sailor and Robin Hood to Noah and the animals and the gods of Greek mythology, people from many ages and cultures live for modern readers through her tales.

Born in England, Williams spent much of her childhood in boarding school, away from her parents. Homesick, she sent her mother and father self-illustrated letters recounting her day-to-day experiences. Sometimes she even wrote a poem to add to her letters. "This is where my career began," she would later quip to *Something about the Author* (*SATA*). Williams's mother, also a writer, had a passion for books, and when the two were together she would often read her daughter excerpts from classics and mythology. "I found [Marcel] Proust and the Greek myths a little hard going," the author recalled. "I was delighted, therefore, to discover later that many of these stories were exciting and amusing. I think this is why I enjoy making classic tales accessible to young children."

Moving from school to school did not make Williams exactly fall in love with reading. "Always the first thing that happened in a new classroom was having to stand up and read in front of your peers to make sure you had reached the required level," she remembered. "I even find the memory of it a torture. Also, there were very few picture books available, so most classics were read from adult versions, not for pleasure but as preparation for a test. It was only when I had my own children that I came to realize the joy of books. So I think I create books now to make up for all those lost years of pleasure, and to give books to others like Alice and myself who can't see the point of books 'without pictures and conversation.'"

While she had always enjoyed writing and illustrating stories and cards for friends, Williams never received formal art training; she viewed her creative outlet as a hobby rather than as a potential career. That would all change after the birth of her second child in the late 1980s. "I was very lucky to visit Walker Books with a Christmas picture on a day they were looking for someone to write and illustrate the Christmas story," she remembered. "When I look back on it now, I find it hard to believe that I had the nerve to present myself, or that the art designer had the nerve to give a book to a complete novice. Maybe he never realized!" The rela-tionship that Williams established with Walker Books

has continued for over a decade. As the illustrator notes, "creating picture books has become as important to me as breathing."

Published in 1988, Williams's interpretation of *The First Christmas* follows the traditional story while also adding images of the way the holiday is celebrated in different parts of the world. Called an "energetic and appealing book" by a *School Library Journal* reviewer, *The First Christmas* would be the first of several books its author would publish on Biblical themes. Her *The Amazing Story of Noah's Ark* closely follows the story from the Book of Genesis and is chock-full of animals and activity, with William's colorful drawings augment-ed by "text ... ingeniously distributed over the illustra-tions," according to a *Junior Bookshelf* critic. Calling the book an "exuberant folk-art treatment," *School Library Journal* contributor Patricia Dooley praises William's adaptation of *Joseph and His Magnificent Coat of Many Colors* for a preschool audience respon-sive to bright colors, animals, and a sense of magic.

From Bible stories, Williams has also moved to the myths of Greece she recalled from her childhood. In the highly praised *Greek Myths for Young Children,* she introduces youngsters to the timeless stories of Pando-ra's Box, Hercules, Daedalus and Icarus, Arachne, and the Minotaur, among others. Using a lighthearted tone to dilute some of the tales' darker moments—such as Icarus being drowned in the sea after flying too close to the sun—Betsy Hearne, writing in in *Bulletin of the Center for Children's Books,* applauded Williams's col-lection for inducing "a broad range of kids to become culturally literate as they pore over [her] comic-strip versions" of otherwise offputting classic myths. The author/illustrator's "brightly colored cartoon figures and the witty asides they trade emphasize the vitality and down-to-earth character of the tales," in the opinion of *School Library Journal* essayist Patricia Dooley. The author continues her lighthearted approach in her retelling of Homer's epic stories in *The Iliad and the Odyssey,* published in 1996. Peter F. Neumeyer, in a *Boston Globe* review, lauded her use of the comic-panel format through which he estimated Williams provided over two hundred illustrations with endpapers compris-ing another forty-two panels, telling a "wartime story both serious and witty." He praised her ability to juggle "a sober, straightforward running narrative" with a "modern-lingo, ironic, and iconoclastic repartee," to-gether with "illustrations that not only elucidate but themselves editorialize with wit and irony." Spanning the ages and the continents, Williams has also turned her attention to the legends of her native Great Britain. In *The Adventures of Robin Hood* she recounts numer-ous escapades of the outlaw of Sherwood Forest in her characteristic witty fashion, making "this rendition of the Robin Hood legend both an easy laugh and an easy read," according to *Booklist* contributor Julie Walton. Praising Williams's use of earthy greens, golds, and browns rather than her usual brilliant colors, a *Publish-ers Weekly* critic noted that *The Adventures of Robin Hood* "may well be her most child-appreciated work yet." The regal King Arthur comes in for much the same

Robin was offended that the sheriff would think someone could outshoot him, so he and Little John hatched a plot of their own. That evening, as the sheriff and his henchmen sat bemoaning their failure, an arrow flew through the window, burying itself in the table. Attached to the arrow was this message:

Now heaven bless thy Grace this day, Say all in sweet Sherwood. For thou didst give the prize away To Merry Robin Hood!

Williams lends a buoyant touch to her rendition of the tales of Robin Hood. (From *The Adventures of Robin Hood,* written and illustrated by Williams.)

treatment at Williams's hands, as the adventures of the sturdy knights of the round table are augmented by quips, jokes, and a steady stream of one-liners. While *Booklist* reviewer Carolyn Phelan noted that the presentation "is not for every taste," critic Deborah Stevenson praised *King Arthur and the Knights of the Round Table* in her review for *Bulletin of the Center for Children's Books* as "an amiable and breezily told introduction to a durable legend, with adventure, broad comedy, and atmosphere aplenty."

Williams considers herself a very disciplined worker; she has been known to devote seven days a week, ten hours a day, to a book project. "I work in my bedroom, so it is sometimes difficult to shut off, but one day I hope to have a studio," the author-illustrator told *SATA*. "I spend a long time getting the story right as, although my books are short on texts, I believe this means the story has to be even stronger to hold the weight of the illustrations." She employs a style of illustration called "comic-strip" style, wherein inked drawings tinted with watercolor flow from scene to scene along a linear "strip," with captions printed below and "bubbles" within each picture providing additional dialogue. This style grew out of her desire to communicate with young readers on more than one level. "A child recently told me that he understood my books perfectly," the illustrator told *SATA*. "The main text and pictures were for him to share with his Mum and Dad, but the speech bubbles were just for him. I was delighted at his perception and the feeling that we had formed this special bond, and of course he was right. The speech bubbles are also a wonderful opportunity to add a bit of anarchic humor and animation to the stories," Williams added, "helping to make them accessible by bringing them into the child's own orbit of experience."

Because of the comic-book style she employs, there is a sense of theatricality about Williams's books that is intentional on the part of the author/illustrator. "I have always loved the theatre and in many ways I see my books as theatre on the page, and I am the lucky one who gets all the parts!" she explained. "Sheer greed and sheer delight. I hope the delight communicates itself to the reader." The books Williams designs are very labour-intensive, "not only for me but also for the whole publishing team, in particular my editor and art designer." She credits the "unstinting support and generosity" of the staff at Walker Books with part of her success.

Text and illustration remain equally important to Williams: "I strive not to use one to reiterate the other, but to weave them together to build up character and atmosphere until they become a satisfying whole." At home in her vocation as author and illustrator, Williams continues to imbue new life in old stories. "I love my work and can't imagine any other career," she told *SATA*. "I enjoy every part of making a book and also enjoy visiting schools and talking to children who are an endless inspiration and always manage to look at things from unexpected angles."

■ Works Cited

Review of *The Adventures of Robin Hood, Publishers Weekly,* January 30, 1995, p. 100.

Review of *The Amazing Story of Noah's Ark, Junior Bookshelf,* February, 1989, p. 15.

Dooley, Patricia, review of *Joseph and His Magnificent Coat of Many Colors, School Library Journal,* April, 1992, p. 102.

Dooley, Patricia, "Beyond Cultural Literacy: The Enduring Power of Myths," *School Library Journal,* June, 1994, pp. 52-3.

Review of *The First Christmas, School Library Journal,* October, 1988, p. 38.

Hearne, Betsy, review of *Greek Myths for Young Children, Bulletin of the Center for Children's Books,* November, 1992, pp. 94-95.

Neumeyer, Peter F., review of *The Classics Illustrated, Boston Globe,* September 7, 1997.

Phelan, Carolyn, review of *King Arthur and the Knights of the Round Table, Booklist,* April 15, 1996, p. 1438.

Stevenson, Deborah, review of *King Arthur and the Knights of the Round Table, Bulletin of the Center for Children's Books,* March, 1996, p. 247.

Walton, Julie, review of *The Adventures of Robin Hood, Booklist,* March 15, 1995, p. 1327.

■ For More Information See

PERIODICALS

Booklist, June 15, 1992, p. 1843; March 1, 1994, p. 1267.

Books for Your Children, spring, 1992, p. 13.

Bulletin of the Center for Children's Books, May, 1995, p. 326; February, 1997, p. 227.

Horn Book, January-February, 1997, p. 82.

Junior Bookshelf, December, 1989, p. 269; February, 1992, p. 35; April, 1993, p. 72.

Kirkus Reviews, March 1, 1994, p. 312.

Magpies, July, 1995, p. 8; September, 1995, pp. 16-17.

Publishers Weekly, August 26, 1988, p. 85; April 27, 1992, p. 267; October 19, 1992, p. 78; March 1, 1993, p. 57; March 11, 1996, p. 66; November 25, 1996, p. 75.

School Librarian, May, 1992, p. 58.

School Library Journal, July, 1989, p. 81; April, 1995, p. 148.

Times Educational Supplement, September 9, 1994.

*   *   *

WOOD, Frances M. 1951-

■ Personal

Born October 30, 1951, in Washington; daughter of Edward C. (an engineer) and Obdulia (Doan) Wood; married Brian J. Morton (an environmental economist), August 30, 1975. *Education:* Attended Brown University, 1969-71; Stanford University, B.A., 1973; University of California, Berkeley, M.L.S., 1976. *Hobbies and other interests:* Hiking, music, pets (a dog and a cat).

FRANCES M. WOOD

■ Addresses

Agent—Frances Kuffel, Jean V. Naggar Agency, 216 East 75th St., New York, NY 10021.

■ Career

Writer and reference librarian.

■ Writings

Becoming Rosemary, Delacorte (New York City), 1997.

■ Sidelights

Frances Wood told *Something about the Author* (*SATA*): "When I graduated from college, all I wanted to do was to write a book and dance. I quickly awakened to the fact that I would have to get a job, earn money, and support myself. So, after writing, dancing, and working at odd jobs for several years, I went back to school and became a reference librarian. It has been a career that has served my writing well. When my husband and I moved to North Carolina, everything that I saw was new to me—the trees, the flowers, the birds, the bugs—but I knew how to look things up, how to research. *Becoming Rosemary* is half love, half research. Did you know that in Rosemary's day, people 'washed' their pots and pans with corncobs and sand?"

Wood's debut book, *Becoming Rosemary,* is a coming-of-age historical novel set in a small North Carolina farming village in the late eighteenth century. The eponymous heroine is a twelve-year-old who must reconcile her family's magical gifts of healing and telepathy with her community's perception of what is "normal." *Booklist* contributor Hazel Rochman maintained that "readers will be caught by the witch-hunting history and by the universal outsider story." A *Publishers Weekly* commentator described *Becoming Rosemary* as a "strong first novel," praising Wood's prose and dubbing the book "a hymn to the pains and joys of special gifts." A *Kirkus Reviews* critic similarly lauded the tale as "nearly flawless" and "an auspicious debut."

■ Works Cited

Review of *Becoming Rosemary, Kirkus Reviews,* November 1, 1996, p. 1610.
Review of *Becoming Rosemary, Publishers Weekly,* December 9, 1996, p. 69.
Rochman, Hazel, review of *Becoming Rosemary, Booklist,* January 1 & 15, 1997, p. 846.

■ For More Information See

PERIODICALS

Bulletin of the Center for Children's Books, May, 1997, p. 338.
School Library Journal, February, 1997, p. 106.
Voice of Youth Advocates, April, 1997, p. 34.

* * *

WRIGHT, Susan Kimmel 1950-

■ Personal

Born January 5, 1950, in Somerset, PA; daughter of Paul L. (a carpenter) and Alice B. (a homemaker; maiden name, Zwick) Kimmel; married David L. Wright (a civil engineer), December 19, 1970; children: Antonio D., Francisca, Maria N. *Education:* University of Pittsburgh, B.A. (magna cum laude), 1971; Duquesne University, J.D. (magna cum laude), 1976. *Religion:* Lutheran. *Hobbies and other interests:* Horseback riding.

■ Addresses

Home—Bridgeville, PA.

■ Career

Writer. Admitted to the bar of Pennsylvania, 1976; Dickie, McCamey, and Chilcote, Pittsburgh, PA, began as law clerk, became partner, 1973-93. Served on the board of Christian education for Zion Lutheran Church and School, Bridgeville, PA. *Member:* Mystery Writers of America, Sisters in Crime/Mysteries for Minors, Society of Children's Book Writers and Illustrators (advisory board, West Pennsylvania Chapter, 1993—), Penn Writers, Allegheny County Bar Association.

■ Awards, Honors

Numerous awards in law school; named writer of the year, 1992, by the Blue Ridge Writers Conference.

SUSAN KIMMEL WRIGHT

■ Writings

JUVENILE FICTION

Secret of the Old Graveyard, Herald Press (Scottsdale, PA), 1993.
Death by Babysitting, Herald Press, 1994.
Dead Letters, Herald Press, 1996.
Dead-End Mysteries, Herald Press, 1996.

OTHER

Also contributor to periodicals and anthologies, including *God's Abundance: 365 Days to a Simpler Life,* Starburst, 1997, and *Unexpected Blessings,* 1998.

■ Work in Progress

Several juvenile and young adult mysteries, including *Against the Law, In a Glass Darkly, The Mystery Next Door,* and *Dead End Road;* a biography of a female Revolutionary War soldier; work on women's air force pilots ("WASP's—World War II-era service pilots, long-denied veteran status"); work on West Pennsylvania farm life, 1920-1940.

■ Sidelights

Author Susan Kimmel Wright had a successful career with a law firm in Pittsburgh, Pennsylvania, while also writing mysteries for young readers. Several of her works were published in periodicals, but it wasn't until 1993 that her first book, *The Secret of the Old Graveyard,* appeared, and her full time writing career began.

Wright's Christian beliefs are displayed in her books, which are published by a Pennsylvanian Mennonite publishing house, Herald Press. In *The Secret of the Old Graveyard,* protagonist Nellie Locke has a problem. Although like most of the members of their Christian community, her parents are, according to Nellie, strange. Unlike other moms and dads, Nellie's parents are vegetarians, dress like hippies, live on a farm, and plan to adopt a three-month-old Colombian orphan. Nellie fears their oddness will scare away Rick Keppler, a boy she has a crush on. To add to her problems, after her parents leave her with her aunt while they pick up her new brother, strange things begin to take place in the old graveyard on her parent's property. Eventually, however, Nellie comes through, teaming with her best friend Peggy to solve the graveyard crimes, growing closer to Rick, and learning to accept her new brother who doesn't resemble anyone else in her family.

Sharon Grover applauded the book in the *School Library Journal,* calling it "a good choice for those looking for recreational reading infused with traditional Christian values." In *Librarian's World,* the official publication of the Evangelical Church Library Association, a critic praised Wright's "touches of humor" and observed that her characters "are not cookie-cutter Christians." A reviewer for another official publication, that of the Christian Booksellers Association, *Bookstore Journal,* also lauded *The Secret of the Old Graveyard.* This critic asserted that "readers will be able to identify with Nellie's feelings about her 'odd' parents," and commanded to Christian booksellers: "Recommend this to preteen and teen customers searching for an excellent rainy day book."

Wright followed *The Secret of the Old Graveyard* with *Death by Babysitting* and *Dead Letters.* She has written other mysteries for young people which are as yet unpublished, and she is working on the biography of a female soldier of the Revolutionary War. She is also planning to write about women air force pilots (WASP's) and West Pennsylvania farm life from 1920 to 1940. Wright is active in several organizations for writers and serves on the advisory board for the West Pennsylvania chapter of the Society of Children's Book Writers and Illustrators.

Wright told *SATA:* "I was born in a fold of the western Pennsylvania mountains and grew up hearing stories— not only the printed stories my mother read to me, but radio serials and early TV shows, stories about people my parents knew, and Bible stories. Both my parents were also fond of quoting poetry, and its music worked its way into my brain and my fingertips.

"My father told me about bringing home a leathery egg he'd found at the edge of a swamp. My mother warmed it by the wood cookstove until one day it began to crack and, to their dismay, out I popped.

"I write every day and everywhere. I write letters and lists, notes and journal entries, articles and books. I write because it is part of me. I write so that certain things, ideas, people, and events will be remembered. I write to entertain and I write to communicate. I write to share ideas and to arouse feelings—of reverence, compassion, reassurance, conviction.

"Publication rarely comes easily, and it didn't for me. But if you write out of the well of love inside you, about what you're compelled to write, that fire will sustain you until publication comes. As Winston Churchill said: 'Never give in, never give in, never, never, never, never—in nothing, great or small, large or petty—never give in except to convictions of honor and good sense.'"

■ Works Cited

Grover, Sharon, review of *Secret of the Old Graveyard, School Library Journal,* November, 1993, p. 111.
Review of *Secret of the Old Graveyard, Bookstore Journal,* June, 1993.
Review of *Secret of the Old Graveyard, Librarian's World,* second quarter, 1993-94.

■ For More Information See

PERIODICALS

School Library Journal, March, 1995, p. 226; September, 1996, p. 208.

Z

ZAWADZKI, Marek 1958-

■ Personal

Born March 9, 1958, in Wroclaw, Poland; son of Zdzislaw (a land surveyor) and Irena (a lawyer; maiden name, Murza) Zawadzki; married Beata Brocka (a photographer). *Education:* Attended Academy of Fine Arts, Wroclaw, Poland, 1978-81; Academy of Fine Arts, Stuttgart, Germany, diploma in graphic design, 1983. *Politics:* "Not affiliated." *Religion:* Roman Catholic. *Hobbies and other interests:* Chess, music (classical, jazz).

MAREK ZAWADZKI

■ Addresses

Home and office—Schrozberger Strasse 22, 70435 Stuttgart, Germany. *Agent*—Verlag J. F. Schreiber, Sirnauer Strasse 50, 73779 Deizisau, Germany.

■ Career

Freelance graphic designer, Stuttgart, Germany, 1984—. *Member:* National Association of Artists (Germany).

■ Awards, Honors

Troisdorfer Award for children's book illustration, 1995.

■ Illustrator

Roswitha Froehlich, *Josephine Baker,* Verlag J. F. Schreiber (Deizisau, Germany), 1993.

Arnica Esterl, *Okino und die Wale,* Verlag J. F. Schreiber, 1994, translation published as *Okino and the Whales,* Harcourt, 1995.

Vladimir Hulpach, *Ahajute und der Wolkenfresser,* Verlag J. F. Schreiber, 1995, translation by Pauline Hejl published as *Ahaiyute and the Cloud Eater,* Harcourt, 1996.

Gisa Kaad, *Ich komm' nicht mit nach Afrika,* Ensslin Verlag, 1995.

■ Work in Progress

Gilgamesh, King of Uruk, based on the Babylonian epic poem; research on the culture of the ancient civilizations of Sumer.

■ Sidelights

Marek Zawadzki told *Something about the Author* (*SATA*): "I have always favored representational and narrative painting. I believe that the artist's style should derive from the essence of a message he intends to deliver. Illustrating children's books allows me to combine my artistic avidity with factual communication.

"In order to satisfy my desire for accuracy and fine detail, I normally expend considerable time and effort researching the subject matter thoroughly prior to beginning the actual illustration. This enables me, not only to express the atmosphere, but also to employ symbolism, which renders a given epoch most appropriately.

"In addition to its purely entertaining function, I hope that my work may contribute to quenching children's curiosity and awakening their fantasy."

Zawadzki provided the illustrations for Arnica Esterl's *Okino and the Whales,* an adaptation of a Japanese tale about a young girl whose curiosity leads her to the distant underwater Kingdom of Iwa. The only way that the girl can be reached is if her mother weaves a coat made of her own hair for the Great Mother of the Ocean. Even though it takes many years for the mother to complete the blanket, she and her adult daughter are eventually reunited. *Booklist* contributor Linda Ward Callaghan praises Zawadzki's "realistic, highly detailed" illustrations and calls his blending of colors "exquisite." The illustrator's contrast of the real world and the underwater kingdom aid in "heightening the sense of fantasy," claims *School Library Journal* reviewer Wendy Lukehart.

■ Works Cited

Callaghan, Linda Ward, review of *Okino and the Whales, Booklist,* October 15, 1995, p. 410.
Lukehart, Wendy, review of *Okino and the Whales, School Library Journal,* January, 1996, p. 83.

■ For More Information See

PERIODICALS

Kirkus Reviews, October 15, 1995, p. 1489; March 15, 1996, p. 448.

Cumulative Indexes

Illustrations Index

(In the following index, the number of the volume in which an illustrator's work appears is given *before* the colon, and the page number on which it appears is given *after* the colon. For example, a drawing by Adams, Adrienne appears in Volume 2 on page 6, another drawing by her appears in Volume 3 on page 80, another drawing in Volume 8 on page 1, another drawing in Volume 15 on page 107, and so on and so on....)

YABC

Index citations including this abbreviation refer to listings appearing in *Yesterday's Authors of Books for Children*, also published by Gale Research Inc., which covers authors who died prior to 1960.

Author Index

The following index gives the number of the volume in which an author's biographical sketch, Brief Entry, or Obituary appears.

This index includes references to all entries in the following series, which are also published by Gale Research.

YABC—*Yesterday's Authors of Books for Children: Facts and Pictures about Authors and Illustrators of Books for Young People from Early Times to 1960*

CLR—*Children's Literature Review: Excerpts from Reviews, Criticism, and Commentary on Books for Children*

SAAS—*Something about the Author Autobiography Series*

May, Robin
  See May, Robert Stephen
Mayberry, Florence V(irginia Wilson) *10*
Maybury, Richard J. 1946- *72*
Mayer, Albert Ignatius, Jr. 1906-1960
  Obituary *29*
Mayer, Ann M(argaret) 1938- *14*
Mayer, Barbara 1939- *77*
Mayer, Jane Rothschild 1903- *38*
Mayer, Marianna 1945- *83*
  Earlier sketch in SATA *32*
Mayer, Mercer 1943- *73*
  Earlier sketches in SATA *16, 32*
  See also CLR *11*
Mayerson, Charlotte Leon *36*
Mayerson, Evelyn Wilde 1935- *55*
Mayfield, Sue 1963- *72*
Mayhar, Ardath 1930- *38*
Mayhew, James (John) 1964- *85*
Maynard, Chris
  See Maynard, Christopher
Maynard, Christopher 1949-
  Brief entry *43*
Maynard, Olga 1920- *40*
Mayne, William (James Carter)
  1928- *68*
  Earlier sketch in SATA *6*
  See also SAAS *11*
Maynes, Dr. J. O. Rocky
  See Maynes, J. Oscar, Jr.
Maynes, J. O. Rocky, Jr.
  See Maynes, J. Oscar, Jr.
Maynes, J. Oscar, Jr. 1929- *38*
Mayo, Gretchen Will 1936- *84*
Mayo, Margaret (Mary) 1935- *96*
  Earlier sketch in SATA *38*
Mays, Lucinda L(a Bella) 1924- *49*
Mays, (Lewis) Victor, (Jr.) 1927- *5*
Mazer, Anne 1953- *67*
Mazer, Harry 1925- *67*
  Earlier sketch in SATA *31*
  See also CLR *16*
  See also SAAS *11*
Mazer, Norma Fox 1931- *67*
  Earlier sketch in SATA *24*
  See also CLR *23*
  See also SAAS *1*
Mazille, Capucine 1953- *96*
Mazza, Adriana 1928- *19*
Mazzio, Joann 1926- *74*
Mbugua, Kioi Wa 1962- *83*
McAfee, Carol 1955- *81*
McAllister, P. K.
  See Downing, Paula E.
McArthur, Nancy *96*
McBain, Ed
  See Hunter, Evan
McBratney, Sam 1943- *89*
  See also CLR *44*
McCafferty, Jim 1954- *84*
McCaffery, Janet 1936- *38*
McCaffrey, Anne 1926- *70*
  Earlier sketch in SATA *8*
McCaffrey, Mary
  See Szudek, Agnes S(usan) P(hilomena)
McCain, Murray (David, Jr.)
  1926-1981 ....*7*
  Obituary *29*
McCall, Edith S. 1911- *6*
McCall, Virginia Nielsen 1909- *13*
McCall Smith, Alexander 1948- *73*
McCallum, Phyllis 1911- *10*
McCallum, Stephen 1960- *91*
McCampbell, Darlene Z. 1942- *83*
McCann, Edson
  See del Rey, Lester
McCann, Gerald 1916- *41*
McCann, Helen 1948- *75*
McCannon, Dindga Fatima 1947- *41*
McCants, William D. 1961- *82*
McCarter, Neely Dixon 1929- *47*
McCarthy, Agnes 1933- *4*
McCarthy, Colin (John) 1951- *77*
McCarthy-Tucker, Sherri N. 1958- *83*
McCarty, Rega Kramer 1904- *10*
McCaslin, Nellie 1914- *12*

McCaughrean, Geraldine 1951- *87*
  See also CLR *38*
  See also Jones, Geraldine
McCaughren, Tom 1936- *75*
McCay, Winsor 1869-1934 ....*41*
McClary, Jane Stevenson 1919-1990
  Obituary *64*
McCleery, Patsy R. 1925- *88*
McClintock, Barbara 1955- *95*
  Earlier sketch in SATA *57*
McClintock, Marshall 1906-1967 ....*3*
McClintock, Mike
  See McClintock, Marshall
McClintock, Theodore 1902-1971 ....*14*
McClinton, Leon 1933- *11*
McCloskey, Kevin 1951- *79*
McCloskey, (John) Robert 1914- *39*
  Earlier sketch in SATA *2*
  See also CLR *7*
McCloy, James F(loyd) 1941- *59*
McClung, Robert M(arshall) 1916- *68*
  Earlier sketch in SATA *2*
  See also CLR *11*
  See also SAAS *15*
McClure, Gillian Mary 1948- *31*
McColley, Kevin 1961- *80*
  See also SAAS *23*
McConduit, Denise Walter 1950- *89*
McConnell, James Douglas (Rutherford)
  1915-1988 ....*40*
  Obituary *56*
McCord, Anne 1942- *41*
McCord, David (Thompson Watson)
  1897-1997 ....*18*
  Obituary *96*
  See also CLR *9*
McCord, Jean 1924- *34*
McCormick, Brooks
  See Adams, William Taylor
McCormick, Dell J. 1892-1949 ....*19*
McCormick, (George) Donald (King)
  1911- *14*
McCormick, Edith (Joan) 1934- *30*
McCourt, Edward (Alexander) 1907-1972
  Obituary *28*
McCoy, Iola Fuller *3*
McCoy, J(oseph) J(erome) 1917- *8*
McCoy, Karen Kawamoto 1953- *82*
McCoy, Lois (Rich) 1941- *38*
McCrady, Lady 1951- *16*
McCraffrey, Anne 1926- *8*
  See also SAAS *11*
McCrea, James 1920- *3*
McCrea, Ruth 1921- *3*
McCue, Lisa (Emiline) 1959- *65*
McCullers, (Lula) Carson
  1917-1967 ....*27*
McCulloch, Derek (Ivor Breashur) 1897-
  1967
  Obituary *29*
McCulloch, Sarah
  See Ure, Jean
McCullough, David (Gaub) 1933- *62*
McCullough, Frances Monson 1938- *8*
McCully, Emily Arnold 1939- *5*
  See also CLR *46*
  See also SAAS *7*
  See Arnold, Emily
McCunn, Ruthanne Lum 1946- *63*
McCurdy, Michael (Charles) 1942- *82*
  Earlier sketch in SATA *13*
McCutcheon, Elsie 1937- *60*
McCutcheon, John 1952- *97*
McDaniel, Becky B(ring) 1953- *61*
McDaniel, Lurlene 1944- *71*
McDearmon, Kay *20*
McDermott, Beverly Brodsky
  1941- *11*
McDermott, Gerald (Edward)
  1941- *74*
  Earlier sketch in SATA *16*
  See also CLR *9*
McDermott, Michael 1962- *76*
McDevitt, Jack
  See McDevitt, John Charles
McDevitt, John Charles 1935- *94*

McDole, Carol
  See Farley, Carol
McDonald, Collin 1943- *79*
McDonald, Gerald D. 1905-1970 ....*3*
McDonald, Jamie
  See Heide, Florence Parry
McDonald, Jill (Masefield)
  1927-1982 ....*13*
  Obituary *29*
McDonald, Lucile Saunders 1898- *10*
McDonald, Mary Ann 1956- *84*
McDonald, Megan 1959- *67*
McDonald, Mercedes 1956- *97*
McDonnell, Christine 1949- *34*
McDonnell, Flora (Mary) 1963- *90*
McDonnell, Lois Eddy 1914- *10*
McDonough, Yona Zeldis 1957- *73*
McElrath, William N. 1932- *65*
McElrath-Eslick, Lori 1960- *96*
McEntee, Dorothy (Layng) 1902- *37*
McEwen, Robert (Lindley) 1926-1980
  Obituary *23*
McFall, Christie 1918- *12*
McFarlan, Donald M(aitland)
  1915- *59*
McFarland, Kenton D(ean) 1920- *11*
McFarlane, Leslie 1902-1977 ....*31*
McFarlane, Peter (William) 1940- *95*
McFarlane, Sheryl P. 1954- *86*
McGaw, Jessie Brewer 1913- *10*
McGee, Barbara 1943- *6*
McGiffin, (Lewis) Lee (Shaffer)
  1908- *1*
McGill, Marci
  See Ridlon, Marci
McGill, Ormond 1913- *92*
McGinley, Phyllis 1905-1978 ....*44*
  Obituary *24*
  Earlier sketch in SATA *2*
McGinnis, Lila S(prague) 1924- *44*
McGough, Elizabeth (Hemmes)
  1934- *33*
McGovern, Ann 1930- *70*
  Earlier sketch in SATA *8*
  See also SAAS *17*
McGowen, Thomas E. 1927- *2*
McGowen, Tom
  See McGowen, Thomas E.
McGrady, Mike 1933- *6*
McGrath, Thomas (Matthew)
  1916-1990 ....*41*
  Obituary *66*
McGraw, Eloise Jarvis 1915- *67*
  Earlier sketch in SATA *1*
  See also SAAS *6*
McGraw, William Corbin 1916- *3*
McGregor, Barbara 1959- *82*
McGregor, Craig 1933- *8*
McGregor, Iona 1929- *25*
McGuffey, Alexander Hamilton
  1816-1896 ....*60*
McGuffey, William Holmes
  1800-1873 ....*60*
McGuire, Edna 1899- *13*
McGuire, Leslie (Sarah) 1945- *94*
  Brief entry *45*
  Earlier sketch in SATA *52*
McGurk, Slater
  See Roth, Arthur J(oseph)
McHargue, Georgess 1941- *77*
  Earlier sketch in SATA *4*
  See also CLR *2*
  See also SAAS *5*
McHugh, (Berit) Elisabet 1941- *55*
  Brief entry *44*
McIlwraith, Maureen 1922- *2*
McIlwraith, Maureen Mollie Hunter
  See Hunter, Mollie
McInerney, Judith Whitelock 1945- *49*
  Brief entry *46*
McInerny, Ralph 1929- *93*
McKaughan, Larry (Scott) 1941- *75*
McKay, Donald 1895- *45*
McKay, Hilary 1959- *92*
  See also SAAS *23*
McKay, Robert W. 1921- *15*
McKeating, Eileen 1957- *81*

T

Wynne-Jones, Tim(othy) 1948- *96*
  Earlier sketch in SATA *67*
  See also CLR *21*
Wynter, Edward (John) 1914- *14*
Wynyard, Talbot
  See Hamilton, Charles (Harold St. John)
Wyss, Johann David Von
  1743-1818 ....*29*
  Brief entry *27*
Wyss, Thelma Hatch 1934- *10*

Y

Yadin, Yigael 1917-1984 ....*55*
Yaffe, Alan
  See Yorinks, Arthur
Yakovetic, (Joseph Sandy) 1952- *59*
Yakovetic, Joe
  See Yakovetic, (Joseph Sandy)
Yamaguchi, Marianne 1936- *7*
Yamaka, Sara 1978- *92*
Yancey, Diane 1951- *81*
Yang, Jay 1941- *12*
Yang, Mingyi 1943- *72*
Yarbrough, Camille 1938- *79*
  See also CLR *29*
Yarbrough, Ira 1910(?)-1983
  Obituary *35*
Yaroslava
  See Mills, Yaroslava Surmach
Yashima, Taro
  See CLR *4*
  See Iwamatsu, Jun Atsushi
Yates, Elizabeth 1905- *68*
  Earlier sketch in SATA *4*
  See also SAAS *6*
Yates, Janelle K(aye) 1957- *77*
Yates, John 1939- *74*
Yates, Philip 1956- *92*
Yates, Raymond F(rancis)
  1895-1966 ....*31*
Yaukey, Grace S(ydenstricker)
  1899-1994 ....*5*
  Obituary *80*
Yeakley, Marjory Hall 1908- *21*
Yeatman, Linda 1938- *42*
Yee, Paul (R.) 1956- *96*
  Earlier sketch in SATA *67*
  See also CLR *44*
Yee, Wong Herbert 1953- *78*
Yeh, Chun-Chan 1914- *79*
Yenawine, Philip 1942- *85*
Yensid, Retlaw
  See Disney, Walt(er Elias)
Yeo, Wilma (Lethem) 1918-1994 ....*24*
  Obituary *81*
Yeoman, John (Brian) 1934- *80*
  Earlier sketch in SATA *28*
  See also CLR *46*
Yep, Laurence Michael 1948- *69*
  Earlier sketch in SATA *7*
  See also CLR *17*
Yepsen, Roger B(ennet), Jr. 1947- *59*
Yerian, Cameron John *21*
Yerian, Margaret A. *21*
Yetska
  See Ironside, Jetske
Yoder, Dorothy Meenen 1921- *96*
Yoder, Dot
  See Yoder, Dorothy Meenen
Yoder, Walter D. 1933- *88*
Yolen, Jane (Hyatt) 1939- *75*
  Earlier sketches in SATA *4, 40*
  See also CLR *44*
  See also SAAS *1*
Yonge, Charlotte Mary 1823-1901 ....*17*
Yorinks, Arthur 1953- *85*
  Earlier sketches in SATA *33, 49*
  See also CLR *20*
York, Andrew
  See Nicole, Christopher Robin
York, Carol Beach 1928- *77*
  Earlier sketch in SATA *6*

York, Rebecca
  See Buckholtz, Eileen (Garber)
York, Simon
  See Heinlein, Robert A.
Yoshida, Toshi 1911- *77*
Yost, Edna 1889-1971
  Obituary *26*
Youd, C. S. 1922-
  See SAAS *6*
Youd, (Christopher) Samuel 1922- *47*
  Brief entry *30*
  See also SAAS *6*
Young, Bob
  See Young, Robert W(illiam)
Young, Clarence [Collective
  pseudonym] *67*
  Earlier sketch in SATA *1*
Young, Dianne 1959- *88*
Young, Dorothea Bennett 1924- *31*
Young, Ed (Tse-chun) 1931- *74*
  Earlier sketch in SATA *10*
  See also CLR *27*
Young, Edward
  See Reinfeld, Fred
Young, Elaine L.
  See Schulte, Elaine L(ouise)
Young, Jan
  See Young, Janet Randall
Young, Janet Randall 1919- *3*
Young, Judy (Elaine) Dockrey
  1949- *72*
Young, Ken 1956- *86*
Young, Lois Horton 1911-1981 ....*26*
Young, Louise B. 1919- *64*
Young, Margaret B(uckner) 1922- *2*
Young, Mary 1940- *89*
Young, Miriam 1913-1974 ....*7*
Young, Noela 1930- *89*
Young, (Rodney Lee) Patrick (Jr.)
  1937- *22*
Young, Percy M(arshall) 1912- *31*
Young, Richard Alan 1946- *72*
Young, Robert W(illiam) 1916-1969 .....*3*
Young, Ruth 1946- *67*
Young, Scott A(lexander) 1918- *5*
Young, Vivien
  See Gater, Dilys
Youngs, Betty 1934-1985 ....*53*
  Obituary *42*
Younkin, Paula 1942- *77*
Yount, Lisa 1944- *74*
Yuditskaya, Tatyana 1964- *75*

Z

Zach, Cheryl (Byrd) 1947- *58*
  Brief entry *51*
  See also SAAS *24*
Zaffo, George J. (?)-1984 ....*42*
Zagwyn, Deborah Turney 1953- *78*
Zahn, Timothy 1951- *91*
Zaid, Barry 1938- *51*
Zaidenberg, Arthur 1908(?)-1990 ....*34*
  Obituary *66*
Zalben, Jane Breskin 1950- *79*
  Earlier sketch in SATA *7*
Zallinger, Jean (Day) 1918- *80*
  Earlier sketch in SATA *14*
Zallinger, Peter Franz 1943- *49*
Zambreno, Mary Frances 1954- *75*
Zappler, Lisbeth 1930- *10*
Zarchy, Harry 1912- *34*
Zarif, Margaret Min'imah (?)-1983 ....*33*
Zaring, Jane (Thomas) 1936- *51*
  Brief entry *40*
Zarins, Joyce Audy
  See dos Santos, Joyce Audy
Zaslavsky, Claudia 1917- *36*
Zawadzki, Marek 1958- *97*
Zebra, A.
  See Scoltock, Jack
Zebrowski, George 1945- *67*
Zeck, Gerald Anthony 1939- *40*

Zeck, Gerry
  See Zeck, Gerald Anthony
Zed, Dr.
  See Penrose, Gordon
Zei, Alki *24*
  See also CLR *6*
Zeier, Joan T(heresa) 1931- *81*
Zeinert, Karen 1942- *79*
Zelazny, Roger 1937- *57*
  Brief entry *39*
Zeldis, Malcah 1931- *86*
Zelinsky, Paul O. 1953- *49*
  Brief entry *33*
Zellan, Audrey Penn 1950- *22*
Zemach, Harve 1933- *3*
Zemach, Kaethe 1958- *49*
  Brief entry *39*
Zemach, Margot 1931-1989 ....*70*
  Obituary *59*
  Earlier sketch in SATA *21*
Zens, Patricia Martin 1926-1972
  Brief entry *50*
Zephaniah, Benjamin (Obadiah Iqbal)
  1958- *86*
Zerman, Melvyn Bernard 1930- *46*
Zettner, Pat 1940- *70*
Zhang, Christopher Zhong-Yuan
  1954- *91*
Zhang, Song Nan 1942- *85*
Ziegler, Jack (Denmore) 1942- *60*
Ziemienski, Dennis 1947- *10*
Zillah
  See Macdonald, Zillah K(atherine)
Zim, Herbert S(pencer) 1909-1994 ....*30*
  Obituary *85*
  Earlier sketch in SATA *1*
  See also CLR *2*
  See also SAAS *2*
Zim, Sonia Bleeker
  See Bleeker, Sonia
Zima, Gordon 1920- *90*
Zimelman, Nathan 1921- *65*
  Brief entry *37*
Zimmer, Dirk 1943- *65*
Zimmerman, Naoma 1914- *10*
Zimmermann, Arnold E(rnst Alfred)
  1909- *58*
Zimnik, Reiner 1930- *36*
  See also CLR *3*
Zindel, Bonnie 1943- *34*
Zindel, Paul 1936- *58*
  Earlier sketch in SATA *16*
  See also CLR *45*
Ziner, (Florence) Feenie 1921- *5*
Zion, (Eu)Gene 1913-1975 ....*18*
Zollinger, Gulielma 1856-1917
  Brief entry *27*
Zolotow, Charlotte S(hapiro) 1915- *78*
  Earlier sketches in SATA *1, 35*
  See also CLR *2*
Zonderman, Jon 1957- *92*
Zonia, Dhimitri 1921- *20*
Zubrowski, Bernard 1939- *90*
  Earlier sketch in SATA *35*
Zubrowski, Bernie
  See Zubrowski, Bernard
Zucker, Miriam S. 1962- *85*
Zudeck, Darryl 1961- *61*
Zupa, G. Anthony
  See Zeck, Gerald Anthony
Zurhorst, Charles (Stewart, Jr.)
  1913- *12*
Zuromskis, Diane
  See Stanley, Diane
Zuromskis, Diane Stanley
  See Stanley, Diane
Zwahlen, Diana 1947- *88*
Zweifel, Frances 1931- *14*
Zwerger, Lisbeth 1954- *66*
  See also CLR *46*
  See also SAAS *13*
Zwinger, Ann 1925- *46*